LONGMAN LINGUISTICS LIBRARY

AN INTRODUCTION TO THE CELTIC LANGUAGES

LONGMAN LINGUISTICS LIBRARY

General editors:
R. H. Robins, *University of London*
Martin Harris, *University of Manchster*
Geoffrey Horrocks, *University of Cambridge*

For a complete list of books in the series see pages v and vi

An Introduction to the Celtic Languages

Paul Russell

LONGMAN
LONDON AND NEW YORK

Longman Group Limited,
Longman House, Burnt Mill,
Harlow, Essex CM20 2JE, England
and Associated Companies throughout the world.

*Published in the United States of America
by Longman Publishing, New York*

© Longman Group Limited 1995

First published 1995

ISBN 0 582 100828 CSD
ISBN 0 582 10081X PPR

British Library Cataloguing-in-Publication Data
A catalogue record for this book is
available fromthe British Library

Library of Congress Cataloging-in-Publication Data
Russell, Paul, 1956 Feb. 23–
An introduction to the Celtic languages / Paul Russell.
p.   cm. — (Longman linguistics library)
Includes bibliographical references and index.
ISBN 0–582–10082–8 (CSD). — ISBN 0–582–10081–X (PPR)
1. Celtic languages.   I. Title.   II. Series.
PB1014.R87   1995
491.6—dc20   94–44203
CIP

Typeset in 10/11 Times by 8M
Produced by Longman Singapore Publishers (Pte) Ltd.
Printed in Singapore

LONGMAN LINGUISTICS LIBRARY

General editors:
R. H. Robins, *University of London*
Martin Harris, *University of Manchester*
Geoffrey Horrocks, *University of Cambridge*

A Short History of Linguistics
Third Edition
R. H. ROBINS

Text and Context
Explorations in the Semantics and Pragmtics of Discourse
TEUN A. VAN DIJK

Introduction to Text Linguistics
ROBERT DE BEAUGRANDE
AND WOLFGANG ULRICH
DRESSLER

Psycholinguistics
Language, Mind, and World
DANNY D. STEINBERG

Principles of Pragmatics
GEOFFREY LEECH

Generative Grammar
GEOFFREY HORROCKS

The English Verb
Second Edition
F. R. PALMER

A History of American English
J. L. DILLARD

English Historical Syntax
Verbal Constructions
DAVID DENISON

Pidgin and Creole Languages
SUZANNE ROMAINE

A History of English Phonology
CHARLES JONES

Generative and Non-linear Phonology
JACQUES DURAND

Modality and the English Modals
Second Edition
F. R. PALMER

Semiotics and Linguistics
YISHAI TOBIN

Multilingualism in the British Isles I:
The Older Mother Tongues and Europe
EDITED BY SAFDER ALLADINA AND VIV EDWARDS

Multilingualism in the British Isles II:
Africa, The Middle East and Asia
EDITED BY SAFDER ALLADINA AND VIV EDWARDS

Dialects of English
Studies in Grammatical Variation
EDITED BY PETER TRUDGILL AND J. K. CHAMBERS

Introduction to Bilingualism
CHARLOTTE HOFFMANN

Verb and Noun Number in English:
A Functional Explanation
WALLIS REID

English in Africa
JOSEF SCHMIED

Linguistic Theory
The Discourse of Fundamental Works
ROBERT DE BEAUGRANDE

General Linguistics
An Introductory Survey
Fourth Edition
R. H. ROBINS

Historical Linguistics
Problems and Perspectives
EDITED BY C. JONES

A History of Linguistics Vol. I
The Eastern Traditions of Linguistics
EDITED BY GIULIO LEPSCHY

A History of Linguistics Vol. II
Classical and Medieval Linguistics
EDITED BY GIULIO LEPSCHY

Aspect in the English Verb
Process and Result in Language
YISHAI TOBIN

The Meaning of Syntax
A Study in the Adjectives of English
CONNOR FERRIS

Latin American Spanish
JOHN M. LIPSKI

A Linguistic History of Italian
MARTIN MAIDEN

Modern Arabic
CLIVE HOLES

Frontiers of Phonology: Atoms,
Structures, Derivations
EDITED BY JACQUES DURAND AND
FRANCIS KATAMBA

An Introduction to the Celtic
Languages
PAUL RUSSELL

To Ben

CONTENTS

Acknowledgements   xv

List of abbreviations   xvi

The periods of the Celtic languages   xviii

1 The Historical background to the Celtic Languages   **1**
  1.0 Introduction   **1**
  1.1 Celtic as an Indo-European language   **2**
  1.2 Continental Celtic   **2**
      1.2.1 Gaul   3
      1.2.2 Northern Italy   5
      1.2.3 The Iberian peninsula   6
  1.3 Insular Celtic   **7**
      1.3.1 Britain and Brittonic   7
      1.3.2 Ireland and Goidelic   9
  1.4 The distinctive features of Celtic languages   **10**
      1.4.1 Phonology   10
          1.4.1.1 Long vowels and diphthongs   10
          1.4.1.2 Loss of /p/   11
          1.4.1.3 IE /gʷ/ > /b/   12
          1.4.1.4 IE */r̩/, and */l̩/ > Celtic /ri/ and /li/   12
      1.4.2 Morphology and syntax   12
          1.4.2.1 Nominal inflection   13
          1.4.2.2 The verbal system   13
          1.4.2.3 Possession   13
  1.5 The distinctive features of Goidelic and Brittonic   **14**
      1.5.1 P and Q Celtic   14
      1.5.2 Word accent   15

1.6   The inter-relationship of the Celtic languages   15
1.7   The Italo-Celtic hypothesis   18

2 The Goidelic languages   25
2.0 Introduction   25
2.1 The sources   25
       2.1.1   Irish   25
       2.1.2   Scottish Gaelic   27
       2.1.3   Manx   28
2.2   General features of the Goidelic languages   28
       2.2.1   Lenition and mutations   28
       2.2.2   The initial accent and its consequences   29
       2.2.3   Other sound changes   32
                2.2.3.1   Long vowels and diphthongs   33
                2.2.3.2   Vowel affection   34
                2.2.3.3   Palatalization   35
                2.2.3.4   Tense and lax resonants and
                          'Mac Neill's Law'   38
       2.2.4   Nominal declension and the loss of final syllables   38
       2.2.5   The chronology of early Irish sound changes
               and Latin loanwords   42
       2.2.6   The verbal system   45
                2.2.6.1   The tenses and moods of the early
                          Irish verb   45
                2.2.6.2   Absolute and conjunct verbal inflection 49
                2.2.6.3   Deponents, impersonals and passives 55
                2.2.6.4   Relative clauses   56
                2.2.6.5   The verbs 'to be'   58
                2.2.6.6   Middle Irish developments   59
2.3   Scottish Gaelic and Manx developments   61
       2.3.1   Phonology   62
       2.3.2   Morphology   65

3 Irish   69
3.1   Types of Irish   69
       3.1.1   Dialects   69
       3.1.2   The survival of Irish   73
3.2   Phonology   74
       3.2.1   The framework of the phonology   74
       3.2.2   Stress patterns   77
       3.2.3   Consonant clusters and epenthesis   79
       3.2.4   Raising, lowering and paradigmatic variation 79
       3.2.5   Palatalization   80
3.3   The nominal system   81
       3.3.1   Gender   81

3.3.2   The case system   82
3.3.3   Number   84
3.3.4   Determination and definiteness   85
         3.3.4.1   The article   85
         3.3.4.2   Demonstratives   85
         3.3.4.3   Possessive adjectives and pronouns   86
3.3.5   Adjectives   87
3.3.6   Pronouns   88
3.3.7   Numerals   90
3.4   The verbal system   **92**
3.4.1   The forms of the verb   92
3.4.2   The verbs 'to be'   96
3.4.3   Tenses, aspect and auxiliary verbs   98
3.4.4   Impersonals and passives   101
3.5   Syntax   **102**
3.5.1   Word order   102
3.5.2   Pre-sentential particles   102
         3.5.2.1   Negatives   102
         3.5.2.2   Interrogatives   103
         3.5.2.3   Declaratives   104
3.5.3   Subordination   104
         3.5.3.1   Reported speech   104
         3.5.3.2   Relative clauses   105
3.5.4   Theoretical treatments of Irish syntax   106

4   The Brittonic languages   **111**
4.0   Introduction   **111**
4.1   The sources   **111**
4.1.1   Welsh   111
4.1.2   Cornish   113
4.1.3   Breton   114
4.2   General features of the Brittonic languages   **115**
4.2.1   Lenition and mutations   115
4.2.2   Other sound changes   116
         4.2.2.1   Long vowels and diphthongs   116
         4.2.2.2   Vowel affection   118
         4.2.2.3   Brittonic /s/ and /i̯/   118
4.2.3   The penultimate accent, its shift and the
         consequences   119
4.2.4   The new quantity system   121
4.2.5   Loss of final syllables   122
4.2.6   The verbal system   125
4.2.7   Compound prepositions   127

4.3 The inter-relationship of the neo-Brittonic languages   127
4.3.1 Phonology   129
4.3.2 Morphology   130
4.3.3 The Brittonic family tree revisited   132

5 Welsh   137
5.0 Introduction   137
5.1 Types of Welsh   137
5.1.1 Modern literary Welsh   138
5.1.2 Modern Welsh dialects   139
5.1.3 Cymraeg Byw and standard spoken Welsh   145
5.2 Phonology   146
5.2.1 The framework of the phonology   146
5.2.2 The central vowel /ə/   151
5.2.3 Final consonantal clusters   154
5.2.4 Phonology and grammatical alternations   156
5.2.5 Theoretical treatments of Welsh phonology   157
5.3 The nominal system   158
5.3.1 Gender   158
5.3.2 Number   159
5.3.3 Determination   160
        5.3.3.1 The article   160
        5.3.3.2 Demonstratives   160
        5.3.3.3 The 'genitive' construction   161
        5.3.3.4 Possessive adjectives and pronouns   161
5.3.4 Adjectives   164
5.3.5 Personal pronouns   166
5.3.6 Numerals   169
5.4 The verbal system   169
5.4.1 The forms of the verb   170
5.4.2 The verb *bod* 'to be'   173
5.4.3 Tenses, aspect and auxiliary verbs   174
5.4.4 Passives   177
5.5 Syntax   179
5.5.1 Word order   179
5.5.2 Pre-sentential particles   181
        5.5.2.1 Negatives   181
        5.5.2.2 Interrogatives   184
        5.5.2.3 Declaratives   186
5.5.3 Subordination   186
        5.5.3.1 Reported speech   186
        5.5.3.2 Relative clauses   188
5.5.4 Theoretical treatments of Welsh syntax   189

6   The orthographies of the Celtic languages   197
   6.1   Orthography and phonology   197
   6.2   The scripts of Continental Celtic   198
      6.2.1   Greek   198
      6.2.2   Celtiberian   202
      6.2.3   The Lugano script of northern Italy   204
      6.2.4   Latin   206
   6.3   The scripts of Insular Celtic   207
      6.3.1   Ogam   208
      6.3.2   Latin   211
          6.3.2.1   British   211
          6.3.2.2   Welsh   213
          6.3.2.3   Breton   219
          6.3.2.4   Cornish   222
          6.3.2.5   Irish   223
          6.3.2.6   Scottish Gaelic   227
          6.3.2.7   Manx   228

**7   Lenition and mutations: phonetics, phonology
and morphology   231**
   7.0   Introduction   231
   7.1   The phonological data   231
   7.2   The grammatical function of the initial mutations   232
      7.2.1   Nouns   232
          7.2.1.1   Feminine nouns   232
          7.2.1.2   Masculine nouns   234
          7.2.1.3   Case forms in Goidelic   234
      7.2.2   Numerals   234
      7.2.3   Possessive pronouns and adjectives   235
      7.2.4   The negative particle   235
      7.2.5   Provection   235
      7.2.6   Initial vowels   236
   7.3   Mutations in the consonantal system   236
   7.4   Theories of lenition and spirantization   238
      7.4.1   Jackson and Greene   239
      7.4.2   Harvey   242
      7.4.3   P. W. Thomas and Sims-Williams   242
      7.4.4   Martinet and Koch   246
   7.5   The grammaticalization of the mutations   249
   7.6   Modern mutations and functional load   252

8   Verbal nouns, verbs and nouns   258
   8.1   Verbs, nouns and verbal adjectives   258
   8.2   Formal characteristics of verbal nouns   260

8.3   Syntactical characteristics of verbal nouns   **263**
   8.3.1   Nominal features   263
       8.3.1.1   Modification by article and adjective   ·   263
       8.3.1.2   Modification by noun and pronoun   263
       8.3.1.3   Modification by prepositions   266
       8.3.1.4   Gender and declension   266
       8.3.1.5   Verbal noun as subject or object of a
                of a verb   267
       8.3.1.6   Neutral to active/passive distinctions   268
   8.3.2   Verbal features   269
       8.3.2.1   Modification by adverb   269
       8.3.2.2   Periphrastic auxiliary verbs and aspect   269
       8.3.2.3   Verbal nouns in subordinate clauses   270
       8.3.2.4   Replacement of finite verb in
                co-ordinated strings   271
8.4   Verbal noun: verb or noun?   **271**
8.5   Verbal nouns and infinitives: the historical
**   background**   **275**

9   Word order in the Celtic languages   **278**
9.0   Introduction   **278**
9.1   The evidence   **281**
   9.1.1   Continental Celtic   282
   9.1.2   Insular Celtic   286
       9.1.2.1   Goidelic   286
       9.1.2.2   Brittonic   292
9.2   The historical background   **300**

References   306

Index   336

Acknowledgements

The original invitation to contribute this volume to the *Longman Linguistics Library* series came from Elizabeth Mann, and I am grateful to her and the editors of the series for their support and encouragement. There would have been no chance of completing the volume on time had not the Warden and Council of Radley College been kind enough to grant me a term's sabbatical during the final stages. I am grateful also to my colleagues for shouldering the extra work my absence entailed. During that term Jesus College, Oxford, provided a congenial place to work, and Ellis Evans displayed characteristic kindness in discussing aspects of my work. John Penney read a final draft of the whole work, and by always asking the awkward questions and raising the telling objections showed me that the draft was less final than I had thought. I have also benefited from discussing aspects of the work with Pierre-Yves Lambert and Peter Smith. As ever, Thomas Charles-Edwards has kindly acted as a sounding-board for ideas, and has supplied clarity of thought and good sense in large measures; he too read a final draft and made many valuable suggestions and corrections. It is a better volume for all their contributions.

My wife, Felicity, has as usual borne the brunt of my labours, particularly in giving me time and space to complete the work; she has provided constant support and encouragement in every way. Ben, my son, has taken a keen and detailed interest in all aspects of the production of 'his' book; it is dedicated to him with love.

PAUL RUSSELL
Radley College

Abbreviations

A	adjective	m.	masculine
acc.	accusative	MB	Middle Breton
AgN	agent noun	MCo	Middle Cornish
AN	abstract noun	MIr	Middle Irish
B	Breton	MnE	Modern English
Cards	Cardiganshire	MW	Middle Welsh
CF	Cois Fhairrge	MnB	Modern Breton
Celtib	Celtiberian	MnCo	Modern Cornish
Co	Cornish	MnIr	Modern Irish
Conn	Connacht	MnW	Modern Welsh
dat.	dative	Mun	Munster
Det.	Determinative	Mx	Manx
Don	Donegal	n.	neuter
Eng	English	Neg.	Negative
f.	feminine	nom.	nominative
Gaul	Gaulish	NM	nasal mutation
GD	Gweedore	NW	Northern Welsh
gen.	genitive	OB	Old Breton
Goth	Gothic	obj.	object
Gk	Greek	OCo	Old Cornish
H	any laryngeal (see	OE	Old English
	Chapter 2, n. 16)	OHG	Old High German
Ir	Irish	OIr	Old Irish
IE	Indo-European	Osc	Oscan
Lat	Latin	OW	Old Welsh
Lep	Lepontic	part.	particle
lit.	literally	Pembs	Pembrokeshire
LN(N)	local name(s)	pl.	plural
LW	literary Welsh	PN(N)	personal name(s)

Pr-C	Proto-Celtic	SpM	spirant mutation
pres.	present	SpW	spoken Welsh
pro.	pronoun	subj.	subject
R	any resonant	SW	Southern Welsh
rel.	relative	T	any consonant
RN(N)	river name(s)	VN(N)	verbal noun(s)
S	any spirant	voc.	vocative
ScG	Scottish Gaelic	W	Welsh
S-EW	South-east Welsh	#	word boundary
sg.	singular	*	reconstructed form
Skt	Sanskrit	**	unacceptable form
SM	soft mutation		

The periods of the Celtic languages

All dates are AD.

Irish	Archaic Irish	500–700
	Early Old Irish	700–800
	Classical Old Irish	800–900
	Middle Irish	900–1200
	Early Modern Irish	1200–1600
	Modern Irish	1600–present
Scottish Gaelic	Early Modern Scottish Gaelic	1100–1700
	Modern Scottish Gaelic	1700–present
Manx	Early Manx	1600–1700
	Classical Manx	1700–1800
	Late Manx	1800–1974
	Revived Manx	Present
Welsh	Archaic Welsh	600–800
	Old Welsh	800–1200
	Middle Welsh	1200–1500
	Classical Modern Welsh	1500–1900
	Modern Welsh	1900–present
Breton	Archaic Breton	500–600?
	Old Breton	600–1100
	Middle Breton	1100–1659
	Modern Breton	1659–present
Cornish	Archaic Cornish	600–800
	Old Cornish	800–1200
	Middle Cornish	1200–1575
	Late Cornish	1575–1800
	Revived Cornish	Present

Chapter 1

The historical background to the Celtic languages

1.0 Introduction

Speakers of the modern Celtic languages, Irish, Scottish Gaelic, Manx, Welsh and Breton, are today only to be found on the western seaboards of the British Isles and France. But they are inheritors of languages which some two thousand years ago were spoken throughout Europe and even in Asia Minor. It is, therefore, important and often useful to retain a historical perspective when considering the Celtic languages. The present volume attempts to provide a general introduction to the Celtic languages for linguists unfamiliar with them. The Celtic languages can seem very difficult and complex to non-Celticists and one good reason for adopting a more historical approach is to show that many of those complexities arose by a comprehensible process of historical development. For example, the phenomenon of the initial mutations which marks out Celtic languages, discussed in Chapter 7, can be shown to be the outcome of a series of reasonably well-understood historical developments, none of which would startle a historical linguist. It is beyond the scope of this volume to provide detailed discussion of every single aspect worthy of consideration, and there are inevitable omissions.[1] However, the detailed bibliographical resources should provide the necessary back-up and support to enable the reader to broaden his or her knowledge in any area. Several multi-author volumes have appeared recently, MacAulay 1992a, Ball and Fife 1993 and Price 1992a, which offer discussions of the individual languages and also, in some, discussion of the earlier stages.[2] Nevertheless, it is very difficult in such a format to maintain a consistency of approach and impossible to capture generalizations about Celtic languages as a group or to discuss common features.

The rest of Chapter 1 considers the Celtic languages in their Indo-European context with particular emphasis on the evidence for the early

Celtic languages of Continental Europe. Chapters 2–5 concentrate on the two main groups of the Insular languages, Goidelic and Brittonic. Chapters 2 and 4 consider the historical development of the two groups, while 3 and 5 examine in detail a modern representative of each, namely Irish and Welsh respectively. The remaining chapters examine a number of general topics – writing systems, mutations, verbal nouns and word order – topics which are often regarded as containing features characteristic of Celtic.

1.1   Celtic as an Indo-European language

The Celtic languages belong to the Indo-European group of languages, members of which include Latin and the Romance languages, Greek, the Indo-Iranian languages (including Sanskrit, Avestan and Persian) Russian, German and English.[3] Speakers of Indo-European languages can, therefore, be found from Iceland and the Hebrides to the mouth of the Ganges even before taking into account the historically more recent migrations to the Americas, Africa and the Antipodes. Even the most simple of lexical comparisons suggests a connection between these languages, e.g. OIr *bráthir* 'brother', Lat *fráter*, Gk *phrátēr*, Goth *broþar* (H. Lewis and Pedersen 1961: 6); OIr *ech* 'horse', Gaul *Epona* < **ekuo-*, cf. Lat *equus*, Gk *híppos*, Skt *aśva* (H. Lewis and Pedersen 1961: 3). The relationship between these languages, however, runs much more deeply than simple lexical correspondences. The Celtic languages show, for example, in various stages of disintegration, a nominal case system similar to that of the classical languages, with phonologically related elements, e.g. OIr *eich* 'horse' (gen. sg.) < **ekuī* cf. Lat *equī*, OIr *fiur* 'man' (dat. sg.) < **uirū* < **uīrō*, cf. Lat *virō*, Gaul *-oui*, Gk *-ōi*; OIr *feraib* 'men' (dat. pl.) < **uirobis*, cf. Lat *-ibus*, Gk *-(o)phi*, Skt *-bhis*; etc. (H. Lewis and Pedersen 1961: 166–7). Furthermore, they have a verbal system which, despite superficial dissimilarities, shares a number of features with the verbal systems of other Indo-European languages; for example, the alternation in Old Irish of *berid* : *·beir* 'he carries' < **bereti/beret* seems to continue an alternation of endings also seen in Skt *bharati* : *(a)bharat* (McCone 1979a: 26–32). Old Irish also shares a reduplicated perfect or preterite formation with Latin, Greek and Indo-Iranian (McCone 1986: 233), and a reduplicated future with Indo-Iranian languages (McCone 1991a: 137–82; for further discussion, see 2.2.6 below).

1.2   Continental Celtic

The evidence for Celtic speaking peoples in Continental Europe is widespread but variable in quality and quantity.[4] Our knowledge of the distribution of Celtic tribes is largely dependent on classical authors

who portrayed the Celts as one of the barbarian tribes who threatened
the peace and stability of the Mediterranean world (Rankin 1987: ch.
6). Their testimony can be misleading; use of the generic term *Keltoi* in
Greek or *Celtae* in Latin does not necessarily refer to speakers of a
Celtic language unless decisive personal names or local names are present. Much of our knowledge of Continental Celtic depends precisely
on such evidence.

Celtic names in Continental Europe are identifiable
by the fact that they contain elements also found in the later languages;
for example, *Vercingetorix*, the name of a Gaulish tribal leader, is
divisible into three elements *ver-* 'over, above', cf. Ir *for*, OW *guor*,
MnW *gor*; *-cingeto-*, cf. Ir *cingid* 'he steps, walks'; *-rix*, cf. Ir *rí* (gen.
ríge), W *rhi*, Lat *rēx*, etc. (D. E. Evans 1967: 121–2); the name may
thus be interpreted literally as 'the king who walks over' but should
perhaps be taken as 'Super-champion' *vel sim.* (Hamp 1977–8: 12).[5]
The Gaulish personal name *Curmisagios* contains the elements *curmi-*
'beer', cf. Ir *cuirm*, W *cwrw*, and *-sagios* 'seeker', cf. Ir *saigid* 'he
seeks', W *haeddu* and *-hai* 'one who seeks . . .' (Ford and Hamp
1974–6: 155–7, Joseph 1987, Russell 1989: 38–9). The precise sense
of the compound is unclear though the more legalistic 'beer-steward' is
more complimentary than 'beer-seeker'.

A combination of ethnographers' accounts and the analysis of personal and local name elements allows us to identify the limits of Celtic
tribal movements, at least in general terms.[6] The high density of Celtic
name elements in Gaul, northern Italy and Spain shows that these
regions were largely, if not entirely, Celtic speaking in the pre-Roman
period, but the ethnographers also record migrations into the Italian and
Balkan peninsulas and even as far as Asia Minor (Rankin 1987:
45–102). In the 3rd and 2nd centuries BC, Celtic tribes migrated across
the Hellespont and settled in Galatia in central Asia Minor (Rankin
1987: 188–207); the tribal name *Tectosages* and the place name
Drunemeton (Strabo xii.5.1) 'oak-shrine' (compare Ir *drú*, W *derw*
'oak', and Ir *nemed* 'shrine, high noble', W *nefed* (Schmidt 1958)) tes-
tify to the Celticity of these immigrants (see Mitchell 1993: 11–58).
The relationship between the languages of these different areas is discussed below (1.6). At present we may consider the evidence of these
languages in more detail.

1.2.1 Gaul

The evidence of ethnography and naming practices can allow us to
define limits, but within the major Celtic speaking areas of western
Europe more evidence is available. Again much but not all the evidence
is onomastic. The presence of a Greek colony at Massalia (Marseilles)
made a writing system available to the inhabitants of southern Gaul
even before the arrival of the Romans.[7] There is a significant number of
Gaulish inscriptions written in Greek script (see Lejeune 1985 and

---

Kassitalos Ouersiknos dede bratou dekanten Ala[ ]*einoui*
'Kassitalos, son of *Ouersos, willingly gave a tithe to A.'

FIGURE 1.1   A Gallo-Greek inscription from southern Gaul. Lejeune 1985: G-206 (pp. 284–7).

6.2.1 below); most seem to date from between the 2nd and 1st centuries BC though some may be older. By far the majority of these 'Gallo-Greek' inscriptions are graffiti on fragments of pots and consist entirely of personal names. The stone inscriptions are fewer in number but often longer and more informative about the language. Most consist of dedications to divinities and, in addition to personal and divine names, contain several Gaulish phrases. Many are fragmentary but an almost complete example (given in Figure 1.1) shows the nature of the evidence. The phrase *dede bratou dekanten* has been convincingly interpreted as 'gave a tithe in gratitude' by Szemerényi (1974 and 1991), where *dede* represents a perfect 3rd singular corresponding in stem form to Latin *dedit* and *dekanten* is the accusative singular of a noun based on **dekan* 'ten' (cf. Ir *déc*, W *deg*, Gk *déka* and Lat *decem*). The inscription also demonstrates a very common feature of Gaulish nomenclature, the use of a suffixed form of a personal name to mark a patronymic (Russell 1988a: 136–7), hence the uncertainty over the basic form of the name in the example in Figure 1.1. Whatever the correct form of the final divine name, it is in the dative case with an ending *-oui*.

However, by far the largest and most important Gaulish inscriptions are not written in a Greek script but in Roman cursive. In January 1971 a lead tablet was found at the site of a sacred spring in Chamalières (Puy-de-Dôme) containing a Gaulish inscription of 336 characters, at the time the longest continuous Gaulish text. Interpretation of the text continues to be debated but it seems probable that it was intended as a curse-tablet (the Latin term is *defixio*) directed at the names listed in the text.[8] Twelve years later in August 1983 a much longer text of 1000 characters and more than 160 words was discovered near Aveyron; it is known as 'le plomb de Larzac'.[9] Again it seems to be a magical text but on this occasion involving women, some of whom appear to be magicians (Lambert in Lejeune *et al.* 1985: 176). Some of the text remains obscure but it makes several significant additions to our knowledge of the Gaulish lexicon and grammar. Notably, since the text deals with women, we acquire a much clearer understanding of the first (*ā*-stem) declension in Gaulish together with the Gaulish words for 'mother' and 'daughter', *matir* and *duxtir* respectively, e.g. *Adiega matir Aiias* 'Adiega, mother of Aiia' and the converse *Aiia duxtir*

Adiegias 'Aiia, daughter of Adiega' (Lejeune *et al.* 1985: 166). *Matir* is entirely expected and corresponds to Ir *máthair* as well as Eng *mother*, etc. On the other hand, *duxtir*, phonetically /duxti:r/, which is cognate with Eng *daughter* and Gk *thugatēr*, etc., has only previously been traced in the archaic Irish name element *Der-/Ter-* where it was unaccented and therefore reduced from the expected but unattested **duchtair* (O'Brien 1956).

In addition to the long inscriptions there is much material in the form of personal names in Latin inscriptions and graffiti on pottery.[10]

1.2.2 Northern Italy

On the other side of the Alps there is also evidence for Celtic languages spoken in northern Italy (the Roman province of Cisalpine Gaul). The valley of the Po began to be Romanized from about the 2nd century BC onwards but the onomastic and inscriptional evidence together with the anecdotal evidence of classical writers suggests that Celtic naming patterns and the language survived for some centuries (Rankin 1987: 153–4). The term used for the earliest Celtic language of Cisalpine Gaul is Lepontic.[11] Lejeune 1971 distinguished two types of Celtic in northern Italy; first, there is a body of evidence from around the Italian lakes which is taken to be a form of Celtic. It is this which he calls Lepontic. Recent finds (Gambari and Colonna 1988) and re-assessment of earlier evidence suggest that the earliest evidence for Lepontic texts dates from as early as the 6th century BC, thus making them the earliest records of Celtic by some way. Secondly, there are a few inscriptions in Italy in Gaulish, which is thought to have been brought into Italy by migrants from Gaul from the early 4th century BC onwards; they are written in a script borrowed from the Lepontic region and it is this group which is presented in Lejeune 1988. The linguistic differences between the two types are slight and it may perhaps be better to think in terms of a gradual infiltration and assimilation by Gaulish speakers rather than full-scale migration. A degree of bilingualism and cultural assimilation among speakers of Gaulish and Latin in northern Italy is implied by one of the most important Cisalpine inscriptions, the bilingual inscription of Todi.[12] The stone which is dated to around 150 BC contains two versions of the same inscription with the Lepontic coming after the Latin; side B is less damaged and is given in Figure 1.2 overleaf. There is a clear difference in word order which indicates that the Lepontic word order was not merely copying the Latin (Koch 1985a: 16); it is also probable that the Latin was translated from the Lepontic and not vice versa (Lejeune 1988: 49–52). As in Gaulish, a patronymic suffix is used, again *-kno-*, in contrast to the Latin *Drutei filius* (Russell 1988a: 136–6). The verbal form *karnitu* seems to be based on the noun found in Irish and Welsh as *carn* 'pile of stones, cairn'. The ending *-tu*, with an apparent plural *-tus* also found in

Latin:
[ATEGNATEI DRVTEI F COI]SIS DRVTEI F FRATER EIVS
MINIMVS LOCAVIT ET STATVIT
'Coisis, son of Drutos, his youngest brother, placed and established (this) for
Ategnatos, son of Drutos'

Lepontic:
ATEKNATI TRVTIKNI KARNITV ARTUAŠ KOISIS TRVTIKNOS
For A.   son of T.   assembled   stones   K.   son of T.
'Coisis, son of Drutos, assembled (these) stones for Ategnatos, son of Drutos'

FIGURE 1.2   The bilingual inscription from Todi (side B). Lejeune 1988: E-5
(pp. 41–52).

Lepontic and in Celtiberian, is problematical (D. E. Evans 1979: 529)
but does not seem to have any correspondent in the insular languages.[13]
The word for 'stones', *ARTUAŠ*, which corresponds to *LOKAN* 'grave'
on side A, seems to have a correspondent in OIr *art* 'stone', a rare glossary word which occurs in a parallel context (Russell 1988b: 29; but cf.
Lejeune 1988: 49).

1.2.3   The Iberian peninsula
Apart from Gaul and northern Italy, the third area which provides clear
evidence of Celtic speakers in the historical period is the Iberian peninsula. It is, however, very difficult to separate the Celtic elements from
other, possibly Indo-European, languages in the region (D. E. Evans
1979: 513–16). Finds of Hispano-Celtic material centre on an area bor-
dered by Burgos in the west and Zaragoza in the east, i.e. central
northern Spain. The identifiable Celtic material consists of a large number of names, and fragments of names, on tesserae, two relatively short
inscriptions from Peñalba de Villastar and Luzaga (Lejeune 1955), and
a recently discovered long inscription from Botorrita.
    The attention of Celticists has in recent years largely concentrated on
the last of these, an inscription found at Botorrita, near Zaragoza, in
April/May 1970. It probably dates from around 100 BC and the text may
well have been influenced in style and content by local Roman munici-
pal laws.[14] The script, which is partly syllabic and partly alphabetic, is
unique to the Iberian peninsula where it was used to write many of the
pre-Roman languages (Eska 1989b: 7–10; see also 6.2.2 below). It
seems clear that the text is juridical or quasi-juridical in content; the
phrasing *neCue . . . liTom . . . neCue liTom* seems to represent a prohi-

bition. In addition, some of the verbal forms seem to be subjunctive or at least modal in form. However, it is still uncertain whether the text on side A is related to the list of names on side B; if they are related, it is perhaps difficult to understand how the tablet was displayed (Russell 1992b: 177), although a wooden frame leaving both sides visible would not be an impossibility. Linguistically, the text not only provides a large number of lexical items and particularly verbal forms but it also offers some valuable insights into the syntax of Celtiberian; the use of *-Cue* 'and', e.g. *Tocoitoś-Cue śaŕniCio-Cue* (side A, lines 10–11) 'of T. and S.', traces of which survive in Old Irish (Binchy 1960), may be familiar from Latin but cannot have been imitated as Latin only uses the single *-que*. Similarly, *-ue* 'or' follows each member of the phrase, e.g. *PouśTom-ue Coŕuinom-ue maCaśi[a]m-ue ailam-ue* (side A, lines 4–5) 'the cow stable or (animal) enclosure or wall (of an enclosure) or (outer) wall' (following Eska 1989a: 179). While there is considerable debate over the interpretation of the inscription as a whole, it is generally agreed that it is Celtic. This agreement is based on a number of lexical items; for example, *Camanom* (side A, line 5) 'road, path' is Celtic in origin, cf. Ir *céimm*, W *cam* 'step', but was borrowed into Latin as **cammīnum*, which gave French *chemin*, Spanish *camino*, etc. (Eska 1989a: 53–4).

It has been reported that a second inscription has been discovered at the Botorrita site; at present it awaits decipherment and analysis (Meid 1992: 57, n. 102).

1.3   Insular Celtic

The Insular Celtic languages are those which are or were spoken in the British Isles. This customary definition also includes Breton spoken in Brittany in mainland Europe. The insular languages divide into the **Brittonic** group, consisting of Welsh, Cornish and Breton, and the **Goidelic** group, made up of Irish, Scottish Gaelic and Manx. The details of the relationship between the groups are discussed below (1.6, 2.1.2 (Goidelic), 4.3 (Brittonic)). First, the distribution of the languages requires consideration. The insular languages are the main object of study of this book and at this point only the barest outlines will be given; further details are found in Chapters 2 to 5.

1.3.1   Britain and Brittonic

In addition to the Celts' activities in Europe, the classical authors also record the close linguistic and tribal ties between Gaul and Britain; Julius Caesar used as one of his excuses for invading Britain the support given to rebellious Gaulish tribes by their relations across the Channel (*de Bello Gallico* (Handford 1951: 119)), while Tacitus noted the close similarities in religion and language between Britons and Gauls (*Agricola* (Mattingly and Handford 1970: 62)). Our evidence for the languages in Britain before the Roman occupation is, as on the Continent, necessarily filtered through the classical writers. During the Roman occupation (from AD 43 onwards) inscriptional evidence provides further information but nevertheless the evidence is still largely onomastic, consisting of personal names of British tribesmen, e.g. *Boudicca*, *Catuvellaunus*, etc., divine names of local cults, e.g. *Maponus*, *Sulis*, etc., and place names mainly from itineraries and early maps.[15] Until recently it had been assumed that Britons in the Roman province of Britain who wished to express themselves in writing would have used Latin since there was no tradition of writing in British (Jackson 1953: 99–100). However, among the large number of curse-tablets found at Bath there are two which may contain Celtic texts (Tomlin 1988: nos. 14 and 18). They are not just lists of names and are clearly not in Latin; the assumption is that they are British although at present they await further analysis (Tomlin 1987; see also Lambert 1994: 174).

The language spoken by the Britons in Roman-occupied Britain, often termed British, was the ancestor of Welsh, Cornish and Breton. To what extent Latin took over from British in the Roman province would have depended on a number of socio-linguistic and geographical factors, such as the degree of Romanization in a particular area, the social status (and therefore level of Romanization) of individual Britons, etc. (cf. Mann 1971, Hamp 1975a). It is highly probable, for example, that in the later centuries of Roman occupation less British would have been heard in the south-east of Britain than in the south-west. However, the large number of Latin loanwords in Welsh, Cornish and Breton indicates a sustained period of contact with Latin which went well beyond the period of Roman occupation.[16] On the other hand, the relatively small number of Celtic loanwords in Old English suggests that the Saxons landed in a south-east Britain which was linguistically Romanized.

Further north it is clear that forms of British survived well into the sub-Roman period. The area of southern Scotland, south of the Forth–Clyde line, and northern England consisted of three kingdoms, Strathclyde (most of south-west Scotland), Gododdin (south-east Scotland between the Forth and the Tyne) and Rheged (Solway basin and Eden valley) (see generally Price 1984: 146–54). Place name evidence from this area indicates a Celtic language, probably related to Welsh, etc., which is termed Cumbric or Pritenic, e.g. *Lanark* (= W *llanerch* 'glade'), *Pencaitland* (cf. W *pen* 'top, summit', *coedlan* 'copse'), *Melrose* (= W *moel* 'bald', *rhos* 'moor'), etc. (Price 1984: 148–9, Jackson 1963). In addition, Cumbric is represented by three lexical items preserved in the *Leges inter Brettos et Scottos* (Loth 1930:

389–400): *galnys* 'blood money for homicide' (= W *galanas*), *mercheta* 'tax paid to a lord by a father on his daughter's marriage' (cf. W *merched* 'girls'), *kelchyn* 'tribute paid when a ruler goes on a progress' (cf. W *cylch* 'circuit').[17] The Brittonic language of northern Britain seems also to have had a strong literary tradition which is reflected in early Welsh literature in the works attributed to Taliesin and Aneirin.[18]

With the westward movement of the Angles in the north and midlands and of the Saxons in the south during the 6th and 7th centuries AD, British speakers were gradually isolated and pushed back into the western peninsulas. Such was the pressure in the south-west peninsula that there was a series of migrations of British speakers across the Channel to Brittany, where a form of British has survived as Breton (see Chadwick 1965 and 1969).[19] Cornish was under constant pressure from English from the 7th century onwards and it therefore comes as some surprise that the last-known native speaker of Cornish died in 1777 (Price 1984: 136). On the other hand, Welsh has survived to the modern day though under considerable pressure from English.

1.3.2 Ireland and Goidelic

Ireland never felt the impact of Rome in quite the same way as Britain; the effect of this is that we have little evidence for the language of Ireland before literacy was introduced in the sub-Roman period. The earliest evidence we have is the list of names on Ptolemy's map (illustrated at Rivet and Smith 1979: 107). They comprise coastal landmarks and river and tribe names; some can be equated with later Irish names, e.g. *Bououinda* /buːu̯inda/ = OIr *Boänd* (the modern River Boyne), *Auteinoi* = the OIr tribal name *Úaithni*, but many are obscure.[20] Despite Ireland's geographical isolation beyond the frontiers of the Roman Empire, there is increasing evidence of regular and continuous contact with both Roman Britain and Roman Gaul (Stevenson 1989: 130–3). A familiarity with Latin both as a spoken and as a written language is implied by recent interpretations of the archaic script called Ogam in which the early inscriptions are written (see McManus 1991, and 6.3.1 below). Irish remained for centuries the main language in Ireland despite invasions by Vikings and the English; it continues to be spoken at least in parts of Ireland to the present day. The related languages of Manx and Scottish Gaelic were established through the migration of Irish speakers from Ireland to the Isle of Man and western Scotland respectively.[21] In Scotland the key event was the establishment of a permanent colony of the Dál Riada from northern Ireland in Argyll and Bute in around AD 500 (Price 1984: 49–50). From there and by further migrations from Ireland Irish speakers spread through the islands and mainland of western Scotland. Jackson (1951:

74–5) has argued that the languages did not begin to diverge significantly until the 10th century or even later (but see 2.3 below). Similarly, settlers seem to have arrived in the Isle of Man from the fifth century onwards (Price 1984: 71–83). Scottish Gaelic still survives although with difficulty in some areas, while the last native speaker of Manx died in 1974.[22]

1.4 The distinctive features of Celtic languages

It is conventional to reconstruct a notional Proto-Celtic ancestor language which is phonologically and morphologically distinct from other Indo-European dialects. The following list of features is not exhaustive but will give some idea of the nature of Celtic languages. Many of the features are found in other Indo-European languages (for example, loss of *p is paralleled in Armenian) but it is the sum of these features which goes to define the Celtic languages.

1.4.1 Phonology

Reconstructed Proto-Celtic represents a stage at which a range of sound changes has already taken place which distinguishes it from other Indo-European languages and is common to all Celtic languages. It is not intended here to present a full historical phonology; four distinctive changes may be used to illustrate the process.[23]

1.4.1.1 Long vowels and diphthongs

Proto-Celtic inherited a system of five long vowels and a series of diphthongs, as presented in Figure 1.3. Within the Proto-Celtic period, i.e. the changes are shared by both Goidelic and Brittonic, this arrangement was re-adjusted in four ways (see Table 1.1). The effect of these re-adjustments was to maintain a five long-vowel system but to reduce the number of diphthongs in Proto-Celtic (see Figure 1.4).

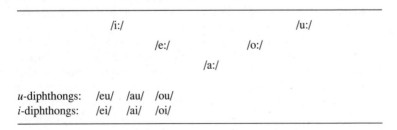

/i:/				/u:/
	/e:/		/o:/	
		/a:/		

u-diphthongs:	/eu/	/au/	/ou/
i-diphthongs:	/ei/	/ai/	/oi/

FIGURE 1.3 The inherited system of long vowels and diphthongs

TABLE 1.1   Proto-Celtic developments to the long vowels and diphthongs

(i)   /e:/ > /i:/, e.g. OIr *rí*, MW *rhi*, Gaul *-rix* 'king' < Pr-C **rīks* < IE **rēks*
       (cf. Lat *rēx*).

(ii) /o:/ > /a:/ in non-final syllables, e.g. OIr *már*, W *mawr* 'great', Gaul
       -maros < Pr-C **māros* < IE *mōros* (cf. Gk *-mōros* 'big, long').
       BUT /o:/ > /u:/ in final syllables, e.g. OIr *cú* 'dog' < Pr-C **kwū* < IE
       *ku̯ō(n) (cf. Gk *kúōn*). Nom. sg. *-u* < *-ō*, e.g. Gaul *Frontu* < Lat *Frontō*.

(iii) /ei/ > /e:/ replacing original /e:/ which had given /i:/ in (i) above, e.g. OIr
       día (gen. sg. *dé*) 'god', Gaul *Devo-* < Pr-C **dēu̯o-* < IE **deiu̯o-* 'divine'
       (cf. Lat *dīvus*, etc.).

(iv) /eu/ > /ou/ > /o:/, e.g. OIr *túath*, MW *tut* 'people' < Pr-C **tōtā* < **toutā* <
       IE *teutā* (cf. Osc *touto*, Goth *þiuda*, Lithuanian *tautà*, etc.).

It has been conventional to include /au/ in this development; but see now Lambert 1990
who argues that /au/ survived as a diphthong into the separate Brittonic languages.

1.4.1.2   Loss of /p/

One of the most striking features of Celtic phonology in an Indo-
European context is the absence of an inherited /p/ (H. Lewis and
Pedersen 1961: 26–7; see Table 1.2 overleaf for examples). However,
the loss of /p/ may well have been relatively late in Proto-Celtic since
in some environments it left traces (McCone 1991b: 46–6, 1992:
14–15); for example, in the cluster /pt/ which gave /xt/, e.g. Ir *secht*, W
saith 'seven', Gaul *sextametos* 'seventh' < IE **sept-*, Ir *necht*, W *nith*
'niece' < IE **neptī-* (cf. OHG *nift*, Skt *napti-*), in the cluster /pn/, e.g. Ir
dúan < **dapno-* (cf. Lat *dapes*, etc. (C. Watkins 1976)), where /p/ survived long enough to create a diphthong in Irish when it was lost (see
2.2.2), and in clusters of /p/ + liquid, e.g. *ebraid* 'he will give' < **pipr-*,
eblaid 'he will drive' < **pipl-* (cf. Lat *pellere*). Furthermore, Ir *cóic*, W

(/e:/, /i:/ >)	/i:/		/u:/ (< /u:/, final /o:/)
(/ei/ >)	/e:/	/o:/ (< /ou/ (including /eu/))	
	/a:/	(< /a:/, non-final /o:/)	

dipthongs:
/au/   /ai/   /oi/

FIGURE 1.4   The Proto-Celtic long vowels and diphthongs

TABLE 1.2   Examples of loss of /p/ in Celtic

Ir *athir* 'father' < IE *patēr* (cf. Lat *pater*, Goth *fadar*, etc.)
Ir *én*, W *edn*, OCo *ethen* 'bird' < IE *pet-* (cf. Lat *penna* 'feather', Gk *pétomai* 'fly')
Ir *for*, OW *guor*, W *gor-*, Gaul *uer-* 'over' < *u̯or < IE *uper* (cf. Gk *hupér*, Latin *super*)
Ir *íasc* 'fish', W RN *Wysg* < *eisko- < IE *peisko-* (cf. Lat *piscis*, Eng *fish*, etc.)

pimp 'five' < *$k^w enk^w e$ < *$penk^w e$ (cf. Gk *pénte*, Skt *pañca*) show an assimilation of *p. . .k^w-* > *k^w. . .k^w-* which would have occurred in Proto-Celtic before the loss of /p/ (see 1.7 below). In theory, therefore, it would be possible for an early Celtic dialect still to retain /p/, although, since loss of /p/ is so embedded in the definition of a Celtic language, it might be difficult to incorporate such a language into any broad definition of the Celtic group.

In later stages of the languages, /p/ re-occurred; in Brittonic languages it arose from /kʷ/ (1.5.1 below), while in Goidelic it first arose from the simplification and devoicing of consonant clusters and then entered the language in loanwords from Latin (2.2.5 below).

1.4.1.3   IE /gʷ/ > /b/
The labialization of /gʷ/ is regular, e.g. OIr *bó*, W *bu* 'cow, ox' < IE *$g^w ou-$ (cf. Lat *bous*, Gk *boûs*, Skt *gauh)*, Gaul *bnanom*, OIr *ben*, W *benyw* 'woman' < IE *$g^w enā$ (cf. Gk *gunḗ* (dialect *bana*)).[24]

*1.4.1.4   IE */r̥/ and */l̥/ > Celtic /ri/ and /li/*
In positions between consonants /r̥/ and /l̥/ are vocalized in all languages though the quality of the vowel varies significantly. In Celtic they are vocalized as /ri/ and /li/, e.g. W *rhyd*, Gaul *Ritu-* 'ford' < *pr̥tu- (cf. Lat *portus*, Eng *ford*), OIr *lethan*, W *llydan*, Gaul *Litano-* 'broad' < *pl̥t-(cf. Gk *platús*) (de Bernardo Stempel 1987).

1.4.2   Morphology and syntax
There are also morphological features common to all the Celtic languages. Most of these are preservations of features found in other Indo-European languages and again it is the combination of features which is diagnostic. There are, however, some features which are unique to Celtic.

1.4.2.1   Nominal inflection
Only the Goidelic languages preserve a case system and show reflexes
of the Indo-European system; for some examples, see 1.1 above.
In addition, both the neuter gender and the dual inflection are
preserved in the earlier stages of the languages, particularly in Old Irish;
for example, *láa mbrátha* 'Day of Judgement' shows the nasalization of
brátha (gen. sg. of *bráth* 'judgement') which reflects the original ending
-on of the word 'day', an ending characteristic of the neuter (cf. Lat
-um, Gk *-on*). Dual forms still occur after OIr *da* 'two', e.g. *da chlaideb*
'two swords' (nom. pl.) beside *claidib* 'swords' (nom. pl.).

1.4.2.2   The verbal system
There is no doubt that Celtic inherited a full range of categories of
tenses and moods (McCone 1986 and 1991a). Diagnostic features are
reduplicated futures, e.g. OIr *cichset* 'they will step' : *cingid* 'he steps'
(McCone 1991a: 137–82), the use of an *r*-ending in passives and
impersonal forms, e.g. *berair* 'it is carried' : *berid* 'he carries', MW
kerir 'it is loved', which is shared by Latin, Hittite and Tokharian
(Cowgill 1983), the use of a *-tio-* suffix for passive past participles
and preterite passives, e.g. *mórthae* 'praised' < **mōr-tio-* : *móraid* 'he
praises', MW *honneit* 'known' (Schmidt 1971).
   Celtic languages also reflect the workings of 'Wackernagel's Law',
which requires that enclitic, unaccented elements, usually sentence particles or pronouns, go in second place in the sentence after the first
accented element (Collinge 1985: 217–19). There is, however, a Celtic
refinement sometimes known as 'Vendryes' Restriction'. The Celtic
refinement seems to require that pronouns, or sometimes in the archaic
language sentence connectives, should either be infixed into compound
or negative verbs or, in archaic Irish only, suffixed to simple verbs
(Breatnach 1977), e.g. OIr *fom·gaib* 'he seizes me': *fo·gaib* 'he seizes',
ním·ben 'he does not strike me' : *ní·ben* 'he does not strike', *beirthi* 'he
carries it' : *berid* 'he carries' (Watkins 1963a, McCone 1979a). There
are traces of the same pattern in early Welsh, e.g. MW *dym-kyueirch*
'he greets me', *rym-goruc* 'he has made me', etc. (H. Lewis and
Pedersen 1961: 206–7, D. S. Evans 1964: 55–7). A striking feature of
Celtic languages which seems to be related to this is the regular initial
verb; this is discussed below (Chapter 9). Whether this is a feature of
all Celtic languages or just a feature of Insular Celtic depends on the
interpretation of Continental Celtic forms, such as *to-so-kote*, *tio-in-*
uoru, *to-med-eclai*, etc. (Lambert 1994: 67–8).

1.4.2.3   Possession
No Celtic language has a finite verb signifying possession equivalent to
English *have*. The constructions used are parallel to Latin *est mihi* or

Greek *estí moi*, both meaning literally 'there is to me'; compare Irish *tá airgead aige* and Welsh *mae arian gyda fe*, both 'he has money' (lit. 'there is money with him'). The use of prepositional forms, it seems, has replaced the use of the dative infixed pronoun. In both Old Irish and early Middle Welsh infixed forms are found, e.g. OIr *ros·mbia lóg* 'they shall have a reward' (lit. 'a reward shall be to them (-*s*)') (H. Lewis and Pedersen 1961: 196–7), MW *chwioryd a'm bu* 'I had sisters' (lit. 'sisters were to me') (D. S. Evans 1964: 57). However, in Cornish and Breton the infixed pattern survived, e.g. MCo *am bes*, MB *em-eus* 'I have' (lit. 'there is to me') (H. Lewis and Pedersen 1961: 210, 213).

1.5   The distinctive features of Goidelic and Brittonic

Most of the features which distinguish Goidelic from Brittonic are phonological. There are morphological differences but they tend to be differences of degree; for example, despite the general loss of final syllables in late Insular Celtic (i.e. not in Continental Celtic nor in Ogam), Goidelic languages retain a functioning, though eroded, case system to the present day, while even in the earliest evidence for distinct Brittonic languages the case system has vanished. The reasons for this are complex and in part at least involve phonological differences between the language groups (compare 2.2 with 4.2 for further discussion). At this point, two examples which distinguish Goidelic from Brittonic will be sufficient.

1.5.1   P and Q Celtic

The most obvious phonological distinction involves the outcome of the unvoiced labiovelar */kʷ/. In phonetic terms it was delabialized in Goidelic in most environments and merged with /k/, but was fully labialized in Brittonic and gave /p/, e.g. Ir *cethar*, W *pedwar* 'four' < *k^wetuores* (cf. Lat *quattuor*), Ir *cía*, W *pwy* 'who?' < *k^weis* (cf. Lat *quis*, etc.), Ir *fliuch*, W *gwlyb* 'wet' < *$u̯lik^w$o-* (cf. Lat *liquor*, etc.). In the environment of /u/, /kʷ/ was delabialized even in Brittonic, e.g. Ir *búachaill*, W *bugail* 'cowherd' < *g^wou-k^wol-* (cf. Gk *boukólos*). Primitive Irish in Ogam script still shows the retention of /kʷ/, e.g. *MAQ(Q)I* 'son' < *mak^wk^wo-* (cf. Ir *macc*, W *mab*), *QRITTI* < *k^writu-* (cf. Ir *cruth*, W *pryd* 'form, shape') (McManus 1991: 121–2).

   This basic difference has given rise to the unfortunate terms P-Celtic and Q-Celtic for Brittonic and Goidelic respectively. It is immediately recognizable but in phonological terms it is relatively trivial (Hamp 1958). The same change occurs in Italic, where Latin preserved -*qu*- but in Oscan and Umbrian */kʷ/ gave /p/ as in Brittonic. In Greek */kʷ/ gave /p/ before /o/ and /a/, /k/ in the environment of /u/, and /t/ before /i/ and /e/. In other words, */kʷ/ is potentially unstable and prone to simplification, and its significance may have been over-rated.

TABLE 1.3   Accent mobility in Gaulish tribal names reflected in modern place names

Rennes < Rédones	:	*Redon < Redónes*
Condes < Cóndate	:	*Condé < Condáte*
Bourges < Bitúriges	:	*Berry < Bituríges*

Furthermore, Whatmough (1963: 110–11) pointed out that acoustically /kʷ/ and /p/ are very similar and it is highly probable that they may have existed as allophonic variants in Proto-Celtic. The close acoustic similarity is supported by the early Irish treatment of /p/ in loanwords as /k/, e.g. *Cothriche < Patricius* (see 2.2.5 below).

1.5.2   Word accent

There are more fundamental differences than *p* and *q*. In Goidelic, accented words are stressed on the initial syllable, while in Brittonic the stress was on the penultimate syllable (H. Lewis and Pedersen 1961: 69–80). This difference produced major variations in word shape and prosodic patterns. Accentuation in Indo-European and thus in Proto-Celtic was extremely complicated but essentially it seems to have had considerable freedom of movement. Evidence for the mobility of the accent is found in the different French reflexes of Gaulish tribal names (see Table 1.3).

The fixing of the accent on the initial syllable in Goidelic produced a reduction and syncope of unaccented syllables in surrounding syllables; for example, compare *samail* 'similar' with the compounded *cosmil* 'similar' which shows syncope of the vowel between the *s* and *m*. Long vowels were reduced, e.g. *marcach* 'horseman' /'markəx/ < *márkāko- (see 2.2.2).

In Brittonic, accentual matters were complicated in different ways. The penultimate stress accent was fixed before the loss of endings. Subsequently, with the erosion of final syllables, the accent shifted back to the new penultimate (see 4.2.3, 4.2.5).

1.6   The inter-relationship of the Celtic languages

The details of the relationship of the languages within Goidelic and Brittonic are discussed below in Chapters 2 and 4. As a preliminary, and with no justification, the traditional family tree is given in Figure 1.5.

Of more importance at this point is the relationship of the Insular Celtic to the Continental languages. However, a prior question concerns the Continental group itself; for it is not clear that there is any agreement about their inter-relationship. Certain isoglosses do present themselves but the evidence for the languages is so fragmentary that lit-

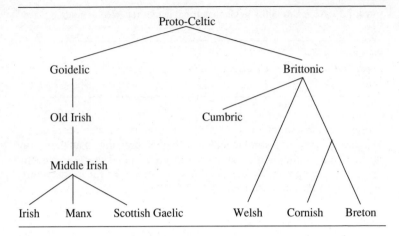

FIGURE 1.5   The traditional family tree of the insular Celtic languages

tle weight can be placed on them. This is particularly the case when one of the isoglosses in question is the vexed *p/q* distinction discussed above (1.5.1). In Gaulish and Lepontic */kʷ/ and */kṷ/ as a rule gave /p/ as in Brittonic, e.g. Gaul *Epo-* 'horse', *petru-* 'four', Lep *-pe* 'and' (cf. Lat *-que*, Gk *te* < **kʷe*), while in Celtiberian it remained as a labiovelar, e.g. *-Cue* 'and', *neCue* 'neither'. But the apparent clear-cut distinction is blurred by a number of Gaulish forms in *-qu-*, e.g. *equos* and *quimon* from the Calendar of Coligny (Duval and Pinault 1986), and the local and tribal names *Sequana* 'Seine', *Sequani, Quariates* 'Queyras', etc. The validity of *p/q* could be rescued by appeal to archaism; that is, the Gaulish forms with *-qu-* could be archaisms, especially those preserved in the Calendar of Coligny, which pre-date the change of /kʷ/ to /p/ (Schmidt 1978–80: 197–8, 1988: 232–5). But it is very difficult to argue for archaism or innovation when it is impossible to establish any dates or relative chronology, or indeed whether these forms should be considered Celtic at all.

     In recent years several scholars have suggested that there is evidence, which goes beyond the *p/q* distinction, that Gaulish and Lepontic and the Brittonic group are more closely related so that one can speak of a Gallo-Brittonic group (Fleuriot 1978, 1980: 51–79, 1988, Koch 1985b: 49–67, D. E. Evans 1988: 220). On the other hand, it is not clear that Celtiberian can be paired with Goidelic despite the fact that both preserved */kʷ/ and */kṷ/. For example, Goidelic has been seen to be distinct from all the other Celtic languages in its treatment of vocalic */m̥/ and */n̥/, e.g. OIr *imb* 'around': W *am*, Celtib/Gaul *ambi-* < **m̥bhi-* (cf. Gk *amphí*, Lat *ambō*, etc.) (McCone 1991b: 57).

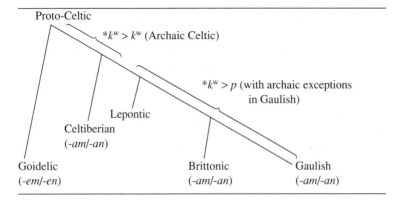

FIGURE 1.6   The emergence of the Celtic languages according to Schmidt 1988

Schmidt 1988 has argued that the Celtic languages emerged in the order presented in Figure 1.6. There are a number of difficulties with this reconstruction. First, it puts a great deal of weight on the *p/q* distinction when this could well have been allophonic for a considerable period. Secondly, it is not clear how significant the Goidelic feature of */m̥/ and */n̥/ > -*em*/-*en* really is; this change has been questioned by some who have argued that */m̥/ and */n̥/ gave -*am*/-*an* in Goidelic which subsequently changed to -*em*/-*en* in certain environments (McCone 1991b: 53–69, cf. Szemerényi 1991), while others have argued that */m̥/ and */n̥/ gave -*em*/-*en* in Gaulish as well (Szemerényi 1978). On balance, the evidence tends to support the former argument; if so, Schmidt's scheme in Figure 1.6 seems fatally damaged.

The range of possibilities is not exhausted by the above discussion. It is at least theoretically possible that all the sub-groups of the Celtic group are to be derived directly from Proto-Celtic, as in Figure 1.7, and

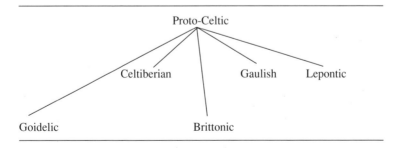

FIGURE 1.7   An alternative view of the relationship of the Celtic languages

that any striking parallels between sub-groups is due to subsequent contact between speakers. To point to one historically documented case,
we know that speakers of Brittonic and Gaulish were in contact in the
1st century BC (see 1.3.1). The difficulty is then merely displaced to
deciding which features represent a genetic relationship as opposed to
those which are simply due to language contact.

The methodological problem with a discussion of this type is to
decide which features are significant; we have seen that much of the
discussion has centred on very fragile alternations. To go further it
would be necessary to consider more thoroughgoing aspects of morphological and syntactic structures. But despite the growing corpus of
Continental Celtic material, these areas of study are still bedevilled by
the fragmentary nature of the evidence and by difficulties in dating the
material. The distinction between the Insular and Continental languages
is purely one of geographical convenience, though still useful, and
probably does not reflect any genetic difference.

1.7   The Italo-Celtic hypothesis

While it is universally agreed that the Celtic languages form part of the
Indo-European group, there is less agreement about whether Celtic
belonged to a sub-group within Indo-European. The prime candidate
for partnership has been Italic (Latin, Faliscan, Oscan, Umbrian). It is,
however, important to establish what kind of connection is being postu-
lated and what kind of evidence can be used to prove or disprove the
hypothesis. Two language groups can share features because of a common genetic origin, i.e. they had a common ancestor at some point in
prehistory. Alternatively, the phonological and morphological structures of two language groups, which have no common genetic ancestry,
might converge on account of geographical proximity. Various intermediate situations can also be envisaged where two related languages
also go through a period of geographical proximity. The question is not
even as simple as deciding between these various scenarios. For Italic
and Celtic it is agreed that they are genetically related through an
ancestral Indo-European and that for some considerable period they
were geographically contiguous, but do the similarities suggest a closer
connection between them than between either of them and other Indo-
European languages? In other words, is there any justification for the
relationship posited in Figure 1.8(a) rather than the one in 1.8(b)?[25] To
these basic questions can be added the structural objection raised by C.
Watkins 1966a that any particular feature must be seen within its own
linguistic system and not just extracted and examined in isolation, as,
for example, with the Celtic and Italic *ā*-subjunctive or *b*-future.
Moreover, at least as much effort should be expended on the differences as on the similarities.

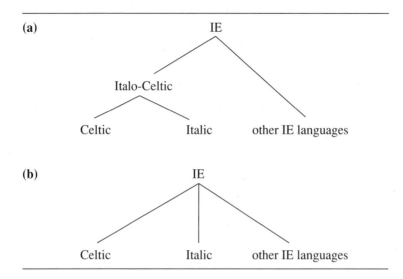

(a)   IE

        Italo-Celtic

    Celtic   Italic   other IE languages

(b)   IE

    Celtic   Italic   other IE languages

FIGURE 1.8   The Italo-Celtic hypothesis

A basic list of features was first produced and then elaborated upon by Meillet (1933: 16–47). The list suffers from the deficiency noted above that it tends to abstract features from their context and over the years has been eroded by the work of other scholars.[26] This is not the place to discuss the features in detail but it may be useful to mention briefly those which have survived the critical onslaught longest.

As was pointed out above (1.4.1.2), Ir *cóic*, W *pimp* 'five' < *$k^w enk^w e$ < *$penk^w e$ (cf. Gk *pénte*, Skt *pañca*) show an assimilation of *p*...k^w- > k^w...k^w-. The same assimilation also occurs in Latin, e.g. *quinque* 'five' < *$k^w enk^w e$, etc. Compare also Lat *coquus*, W *pobi* 'cook' < *$k^w ok^w$- < *pok^w- (cf. Gk *péttō* < *pek^w-). It has been argued that this assimilation goes back to a period of Italo-Celtic unity. However, C. Watkins 1966a: 33–5 has demonstrated that there is a problem of chronology in relation to the change of *-$k^w u$- to *-*ku*-. The case of Lat *quercus* 'oak' < *$perk^w u$- is central to the argument. The ancient name for the Hercynian Forest of central Europe, Gk *Herkúnia*, which is connected with Lithuanian *Perkūnas* 'a thunder god', shows it to be a derivative of *$perk^w u$- 'oak'. Lat *quercus* shows that the assimilation took place before the change of *-$k^w u$- to *-*ku*- in Italic, since *p*...*ku*- would not have undergone assimilation. However, Gk *Herkúnia*, which is to be regarded as reflecting a Celtic original because of the loss of *p*-, indicates that in Celtic *-$k^w u$- went to *-*ku*- before the assimilation and *p*- was thus preserved and later lost. The conclusion must be that the assimilation took place independently in each language group and does not indicate a period of unity.[27]

It has long been argued that the Latin *amabo*-type future is to be related to the *f*-future of Old Irish, e.g. *léicfea* 'he will leave' : *léicid* 'he leaves'. Problems have arisen over the phonology of the equation and the precise formation of the Latin tense. Despite valiant attempts (e.g. Quin 1978), the Latin *b* cannot correspond to Old Irish *f*. Moreover, in principle it is difficult to equate the tenses when the *f*-future only occurs in Old Irish and not in Brittonic or the Continental languages; independent innovation in Irish seems a more likely prospect (*pace* C. Watkins 1966b), though the most recent explanation along these lines is not convincing (McCone 1991a: 176–82, Russell 1993a: 165–7).

Cowgill 1970 argued that the superlative formations in Italic and Celtic reflect a suffix *-is-ṃmo-* as opposed to *-is-to-* found elsewhere, e.g. OIr *sinem*, OW *hinham* 'oldest' < *sen-is-ṃmo-* , Latin *maximus* 'biggest' < *mag-is-ṃmo-*. His arguments were examined by De Coene 1976–8: 409–11, who argued that his case was not sufficient to regard *-is-ṃmo-* as a common innovation as against a parallel but independent innovation.

Even the claimed common innovations are open to objections; in particular they do not fulfil the criterion of demonstrating a close genetic origin as opposed either to a more distant genetic origin or to mutual influences when in close geographical proximity.

Contacts were not limited to the prehistoric period. As the official language of the western half of the Roman Empire, Latin influenced many of the languages of Europe and was influenced by them, especially at the lexical level. Contact with the Gauls of northern Italy and Gaul itself brought about considerable lexical acquisition, particularly in terminology unique to Celtic tribes, e.g. *bracae* 'trousers', *cervesia* 'beer', *cucullus* 'cloak', *essedum* 'chariot', *carrus* 'wagon', *gaesa* 'javelin', *bardus* 'bard', *druidae* 'druids', etc. (Palmer 1954: 52–3, Lambert 1994: 185–204). The Gaulish substratum also influenced the Vulgar Latin of Gaul and, it has been argued, can be used to explain not only lexical variation (Ewert 1961: 289–90, Pope 1934: 5) but also perhaps the vigesimal counting system (Ewert 1961: 147–8; see 3.3.7 and 5.3.6 below).

Roman contact with Britons brought about lexical influence on the Brittonic languages and also, primarily through ecclesiastical channels, on the Goidelic languages (McManus 1983, 1984). Mac Cana 1976 has further suggested that Latin influence may account for the form of the pluperfect tense in Brittonic languages and have something to do with the proliferation of compound prepositions in Brittonic but not in Goidelic (for the latter, see 4.2.7 below).

Notes

1. One omission is any detailed discussion of sociolinguistic aspects of the languages (though there are passing references). These have been dealt with in far greater detail in recent works, such as Ó Murchú 1993 (Modern Irish), Mackinnon 1993 (Scottish Gaelic), R. O. Jones 1993 (Modern Welsh), Humphreys 1993 (Modern Breton), George and Broderick 1993 (Cornish and Manx respectively). While a section is devoted to the fate of Irish (3.1.2) there is no similar section on Welsh; however, the 1991 Census figures are now discussed by Aitchison and Carter 1994.

2. For a review, see Müller 1994; and for a less satisfactory introduction, see Gregor 1980.

3. For a basic introduction to the Indo-European languages, see Lockwood 1969 and 1972 (for Celtic see 1969: 140–51 and 1972: 62–94). For more advanced introductions to comparative Indo-European linguistics, see Meillet 1937 and Szemerényi 1990.

   The only full bibliography of the Celtic languages was *Bibliotheca Celtica* (National Library of Wales 1909–84), which has now ceased publication. Annual bulletins appear in the *Proceedings of the Modern Languages Association, Studia Celtica*, and *Die Sprache* (vol. 13 (1967) onwards). Best 1913 and 1942, and Baumgarten 1986 provide the fullest bibliography for Irish (a volume up to 1986 is in preparation). For Welsh, see J. E. C. Williams and Hughes 1988. For Breton, Hemon 1947 is useful for earlier material; see also Le Bihan 1957 on early printed material. For literature, Bromwich 1974 provides a select bibliography; see also Matonis 1987. A bibliography of Continental Celtic is in the course of preparation by Eska. For Latin material from Celtic sources, see Lapidge and Sharpe 1985.

4. D. E. Evans 1979 has a full discussion of the difficulties of interpretation and also provides a useful history and bibliography of the scholarship; for a general discussion, see Schmidt 1977a. The largest but very unreliable collection of Continental Celtic onomastics is Holder 1891–1913; see now Billy 1993. Whatmough 1970 provides a more up-to-date collection for the Roman provinces of Gaul. Dottin 1920 was the best introduction to Gaulish, but has now been superseded by Lambert 1994. For Galatia, see now Mitchell 1993: 11–58.

5. The difficulties of personal name interpretation are notorious; see D. E. Evans 1967: 40–2, 296–7, and 1970–2: 415–17.

6. For a collection of the main texts from Athenaeus, Diodorus Siculus and Strabo, see Tierney 1960. In addition there are detailed but probably derivative accounts in Caesar's *Gallic Wars* (text in Du Pontet 1900, translation in Handford 1951); for the problems of the transmission of personal and local names in Caesar, see D. E. Evans 1967: 21–31. The attitudes of classical authors to the Celts are discussed by Rankin 1987: 103–52.

7. On the early history of southern Gaul, see Rivet 1988: chs. 1–3.

8. The text of the inscription was published by Lejeune and Marichal 1976–7: 156–68. Subsequently, interpretative discussions have been contributed by Fleuriot 1976–7, Lambert 1979a and 1987 and Schmidt 1980–2; see also

Meid 1992: 38–40 and Lambert 1994: 150–9. A full edition of all the Gaulish inscriptions in Roman cursive is in preparation in the same series as Lejeune 1985 and 1988. For similar texts from Britain (almost entirely in Latin), see Tomlin 1988.

9. The text of the inscription was published together with interpretative discussions by Lejeune *et al*. 1985; see also Schmidt 1990, Meid 1992: 40–6.
10. See, for example, Marichal 1988 (Graffiti of Graufesenque) and Duval and Pinault 1986 (Calendar of Coligny).
11. A major difficulty in this area is distinguishing the number of different languages, such as Venetic, Etruscan and Latin, not to mention the large number of language names invented by scholars, e.g. Ligurian, Proto-Ligurian, Celto-Ligurian, Lepontic, Luganian, Gallic, Celtic, etc. (D. E. Evans 1979: 517–20). In the main collection of Cisalpine Celtic material, Lejeune 1971 used the term Lepontic, though with some reservations (see Lejeune 1972), and that is the term used here; the best edition of the main texts is now Lejeune 1988.
12. Rhŷs 1906: 69–74, Conway *et al*. 1933: no. 339, Lejeune 1971: 385–92, Koch 1985a: 16–19, Lejeune 1988: E-5 (pp. 42–52), Meid 1992: 12–15. Lambert 1994: 74–6.
13. It is generally agreed that the *-s* is a plural marker, which can either be derived from the nominal ending or perhaps from the 1st plural *-mos*. The ending *-tu* has been variously interpreted as a preterite (Lejeune 1971: 430–6, 1988: 21), as an imperative (Schmidt 1976a: 392, 1978–80: 193–4), as a future imperative (Eska 1989a: 169, 1989b), or as a rather more vaguely defined modal form (Fleuriot 1979: 130–1). The difficulty with the modal explanations is that they cannot apply to all the examples, especially not to the Todi inscription; Eska 1989b, for example, is happy that the Celtiberian examples should have a separate explanation from Lepontic *karnitu*, etc. See also Lejeune 1971: 449–52 and Eska 1990b.
14. The clearest transcription and photographs of the cleaned text are in Beltrán and Tovar 1982. Interpretative studies are numerous; the most important are Lejeune 1973, de Hoz and Michelena 1974, Fleuriot 1975, Schmidt 1976a and 1976b, Fleuriot 1988, Eska 1989b, Eichner 1989: 23–56. Earlier finds of 'Celtiberian' material are collected in Lejeune 1955. A definitive edition of the pre-Roman linguistic remains of the Iberian peninsula, and not only Celtiberian, is in progress; the sections published so far are Untermann 1975, 1980 and 1990.
15. The inscriptions of Roman Britain are still in the process of publication. The stone inscriptions are in Collingwood and Wright 1965, with indexes in Goodburn and Waugh 1983. The inscriptions on *instrumenta domestica* are being published by Frere *et al*., 1990 and Frere and Tomlin 1991a, 1991b, 1992, 1993 and 1994. Recent inscriptions are usually published in the journals *Britannia* or *Journal of Roman Studies*. For what is known of the Celtic population, see Birley 1979. The standard work on place names in Roman Britain is Rivet and Smith 1979. There is no reference work similar to D. E. Evans 1967 for the personal names of Roman Britain though he provides much of the documentation for Roman Britain as well as Gaul. The recent publication of the large find of curse-tablets from Bath

has brought to light another rich collection of Celtic names (see Tomlin 1988).

16. For a full survey, see D. E. Evans 1983. Loanwords in the Brittonic languages are collected in Loth 1892, with more specialized collections in Lewis 1943 and Haarmann 1970 for Welsh, and Haarmann 1973 for Breton.

17. See Jackson 1953: 9–10, 1980: 88, Price 1984: 148. It is not clear from Jackson's discussion that the *Leges inter Brettos et Scottos* are a set of laws between British speakers and speakers of a Goidelic language in Scotland; in addition to the three items mentioned, there are four Goidelic words *cro* 'compensation for homicide' and *enach* 'honour' (lit. 'face'), *turhocret* (= OIr *turfochraic* 'compensation'), *octhiern* (= OIr *ócthigern* 'lower grade of noble') (Loth 1930: 392–9).

18. See Williams 1968 and 1938 respectively. For a translation of Aneirin, see Jackson 1969 and Jarman 1988. For recent discussions of the manuscript and text, see Roberts 1988.

19. The question has been raised by some scholars as to the extent that Breton represents not only the language of migrants from Britain but also the survival of Gaulish; the question is examined below (4.3).

20. The only full discussion of the Irish part of Ptolemy's map – T. F. O'Rahilly 1946: 1–42 – must be used with care.

21. On the pre-Goidelic Pictish population of Scotland, see the collection of essays in Wainwright 1980, and especially Jackson 1980, and more briefly Price 1984: 155–7.

22. See R. L. Thomson 1969, and for a recent description of late spoken Manx, see Broderick 1984–6.

23. None of what follows in this section is controversial and further examples may be found in the standard historical grammars such as Pedersen 1909–13 and H. Lewis and Pedersen 1961.

24. For the controversy over the Celtic outcome of $*g^wh$, see the main discussions by Cowgill 1980 and Sims-Williams 1982, and the subsequent comments by McCone 1991b: 38–45 and Koch 1992.

25. Such questions also presuppose the notion both of a unitary Celtic proto-language and a unitary Italic proto-language. We have seen above that a Proto-Celtic can be posited though the precise inter-relationships remain unclear. Doubts have also afflicted Italic scholars such as Beeler 1966 and Jeffers 1973. Walde 1917 even went as far as to split both Celtic and Italic, and link Oscan and Umbrian with Brittonic and Latin with Goidelic.

26. C. Watkins 1966a launched the most devastating modern attack on the theory, though Cowgill 1970 attempted to rescue the superlative formations from the wreckage, and Kortlandt 1981 has attempted unconvincingly to adduce further evidence. De Coene 1972–4 and 1976–8 has added further points in support of Watkins, and more recent discussions, for example by Bednarczuk 1988 and Schmidt 1991, have remained suitably sceptical.

27. Hoenigswald 1973 has argued that the difference in relative chronology may be illusory and that Lat *quercus* may be the outcome of an analogical restructuring of the paradigm with a nom. sg. $*perkus$ (< $*perk^wus$) : gen. sg. $*perk^weus$. In the nom. sg., $/k^w/$ was simplified to $/k/$ next to $/u/$; in the gen. sg., $/p/$ was assimilated to $/k^w/$ to produce a skewed paradigm $*perkus$:

*k^werk^weus. The oblique stem *k^werk^w- would then have been generalized to the whole paradigm, replacing the nom. sg. in p-. At best Hoenigswald's argument offers an alternative scenario which removes this feature from the debate since there are no criteria for deciding between the alternatives. On the other hand, it depends on an *ad hoc* re-arrangement of the paradigm of *quercus*.

Chapter 2

The Goidelic Languages

2.0 Introduction

This chapter considers the Goidelic languages as a whole, Irish, Scottish Gaelic and Manx, and focuses on common features of these languages and their inter-relationship. While we have little or no evidence for the common language lying behind the individual Brittonic languages (see Chapter 4), Scottish Gaelic and Manx seem to have separated from Irish in the Middle Irish period, and so the three languages thus have a common, well-documented past in Old Irish. Since Irish is the subject of Chapter 3, the focus here will be firstly on Old Irish and then on Scottish Gaelic and Manx.

2.1 The sources

2.1.1 Irish[1]

The earliest evidence for a Celtic language in Ireland is to be found on stone inscriptions written in the Ogam script (for details of the script, see 6.3.1).[2] Inscriptions in Ogam are also found in western Britain. They date from the 5th-6th centuries, and perhaps in a few cases from the late 4th century. Most are memorial inscriptions and tend to have the form 'A, son/descendant of B', or the like, e.g. *GRILAGNI MAQI SCILAGNI* (McManus 1991: 44–52). The Ogam inscriptions are crucial to our understanding of Irish phonology since they span the period of fundamental changes in the language, such as lenition, vowel affection and the loss of final syllables, etc. Evidence from these inscriptions will, therefore, feature heavily in subsequent sections. Although phonologically very useful, they tell us little about the morphology of Archaic Irish; case forms are limited to nominatives and genitives, and there are no verbs or prepositions.

The earliest strings of continuous Irish date from the 7th century and are in Old Irish.[3] The fullest range of early material consists of a vast number of glosses and longer commentary on biblical and grammatical texts in Latin; much of this material was not written in Ireland but by Irish monks in ecclesiastical centres on the Continent. The three main collections, conventionally named after the modern location of the manuscript, are the Würzburg glosses on the Pauline epistles, the Milan glosses on a commentary on the Psalms, and the St. Gall glosses on Priscian (Stokes and Strachan 1901–3). The Würzburg glosses are the earliest (mid 8th century) and are of particular interest in that the first glossator (the *prima manus*) used a somewhat different orthography to the other glossators (see 6.3.2.5 and Table 6.14). In addition, there are some short passages written in Old Irish in the Book of Armagh and in a Cambrai manuscript which are linguistically earlier than the Würzburg glosses (Stokes and Strachan 1901–3: II, 38–43 and 244–7 respectively). The value of this material is that it has come down to us in contemporary manuscripts and has not, therefore, been subject to modification and modernization like so much of the rest of the Old Irish material. For this reason, Thurneysen's grammar of Old Irish (Thurneysen 1946) was almost entirely based on this material.[4]

In addition, there are miscellaneous Old Irish verses written in the margins of Latin texts (Stokes and Strachan 1901–3: 290–7) and incorporated into genealogical tracts (O'Brien 1962) found in later manuscripts. This is only part of a vast range of material which has also been attributed to the Old Irish period but which is only found in the great manuscript collections of the 12th-14th centuries, such as *Lebor na h-Uidre* 'The Book of the Dun Cow' (Best and Bergin 1929) and the Book of Leinster (Best, O'Brien *et al.* 1954–83). The difficulty with much of this material for the linguist is that it has been copied by later scribes and has been subject to alteration and modernization; the texts may well display Old Irish features among the Middle and Early Modern Irish features, but it is not easy for the editor to restore the Old Irish text. The editor must also bear in mind that some of the scribes were adept at archaizing and were capable of creating Old Irish features in a later text. The dating of a text cannot, therefore, be based entirely on linguistic features, but has to take into account historical references and the manuscript sources of the text. The mixed language of these texts is, nevertheless, interesting in its own right as a stage in the development of a literary language, but it is difficult to extract from it information either about Old Irish or about the spoken language of this later period.

One group of texts was perhaps less open to modernization. There is a large corpus of early Irish legal texts which were treated rather differently. Because of their canonical nature and their inherent difficulty, later scribes were less prone to attempt to modify them, but instead added glosses and commentary around the core text, which as a result survived relatively unscathed.[5]

Middle Irish is usually taken to begin with the epic biblical poem *Saltair na Rann* 'The Psalter of Staves' (Stokes 1883) composed in the 10th century. Various redactions of the great prose tale *Táin Bó Cúailnge* 'The Cattle Raid of Cooley' also date from this period, though parts of it are likely to be earlier. We encounter here the other end of the problem discussed above of adapted and modernized material in large manuscript collections. From 1200 onwards the growth of bardic schools brought about the standardization of the poetic language which remained fixed for the next four hundred years.[6] During this period the preservation and renewal of the literary tradition was in the hands of a group of learned families (for details in the context of legal texts, see F. Kelly 1988: 250–63); they were concerned not only with copying manuscripts and maintaining the Irish tradition but also with making the literature of the Continent available in Ireland. Translations were made of the *Aeneid*, the *Thebaid* of Statius and Lucan's *Bellum Civile* (J. E. C. Williams and Ford 1992: 119–52). From 1600 Irish literature struggled against the pressure of English and it was only with the revival of interest in Irish culture in the 19th century that Irish began to flourish again as a literary language (J. E. C. Williams and Ford 1992: 255–338).

The spoken language survives to this day in the specially designated areas (*Gaeltachtaí*) but the most recent study (Hindley 1990) is pessimistic about its chances of survival. One aspect which in some way militates against its survival is the strong loyalty to dialect distinctions, which slows down any attempts to develop a standard spoken form of Irish. Dialect studies have been a productive area of scholarship in this century and have ensured that the details will be preserved (see 3.1.1).[7]

2.1.2 Scottish Gaelic

Although Scotland was settled from Ireland from the 5th century onwards, it has been argued that Irish and Scottish Gaelic 'remained substantially identical, in fact a single language, until at least the tenth century, and in most respects the thirteenth' (Jackson 1951: 74–5; but see 2.3). The difficulty about establishing when and how Scottish Gaelic began to diverge from Irish is that there are no documents written in Scottish Gaelic before the 12th-century Gaelic entries in the *Book of Deer*, which is associated with the abbey of Deer in Buchan. Jackson 1972 concluded that these entries, a short origin legend and some other brief notes, were written in a form of Gaelic indistinguishable from Middle Irish despite the differences in orthography (see 6.3.2.6). Indeed, the Gaelic literature of Scotland between the 12th and 17th centuries was written in a standardized form of Early Modern Irish with little or no hint of the underlying spoken language (Gillies 1993:

145–6). The only exception is the *Book of the Dean of Lismore*, an early 16th century manuscript from Perthshire, which was written in a Scots orthography and so allows us a glimpse of the colloquial pronunciation of the language (see 6.3.2.6). The bulk of literature in Scottish Gaelic emerges from the 17th century onwards, much of it in verse (D. S. Thomson 1989, 1992).

Scottish Gaelic is rich in dialectal variation. There is no overall survey, but there are several studies of particular dialects.[8] In addition to the decreasing numbers of Scottish Gaelic speakers in the Islands and western seaboard, there is a substantial emigré speech community in Nova Scotia, a relic of the 19th-century Highland clearances (MacAulay 1992b: 148–9).

2.1.3 Manx

The earliest evidence for Manx is John Phillips' translation of the Book of Common Prayer (c. 1610) and his Bible translations (Moore and Rhŷs 1893–4), though the historical poem known as the Manx *Traditionary Ballad*, preserved in 18th-century manuscripts, has been dated to the early 16th century (R. L. Thomson 1961).[9] Phillips' translation was not printed until 1894, and the first printed Manx was Bishop Thomas Wilson's *Coyrle Sodjeh* 'further advice', in its English version *Principles and Duties of Christianity*, which appeared in 1707. The 18th century saw a number of Manx works including a Manx Bible. Up to this point, Manx publications had been entirely religious in character, but in the late 18th century and early 19th there appeared a number of traditional songs, both secular and religious, initially in manuscript form, some of which dated from the late medieval period. From the late 19th century, Broderick 1981, 1982 has published probably the last example of native vernacular Manx, the folktales of Ned Beg Hom Ruy.

2.2 General features of the Goidelic languages

The presentation of phonological features in this section is necessarily piecemeal and not always in chronological order. It seems clearer, for example, to deal with all the developments associated with the initial accent together even though they may span a considerable period when other changes were taking place as well. The changes discussed are summarized at the beginning of section 2.2.5 and in Table 2.10.

2.2.1 Lenition and mutations

The most fundamental change affecting the Celtic languages was probably lenition, a reduction in articulation affecting all single intervocalic consonants. It cannot, however, be seen as a Proto-Celtic development, since the outcome was different in the two main branches of Insular Celtic and there is no clear evidence that it affected Continental Celtic

GENERAL FEATURES OF THE GOIDELIC LANGUAGES

29

TABLE 2.1   Examples of lenition in Old Irish

OIr *cath* 'battle' /kaθ/ < **catu-* (cf. Gaul *Catu-*)
OIr *locharn* 'lightning' /'loχərn/ < **leuk-* (cf. Lat *lucerna*, etc.)
OIr *abann* 'river' /'avəN/ < **abon-* (cf. British *Abona*)
OIr *mid* 'mead' /mið/ < **medu-* (cf. Skt *mádhu*, Eng *mead*)
OIr *tugae* 'thatch, roof' /'tuɣə/ < **tog-i̯ā* (cf. Lat *toga*)

in any systematic way (see 7.4.4). It seems most likely that the two
branches inherited a tendency to reduce articulation which was realized
in different ways. The Brittonic changes are summarized in 4.2.1, and
the whole question is dealt with in detail in Chapter 7, particularly in
the light of recent new theories (for resonants in Irish, see 2.2.3.4
below).

In about the 5th century, intervocalic single consonants underwent a
spirantization, i.e. /t k/ > /θ χ/ and /b d g/ > /v ð ɣ/ respectively (see
Table 2.1 for examples). These changes affected all intervocalic consonants, whether they were word internal or initial; if one word ended in a
vowel, the initial consonant of the following word would be in a position to be lenited. This is the origin of the series of initial mutations
which became important markers of grammatical information in the
later stages of the languages (see 7.5).

2.2.2   The initial accent and its consequences
Goidelic had an initial stress accent. This may not have been the case in
Insular Celtic, since Brittonic languages have a penultimate accent. The
Proto-Celtic situation seems unrecoverable (see 1.5.2; cf. also Salmons
1992 and Russell 1994). Modern Irish itself still largely has an initial
stress, though changes have occurred in some dialects (see 3.2.2). Our
evidence for early Irish is derived from the effect which the initial
stress accent had on the unaccented syllables. The Ogam evidence
shows no indication of these effects, though this may be a matter of
orthography, and we have to look at the early manuscript texts for our
first indications. The fixing of the accent on the first syllable affected
the surrounding unaccented syllables: in preceding syllables vowels
were reduced to /ə/ and the articulation of consonants was reduced
leading to voicing or spirantization; in following syllables vowels were
reduced and in some syllables syncopated.

Archaic Irish had a full system of both long and short vowels. One
effect of the accent was to reduce unstressed long vowels; for example,
Lat *molīna* 'mill' was borrowed as /moli:nah/ which was reduced to
/'molinah/, giving ultimately OIr *muilen* (Latin loanwords are useful
examples as they provide a reasonably clear starting point; for their

importance in Irish, see 2.3 below). The immediate outcome was that long and short vowels were only distinguished in accented syllables, i.e. in monosyllables and the initials of polysyllables. However, at a later stage after apocope, the loss of final syllables, new unaccented long vowels arose from clusters of spirant and resonant; essentially, a cluster of -VSR gave V:R, e.g. *anatlo- > */'anaθl/ > /'ana:l/ *anál* 'breath' (cf. W *anadl*), Lat *signum* > Archaic Irish /seɣn/ > OIr /se:n/ *sén* 'sign, omen'. The change can be seen as one of a number of ways in which awkward final clusters arising after the loss of final syllables were accommodated into the early Irish phonological system (see 5.2.3 below and Russell 1984, 1985a for examples from Welsh). An alternative strategy was the development of an epenthetic vowel in the cluster; for example, *dubno- gave /dov̄n/ > OIr /dovən/ *domun* 'world' by the insertion of a vowel to break up the cluster.

At a later stage after the loss of final syllables (see 2.2.4), a more wide-ranging change occurred which affected all polysyllabic words and together with apocope of final syllables drastically reduced the length of words in Old Irish, namely syncope. The changes are schematized in Table 2.2. The loss of final syllables reduced most words by one syllable; for exceptions, see Tables 2.7 and 2.8 below. The subsequent syncope of a short vowel immediately following the stressed syllable left words with, at this stage, two and three syllables unaffected, but reduced longer words by one or two syllables depending on the length. For example, OIr *samail* /'saval'/ 'similar' (cf. Lat *similis*) had a compound form originally *cosamail* /'kosaval'/ which was reduced to *cosmail* /'kosv̄əl'/ with syncope of the second syllable. Latin *Nātālicia* was borrowed into British and gave Archaic Welsh /nod'olig/ 'Christmas', whence it was taken over into Irish and subjected to syncope, producing OIr *Notlaic* /'nodlig/.[10] It was possible, therefore, with the loss of final syllables and the effects of the initial accent for a four-syllable Proto-Celtic word to be reduced to two in Old Irish, e.g. *teglach* 'family' < *tego-slougo- (lit. 'house-host').

The regular loss of the second syllable often created consonant clusters which required modification. For example, Celtic had an adjectival suffix *-odi̯o- which gave W -aidd. The form of the suffix in Old Irish depended on the number of syllables in the base of the derivative. When the base was a monosyllable, then the suffix took the form -dae /-ðe/ with the loss of the first vowel of the suffix, e.g. *rí* /r'i:/ 'king' : *rígdae* /r'i:ɣðe/ 'royal' (< *rīg-odi̯o-) (Thurneysen 1946: 321–2). Where the base of the derivative ended in an unvoiced consonant, the cluster was modified, e.g. *líth* /l'i:θ/ 'festival' : *lítae* /l'i:t'e/ < /l'i:θðe/ 'festive'. When the base was disyllabic, the first vowel of the suffix remained since it was not the second, post-tonic, syllable, e.g. *blíadain* /'bl'iaðən'/ 'year' : *blíadnaide* /'bl'iaðnəð'e/; in this case the second syllable of the base suffered syncope.

TABLE 2.2   Schematized illustration of the affects of apocope and syncope in Archaic Irish

	Apocope	Syncope
TV_1TV_2T (2)	TV_1T	TV_1T (1)
$TV_1TV_2TV_3T$ (3)	TV_1TV_2T	TV_1TV_2T (2)
$TV_1TV_2TV_3TV_4T$ (4)	$TV_1TV_2TV_3T$	TV_1TTV_3T (2)
$TV_1TV_2TV_3TV_4TV_5T$ (5)	$TV_1TV_2TV_3TV_4T$	$TV_1TTV_3TV_4T$ (3)
$TV_1TV_2TV_3TV_4TV_5TV_6T$ (6)	$TV_1TV_2TV_3TV_4TV_5T$	$TV_1TTV_3TTV_5T$ (3)

T = any consonant, V = any vowel.

The reduction in articulation in unaccented syllables did not only affect vowels; distinctions between groups of consonants were also lost. In Early Old Irish /θ/ (< lenited /t/) and /ð/ (< lenited /d/) were distinct at the end of unaccented syllables, but by about 700 they had become indistinguishable and in standard Old Irish orthography both were written as d (Sharpe 1991: 326–7). The confusion can be seen in cases where -th is used where etymologically /ð/ would be expected and vice versa, e.g. dílgud 'forgiving' (with -d for original /θ/) beside a genitive singular dílgotho, later dílguda (Thurneysen 1946: 82). A similar alternation or confusion seems to operate with /χ/ and /ɣ/ but is far less regular; even so, it is rare to find a palatal /χ'/ in an unaccented syllable where /ɣ'/ is usual.

Unaccented syllables do not only occur after the accent. Prepositions, the article, conjunctions, possessive adjectives inter alia do not have a stress accent independently of the word with which they are linked; for example, in Old Irish do lám /də 'la:ṽ/ 'your hand' the phrase only has one stress accent. Early Irish scribes frequently wrote such accentual units as a single string of letters with no word spacings. The same reduction in articulation occurs here as in other unaccented syllables. The clearest example involves the reduction of /t/ to /d/. The possessive pronoun do 'your' (sg.) derives from *toṷe (cf. Lat tuus, etc.); the early form survives in saints' names as To, Tu-, Do-, e.g. Tu Enóc, etc. (see Russell 1990: 111–12). The form do arose in unaccented position. Similarly, the preverb to was used to form verbal compounds; the alternation between the accented and unaccented version of to is clear in deuterotonic and prototonic forms of the same compound verb (for the terminology, see 2.2.6.2): do·beir /do'ber'/ 'he gives' beside ní·tabair /ni:'tavər'/ 'he does not give'. The /t/ remains in stressed syllables but is reduced to /d/ in unstressed syllables. This development is not indicated in the earliest literary sources which still have to/tu in unaccented position, e.g. tond·eccomnuccait, tu·esmot (Stokes and Strachan 1901–3: II, 247.11–12 and 19 respectively). McCone 1981 identified a similar development in syllables following the stress and summarized the rule to include fricatives as follows: 'a voiceless dental stop or fricative on the word boundary was regularly voiced in contact with an unstressed vowel, but otherwise remained unvoiced' (McCone 1981: 44).

As is clear from rhyming patterns within Old Irish, unaccented vowels retained distinct quality, but in late Old Irish and Middle Irish all unaccented vowels, irrespective of origin, were gradually reduced to /ə/. Thus, for example, in the Middle Irish period Old Irish *céle* (nom. sg.), *céli* (gen. sg.), *céliu* (dat. sg.) would all have been pronounced /k'e:l'ə/ and written indiscriminately *céli* or *céle* with potentially chaotic consequences for the case system.

But even in Old Irish it is not clear that all the vowel distinctions made in accented syllables had been maintained in unaccented syllables. It would appear that they had been reduced to two distinct vowels, one front, one back, (see Table 2.3 (a)). The written forms of the vowels were determined by the surrounding consonants; *e* or *i* resulted from contact with a palatal consonant, *a* in contact with non-palatal consonants (Table 2.3 (b); see also Thurneysen 1946: 63–6; for palatalization, see 2.2.3.3). It is clear that the phonetic quality of the vowels as either front or back was maintained at this stage because it is crucial for the quality of the consonant clusters arising from syncope (see 2.2.3.3).

TABLE 2.3 The phonology and orthography of reduced vowels in unaccented syllables

---

(a) Phonology
/a/, /o/, /uT/ > back vowel /A/
/e/, /i/, /uT'/ > front vowel /I/

/A/ and /I/ represent indeterminate back and front vowels respectively.

(b) Orthography
T*a*T, e.g. *as·rubart* /əs'ruvArt/ 'he has said'
T'*e*T, e.g. *tuirem* /'tur'Iṽ/ 'relating'
T*i*T' (later T*ai*T'), e.g. *reth(a)it* /'r'eθId'/'they run'
T'*i*T', e.g. *berid* /'ber'Iδ'/ 'he carries'

2.2.3 Other sound changes

It may be helpful to gather together a number of the more important sound changes which belong to this early period and are reflected in all the Goidelic languages.

2.2.3.1   Long vowels and diphthongs

In 1.4.1.1 the Proto-Celtic development of long vowels and diphthongs was charted. It had a system of five long vowels and three diphthongs (see Figure 2.1).

Within Irish, further changes occurred. The long vowels /i:/, /u:/ and /a:/ remained, but within Archaic Irish /e:/ and /o:/ were diphthongized to /i:ə/ *ía* and /u:ə/ *úa* respectively before non-palatal consonants. The chronology of this change is fairly clear. There is no sign of it in the Ogam inscriptions, e.g. *NETTASLOGI* (= OIr *Nad-Slúag*), *TOTAVALI* (= OIr Túathal), *CERAN[I]* (= OIr *Cíarán*) (McManus 1991: 120–1). Moreover, in the Early Old Irish period the long vowels are still retained in the orthography, e.g. *fédot* for later *fíadat* 'they lead', PN *Tóthal* for later *Túathal*, and occasionally doubled to indicate length, e.g. *Feec* for *Fíacc* (see also 6.3.2.5) (from written Old Irish onwards, the usual marker of length was an acute accent over the vowel). There are also occasional spellings such as *oa* and *ea*, e.g. *óas* for *úas* (Thurneysen 1946: 40), *Leathain* for *Líathain* (Anderson and Anderson 1991: lxxvii) which probably indicate an intermediate stage between the long vowel and the diphthong. Subsequently, as we have seen (2.2.2), the gap in the long-vowel system was filled by new long vowels from final clusters of consonant and resonant.

The diphthongs /ai/ and /oi/ are conventionally written *aí* and *oí* to distinguish them from long vowels followed by a palatal glide, i.e. *ái* and *ói* (for palatal glides, see 6.3.2.5). Greene 1976 has shown that the number of diphthongs increased markedly during the Archaic Irish and Early Old Irish periods due to the loss of intervocalic /i̯/, /u̯/ and /s/ which brought together pairs of vowels; to begin with, the two vowels were in hiatus but they then fell together to form new diphthongs. On the other hand, from Classical Old Irish onwards there seems to have been a trend towards a reduction in their number.[11]

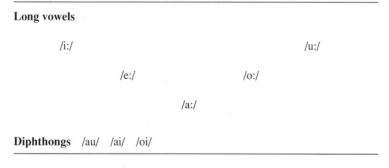

Long vowels

/i:/	/u:/
/e:/	/o:/
/a:/	

Diphthongs   /au/   /ai/   /oi/

FIGURE 2.1   Proto-Celtic long vowels and diphthongs

2.2.3.2   Vowel affection

Vowel affection, otherwise known as metaphony or umlaut, is the process whereby the quality of a short vowel in one syllable is affected by the quality of the vowel in the next; essentially, it is a form of assimilation or vowel harmonization. Both the Goidelic and Brittonic languages independently underwent this kind of change. In Irish terms it has to do with the 'lowering' of /i/ and /u/ to /e/ and /o/ respectively when the following syllable contained /o/ or /a/, and the 'raising' of /e/ and /o/ to /i/ and /u/ respectively when followed in the next syllable by /i/ and /u/ (see Table 2.4)[12] It is clear that vowel affection began with the stressed syllable; for example, OIr *uilen* 'elbow' went through several stages from */oli:na:/, i.e. > */olina/ (reduction of unstressed long vowel) > */ul′ina/ (raising of /o/) > */ul′ena/ (lowering of /i/). Had /i/ been lowered to /e/ before the raising of /o/, **oilen* would have been the expected outcome (McManus 1991: 87). Vowel affection is detectable in some Ogam inscriptions but not in others, e.g. without vowel affection *GRILAGNI* (= OIr *Grellán*), the name element *-CUNAS* (= OIr *-con*), and with vowel affection *VERGOSO* (gen.) (= OIr *Fergus*) < **u̯ira-guso-*, the ending *-EAS* (= OIr *-e*) < **-ii̯as* < **-i̯os* (McManus 1991: 87–8). Both in Table 2.4 and in the examples above, it is indicated that vowel affection is caused by the endings **-as* or **-an* arising from **-os* and **-on* rather than by original **-os* and *-on*, etc. The only evidence for the change of /o/ to /a/ in final syllables is in the Ogam inscriptions, e.g. *DECCEDDAS* (< **Dekantos*), etc., where *-OS* is not attested.

Another important type of vowel affection was also in operation, namely *u*-affection. The account given by Thurneysen 1946 is confused by the fact that he regarded it as being on the same level as palatalization (see 2.2.3.3); he thought Irish had three types of consonant

Table 2.4: Vowel affection in Irish

Lowering

T*i*T*o*- > T*e*T(*o*)-, e.g. OIr *fedo* (gen.) 'wood' < */u̯ido:s/.
T*i*T*a*- > T*e*T(*a*)-, e.g. OIr *fer* 'man' < */u̯irah/ < */u̯iros/
T*u*T*o*- > T*o*T(*o*)-, e.g. OIr *mogo* (gen.) 'slave' < */mugo:s/
T*u*T*a*- > T*o*T(*a*)-, e.g. OIr *cloth* 'fame' < */klutan/ < */kluton/

Raising

T*e*T*i*- > T*i*T(*i*)-, e.g. OIr *mil* 'honey' < */meli/
T*e*T*u*- > T*i*T(*u*)-, e.g. OIr *mid* 'mead' < */medu/
T*o*T*i*- > T*u*T(*i*)-, e.g. OIr *mruig* /mrug′/ 'land' < */mrogi/-
T*o*T*u*- > T*u*T(*u*)-, no clear examples

( ) indicate the syllable lost by apocope.

quality – non-palatal, palatal and *u*-coloured. Greene 1962 presented compelling arguments against this view and showed (Greene 1976: 28–30) that this *u*-colouring is another form of vowel affection. It can affect stressed syllables; for example, OIr *caurad* (gen. sg.) /'kaurəð/ 'warrior' derives from an earlier */karuθah/ < *karutos. But its most obvious impact is seen in the original declensional endings containing /u/; for example, the masculine dative singular ending was -/u/ (< */u:/ < *-/o:/ (see 1.4.1.1)) and so these case forms are regularly marked by *u*-colouring, e.g. *fiur* (dat. sg.) 'man' < */u̯iuru/ < */u̯iru/.

2.2.3.3 Palatalization

Palatalization is one of the most striking features of early Irish phonology, and marks out the Goidelic languages from Brittonic. It was also an important factor in the preservation of a functioning case system in Goidelic after the loss of final syllables (see 2.2.4). Essentially, it involved the development of a series of palatal consonants (consonants with a following /i̯/ glide, marked in phonetic script by ′) beside the pre-existing non-palatal series. Again, as with vowel affection, it began as an assimilatory process; a following front vowel, /e/ or /i/, is anticipated in the articulation of a consonant by raising the tip of the tongue closer to the hard palate than it would be in the articulation of a non-palatal consonant. To begin with, the alternation of non-palatal and palatal consonants was at the phonetic level, and simply allophonic; the realization was determined by the following vowel. But when the vowels were either lost or obscured, the distinction became phonemic and subsequently an important marker of grammatical categories.

It is, however, clear that the conditions for palatalization were more complicated than the simple outline presented above; otherwise we would not expect to find Old Irish forms such as *tugae* /tuɣə/ 'roof' (< */tugii̯a/) without palatalization. Greene 1973 has demonstrated that palatalization was a gradual process and that the quality of the vowel following the consonant was only one factor involved; the nature of the consonant itself and the preceding vowel were also crucial. Greene 1973: 130–1 distinguished the four different types, which he termed the 'first palatalization' (see Table 2.5). The crucial factors which do not permit palatalization are labial and guttural consonants and a following /e/ or /e:/. The blanket 'front vowel' description is, therefore, too broad.

Up to this point, palatalization is merely allophonic but the effects of vowel affection (see 2.2.3.2) must have started the process of phonemicization. For example, the palatal /l′/ in */al'ii̯ah/ (> OIr *aile* 'other') is conditioned by the following /i/ under (c) in Table 2.5, but after vowel affection, which produced */al'ei̯ah/ (see Table 2.4) the palatalization was now no longer conditioned but contrasted phonemically with the non-palatal /l/ of, for example, */kaleθah/ (> OIr *calad* 'hard); the conditions are now the same but in one we find /l/ and in the other /l′/.

TABLE 2.5   The environments affected by the 'first palatalization'

(a) VTV > VT'V (where both vowels are front), e.g. OIr *beirid* /ber'ið'/ 'he carries' < */ber'eθi/.

(b) VTV > VT'V (where V- is /u/, -V is front and C is not a labial or guttural), e.g. OIr *buiden* /buð'en/ 'army' < */bud'ina/.

BUT VTV > VTV (where T is a labial or guttural), cf. *tugae* above.

(c) VTV > VT'V (where V- is /a/ and -V is /i/ or /i:/, e.g. *gaibid* /gav'ið'/ 'he takes' < */gaviθi/.

BUT VTV > VTV (where V- is /a/ but -V is /e/ or /e:/, e.g. *calad* /kalað/ 'hard' < */kaleθah/.

(d) VTV > VT'V (where V- is /a:/, /o/, /o:/ or /u:/, -V is /i/ or /i:/, and T is not a labial or guttural), e.g. *túaithe* (gen. sg.) /tu:əθ'e/ 'tribe' < */to:θ'iịah/.

BUT VTV > VTV (where the environment is the same except that T is a labial or guttural, e.g. *úammae* /u:əme/ < */o:miịah/.

The consonant in question is in bold.
See Greene 1973: 130–1.

    Palatalization was a gradual process and there was a second stage which followed vowel affection but preceded the loss of final syllables (see stage 7 in Table 2.10 below). In contrast to the first stage, there is a distinction between the effects of long and short front vowels but no account taken of consonant types. Effectively, /e/ and /i/ (but not /e:/ and /i:/) were reduced to a short front vowel /I/ which caused palatalization (see 2.2.2 and Table 2.3 above); the result was that some consonants which had previously evaded palatalization were now caught up in it (Greene 1973: 132–3). For example, after the first stage the genitive and vocative singular of Old Irish *ball* 'limb' were distinct, but after the second stage the distinction was lost (see Table 2.6). The subsequent loss of final syllables again removed the conditioning factors for the palatalization and produced the system attested in Old Irish where palatal and non-palatal consonants are in phonemic opposition.

    Palatalization also had a role to play in the process of syncope (see 2.2.2). In Table 2.2 a schematized illustration of the effects of syncope was presented. It can be seen that the second syllable and, in long enough words, the fourth syllable were vulnerable to syncope. It would appear that vowels in unstressed syllables were reduced to either a front vowel or a back vowel (see Table 2.3). The consonant quality of the cluster resulting from syncope was determined by the quality of that syncopated vowel, e.g. OIr *toirthech* /'tor'θ'əχ/ 'fruitful' < */torIθəχ/ < **toret-āko-* : *torad* 'fruit' < */toreto/-, *debthach* /'d'evθəχ/ 'contentious'

TABLE 2.6   The effects of the two stages of palatalization.

	Stage 1	Stage 2	Old Irish
Nom. sg.	*/baLah/	*/baLah/	*ball* /baL/ `limb'
Gen. sg.	*/baL'i/	*/baL'i/	*baill* /baL'/
Voc. sg.	*/baLe/	*/baL'i/	*baill* /baL'/

< */devAθəχ/ < *debut-āko-* (for the notation, see Table 2.2). One further example illustrates the stages in the process: OIr *coicsed* /ˈcogˈsˈəð/ 'suffering' < */kogˈIsəð/. An early form of the word is attested as *coicsath* (Stokes and Strachan 1901–3: II, 245.13) with the early *th* for /θ/ (see 2.2.2). It shows the *i*-glide marking the palatal *c* but, to judge from the following *a*, rather than *e*, the /s/ is still unpalatalized.

It would appear, then, that the palatalization of these clusters arising from syncope was a gradual process spreading from the first to the second element (Greene 1973: 134–5; for palatalization in Middle Irish see 3.2.5).

The main thrust of Greene's arguments was designed to counter Thurneysen's claim (1946: 103–4) that palatalization was a wholesale and thoroughgoing development and that cases of non-palatalization were the result of subsequent depalatalization. There are indeed examples of depalatalization, particularly in unaccented forms; we have seen (2.2.2) that one effect of the removal or absence of the stress accent was the reduction of articulation, one consequence of which was the voicing of unvoiced consonants. Depalatalization was another. For example, a by-form of the verbal noun *toichim* /ˈtoχˈimˈ/ 'going' developed into an unstressed preposition meaning 'towards'; the removal of stress produced the form *dochum* /doχəm/ (> MnIr *chum*) which displays both devoicing and depalatalization.

In contrast to Thurneysen, Greene held that palatalization was a gradual process, and it can be seen to continue its spread even after the Old Irish period. Martinet 1955: 199–211 and Kuryłowicz 1971 have likewise argued that the palatal form was always likely to be generalized as the more marked variant, and Kuryłowicz 1971: 69 used the example of the spread of the palatal form of the *f*-future suffix, i.e. -/fˈa/- at the expense of -/fa/-. The spread of palatal variants continued into Middle Irish and into the modern language in many grammatical categories. For example, there was a tendency from Middle Irish onwards to use palatalization to mark gender so that in Modern Irish there is a general and growing tendency for feminine nouns to be marked by a final palatalized consonant and masculine nouns by a neutral, non-palatal consonant (see 3.3.1). Already in Middle Irish it was common for the accusative/dative singular form with a final palatal consonant to be used as a nominative (see Dottin 1913: I, 48, Jackson 1990: 84–8). Confusion between palatal and non-palatal forms is also evident in derivatives of feminine nouns (Russell 1990: 97–101).

2.2.3.4   Tense and lax resonants and 'Mac Neill's Law'

As was noted above (2.2.1) and is discussed in Chapter 7 below, inter-vocalic consonants underwent a reduction in articulation known as lenition. It can be characterized as a reduction of the tenseness in the articulation of the stop. Resonants were also affected by lenition (tense resonants are conventionally written /N R L/ beside the lax forms /n r l/). Basically, the pattern was /N/, etc. in non-leniting position and /n/, etc. in leniting position. The tense/lax distinction in resonants was par-tially lost in the modern period (see 3.2.1), and may have been reduced at an earlier stage since from the period of phonemic palatalization (see 2.2.3.3) each resonant would have had four different realizations, i.e. /N/ : /N'/ : /n/ : /n'/.

There was, however, one exception: 'After short vowels *l* and *n* are also delenited at the end of unstressed syllables beginning with *r*, *l*, *n* or unlenited *m*' (Thurneysen 1946: 89). Put schematically, /'TVnVN/ occurs where we would expect /'TVnVn/; orthographically a tense res-onant is frequently written as *nn* or *ll*, e.g. *Érenn*, gen. sg. of *Ériu* 'Ireland', PNN *Conall*, *Domnall* beside *Túathal*, *Bresal*, etc. where the required conditions are not met. The conditions are precise; thus, we find *nadmann* /'naðməN/, nom./acc. pl. of *naidm* 'binding', where the unaccented syllable begins with unlenited /m/, beside *Muman* /'muṽən/, gen. of *Mumu* 'Munster', where it begins with /ṽ/ (lenited /m/). This exception to the usual pattern was first sketched out by Mac Neill 1909 and is thus known as 'Mac Neill's Law'; it has received further refine-ment from Hamp 1974.[13]

2.2.4   Nominal declension and the loss of final syllables

The loss of final syllables is usually regarded as the change which marks off earlier forms of the language from Old Irish. However, unlike the similar development in Brittonic (see 4.2.5), it was not asso-ciated with loss of declension. The aim of this section is firstly to integrate the loss of final syllables into the discussion of early Irish phonology, and secondly to consider how declension was maintained when the endings had been lost.

The loss of final syllables is a convenient shorthand term for a series of changes which ultimately resulted in the loss of most but not all final syllables (McCone 1982: 24–5). Some were preserved, e.g. the 3rd sg. conjunct passive ending -(th)ar, the 3rd pl. conjunct active ending -at -/əd/ (< *-ont) (for 'conjunct', see 2.2.6.2), the *o*-stem acc. pl. ending -u

(< *-ōs). Moreover, traces of lost syllables are preserved in the nasalization or lenition of a following word (see 2.2.1 and Chapter 7).

A glance at the declensional patterns of other Indo-European languages shows that, in the nominal declension at least, most endings have a final vowel, final -/s/, final nasal, or final dental (see Szemerényi 1990: 169). The Celtic declensional patterns largely run in parallel and so we should focus on the fate of these endings.

McCone 1979a: 16 and 1982: 24–5 has listed in chronological order of application the changes involved, most of which have figured in previous sections of this chapter (see Table 2.7); these changes are exemplified in Table 2.8.

The loss of final syllables was not, therefore, a single calamitous loss of endings but a gradual, long-term change. In the Ogam inscriptions forms are attested which illustrate most of the stages. For example, the development of the original ending *-i̯os, i.e. -/ii̯os/ > /ii̯as/ > (a) -/ei̯ah/ > (b) -/e(i̯)a #h/- > (d) -/e/ (letters refer to the stages listed in Tables 2.7 and 2.8), is mirrored in the following Ogam forms *MAQIERCIAS, MAQI-RITEAS, MAQI-ESEA, MAQI-RITE* for the last four stages respectively. Similarly, the change of */o:s/ to */o:/ is reflected in *BRUSCCOS* beside *BRUSCO* (McManus 1991: 88). It does not follow, however, that the inscriptions containing these forms may be dated relatively since it is necessary to be aware of the possibilities of conservative orthography (see McManus 1991: 81–3).

Celtic inherited from Indo-European a series of declensions corresponding to those found in other Indo-European languages, *ā*-stem, *o*-stem, *i̯o*-stem, *u*-stem, consonant stem, etc. (see Thurneysen 1946: 176–217 for details). The difference between Irish and other Indo-European languages such as Latin, Greek, Sanskrit, etc. is that it succeeded in maintaining a functioning case system even though final syllables, the primary carriers of grammatical distinctions, had been largely lost. Its success had to do with the effects of many of the sound changes discussed above. Three examples may make the point. Table 2.9 shows the basic development of the *o*-stem, *ā*-stem and *i̯o*-stem singular declensions for *fer* 'man', *túath* 'tribe' and *duine* 'man'.

By a combination of vowel affection, presence or absence of palatalization, and the mutation of a following word, sufficient distinctions could be made for a case system to function. At points in the system the distinctions seem slight; if, for example, there was no following word in close connection to be marked by mutation, the nominative and accusative singular and genitive plural of *o*-stems and *i̯o*-stems would be identical. Confusion is less likely than might appear; a genitive plural would only follow another noun and may itself be marked by

TABLE 2.7   Stages in the loss of final syllables in Irish

(a) Reduction of final /s/ to /h/.

(b) Shortening of long vowels in absolute final position, i.e. -/V:/ > -/V/ but -/V:T/ (including -/V:h/) remained.

(c) Shift of syllable/word boundary: -/Vh # V/- > -/V # hV/, -Vn # V/- > -/V # nV/- and -Vn # T/- > -/V # nT/. This resulted in nasalization and the prefixing of h to vowel-initial words (see 7.1–2).

(d) Loss of most final consonants, except liquids and unlenited stops, such as -/θar/ > -thar, and -/od/ > -at (see above).

(e) Loss of all short vowels in absolute final position (long vowels remain).

(f) Surviving long vowels in final position are shortened in the absence of any phonemic contrast.

TABLE 2.8   Examples illustrating Table 2.7

	(a)	(b)	(c)	(d)	(e)	(f)	Old Irish
*/berod/	–	–	–	/berod/	/berod/	–	berat 'they carry'
*/ɸiru:s/	/ɸiru:h/	–	/ɸiru: #h/	–	/ɸiru:/	/ɸiru/	firu 'men' (acc. pl.)
*/du:non/	–	–	/du:no #n/	–	/du:n/	–	dún 'fort'
*/to:θa:s/	/to:θa:h/	–	/to:θa: #h/	–	/to:θa:/	/to:θa/	túatha 'tribes'
*/bra:θi:r/	–	–	–	/bra:θi:r/	/bra:θi:r/	/bra:θi:r/	bráthir 'brother'
*/su:lis/	/su:lih/	–	/su:li #h/	–	/su:l'/	–	súil 'eye'
*/ɸiru:/	–	/ɸiru/	–	–	/ɸ'iur/	–	fiur 'man' (dat. sg.)
*/ɸeras/	/ɸerah/	–	/ɸera #h/	–	/ɸ'er/	–	fer 'man' (nom. sg.)
*/al'ejas/	/al'ejah/	–	/al'eja #h/	–	/al'e/	–	aile 'other'

TABLE 2.9   Examples to illustrate the development of the Old Irish declension

	Proto-Celtic	Proto-Irish	Old Irish
_o_-stem			
Nom.	ụiros	ụerah	*fer*
Voc.	ụire	ụire	*fir*[L]
Acc.	ụiron	ụeran	*fer*[N]
Gen.	ụirī	ụiri	*fir*[L]
Dat.	ụirū	ụiuru	*fiur*[L]
_ā_-stem			
Nom.	tōtā	tōta	*túath*[L]
Voc.	tōtā	tōta	*túath*[L]
Acc.	tōten	tōten	*túaith*[N]
Gen.	tōtiịās	tōteịah	*túaithe*
Dat.	tōtai	tōti	*túaith*[L]
_ịo_-stem			
Nom.	doniịos	duneịah	*duine*
Voc.	doniịe	duniịe	*duini*[L]
Acc.	doniịon	duneịan	*duine*[N]
Gen.	doniịī	duniịi	*duini*[L]
Dat.	doniịū	duniịu	*duiniu*[L]

Superscript letters indicate the mutation which follows each case form: [N] = nasalization, [L] = lenition (see Chapter 7).

mutation. The distinction of nominative and accusative could be indicated simply by word order; briefly, Old Irish word order was regularly [verb + subject + object], and so the object may be identified from its position and context (Greene 1974: 191; see also Chapter 9 below).

As regards _ịo_-stems, the burden falls on the final vowels, which remained distinct during the Old Irish period. But, as was noted above (2.2.2), the final vowels coalesced to give /ə/ in late Old Irish and

Middle Irish. Greene 1974 has demonstrated that the main preoccupation of noun morphology in that period was to avoid homophony,
especially between singular and plural (see also Strachan 1903–6).
Even in Old Irish, accusatives and genitives could be identified by their
position in the sentence and the dative was largely restricted to prepositional phrases. But for some declensional types, singular and plural
distinctions were not always clear; the problem was most acute among
neuters, e.g. *cride* 'heart(s)' (neuter nom. sg./pl.). In Old Irish itself
there was a tendency to generalize a nominative plural *-a* beyond its
original scope to other classes of neuter nouns (Greene 1974: 191–2).
The longer plural forms were most common where there was no other
mark of plurality such as the article or a numeral (Thurneysen 1946:
177). However, by Middle Irish such strategies were rendered redun-
dant since all absolute final vowels had became /ə/. At this point a
further strategy was adopted, namely the use of a consonant-stem plural
marker which was in various forms to be adopted at different stages of
Irish up to the present (see Hickey 1985). In Middle Irish the most
common ending was *-eda* /eðə/ derived from the lenited dental stem
nouns (Thurneysen 1946: 205–7), e.g. sg. *slige* 'path' : pl. OIr *slige*,
MIr *sligeda*, sg. *gilla* 'boy' : pl. OIr *gilli*, MIr *gilleda* (see Strachan
1903–6: 2–24 for further examples). It is noteworthy that this ending
was not exploited in Scottish Gaelic or Manx, where an ending *-(a)n* is
generalized (Greene 1974: 197–8); it looks as if it may have been generalized from *n*-stem nouns, but Howells 1971: 95–7 has argued that it
derives from the Old English plural ending *-en*.

The general confusion in Middle Irish declensional patterns is also
evidenced in nominal derivatives. The normal pattern for a consonant-
stem noun is that a derivative would be based on the oblique stem, not
the nominative stem, e.g. nom. sg. *foditiu* : oblique stem *foditen-*
'endure' : adjective *foditnech* 'enduring'. However, it is common in
Middle Irish to find derivatives based on the nominative stem, i.e.
foditech; the implication is that the system had broken down to such an
extent that the nominative could be interpreted as a vowel-stem noun
and therefore used as the base for the derivative (Russell 1990: 119–21).

2.2.5 The chronology of early Irish sound changes and Latin loanwords

The preceding sections have discussed a series of sound changes in
early Irish, and not necessarily in chronological order. It may be helpful, therefore, to provide a chronology of the changes discussed above.
Table 2.10 provides a relative chronology, but not an absolute chronology; the actual, or possible, dating of these changes is a complicated
matter which forms the subject of the rest of this section.

The absolute chronology of these sound changes has until recently
been anchored by the claim, made by Jackson 1953: 560–1, that Irish

TABLE 2.10   A summary of the relative chronology of early Irish sound changes.

---

1. /nt/, /nk/ > /dd/, /gg/ (2.2.4)
2. Lenition (including /s/ > /h/) (2.2.1 and Chapter 7)
3. Reduction of unstressed long vowels (except in final syllables ending in /h/) (2.2.2)
4. Vowel affection in stressed syllables (2.2.2)
5. Palatalization (stage 1) (2.2.3.3)
6. Vowel affection in unstressed syllables (2.2.2)
7. Palatalization (stage 2) (2.2.3.3)
8. Loss of unstressed final short vowels (2.2.4)
9. Shortening of unstressed final long vowels (2.2.4)
10. Rise of secondary long vowels (2.2.2)
11. Reduction of unstressed vowels to /A/ or /I/ (2.2.2)
12. Syncope (2.2.2)
13. Palatalization (stage 3) (2.2.3.3)

( ) refer to the sections where there is discussion of the change.

lenition took place in the second half of the 5th century. His argument rests on the form of certain Latin loanwords in Irish. More recently, his arguments have been re-assessed by McManus 1983, Sims-Williams 1990 and Koch 1990 who have questioned aspects of his dating. Latin loanwords are at the centre of the debate, and it may be helpful to begin with a brief survey of their significance. Jackson was not the first to note that Latin loanwords into Irish could take more than one form (see McManus 1983: 21–7). For example, Latin /p/ could appear as *c* or *p* (the relevant consonants are marked in bold), e.g. *Patricius* > *Cothriche*/*Pátraic*; Latin intervocalic /t/ and /k/ could appear as *th* /θ/ and *ch* /χ/ or as *t* /d/ and *c* /g/, e.g. Lat *puteus* 'well' > OIr *cuithe* : Lat *Natalicia* > OIr *Notlaic* 'Christmas', Lat *cucullus* 'cloak' > OIr *cochall* : Lat *pācem* > OIr *póc* 'kiss' (see Jackson 1953: 126 and Table 2.11 for a summary).

TABLE 2.11   Variation in the realization of intervocalic consonants in Latin loanwords in Old Irish

---

Latin		Old Irish	
/p/	>	*c* /k/	: *p* /p/
/t/, /k/	>	*th* /θ/, *ch* /χ/	: *t* /d/, *c* /g/
/nt/, /nk/	>	*nd* /nd/, *ng* /ŋ/	: *nt* /nt/, *nc* /nk/
/ius/	>	*-e* /e/	: *-* /Ø/
/a:/	>	*á* /a:/	: *ó* /o:/
/f/-	>	*s-* /s/	: *f-* /f/

Jackson 1953: 122–45 argued that the different treatments in Irish were the result of a chronological distinction between the two groups. Essentially, words of the first group, termed by Jackson *Cothriche*-words, after its most famous member, were borrowed at a stage when Irish had no /p/ and there was a substitution of /kʷ/, which later gave OIr *c* /k/ (see 1.5.1). They were also borrowed before lenition, before secondary /nt/, etc. had gone to /nd/ (original /nt/ had already gone to /dd/ at an early stage) and before Irish -/iịos/ gave -/e/. Words of this group, therefore, underwent these changes along with native Irish words. The second group, termed *Pátraic*-words, were borrowed later and so avoided being caught up in these changes. However, they had come into Irish via British and had, therefore, undergone British sound changes. Thus, for example, Latin /t/ as Irish /d/ and /k/ as /g/ was the outcome of British lenition, which produced different results to Irish lenition (see 4.2.1 and 7.1). The upshot is that Jackson saw two groups, admittedly with some small sub-groups, the first arriving before lenition and the bulk of the second after the loss of final syllables and syncope (see Table 2.9) with a blank and unexplained intervening period when no borrowing took place.

McManus 1983, 1984, however, has demonstrated that the absorption of Latin loanwords was a continuous process and that a two-group pattern is untenable; for there is a number of hybrid forms which show features of both groups. For example, OIr *nótire* 'professional scribe' < Lat *nōtārius* shows British lenition of the *Pátraic* type but the treatment of the Latin suffix -*ārius* as -*ire* is characteristic of the earlier stratum of loanwords (McManus 1983: 32–3). It has, therefore, become necessary to regard the arrival of Latin loanwords in Irish as a continuous process. From the point when they were absorbed into Irish they took part in Irish sound changes but were not affected by changes which had occurred before their arrival.

Sims-Williams 1990 accepts McManus' re-analysis and takes the discussion further on the question of lenition. His contribution to this aspect of the question is discussed below (7.4.3), but he also has some interesting comments on the question of dating. McManus' revision of Jackson's arguments retained the traditional dating. But Jackson's arguments hang on a few apparently fixed points in Irish phonology which have been re-examined by Sims-Williams 1990: 225–70. One of these fixed points lies at the heart of our discussion. Jackson's dating of lenition is based on the equation of *Cothriche* and *Pátraic* (< *Patricius*) with St Patrick.[14] He assumes that St. Patrick and his British companions would have been the first to introduce Christian loanwords into Irish, the first of which entered before Irish lenition. However, we know that in the pre-Patrician period, in AD 431, Pope Celestine sent Palladius *ad Scottos in Christum credentes* 'to the Irish believing in Christ' to be their first bishop. It would appear, then, that there were already Christian Irish in Ireland before 431, and so loanwords could have entered Irish well before St Patrick began his mission. Moreover, it would be reasonable to suppose that Latin words may have reached Ireland through traders at an even earlier period. Nevertheless, the entry of *Cothriche* into Irish could still be contemporary with the arrival of Patrick, if the name is to be associated with him (see Koch 1982–3). But Harvey 1985 has attempted to reject the equation of *Cothriche* and St Patrick (though the only evidence for *Cothriche* is in connection with St Patrick), while Sims-Williams 1990: 229 has claimed that *Patricius* was a sufficiently common name for it to have entered Irish before *the* Patrick arrived in Ireland. On the other hand, Koch 1990: 185–6 denies that *Patricius* had any wide currency independently of the saint (see also Russell 1991–2: 265–6). It should be added that the Patrician question remains a thorny problem, and it is clear that neither the date of Patrick's mission nor the legitimacy of linking *Cothriche* and Patrick are agreed facts.[15]

In conclusion, the use of Latin loanwords as the basis of an absolute chronology for Irish sound changes is less certain now than it has been. There are two different trends operating at present, either to see these changes as happening earlier than has previously been thought (see Sims-Williams 1990 and 7.4.3 below) or to argue for a later St Patrick (see Dumville 1993).

2.2.6 The verbal system

No other part of early Irish grammar has caused scholar and student so much pain and anguish as the verbal system. One of the main problems is the complex mixture of archaism and innovation. At the same time it was a constantly changing system and attempts to codify it have not always taken those changes into account. Further confusion has been caused by conflicting methods of referring to the classes of the finite verb. Three systems exist, Thurneysen 1946, Strachan and Bergin 1949, and McCone 1987 (see Table 2.12 overleaf); the first is employed here. Unlike Latin or Greek, it is conventional to use the 3rd singular present active as the reference form.

2.2.6.1 *The tenses and moods of the early Irish verb*

Old Irish verbs are traditionally divided into two types: 'weak' verbs where the verbal stem ends in a vowel and 'strong' verbs where it ends in a consonant. The former type was the regular, productive category in which new verbs were created; because of the stem-final vowel, the addition of suffixes and tense markers caused no phonological problems in terms of consonant clusters, etc. On the other hand, the strong

TABLE 2.12   The classification of Old Irish verbs

Thurneysen (1946)	Strachan-Bergin (1949)	McCone (1987)	Description and examples
AI	B(1)	W1	weak *a*-stem, e.g. *móraid* 'he praises'
AII	B(2)	W2	weak *i*-stem e.g. *léicid* 'he leaves'
AIII		H1	*a*-stem hiatus e.g. *raïd* 'he rows'
		H2	*i*-stem hiatus e.g. *gniïd* 'he does'
		H3	*e/o/u*-stem hiatus e.g. *soïd* 'he turns'
BI	A(1)	S1	strong - non-palatal e.g. *berid* 'he carries'
BII	A(2)	S2	strong - palatal e.g. *gaibid* 'he takes'
BIII	A(1)	S1	nasal infix e.g. *bongid* 'he strikes'
BIV BV	A(1)	S3	non-radical *n* e.g. *benaid* 'he strikes'

type tended to be irregular and unproductive, and the repository of the more archaic patterns.

An Old Irish verb has a present, imperative, imperfect, future, conditional (past future) and a preterite indicative, and a present and past subjunctive; there are active and passive forms of all these tenses, the latter only in the 3rd person (see 2.2.6.3). For each person of many tenses and moods there are two forms, absolute and conjunct (see 2.2.6.2). Furthermore, a perfect tense ('I have done') could also be formed by prefixing the particle *ro* to the preterite. Relative clauses were not generally marked by a relative pronoun but by the use of a special verbal form (see 2.2.6.4). In addition to these finite forms, each verb has a past participle passive, a verbal of necessity (in some ways parallel in function to a Latin gerund) and a verbal noun (see Chapter 8). There is also a separate class of deponent verbs which, like Latin deponent and Greek middle verbs, resemble the passive in form but are active in meaning; however, unlike the passive they have forms for all persons and they do differ in some forms from the passives. The tense markers vary from type to type. Table 2.13 summarizes the situation, while Table 2.14 provides a sample paradigm for a weak verb (for a

Table 2.13 Tense markers in the Old Irish verb

	Preterite	Subjunctive	Future
Weak verbal stems			
AI/AII	-s-	-a-	-f-
AIII (H1)	redupl. + -s	-a-	redupl. + -a-
AIII (H3)	-s-	-a-	-f-
Strong verbal stems			
Final dental	redupl.	-s-	redupl. + -s-
Final guttural	redupl.	-s-	redupl. + -a-
Final resonant	-t-	-a-	redupl. + -a-
The rest	redupl.	-a-	redupl. + -a-

redupl. = reduplication of the initial consonant of the stem (reduplication can be replaced in certain categories by a long stem vowel).

TABLE 2.14   A sample paradigm of an Old Irish weak verb

AII *léicid* 'he leaves'

	Absolute	Conjunct	Relative
Indicative			
Present active	*lécid*	*·léci*	*léces*
Present passive	*léicthir*	*·léicther*	*léicther*
Imperfect active	–	*·léced*	–
Imperfect passive	–	*·léicthe*	–
Future active	*léicfid*	*·léicfea*	*léicfes*
Future passive	*léicfidir*	*·léicfider*	*léicfedar*
Conditional active	–	*·léicfed*	–
Conditional passive	–	*·léicfide*	–
Preterite active	*lécis*	*·léic*	–
Preterite passive	*léicthe*	*·léced*	–
Subjunctive			
Present active	*lécid*	*·lécea*	*léces*
Present passive	*léicthir*	*·léicther*	*léicther*
Past active	–	*·léced*	–
Past passive	–	*·léicthe*	–

paradigm of a strong verb, see Strachan and Bergin 1949: 35–68)
    The tense markers have been the subject of detailed scrutiny over the years, particularly in regard to their origin (see in particular C. Watkins 1962 and McCone 1986, 1991a). They have been exploited

to prove or disprove the Italo-Celtic hypothesis (see 1.7); the *f*-future and *a*-subjunctive in particular have been examined in this respect, since they have been thought to be related to the *b*-future and *a*-subjunctive of Latin respectively. The patterns of reduplication and the *s*-markers have been used to demonstrate the close unity of Celtic with other Indo-European languages. The most recent treatment, McCone 1991a presents full discussion of earlier theories together with new insights and analyses (see Russell 1993a).

The most wide-ranging marker is -*s*-, which as a preterite marker for weak verbs is an inherited aorist suffix that shows up in the most common type of Greek aorist, e.g. *élusa*, and in some forms of the Latin perfect, e.g. *rēxī : regō*, etc. C. Watkins 1962: 156–74 has demonstrated that the *t*-preterite formed on stems with a final resonant, e.g. ·*bert* 'he carried', derives from the *s*-aorist; the expected 3rd sg. would have been **ber-s-t*, which regularly gave *bert* through loss of /s/ in that position, and a new paradigm was based on the 3rd sg. *bert*- thus giving rise to a whole new type of aorist.

If the *s*-marker was originally an aorist marker, its occurrence in subjunctive and future forms requires explanation. It is now accepted that they derive from the subjunctives of *s*-aorists (McCone 1991a: 137–74). It has also been convincingly argued by McCone that the *a*-subjunctive is of similar origin. It is to be derived from the subjunctive suffix -*se*- added to roots with a final laryngeal, schematically TVRH*se*- which underwent a resegmentation to TVR-H*se*- when the laryngeal was interpreted as part of the suffix.[16] Laryngeals developed into /a/ in Celtic and so the suffix -*ase*- underwent the usual loss of intervocalic /s/ to give -*a(h)e*- > -*ā*-. The effect of this interpretation is firstly to unite all the subjunctive and future suffixes in one explanation and, secondly, to remove any link between the *a*-subjunctive and the corresponding Latin formation.

The other widespread aspect of these different tenses is reduplication. Again it is a feature of Indo-European date; we may compare, for example, the use of reduplication in Latin and Greek perfects, e.g. Lat *momordī* 'I have bitten' : *mordeō*, *meminī* 'I remember' : e.g. *mens* 'mind', Gk *léluka* 'I have set free' : *lúō*. The Irish preterite system contains reflexes of both Indo-European perfects, marked by reduplication and a particular set of endings, and aorists (preterites), frequently marked by *s*. Likewise, in Latin, original perfects and aorists fell together, while in Greek they remained separate. It is striking, as an aside, that there seems to have been a need felt for the preterite/perfect distinction; Celtic maintained and re-marked it by the addition of *ro* to the preterite, while Late Latin produced a periphrastic perfect (*habeō* + past participle). The Irish preterite to most strong verbs shows reduplication, e.g. *cechan*- : present *canid* 'sing', *gegon-* : *gonaid* 'wound', etc., or a lengthened vowel in the stem, e.g. *gád-* : *guidid* 'pray', *ráth-* : *rethid* 'run', etc. McCone 1986: 235–7 has argued that the latter also originally had reduplication which was lost in western Indo-European by a process of compensatory lengthening, i.e. $T_1 e T_1$-T_2- > $T_1 \bar{e} T_2$- (for the development of /a:/, see McCone 1986: 236–7). McCone 1991a: 168–74 has furthermore claimed that the reduplication associated with futures (e.g. *memais* 'he will break' : pres. *maidid*; *gigis* 'he will pray' : pres. *guidid*) is also of Indo-European date, and to be associated with similar forms in Indo-Iranian. Here again lengthened stem vowels in place of reduplication are likely to be the result of subsequent phonological developments, though the details are unclear (McCone 1991a: 173–4 but also Russell 1993a: 165).

The final category to be considered here is the *f*-future. Generations of scholars have found a link between it and the Latin *-bo*-future almost irresistible despite the phonological impossibility of the correspondence (see McCone 1991a: 176–82 for details). It is clear that the solution to its origin lies within Celtic but there is no obvious answer at present (for McCone's solution, see Russell 1993a: 165–7).

Most of the archaic patterns discussed in this section are associated with the strong verbs. The weak verbs with their clearer and more regular pattern, remained the productive category, largely as denominative and de-adjectival verbs. Simple forms without suffixes arose in Old Irish, e.g. *glan* 'pure' : *glanaid* 'he purifies', *rád* 'speech' : *ráidid* 'he speaks', etc. But the most common type involved the addition of the deponent suffix *-aigidir* -/əɣ'əð'ər'/, e.g. *lobur* 'ill' : *·lobraigedar* 'weaken, is ill', *béo* 'alive' : *·béoigedar* 'vivify', *aile* 'other' : *·ailegedar* 'alters', etc. (Thurneysen 1946: 337–8).

2.2.6.2 *Absolute and conjunct verbal inflection*

The Celtic languages are unique in having for many tenses of the verb a double system of inflection. The system is most clearly visible and functioning in Old Irish, though there are sufficient traces of the same patterns in Brittonic languages (see 4.2.6) for it to be considered an inheritance from Insular Celtic.

The system essentially operates as follows: when a simple verbal form is used in a declarative statement with no negative or interrogative particle or conjunction it goes in first position in the sentence and takes the absolute form, e.g. *léicid* /'l'e:g'ið'/ 'he leaves', but if it is preceded by a particle of any sort it takes the conjunct form, e.g. *ní·léici* /n'i:'l'e:g'i/ 'he does not leave', etc. (see Table 2.14). Old Irish also has compound verbs formed by adding preverbs to the front of the simple verb. They have the same effect as the negative or other particles; they require the conjunct form of the verb, e.g. *do·léci* /do'l'e:g'i/ 'he throws'. Single particles and preverbs are pretonic, i.e. the stress accent rests on the first syllable of the verb; thus, /do'lʹeːgʹi/ has the same stress pattern as /nʹiːˈlʹeːgʹi/. However, when *do·léci* is negated, the stress remains in the same place and the preverb *do* is amalgamated with the verb, thus *ní·téilci* /nʹiːˈtʹeːlʹgʹi/. The verbal compound *·téilci* shows all the features of Irish phonology discussed in 2.2.2, such as syncope of the post-tonic syllable and the stressed form of the preverb **to*, as opposed to the unstressed *do*; compare, for example, *do·berat* /do'bʹerəd/ 'they give' with *ní·tabrat* /nʹiːˈtavrəd/ 'they do not give' (see Table 2.15 for a sample paradigm). Similarly, when a verbal stem is preceded by two preverbs, the accent rests on the second syllable and the first preverb is pretonic, e.g. *as·ingaib* /asˈingavʹ/ 'it exceeds' (< *as* + *in* + *gaib-* 'take').

The terms 'deuterotonic' and 'prototonic' are used to describe these two types of compound verb, and are a useful mnemonic: *deuterotonic* (lit.) 'second stress' describes the situation where the accent is on the second syllable of the compound, i.e. /do'lʹeːgʹi/, while *prototonic* (lit.) 'first stress' indicates that the accent is on the first syllable, i.e. *·téilci* /ˈtʹeːlʹgʹi/. As can be seen from Table 2.14, this system operates across much of the verbal system with the exception of forms based on the imperfect stem, i.e. the imperfect, conditional and imperfect subjunctive. When the imperfect is preceded by a negative or another pretonic particle, or when it is a compound verb, there is no difficulty, but when a simple verb is used in a positive statement, it has to be preceded by the meaningless particle *no*, e.g. *ní·léced* 'he was not leaving' : *no·léced* 'he was leaving'.

The pretonic particles are also used to carry infixed pronouns. In Classical Old Irish object pronouns are enclitic, i.e. they do not carry an accent (for the forms, see Table 2.16). As was pointed out in 1.4.2.2, there was a widespread rule in Indo-European languages, known as Wackernagel's Law, that enclitic particles are placed in second position in the sentence. In Celtic there was a particular corollary to it, called Vendryes' Restriction, which required that the enclitics should be infixed into the verb; the result of this is that the verb was initial or, at least, the first accented unit. Pronouns, therefore, are infixed into compound verbs, or between the negative and the verb, e.g. *do·beir* /do'bʹerʹ/ 'he gives' : *dom·beir* /dom'vʹerʹ/ 'he gives me (obj.)' : *ním·thabair* /nʹiːmˈθavər/ 'he does not give me (obj.)'.

However, the situation is different in simple verbs; pronouns can be inserted with ease into negative verbs, e.g. *ním·théilci* 'he does not throw me', but there is nothing to 'carry' the pronoun in the positive form. In Early Old Irish the pronoun was suffixed to the verb, e.g. *sástum* (lit.) 'it feeds me' (< *sásaid* + 1st sg. pro.), *léicthi* '(he) leaves it' (< *léicid* + 3rd sg. m. pro.), *bertius* '(he) carried them' (< *bert* + 3rd pl. pro.) (Breatnach 1977). This may be an archaic pattern; Gaul *buetid* has been analysed by McCone 1991a: 118 as containing a suffixed pronoun

TABLE 2.15   A sample of the absolute and conjunct inflections for a simple and compound verb

	Absolute	Conjunct
Simple verb		
1st sg.	léicim 'I leave'	ní·léicim 'I do not leave'
2nd sg.	léci	ní·léci
3rd sg.	lécid	ní·léci
1st pl.	léicmi	ní·lécem
2nd pl.	léicthe	ní·lécid
3rd pl.	lécit	ní·lécet
Compound verb		
1st sg.	do·léicim 'I throw'	ní·téilcim 'I do not throw'
2nd sg.	do·léci	ní·téilci
3rd sg.	do·léci	ní·téilci
1st pl.	do·lécem	ní·téilcem
2nd pl.	do·lécid	ní·téilcid
3rd pl.	do·lécet	ní·téilcet

TABLE 2.16   Old Irish infixed pronouns

	A	B (with /d/)	C (with /ð/)
1st sg.	$-m(m)^L$	$-dom^L$	$-dom^L$
2nd sg.	$-t^L$	$-dot^L$	$-dat^L$
3rd sg.	m. $-a^N\ (-^N)$	$-d^N$	$-(i)d^N,\ -^N$
	f. $-s^N\ (-s)$	$-da$	$-da$
	n. $-a^L\ (-^L)$	$-d^L$	$-(i)d^L,\ -^L$
1st pl.	$-n(n)$	$-don$	$-don$
2nd pl.	$-b$	$-dob$	$-dob$
3rd pl.	$-s^N\ (-s)$	$-da$	$-da$

Superscript letters indicate the mutation which follows each case form: ^{N} = nasalization, ^{L} = lenition (see Chapter 7).

Type B is found after preverbs ending in a consonant; type C is found in relative clauses (see 2.2.6.4).

$-(i)d$ though the analysis remains uncertain (see Lambert 1994: 157). Within the Old Irish period the suffixed pronoun had been replaced by pronouns infixed in the 'empty' no, e.g. nom·léici 'he leaves me', nom·beir /nom'v'er'/ 'he carries me' (for details, see Thurneysen 1946: 255–64).

The historical background to these patterns is complex and has been much debated. There are a number of different aspects to the matter which require consideration. There is the question of word order and how the verb came to be in initial position. Why is there is no lenition in *do·beir* /do'b'er'/ when *do* causes lenition elsewhere? After all, protototonic *·tabair* /'tavər'/ shows lenition, and infixed pronouns can cause lenition, e.g. *dom·beir* /dom'v'er'/ 'he gives me (obj.)'. And how do we account for the different sets of endings for absolute and conjunct forms? It has been claimed that all these factors are connected and require solutions in order to produce a coherent explanation of the absolute/conjunct phenomenon.[17]

Word order is the subject of Chapter 9 and is not discussed in detail here, since it requires consideration of all the Celtic languages. The question of endings is crucial to the argument; for it is clear that one major formal difference between absolute and conjunct forms is that the absolute forms look as if they are derived from pre-forms which are a syllable longer than the corresponding conjunct form. In Indo-European terms the difference of a syllable in the length of a verb could be explained in two ways. The reconstructed Indo-European system operated with a distinction between athematic and thematic verbs; in the former, the endings, e.g. 1st sg. *-m*(i), 2nd sg. *-s*(i), etc., were added directly to the stem, in the latter a vowel *e* or *o* intervened (see Table 2.17 and also Szemerényi 1990: 244–9). Secondly, both a thematic and an athematic conjugation could take either primary or secondary endings, i.e. *-mi* or *-m*, *-si* or *-s*, etc. (see Table 2.17). Either a thematic/athematic or a primary/secondary alternation could provide the variation in a syllable seen in the Old Irish absolute and conjunct verbal forms. Both possibilities have been canvassed; Kortlandt 1979 argued that the Old Irish situation arose in part from an alternation between thematic and athematic forms, while Boling 1972 sees the primary/secondary alternation as crucial. Cowgill 1975b: 280–30, however, has cast doubt on the likelihood that any language would use primary endings for an initial verb and secondary endings when it was preceded by a particle; the unanimous evidence of the other Indo-European languages, which preserve both primary and secondary endings, is that the present tense had primary endings wherever it occurred in the sentence. Cowgill 1975a, followed by McCone 1979a, argues that the primary endings alone survived into Celtic, and that the *-i* was lost within Celtic by a late apocope of final short /i/ (McCone 1978: 35–7). The absolute endings which were the outcome of the original primary endings were somehow protected from the loss of final *-i*; how that happened is where Cowgill and McCone part company.

Cowgill belongs to an illustrous group, going back at least as far as Thurneysen 1907 (and including Dillon 1943 and Boling 1972), who have argued that the lack of lenition in *do·beir* is due to the presence of

TABLE 2.17   The reconstructed endings of the Indo-European verb.

	Primary	Secondary
Athematic		
1st sg.	TVT-*mi*	TVT-*m*
2nd sg.	TVT-*si*	TVT-*s*
3rd sg.	TVT-*ti*	TVT-*t*
Thematic		
1st sg.	TVT-*ō*	TVT-*om*
2nd sg.	TVT-*esi*	TVT-*es*
3rd sg.	TVT-*eti*	TVT-*et*

a particle **es* between the preverb and the verb. Thurneysen and others have identified it with the 3rd sg. **est* 'is', which is generally agreed to be present in *ní* 'not' (< **ne est*). Cowgill 1975a prefers to leave the etymology and semantics of the particle to one side, and argues not only that the particle was responsible for the non-lenition in *do·beir* but also that in simple verbs it came after the verb, thus protecting the ending from atrophy; thus, *do·beir* < **to-es beret* : *berid* < **bereti-es*. In other words, this enclitic particle followed Wackernagel's Law in always coming in second position in the sentence.

McCone 1979a: 4–5 raised substantial phonological objections to the above analysis, notably that the reflexes of infixed pronouns gave no indication that there had been a particle containing /s/ in that position.[18] McCone's explanation, followed with modifications by Sims-Williams 1984, allots a much greater role to personal pronouns. Rather than depending on a meaningless particle, McCone argues that the primary and secondary endings of simple verbs were protected from loss in cases where there was a suffixed object pronoun (see above and Breatnach 1977), eg. **bereti-me* 'he carries me' : **beret(i)* 'he carries' > OIr **beirthium* : *·beir*. At the same time, the enclitic pronoun was in second place in compounds, e.g. **to-me bereti*. The subsequent stages in the development are based on a view of Celtic word order first outlined by C. Watkins 1963a which was designed to explain why Celtic has a sentence-initial verb (see Chapter 9 below for a fuller discussion). In essence, Celtic word order was heavily influenced, more so than other Indo-European languages, first by the need to keep enclitics in second position and secondly by the close association of enclitics with verbs (Vendryes' Restriction). According to Watkins, Celtic originally had a sentence-final verb, as in, for example, Latin, but this verb could be pulled to the front of the sentence by the presence of an enclitic (see Table 2.18); thus, types (a), (b), (c) and (d) were in complimentary dis-

TABLE 2.18   Sentence types in Proto-Celtic

(a)   # ... 'V#
(b)   #'VE ... #
(c)   # ... 'P(P₂)V#
(d)   #'PE ... '(P₂)V# (> #PE'(P₂)V ... #)
(e)   #'C(E) ... '(P)V# (> #'C(E)'(P)V ... #)

V = verb, E = enclitic, P = preverb, ' = stress, C = conjunction, () = optional element

All five types are attested in early Old Irish; for examples, see 9.2.2.1 below.

tribution. The key factor was 'univerbation' whereby separated preverbs and verbs were united as in the outcome of types (d) and (e) in
Table 2.18. The direction of univerbation, towards the front of the sentence, was determined by the need to keep enclitics in second place,
which put types (a) and (c) under pressure to conform to the verb-initial
position. The rise of the deuterotonic pattern, so Watkins and McCone
argue, is a consequence of the shift of type (c) to the front of the sentence; a straight shift would have resulted in an opposition of #'P(P₂)V
... # : (d) #PE'(P₂)V ... # (after univerbation) with different stress patterns. The solution seems to have been to regularize the pattern in
favour of the latter; in other words, by taking the model of (d) and (e)
and deleting the enclitic and its accompanying mutation, we can produce the analogical proportion set out in Table 2.19. Similarly, instead
of simply fronting type (a), the enclitic was deleted from type (b)
(where the primary ending had been protected by the enclitic), thus,
*bereti-me → *bereti (> OIr berid). Although the simplest solution
might have been to generalize the forms with the initial accent, Sims-
Williams 1984: 171 sees additional motivation in the potential
confusion between indicatives and imperatives; by opting for a different stress pattern it was possible to differentiate between do·berat 'they
give' and tabrat 'let them give'.

Despite its complexity, the theory can account for an impressive
range of problems in early Irish verbal morphology; for example, the
distinction between absolute and conjunct endings, the lack of lenition
in do·beir, etc. Not all aspects, however, are equally convincing; for
example, the analogical development proposed by McCone requires the
deletion of the enclitic and its mutation, i.e. *to-v̄ere → *to-bere; but
since *to would itself cause lenition of the initial of the verb, should we
not expect *to-vere?

More recently, Koch 1987 has offered an explanation which depends
first on a very different view of the status of the verb in Indo-European
than that underlying the Watkins/McCone theory, and secondly on
prosodic patterns in Celtic. The Indo-European background is discussed
in 9.2; for the prosodic aspects, see Lindeman 1992.

TABLE 2.19   Analogical proportion to explain non-lenition in deuterotonic
verbal forms in Old Irish

---

*nī-me '*θ*overe* (> OIr *ním·thabair*) : **nī-'tovere* (> OIr *ní·tabair*)
:: **to-ṽe 'vere* (> OIr *dom·beir*) : x (x = **to-'bere* (> OIr *do·beir*))

See McCone 1979a: 16.

2.2.6.3   Deponents, impersonals and passives

The pattern of passives and deponents in Celtic is of particular interest
as it has developed from an Indo-European background in an unex-
pected direction (see Cowgill 1983 for the fullest discussion). As in
Latin and Greek, Celtic had a type of verb, called 'deponent', which
was characterized by a different set of endings which correspond to the
medio-passive endings in other Indo-European languages. In terms of
meaning, they are active just like normal non-deponent verbs, e.g. OIr
sechithir 'he follows', *foillsigithir* 'he reveals', *ro·fitir* 'he knows', etc.
As Cowgill 1983: 73 observes, they are a lexical category, not a grammatical category. There was a tendency within the history of Irish for
deponent verbs to be replaced by active verbs; this development was
well under way in Middle Irish and is virtually complete in Modern
Irish. There are traces of a similar pattern in Brittonic, notably in one
verb, W *gwyr*, C *gor*, B *goar* 'he knows' (cf. OIr *ro·fitir*).

On the other hand, every verb, whether active or deponent, can have
a passive. In historical terms, the passive, defined as the raising of the
object of the corresponding active sentence to subject position in the
passive version, is a secondary development, arising later than the
active and middle. Many Indo-European languages subsequently discarded the middle, though traces remain in, for example, the Latin
deponent inflection. Celtic seems not to have gone down the road of
acquiring a fully inflected passive. The Celtic impersonal is not formally identical to the deponent nor does it operate like passives in other
languages, where it usually has a fully inflected paradigm; only the 3rd
person forms are found, e.g. OIr *coscaitir* 'they are punished',
marbthair 'he is killed', etc. For other persons, the subject takes the
form of an infixed pronoun, e.g. *not·marbthar* 'you (sg.) are killed' (lit.
'there is a killing for you'), *nom·mórthar* 'I am praised'; the 'subject'
seems to be functioning as the grammatical object; this is clear in the
modern language where the independent pronouns, which replaced the
infixed forms, take the object form (see 3.4.4). Passives can only logi-
cally be formed by transitive verbs since they involve the
re-arrangement of an active sentence containing a direct object which is
promoted to subject. Intransitive verbs do not, therefore, have passives.
In Celtic, however, intransitive verbs do have an impersonal form, e.g.

OIr *tíagair* 'on va' (lit. 'there is a going'). In Old Irish these impersonals only have one form per tense which can be equated with the 3rd singular form. So, while passives have two forms, singular and plural (each with an absolute and conjunct form (see 2.2.6.2 and Table 2.14)), the impersonals to intransitive verbs only have the one. A similar arrangement seems to have operated in early Brittonic languages, though certainly in Welsh it was replaced by a periphrastic passive (5.4.4). In Middle Irish the impersonal forms to transitive verbs seem gradually to have gone the way of the intransitive impersonal so that in Modern Irish they have become a single impersonal, subjectless form, e.g. *búailtear é* 'he is struck' (lit.) 'on le frappe') : *búailtear iad* 'they are struck' (lit. 'on les frappe'). Beside these true, passive forms have developed in periphrastic verbal constructions (see 3.4.4 below).

2.2.6.4 Relative clauses

The modern Celtic languages have relative clauses marked by particles which do duty for the relative pronoun of other languages, namely MnIr *a*, ScG *na*, W *a/y*, MnB *a*; it is not marked for person, gender, case or number and is thus potentially confusing. For example, MnIr *an fear a chonaic an bhean* is ambiguous, either 'the man who saw the woman' or 'the man the woman saw'. The widespread use of a relative marker is a recent Celtic development; at earlier stages of the language a clear relative particle is restricted to certain constructions and relativity was marked by a combination of special verb forms, mutations and different negatives.[19] The Old Irish relative system is summarized in Table 2.20; the type of the relative is determined by the antecedent. When the antecedent is the subject or object of the verb, a compound verb shows lenition of the accented verb, e.g. *fo·ceird* 'he puts' : *fo·cheird* 'who puts/which he puts'. In historical terms, therefore, there seems to be some form of zero particle which causes lenition infixed in the verbal complex in the same place as an infixed pronoun might go. In compounds containing *imm* 'around' the particle is found as *-e* or *-a*, e.g. *imm·téit* 'he goes around' : *imme·théit* 'who goes around/which he goes around'. Simple verbs had special relative forms for some persons (see Table 2.21), but for the other persons they behaved like compound verbs, using *no* to carry the zero relative marker, e.g. *berid* 'he carries' : *beres* 'who carries/which he carries' but *berim* 'I carry' : *no·berim* /no'v'er'im'/ 'I who carry/which I carry'. The ambiguity was gradually resolved within Old Irish by the increasing use of nasalizing relative clause to mark object antecedents, i.e. where the initial of the accented verbal unit was nasalized. For example, while *as·beir* /as'v'er'/ is ambiguous (as opposed to *as·beir* /as'b'er'/ 'he says') in that it could mean 'who says' or 'which he says', *as·mbeir* is unambiguously 'which he says'. Nasalizing relative clauses where also used in compound verbs were the antecedent is a prepositional phrase or an adverb.

TABLE 2.20   Summary of relative clause usage in Old Irish.

Antecedent	Simple verbs	Compound verbs
Subject	{ Special verb forms { *no* + lenition	Lenition
Object	{ Special verb forms { *no* + lenition	{ Lenition { Nasalization
Prepositional phrases } Adverbs }	Non-relative forms	Nasalization

The negative form in all relative clauses is *na(d)* or *na(ch)*.

TABLE 2.21   The relative forms of the regular Old Irish verb

Present indicative of *caraid* 'love'

	Non-relative	Relative
1st sg.	*caraim*	*no·charaim*
2nd sg.	*carai*	*no·charai*
3rd sg.	*caraid*	*caras**
1st pl.	*carmai*	*carmae**
2nd pl.	*carthae*	*no·charaid*
3rd pl.	*carait*	*cartae**

* indicates a special relative form.

For relative forms of other tenses, see Thurneysen 1946: 352–440, Strachan and Bergin 1949: 34–68.

Relativity was also marked by a different negative form – *na(d)* instead of *ní*, e.g. *ní·ceil* /niː'kʲelʲ/ 'he does not hide' : *nad·cheil* /nad'χʲelʲ/ 'which he does not hide'.

However, since the zero relative particle seems to have occupied the same position as the infixed pronoun, the relative marker was deleted when an infixed pronoun occurred, e.g. *not·beir* /nod'vʲerʲ/ 'he carries you' or 'which/who carries you'. Ambiguity could be avoided by using a different set of pronouns (Class C (see Table 2.16)) containing /ð/ which were used optionally in the 1st and 2nd persons but compulsorily in the 3rd person; thus, for example, *nom·beir* 'he carries me' : *nodom·beir* 'who carries me', *nos·beir* 'he carries them' : *noda·beir* 'who carries them'.

The only place where there is a clear relative particle is in combination with a preposition, e.g. *cosa·mbeir* 'to whom he carries', *lasa·téit* 'with whom he goes', *fua·tabair* 'under which it is brought', etc. It is likely that the relative particle of Middle Irish has developed from this type of pattern.

The origin of Celtic relative markers is clarified by the presence in Gaulish of two forms *dugiiontiio* and *toncsiiontio*. They seem to be 3rd plural but with a further suffix *-io*; contextually, it is possible for them to be relatives. An ending *-io* -/i̯o/ would account for a 3rd plural relative *cartae* < *caront-i̯o* and a Welsh relic of the same system MW *yssyd*, MnW *sydd* /sið/ 'which is' < *esti-i̯o-*. Breatnach 1980: 8–9 has suggested that the nasalizing relative may be explained by reference to a relative particle *-i̯om*, a case form of the form noted above. However, McCone 1980: 18–21 has argued that the relative *-io* was uninflected and was not sensitive to case or gender variation.

A relative particle of that form would, like other enclitics in Celtic, have been infixed in compound verbs in order to remain in second position; the outcome would then have been the pattern of lenition outlined above. Not all is as clear. The origin of the *-s* ending of the 3rd singular relative and the dental element in the Class C infixed pronouns remain problems.

2.2.6.5 The verbs 'to be'

Irish has two fully conjugating verbs 'to be', distinguished both in form and in function (see Table 2.22). They are traditionally known as the substantive verb and the copula.[20] In Welsh the two types have been incorporated into a single verb 'to be', although there are traces in Brittonic of the same highly developed system found in Irish (D. S. Evans 1964: 138–45), as, for example, in the use in southern Welsh of *taw* 'is' related etymologically to Irish *tá*, MW *ys* 'is', e.g. *ys da y gwr* 'that man is good'.

The substantive verb in Old Irish is an accented verb. The present ·*tá* 'it is' is etymologically related to Latin *stāre*, etc., while the other tenses are based on the **bhu*-root of Eng *be*, Lat *fui*, etc., e.g. imperfect ·*bíth*, future *bied*, preterite ·*boí*, etc. (Thurneysen 1946: 476–83). On the other hand, the copula *is* 'is' (< **esti*) is unaccented; the forms outside the present tense are again based on the *b*-forms of the verb 'to be', though, being unaccented, they are much reduced, especially in combination with conjunctions, e.g. *ma* 'if' : *mad* 'if it is', *cé/cía* 'although' : *cid* 'although it is', *ní* 'it is not', *ar* 'is it?' (for the forms in Modern Irish, see 3.4.2 and Table 3.18).

The functional differences between substantive verb and copula are most easily approached from the copula. It essentially denotes a connection between the subject (S) and the predicate (P); the predicate always immediately follows the proclitic verb, thus *is P S* 'P is S', e.g. *is fer Conchobar* 'C is a man', *is mór in fer* 'the man is big'. The predicate in Old Irish can be a noun or an adjective, though in Modern Irish the use of the copula with an adjectival predicate is restricted to a few adjectives, e.g. *is ionann iad* 'they are the same', and to exclamations, e.g. *is maith é* 'he is good!', etc. (Ó Siadhail 1989: 229–30). In

TABLE 2.22 A summary of the Old Irish forms of the copula and substantive
verb

(a) Third singular forms

	Copula		Substantive verb	
	Absolute	Conjunct	Absolute	Conjunct
Present indicative	*is*	-*id*, etc.	*at·tá*	*·tá*
Habitual present		*·bi*	*bíid*	*·bí*
Present subjunctive	*ba*	*·b(o)*	*beith*	*·bé*
Past subjunctive	*bed*	*·bed*		*·beth*
Imperative (2nd sg.)		*ba*		*bí*
Future	*bid*	*·ba*	*bid*	*·bia*
Secondary future	*bed*	*·bad*		*·biad*
Past	*ba*	*·bo*	*boí*	
Perfect	*ro·bo*	*·rbo*	*ro·boí*	*·robae*

There are full conjugations for every form; for details, see Strachan and Bergin 1949:
72–3 (copula), 68–71 (substantive verb), Thurneysen 1946: 483–94 (copula), 476–83
(substantive verb).

(b) Full conjugation of the present indicative

	Copula	Substantive verb
1st sg.	*am*	*at·tó*
2nd sg.	*it*	*at·taí*
3rd sg.	*is*	*at·tá*
1st pl.	*ammi*	*at·taam*
2nd pl.	*adib*	*at·taaid*
3rd pl.	*it*	*at·taat*

Modern Irish adjectival predicates usually take the substantive verb,
e.g. *tá sé maith* or *tá sé go mhaith* 'he is good'.

The substantive verb is used in most other cases where the verb 'to
be' occurs, such as in statements of existence, position or condition. A
crucial difference is in word order; the substantive verb follows the
same order as finite verb sentences, i.e. *tá Seán anseo* 'Seán is here', *tá
fear ann* 'there is a man there' or 'a man exists', *tá an fear ag péinteáil
cathaoir* 'the man is painting a chair', etc. (for details of the Modern
Irish structures, see 3.4.2 and 3.4.3 for periphrastic verbs).

2.2.6.6 Middle Irish developments
The key factor in the development from the Old Irish verbal system
into Modern Irish is a massive simplification of categories which was

motivated in part at least by sound changes in late Old Irish and Middle Irish (see McCone 1987: 176–266). For example, the reduction of all unaccented vowels to /ə/ together with the loss of the neuter gender created havoc in the infixed pronoun series, since it obscured important vocalic distinctions. The ultimate outcome was the Modern Irish system of independent object pronouns.

The complicated alternations of absolute and conjunct verbal inflection (2.2.6.2) were ripe for remodelling. The most widespread Middle Irish strategy was to create new simple verbs from suitable prototonic parts of the Old Irish compound verb, e.g. OIr *do·léici* : *·téilci* 'throws' > MIr *téilcid*, *do·sluindi* : *·díltai* 'denies' > MIr *díltaid*, etc. (McCone 1987: 207–9). An alternative strategy was the creation of new verbs from verbal nouns (see 8.2); indeed, it is often difficult to distinguish the outcomes of these two strategies.

The paradigm was further simplified by the development of a clear, single set of endings, of which the most notable creation was a 3rd singular ending *-enn/-ann*, the predominant 3rd singular ending in modern spoken Irish. With the loss of distinct unaccented vowels, the 3rd singular conjunct endings to weak verbs, i.e. *·marba*, *·léici*, became indistinguishable from 3rd singular subjunctives and 2nd singular indicatives. The new ending was generalized from compounds of BIV verbs (see Table 2.12), such as *renaid* 'sell'; the compound *as·ren* : *·éirenn* 'sells' had a subjunctive *·éire* and by analogy with this *léicid* : *·léici* (subjunctive *·léice*) developed a present *léicenn* (McCone 1987: 224–7).

The weak/strong dichotomy in the Old Irish system with its associated confusion of tense markers (see Table 2.13) was also vulnerable to simplification. The developments have been discussed in detail by McCone 1987: 228–66. At this point, we may consider as an example the changes in future tense marking. Depending on the verb class, the Old Irish future was marked by an *f*-suffix, reduplication and an *a*-suffix, or by a lengthened stem vowel. The *f*-future was the weak verb marker, while the long vowel, frequently /e:/, was characteristic of strong verb stems ending in a liquid or a nasal (see Table 2.13), e.g. *·béra* 'he will carry'; : present *berid*, *·géra* 'he will call' : *gairid*, etc. (Thurneysen 1946: 404–5). Middle Irish displays a confused situation where both types are being generalized often at the expense of each other as much as the other more vulnerable types. The Modern Irish tense has an *f*-marker /h/ but also an ending *-óidh/-eoidh* /oːi̯/. The latter has developed from the generalization of the long vowel future to denominative verbs in *-aig-* which in Old Irish had an *f*-future, thus *-ég-* and *-eóg-* (see McCone 1987: 241–50, and 3.4.1 below for further discussion).

2.3 Scottish Gaelic and Manx developments

The above sections of this chapter have attempted to delineate the main developments in early Irish. The following chapter considers Irish. This section, therefore, briefly examines some of the changes which distinguish Scottish Gaelic and Manx from Irish, in other words the changes which occurred independently after they had separated from Irish.[21] As was pointed out by Jackson 1951, and noted above (2.1.2), the difficulty in establishing when Scottish Gaelic and Manx can be seen as separate dialects is complicated by the complete lack of early Celtic material from Scotland or Man, and even when we do have some evidence, it has been influenced by the standardized language of elevated court poetry. But side by side with the Classical forms a colloquial language was developing which had more rapidly separated from Irish. Jackson 1951: 79 discusses the methodology required to establish the date of the linguistic separation. Essentially it involves finding some features common to Scottish Gaelic and Manx which are not found in Irish, and likewise some features which are unique to Irish. The latter are datable by reference to dated material in Irish, while the former are not. Moreover, it is often the case that a full-scale change in one dialect is paralleled by vague tendencies in the other; this suggests a change which had just begun before the split but was only fully developed in one of the branches.

There is, however, another approach to this material which does not envisage a great split between Western Gaelic (Irish) and Eastern Gaelic (Scottish Gaelic and Manx). There is no doubt that there are substantial similarities between northern dialects of Irish and southern dialects of Scottish Gaelic, such as the negative *cha* (3.5.2.1), the maintenance of distinct vowels in unaccented syllables, e.g. Don -/aχt/ beside -/əχt/ in other Irish dialects (3.2.2; see generally C. Ó Baóill 1978). T. F. O'Rahilly 1932: 45–8, who took a firmly regional view of the matter, claimed that the similarities between Donegal Irish and Scottish Gaelic were due to the influence of Scottish Gaelic on the northern dialects of Irish. This view has been sharply rejected by Ó Buachalla 1977: 92–101, who stresses the essential unity of the Gaelic speaking areas: 'The present-day fragmentary pattern of the Gaelic speaking districts should not obscure the fact that historically we are dealing with a linguistic continuum from Cape Clear to Lewis, within which there were only transitions between gradually differentiated dialects' (Ó Buachalla 1977: 96).

The geographical divide between Ireland, Scotland and the Isle of Man has been assumed to imply a linguistic divide. Our lack of knowledge of the Irish dialect of Co. Down and the Gaelic dialect of Galloway may have helped to perpetuate the notion of dialectal divides;

had these dialects survived, the linguistic continuum might have been more easily perceived. However, modern dialectology would lead us to suppose that there would be some features which Donegal Irish would share with Scottish Gaelic, just as there are some which it shares with Mayo dialects (see 3.1). In other words, a clear-cut split between Western and Eastern Gaelic is perhaps not the most helpful view of the situation. It is perhaps more readily analysed as a continuum of partially overlapping isoglosses, some of which would bring together Donegal Irish with dialects of Scottish Gaelic.

The following sections are concerned with developments common to Scottish Gaelic and Manx.[22]

2.3.1 Phonology

In Irish, stressed disyllabic words with hiatus arising from the loss of /s/ or /u̯/, etc. had contracted into a diphthong or long vowel by the 10th century, but in Scottish Gaelic the hiatus remained to be marked in the orthography by an unpronounced and unetymological consonant, e.g. OIr *fiäch* 'raven' /fiəχ/ > MIr *fíach*, ScG *fitheach* (for further examples, see 6.3.2.6). T. F. O'Rahilly 1932: 143, however, noted that some dialects of Scottish Gaelic had removed the hiatus, hence doublets such as *óisg* : *othaisg* 'dry ewe', *bruach* : *bruthach* 'bank'.

In all dialects of Scottish Gaelic, except in the south-west, unstressed palatalized /ɣ'/ was devoiced to /χ'/, e.g. *doilich* /dol'iχ'/ 'difficult' (cf. MIr *doiligh*); there are traces of a similar devoicing in The Book of Armagh (7th century orthography) and in northern dialects of Irish (O'Rahilly 1932: 56). In Manx all final spirants were lost, e.g. *doilee*, so it is impossible to tell whether Manx shared this development. The interesting point about this development is that it can be dated reasonably precisely. The change only affected original /ɣ'/ and not /ð'/, and so must pre-date the general collapse of /ɣ/ and /ð/. In Irish /ɣ'/ and /ð'/ fell together in the 12th and 13th centuries and /ɣ/ and /ð/ slightly later, but in Scottish Gaelic /ɣ'/ went to /χ'/ but /ð'/ remained at least long enough to be preserved in the orthography.

One of the consequences of the initial stress accent in Irish was the reduction of unstressed long vowels. Subsequently, new long vowels arose in unaccented syllables from clusters of consonants and resonants and in loanwords (see 2.2.2). These secondary long vowels survived in Irish, notably in the series of suffixes, *-án* -/a:n/, *-óg* -/o:g/, etc. In Scottish Gaelic all such secondary vowels were shortened; thus, Irish *-án* and *-óg* appear as *-an* and *-ag*, e.g. ScG *caman* 'hurling-stick' (= Ir *camán*), *ciotag* 'left-handed' (= Ir *ciotóg*), etc. (T. F. O'Rahilly 1932: 125–6). This development is relatively late as it also affects long vowels arising from the loss of spirant, e.g. *fearail* 'manly' (= Ir *fearúil* < OIr *feramail* /'f'erəvəl'/), *cunnart* 'danger' (= Ir *cuntúirt* < OIr *cuntabart* /'kuntəvərt/), etc. O'Rahilly 1932: 126–7 suggests that it was a feature of the spoken language which took a long time to penetrate the written forms. For example, the Scottish poetry of the early-16th-century *Book of the Dean of Lismore* still shows in its unique orthography (see 6.3.2.6) long vowels in unstressed syllables, e.g. *beggane* (= Ir *beagán*, ScG *beagan*), *eddoyk* (= Ir *fheadóig*, ScG *fheadaig*). The evidence, however, can mislead; the poetry of this period composed in Scotland was subject to the influence of Early Modern Irish, and is not always a reliable guide to the spoken language.

While unaccented long vowels of various origins were reduced in Scottish Gaelic, secondary /e:/ in accented syllables was frequently 'broken', giving /iə/; for example, ScG *feur* 'grass' (Ir *féar*) can occur in some areas as /fiər/ or /fiar/ (Jackson 1968). In Irish this /e:/, which arose from clusters of -VCR > -V:R (see 2.2.2), generally remained as a long vowel, though T. F. O'Rahilly 1932: 194 notes examples such as /sk'iəl/ for *scél* 'story, news' in southern dialects. Jackson 1968 has shown that 'breaking' is a widespread feature of central Scottish Gaelic dialects though less common on the fringes of the Gaelic speaking area (Jackson 1968: 68 (map)). Even where it is common, the change does not always affect all words containing /e:/ but seems to have spread gradually through the lexicon.

One of the most wide-ranging developments to affect Scottish Gaelic and also to a certain extent Manx is the wholesale shifts in the articulation of consonants.[23] These changes have nothing to do with lenition, which occurred at a much earlier stage. This second set of changes is summarized in Table 2.23. In unstressed syllables /b d g/ were devoiced. This has already occurred in the *Book of the Dean of Lismore*, e.g. *dermit* (= Ir *Diarmaid*), *ynnit* (= Ir *ionad*), *corik* (= Ir *comhrag*), etc. The standard Irish-type orthography used for Scottish Gaelic does not reveal this change, hence the value of the *Book of the Dean of Lismore* with its non-standard spelling system. Traces of a similar development can be found in the northern dialects of Irish and in Manx; for example, Ir *Pádraig* occurs as *Pádraic, Páraic* or *Parick* in Manx. In stressed syllables /b d g/ were also devoiced, while initial /p t k/ were aspirated and final /p t k/ were heavily pre-aspirated.

TABLE 2.23   Consonantal shifts in Scottish Gaelic and Manx

Stressed syllables
/b d g/ > /p t k/ (written *b d g*)
/p t k/ > initial /pʰ tʰ kʰ/
      final /hp ht hk/ or /χp χt χk/ (written *p t c*)

Unstressed syllables
/b d g/ > /p t k/ (written *b d g*)

Although /b d g/ were devoiced, the contrastive feature seems to have been lack of aspiration rather than voice, thus ScG *bás* 'death' is [b̥a:s] rather than [pa:s]. The pre-aspiration can vary considerably from dialect to dialect; it can range from no pre-aspiration to slight pre-aspiration, i.e. /ʰp ʰt ʰk/, to a more pronounced form, i.e. /hp ht hk/, to a homorganic consonant before /k/, i.e. /hp ht χk/, to /χ/ appearing before all consonants, e.g. /χp χt χk/ (MacAulay 1992b: 155). The distribution shows that the full consonantal form is concentrated in the central dialects while 'fringe' dialects tend to show the lesser stages of pre-aspiration (MacAulay 1992b: 156 (map)). Thus, for example, *macc* 'son' can be realized as /mak/, /maʰk/, /mahk/ or /maχk/.

There are also some changes which separate Manx from Scottish Gaelic. Most notably, intervocalic stops in late spoken Manx were voiced or spirantized, i.e. /p t k/ > /b d g/, /b d g/ > /v ð ɤ/; for example, OIr *capall* /kabəL/ was spelt as *cabyll* in Manx but became /kaviL/ in the latest stages of the language (R. L. Thomson 1992: 128–9); compare also OIr *bratóg* /brado:g/ beside Mx *braddag* > late spoken Manx /braðag/.

There are also a number of other changes specific to Manx (see R. L. Thomson 1992: 125–30, Broderick 1993: 235–6). Initial clusters of /kn gn tn dl tl/ had fallen together with /kr gr tr dr/ by the end of the 17th century, e.g. Early *knaid* : Late *kraid* 'mockery', *gnwis* : *grooish* 'face', etc. The length of unlenited resonants, i.e. /R L N/, was frequently shifted to the preceding vowel, causing either lengthening or diphthongization, e.g. *kione* /k'o:n/ 'head' : Ir *ceann*; *baare* /ba:r/ 'tip' : Ir *barr* /baR/; *eeym* /i:m/ 'butter' : Ir *im* /iM/, etc. (for similar developments in Irish, see 3.2.1 below). On the other hand, lenited nasals at the end of a monosyllable developed a preceding homorganic stop with reduction of a long vowel, e.g. /k'o:n/ > /k'odn/ 'head', /tro:m/ > /trobm/ 'heavy', /loŋ/ > /logŋ/ 'ship'; we may compare the similar development in Late Cornish, e.g. *pedn* < *penn* (George 1993a: 429).

Manx shared with Scottish Gaelic the reduction of secondary unaccented long vowels. But there was more than one stress pattern in Manx; at an earlier stage, like some dialects of southern Irish, Manx acquired a number of loanwords with final stress, e.g. *resoon* 'reason' (= Ir *reusún*), *shirveish* 'service' (= Ir *servís*). They seemed to bring about a shift of stress in some native words with a long vowel in the second syllable, e.g. *faagail* /fag'a:l/ 'leaving' (= Ir *fagbáil*), *Trinaid* /tr'i'na:d'/ 'Trinity' (= Ir *Trionóid*), etc. When the reduction of unaccented long vowels occurred, these remained unaffected. Consequently, Manx has retained two reflexes of Irish long vowel suffixes; for example, Ir *-óg* /o:g/ corresponds to Mx *-ag* /ag/ in words with initial stress, but to *-aag* /a:g/ in those with final stress (R. L. Thomson 1992: 131, Broderick 1993: 236).

2.3.2 Morphology

The morphological differences between Irish and Scottish Gaelic are substantial. This section only briefly touches upon a series of changes already considered from the Irish point of view.

The Irish negative *ní* contrasts with ScG *cha*, which is derived from the Middle Irish variant *nocha*, itself corresponding to OIr *nícon*, a variant of *ní* (Thurneysen 1946: 538). Similarly, the Scottish Gaelic and Manx relative particle *na*, *ny* is derived from MIr *ina*, a variant of *a* which became the standard Irish relative marker (see 2.2.6.4). It was noted above (2.2.4 above) that in Middle Irish a plural marker was generalized from the dental stems; this development did not occur in Scottish Gaelic where there was a tendency for a nasal ending *-an* to spread as a plural marker (Gillies 1993: 173–7, Howells 1971; see also 2.2.4). Scottish Gaelic and Manx have also preserved, much more so than Irish, the absolute/conjunct distinctions of Old Irish (see Table 2.24). The preservation of these patterns has been aided by the absence of any development parallel to the rise of a clear 3rd singular present in *-enn/-ann* in Early Modern Irish (see 2.2.6.6); Gleasure 1990: 186–7 has shown that *-(e)ann* only occurs in the literary forms of Scottish Gaelic. There are very few personal endings; they are marked almost entirely by personal pronouns. A further development in the verbal system is the collapse of present/future and imperfect/conditional distinctions. This was due to the loss of the *f*-marker in the future and in some cases has led to the use of the same forms for both tenses (Ó Buachalla 1977, 1985).

TABLE 2.24   Scottish Gaelic *gabh-* 'take': a summary paradigm

Habitual present/future

Independent (absolute)	*gabhaidh*
Dependent (conjunct)	(*nach*) *gabh*
Relative	*a ghabhas*

Habitual past/conditional

Independent (absolute)	*ghabhaidh*
Dependent (conjunct)	(*nach*) *gabhadh*
Relative	*a ghabhadh*

Simple past

Independent (absolute)	*ghabh*
Dependent (conjunct)	(*nach*) *do ghabh*
Relative	*a ghabh*

See Gillies 1993: 191

Notes

1. For full bibliographies of Irish literature and language, see Best 1913, 1942 and Baumgarten 1986. For a general discussion of Irish literature, see J. E. C. Williams and Ford 1992; see also Ó Riain 1992 and S. Mac Mathúna 1992.
2. McManus 1991 is the best introduction to Ogam; see also now Ziegler 1994. The original collection of Ogam inscriptions was made by Macalister 1945–9. For the British inscriptions, see Nash-Williams 1950, and for south-west Britain, Okasha 1993. For a general discussion of the British inscriptions, see C. Thomas 1994.
3. Much Old Irish material is collected in Stokes and Strachan 1901–3. In addition, Irish names occur in the earlier Latin hagiography deriving from Ireland, such as Adomnán's *Life of Columba* (Anderson and Anderson 1991; see also now Charles-Edwards 1993) and the Patrician lives by Muirchú and Tirechán (Bieler 1979). On the hagiographical material generally, see Sharpe 1991.
4. Thurneysen 1946 is a translated and revised version of Thurneysen 1909. This remains by far the best grammar of Old Irish; but see also Pokorny 1969, Vendryes 1908, Richards 1935. For an elementary listing of paradigms, see Strachan and Bergin 1949. Pedersen 1909–13 contains a vast amount of Old Irish particularly in the list of verbs (II, 450–658 = H. Lewis and Pedersen 1961: 334–403). The best dictionary of the early language is Quin *et al.* 1913–76; for the modern language, see O Dónaill 1977; Dinneen 1934 is dated, though useful for dialect words. There has been no full history of the Goidelic languages, but see now McCone et al. 1994; this work appeared too late for detailed references to be incorporated elsewhere.
5. The texts are collected in Binchy 1978. For a survey of Irish law, see F. Kelly 1988.
6. For Irish bardic poetry of this period, see Bergin 1970.
7. For bibliographical details on Irish dialects, see Chapter 3, n. 2.
8. See Borgstrøm 1937 (Barra), 1940 (Outer Hebrides), 1941 (Skye and Ross-shire), Oftedal 1956 (Leurbost), Holmer 1962 (Kintyre), 1957 (Arran), Mac Gill-Fhinnain 1966 (South Uist), Dorian 1978 (East Sutherland), Ó Murchú 1989 (East Perthshire). For a historical survey of Scottish Gaelic dialect studies, see Bosch 1990.
9. For a general discussion of Manx literature, see R. L. Thomson 1969; see also R L Thomson 1992a: 100–1, 1992b, Broderick 1993: 228–9.
10. For the role of Welsh or British in Latin loanwords into Irish, see 2.3 below.
11 For details, see Greene 1976; some aspects of diphthongs are discussed in 2.3.1 below in relation to Scottish Gaelic.
12 The spatial terminology of 'raising' and 'lowering' is best understood by reference to the conventional arrangement of vowels:

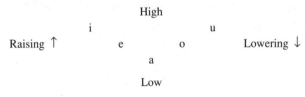

13. McCone 1981 has argued that this resistance to a reduction in articulation in syllables beginning and ending with homorganic consonants is more widespread and affects other consonants as well.

14. The other two fixed points are the following. A bilingual inscription from Dyfed has Ogam *VOTECORIGAS* beside *VOTEPORIGIS* in Latin script; the name has been equated with the similar name *Vortepori* in Gildas and therefore dated to about AD 550. However, the equation is inexact and remains doubtful.

    The change of /nt/ and /nk/ to /dd/ and /gg/ respectively had already taken place before the time of the Ogam inscriptions. Jackson dated the invention of Ogam to the late 4th century, but this is perhaps too late; McManus 1991: 40–1 appears to suggest a 3rd- or early 4th-century date as a *terminus post quem non*.

15. For an up-to-date discussion of Patrician material, see Dumville 1993. For a detailed bibliography, see Lapidge and Sharpe 1985: 9–11.

16. 'Laryngeals' (conventionally written as H) are a series of hypothetical vowels, usually three in number, which have been reconstructed by Indo-Europeanists to account for various anomalies in the correspondences between languages. Despite their name their exact phonetic nature is unclear although their effects are reasonably well understood. Essentially they had the effect of lengthening vowels and in most environments were realized as vowels, although traces of a consonantal resolution appear in Anatolian languages. For a general survey, see Lindeman 1987; for laryngeals in Celtic, see Hamp 1965.

17. On questions of word order, see C. Watkins 1963a and Russell 1988e: 160–7. On the origin of the absolute/conjunct distinction itself, see Dillon 1943, Meid 1963, Boling 1972, Cowgill 1975a, 1975b, Kortlandt 1979, McCone 1979a, and for a detailed summary of the state of the question, Sims-Williams 1984; see also Isaac 1991, 1993. On the form of preverbs, see Russell 1988c, 1988e. On the form of the endings of the Old Irish verb, see McCone 1982.

18. McCone also objects to the lack of any etymology or grammatical status for the *(e)s* particle. However, one possibility is raised by the work of Russell 1988c, 1988e, who has argued that Celtic preverbs had forms with and without /s/, e.g. OIr *fris·gair* 'he answers' : *ní·frecrae* 'he does not answer', where it can be shown that the preverb in the latter form does not contain /s/ (see also 9.2 below). Such a possibility may be exploited to explain the lack of lenition in *do·beir* but not the alternation of absolute/conjunct endings; there is, however, no clear reason why the same explanation should be required to cover both phenomena.

19. For Old Irish, see Thurneysen 1946: 312–25, McCone 1987: 15–18. For specific discussions, see Breatnach 1980, McCone 1980. For Old and Middle Welsh, see D. S. Evans 1964: 60–8.

20. See Thurneysen 1946 475–94. Strachan and Bergin 1949: 68–73 provide a useful collection of forms. T. Ó Máille 1911 discusses the Middle Irish and modern evidence in the context of the Old Irish situation, and also has an interesting comparison with the Spanish usage of *ser* and *estar*. For the Modern Irish copula, see Ó Siadhail 1989: 219–52; and for the forms, see Table 2.22 above.

21. The best discussion of Scottish Gaelic is Gillies 1993; but see also MacAulay 1992b, MacInnes 1992.
22. The treatment here is not exhaustive; for further details, see T. F. O'Rahilly 1932: 122–60, Jackson 1951: 86–91, MacAulay 1992b: 150–9, Gillies 1993: 147–77.
23. See MacAulay 1992b: 154–6, Gillies 1993: 147–62 and Shuken 1976. For further details, see the dialect monographs listed above in n. 8.

Chapter 3

Irish

3.1 Types of Irish

In Chapter 2 the earlier stages of the Goidelic languages were discussed together with developments in Scottish Gaelic and Manx. The present chapter is concerned with the other modern reflex of Goidelic, namely Irish. The aim of this chapter is to provide a description of the modern language which complements the discussion so far and focuses on the features discussed above.[1] Unlike Welsh (see 5.1), there is no generally accepted and widely spoken standard form of the language and most speakers would identify their speech with one of the main dialect groups. It may be helpful, therefore, to consider the dialect situation as a whole.

3.1.1 Dialects

The dialects of Irish are traditionally divided into three groups known by the three regional terms, Donegal, Connacht and Munster (see Map 3.1), though T. F. O'Rahilly 1932: 17 preferred to see a simple split into Southern (Munster) and Northern (Connacht and Donegal) Irish; Table 3.1 (a) shows the distribution of a number of lexical items which illustrate the basic dialectal divergences.[2] But it is clear that, however one labels the dialect groupings, there is a continuum of dialects running from north to south; for example, southern dialects of Connacht Irish share features with northern Munster dialects, particularly in Co. Clare where a number of isoglosses seem to meet; Table 3.1 (b) provides some lexical items which illustrate these finer dialectal splits, particularly in Connacht Irish. It is clear that within the main dialect groups there are significant differences between northern and southern types. However, the modern situation can only give us a partial picture of the original inter-relationship of the dialects; our lack of information from eastern and central Ireland where the language has died out gives

MAP 3.1   The main dialect areas and places which have been surveyed in detail

After Ó Siadhail 1989: 3.

TABLE 3.1   Lexical items illustrating dialect differences

		Donegal	Connacht	Munster
(a)	**Items illustrating the basic dialect divergences**			
17	'calling'	*scairtigh*	*glaodach*	*glaodach*
19	'milking'	*blighe/bleaghan*	*bleaghan*	*crúdh*
42	'fox'	*madadh rúadh*	*sionnach*	*madra rúadh*
72	'cabbage'	*cál*	*gabáiste*	*gabáiste*
78	'pot'	*pota*	*pota*	*corcán*
99	'porridge'	*brochán*	*brochán*	*praiseach*
171	'plough'	*seisreach*	*céachta*	*céachta*
245	'hill'	*cruc*	*cruc*	*cnuc*
249	'nettle'	*cúl fáith*	*neanntóg*	*neanntóg*
(b)	**Items illustrating splits within the basic dialect groups**			
4	'castrating'	*spochadh*	N *spochadh/baint as* S *baint as/coilleadh*	*coilleadh*
95	'earning'	N *cosnadh* S *sathrú*	*sathrú*	*tuilleamh*
106	'grandmother'	*máthair mhóir*	N *máthair mhóir* S *seana mháthair*	*seana mháthair*
107	'people' (of Ireland)	N *muinntear* S *bunadh*	*muinntear*	*muinntear*
114	'Irish'	*Gaedhilc*	N *Gaedhilc/* *Gaedhilge* S *Gaedhilge*	*Gaedhilge*
144	'closing'	*druid*	N *druid* S *dúnadh*	*dúnadh*
160	'smoke'	*toit*	N *toit* S *deatach*	*deatach*

Numbers refer to Wagner 1958–69, vol. I.

no indication, for example, as to how far north Munster-like dialects spread, or how they were related to the dialects of Leinster, or how far east the Co. Clare 'border' area extended (see Wagner 1958–69: I, xxviii). Figure 3.1 shows a series of stemmata demonstrating the sub-divisions of the dialects. It is most easy to demonstrate dialect differentiation at the superficial level of lexical items but the differences run much more deeply. Ó Dochartaigh 1992: 30 observes that Munster Irish tends to be the most conservative in its morphology, while its phonology is most innovative. On the other hand, northern dialects, and in particular Donegal, tend to be most conservative in their phonology but most innovative in their morphology. For example, it is well established that Munster dialects preserve synthetic forms of the

(a) Donegal

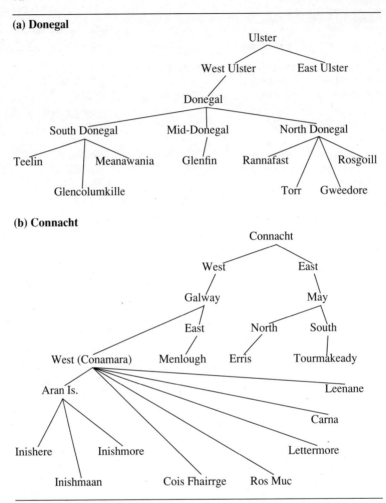

(b) Connacht

Figure 3.1: Stemmata demonstrating the sub-divisions of the dialects.

verb, while elsewhere they have been replaced by analytic forms, e.g. Mun *dhíolas* /ˈi̯ələs/ 'I sold' : elsewhere *dhíol mé* /i̯əl mˈeː/, Mun *cheannuigheamair* /χˈaˈNiːmər/ 'we bought' : elsewhere *cheannuigh muid* /ˈχˈaNə midˈ/ (Wagner 1958–69: I, 1 and 50 respectively); the analytic forms consist of a basic lenited verbal stem used in the preterite and a personal pronoun (see 3.4.1 below). Connacht dialects show a preference for highly marked plural forms, while Munster tends to preserve the shorter form, e.g. Mun *uibh* /iː/ : Conn *uibheachaí* /ˈivəχiː/ 'eggs' (Wagner 1958–69: I, 45). At the phonological level,

(c) Munster

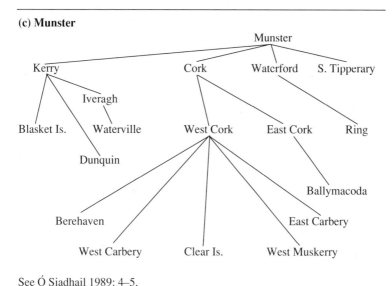

See Ó Siadhail 1989: 4–5.

Figure 3.1: *continued*

word stress is a crucial distinguishing feature. Northern dialects most clearly preserve the original pattern of initial stress, whereas Munster Irish has virtually settled into a system where vowel length and stress are coextensive, e.g. *bradán* 'salmon' Mun /brə'daːn/ with reduction of the pretonic vowel (see 3.2.2 below). Further examples are discussed in the following sections, in which aspects of the phonology, morphology and syntax of Modern Irish are considered. The approach adopted here is to take full account of the dialectal variation and not to concentrate exclusively on one dialect; there is always the danger that such an approach fails to provide a clear picture of any one dialect. However, there are numerous dialect descriptions which offer that, while it is hoped that this chapter will provide a clear introduction to the language as a whole.

3.1.2 The survival of Irish

Concern over the survival of the language has been the subject of considerable discussion over the years.[3] Ó Murchú has recently taken a reasonably upbeat view:

> There is thus in the community as a whole with regard to Irish a solid core of active competence and use and a widespread passive competence. On the other hand, its continuing low ranking on a pragmatic scale leaves Irish constantly vulnerable to extensive abandonment in any period of rapid

socio-economic change. For the present, though, it still fulfils an ideological and ethnic need for a majority in the population . . . (Ó Murchú 1993: 489).

However, Hindley 1990 has presented a much more pessimistic analysis of the present state of the language and a very gloomy view of its future. He has attempted to get behind the Census statistics about numbers of Irish speakers and to consider actual daily use of the language on the ground. His conclusion gives cause for grave concern:

> There is no room for honest doubt that the Irish language is dying. The only doubt is whether the generation of children now in a handful of schools in Conamara, Cloch Chionnaola and Gaoth Dobhair, and Corca Dhuibhne are the last generation of first-language speakers or whether there will be one more. The reasons . . . relate primarily to economic forces which have promoted the modernization of the Gaeltacht economy and the mobilization of its people (Hindley 1990: 248).

Hindley's approach was not only to examine the Census figures in an appropriately sceptical manner but also to make use of recent *deontas* figures, the grant given for every schoolchild in the Gaeltacht, the officially designated Irish speaking areas, for whom it can be verified that Irish is the language of the home (Hindley 1990: 48–62). In 1985–6 the number of children receiving the *deontas* in schools where the majority of pupils receive it was 2858 in 56 schools in 1985–6 (Hindley 1990: 249). It is clear that the majority need to receive it for the children to be growing up in a predominantly Irish speaking environment. But if one then looks at schools where 70 per cent of the children receive the *deontas*, rather than just a simple majority, the figures plummet alarmingly to 1473 children in 33 schools. A sceptical study of the individual areas of the Gaeltacht and of the statistical information brings Hindley to the conclusion that the current numbers of habitual native speakers should be set at about 10 000 as the upper limit. The 1981 Census produced a figure of 58 000 Irish speakers in the Gaeltacht but the majority are second language learners and show no signs of passing the language on to their children. A major difficulty, as Hindley sees it, is the fragmentation of the *deontas*-majority areas; instead of one large core area, they are divided into ten or eleven small pockets, each of which is much more vulnerable to Anglicization than one large area would be.

3.2 Phonology

3.2.1 The framework of the phonology[4]

There are huge differences in the surface realization of particular sounds in the Irish dialects and it is, therefore, very difficult to produce an overview without going into great detail. It is proposed here to follow the approach of Ó Siadhail 1989 who sets up a slightly more abstract phonological system from which the surface realizations can be

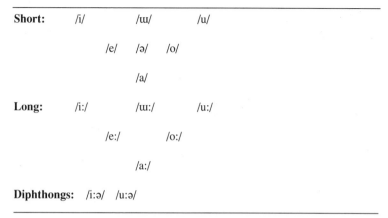

Short:	/i/		/ɯ/	/u/
		/e/	/ə/ /o/	
			/a/	
Long:	/iː/		/ɯː/	/uː/
		/eː/	/oː/	
			/aː/	

Diphthongs: /iːə/ /uːə/

Figure 3.2: Modern Irish vowel and diphthong phonemes

generated by the application of dialect-specific rules; thus, the vowel
and consonant system presented below will not necessarily apply to a
single dialect in its entirety. Throughout this section examples will be
given of the rules which need to be applied in order to produce the surface realizations; but at each stage only a few examples are given and
further information can be extracted from Ó Siadhail 1989.

The underlying Modern Irish vowel system has seven short and six
long vowels, and two diphthongs (as presented in Figure 3.2). Not all
dialects maintain all these distinctions and there is considerable variation in the phonetic realizations. The fullest range of distinctions is only
found in the stressed syllable; elsewhere most vowels are /ə/. The quality of the vowels is very much at the mercy of the quality of
surrounding consonants; for example, /a/ is raised to /e/ before a palatal
consonant in different case forms, e.g. /N′ad/ *nead* 'nest' : gen. sg.
/N′ed′ə/ *neide* (see 3.2.4 below).

There is a consistent development of long vowels and more diphthongs from original short vowels. A few examples are considered here
(for further details, see Ó Siadhail 1989: 48–56). Syllable lengthening
occurs regularly before an original tense /R/, /L/ or /N/; there is an
associated reduction in the tenseness of the resonant. It is usually realized as a long vowel in northern dialects but as a diphthong further
south, e.g. *gann* 'scarce' Conn /gaːn/, Mun /gaun/, etc. (for a similar
development in Manx, see 2.3.1). Before a voiced stop + liquid there is
regular lengthening or diphthongization, e.g. *eaglais* 'church' /aːgləs′/,
paidrín 'rosary' /pa:d′r′iːn/, and similarly before nasal + stop, e.g.
muinntear 'people' Conn /mi:N′t′ər′/, Mun /mi:n′t′ər′/ or /main′t′ər′/,
teampall 'Protestant church' Don /t′aːmpəL/, Mun /t′aumpəL/, etc.
New diphthongs and long vowels also developed from the merging of

semi-vowels (which derive originally from *bh/mh* and *dh/gh* (see below)) with adjacent vowels, e.g. *páighe* 'pay' /pa:i̯ə/ > Conn /pa:i:/, *nuaidheacht* 'news' /nu:əi̯əχt/ > Conn /nu:i:χt/, *talamhan* gen. sg. 'earth' /taləu̯ən/ > Conn /talu:n/, *leabhar* 'book' /L'au̯ər/ > Conn, Mun /L'aur/, etc. (Ó Siadhail 1989: 71–5). In Connacht, and especially in Cois Fhairrge, long vowels arise from the loss of /h/ and the coalescence of the two vowels, e.g. *bóthar* 'road' /bo:r/ (< /bo:hər/), *cuthach* 'rage' /ku:χ/ (< /ku:həχ/). Not all possible combinations of vowels coalesce; for example, /a/ or /e/ before a high vowel /i:/ or /u:/ forms a diphthong, e.g. *cathaoir* 'chair' /kair'/ (< /kahi:r'/), *beithígh* 'cows' /b'ei/ (< /b'e:hi:i̯/).

The fullest version of the consonantal system has two sets of consonants, palatal (slender) and non-palatal (broad) (see Table 3.2; for the historical background to the double set of consonants, see 2.2.3.3). Some distinctions require explanation. The minimal distinction between /u̯/ *bh* and /ũ̯/ *mh* is important in all dialects, even though the surface realization might be different, e.g. *romhat* 'before you' Conn, Mun /ru:t/ but Mayo, Don /ro:t/. In Mayo /ũ̯/ is frequently preserved, while /u̯/ is diphthongized, e.g. *sleamhain* 'slippery' /s'l'au̯ən/ but *leabhar* 'book' /L'aur/. Palatal versions of /u̯/, /ũ̯/ and /ɤ/ are realized as [v'], [ṽ'] and [i̯] respectively, and for convenience are indicated as such, rather than the more misleading /u̯'/, /ũ̯'/ and /ɤ'/. The realization of palatal /u̯'/, /ũ̯'/ as [v'] and [ṽ'] is in practice only found in the north; further south they disappear, leaving vowel lengthening or diphthongization.

Among the liquids and nasals, there appears to be a heavy overloading of the system with palatal and non-palatal variants of both the tense and lax consonants (for the historical background, see 2.2.3.4). In short, /l/ and /n/, etc. occur in leniting position and /L/ and /N/ elsewhere. The tense/lax opposition is preserved in mutating environments, i.e. initially, but elsewhere in the word the fourfold opposition has been reduced usually by the partial removal of the tense/lax contrast. For example, in many parts of Conamara the tense/lax opposition is maintained in the palatal forms, i.e. /L'/ : /l'/, /N'/ : /n'/, etc. but in non-palatal forms there is only /N/ and /L/, e.g. *ball* 'place' /ba:L/ and

TABLE 3.2 Irish consonant phonemes

/p/ : /p'/	/b/ : /b'/	/f/ : /f'/	/m/ : /m'/
/t/ : /t'/	/d/ : /d'/	/s/ : /s'/	
/k/ : /k'/	/g/ : /g'/	/χ/ : /χ'/	/h/ : /h'/
/u̯/ : /v'/	/ũ̯/ : /ũ̯'/	/ɤ/ : /i̯/	
/l/ : /l'/	/n/ : /n'/	/r/ : /r'/	
/L/ : /L'/	/N/ : /N'/	/R/ : /R'/	

baladh 'smell' /ba:Lə/ beside *buille* 'blow' /buL'ə/ but *buile* 'anger'
/bil'ə/ (Ó Siadhail 1989: 93–5 for further examples).

3.2.2 Stress patterns

It has already been observed (2.2.2) that in early Irish the stress accent
fell on the initial syllable of the word and that this had serious effects
on the following unaccented syllables in terms of syncope and vowel
reduction. It is generally assumed that variation in stress patterns in
later Irish are divergences from that. However, given the innate conservatism of the Irish writing system, different stress patterns could have
developed relatively early in the history of the language and simply not
been marked in the orthography.

There are two ways in which the stress pattern varies from an initial
accent. They are more or less restricted geographically. First, there is
the relatively widespread change in words of the shape TVRVTVT-
(where R = /l n r/ and all the vowels are short (see Table 3.3 (a) for
examples); the vowel in the first syllable is higher than /a/ and typically
the vowel in the second syllable is epenthetic in origin (see 3.2.3
below). In this type the accent shifts to the second syllable and the initial syllable, now unaccented, is reduced and usually subject to
syncope. This pattern only seems to operate in Donegal in particular

TABLE 3.3 Accent shifts in Modern Irish

(a)	**Accent shift**	**Syncope**
bolgam 'mouthful':		
/ˈboləgəm/	→ /bəˈlogəm/	→ /blogəm/
tiormaigh 'dry' :		
/ˈt'irəməi̯/	→ /t'əˈroməi̯/	→ /ˈt'r'oməi̯/
furasta 'easy';		
/ˈfurəstə/	→ /fəˈrustə/	→ /ˈfrustə/

(b)
corcán 'pot' /kərˈka:n/
cailíní 'girls' /kaˈli:ni:/
óganach 'youth' /o:ˈga:nəχ/
spealadóir 'mower' /sp'ələˈdo:r'/

(c)
coileach 'cockerel' /koˈl'aχ/
beannacht 'blessing' /b'(ə)ˈNaχt/
BUT
feargach 'angry' /ˈf'arəgəχ/
báisteach 'rain' /ˈba:s't'əχ/

After Ó Siadhail 1989: 28–9.

lexical items such as *tiormaigh* 'dry' /t′r′umiː/ and *urball* 'tail' /rubəL/, but is more widespread in Connacht; in Munster it also affects words where the second syllable does not contain an epenthetic vowel, e.g. *tarathar* 'auger' /ˈtraːhər/, *iomarca* 'excess' /morkə/, *salach* 'dirty' /slaχ/ (Ó Siadhail 1989: 28–9). This more widespread application in Munster may well be related to the second development to be considered here.

In Munster, the stress accent tends to be attracted to a non-initial long vowel (see Table 3.3 (b) for examples). The attraction is not absolute; for example, in *méaracán* 'thimble' /ˈm′eːrəkaːn/ the stress remains initial rather than jump the intervening short vowel to the final long vowel. This accent shift affects a large number of derivatives in *-án* and *-ín*, particularly disyllabic forms where there are no restrictions on the accent shift (Doyle 1992: 115–32). Another element in this shift is the movement of the stress to final /aχ/ or /aχt/ but only when the suffix is preceded by a short vowel (see Table 3.3 (c) for examples). This pattern is centred on Munster but there are traces of a similar (perhaps optional) pattern in parts of Connacht (Wagner 1958–69: 284) where the shift is restricted to cases where the profile of the beginning of the word is (T)VRa:- (where R = /l r/ and the vowel is short), e.g. *arán* 'bread' /ˈaraːn/ > /əˈraːn/, *coláiste* 'college' /ˈkolaːs′t′ə/ > /koˈlaːs′t′ə/ > /klaːs′t′ə/, etc. Even in Donegal /N′iːn/ *iníon* 'daughter' suggests a more widespread feature, even if restricted to certain lexical items; furthermore, Ó Siadhail 1989: 33–4 points out a number of related features in Donegal Irish, such as the fact that in Donegal final /əχt/ is realized as /aχt/. Similarly, unstressed long vowels are shortened, e.g. *arán* 'bread' /ˈaran/, *galún* 'gallon' /galun/, but not reduced to /ə/. There seem to be two forces at work here, the maintenance both of a strong initial stress and of vowel quality in unaccented syllables. These Donegal features are also found in Scottish Gaelic (see, for example, Holmer 1962: 47) and provide a useful reminder that the dialect continuum does not stop short at Donegal but also involves the Scottish Gaelic dialects (see A. J. Hughes 1992: 163).

These accent shifts are not rigid but are affected by the position of the word in phrases. For example, the shift to a final stress in a disyllabic word may well be prevented by a dependent adjective, e.g. *cipín* 'stick' Mun /k′əp′iːn′/ but *cipín dearg* 'a red stick' /ˈk′ip′iːn′ ′d′arəg/ (Ó Siadhail 1989: 31–2). Given that words are rarely uttered in isolation, the above discussion of stress shift, particularly in Munster but elsewhere too, amounts to saying that there is an increasing degree of accentual flexibility developing in Irish, a feature which is not going to decrease in view of the continual influx of English loanwords with a wide range of accentual patterns.

3.2.3 Consonant clusters and epenthesis

Certain internal and final clusters of resonant + stop, or stop + resonant
are regularly broken up by the insertion of an epenthetic vowel /ə/ (Ó
Siadhail 1989: 20–3; see also Ó Dochartaigh 1976). It will be recalled
that in early Irish, new long vowels arose from the reduction of similar
clusters in final position (2.2.2; for the range of reactions to consonant
clusters in Welsh, see 5.2.3). Subsequently, clusters of non-homorganic
resonant + stop were broken up (Table 3.4 exemplifies the possible
combinations). Since /l n r/ are essentially dental in terms of articulation, the combinations concerned with epenthesis usually involve
non-dentals. The alternative strategy whereby there is an assimilation
of the resonant to the stop is uncommon; the only specific example is
where /ng/ becomes /ŋg/ and as homorganic elements there is no
epenthesis. On the other hand, epenthesis is rare with the unvoiced
stops, thus *corp* 'corpse' [korp], *corc* 'cork' [kork]. A second, less
common type of epenthesis occurs in clusters of stop + resonant, e.g.
eagla 'fear' [agələ], *madra* 'dog' [madərə], etc.

   Because these epenthetic vowels do not impinge on the orthography
of Irish, it is difficult to know whether they are a modern phenomenon
or not. The changes which produced these clusters, i.e. syncope and
loss of final syllables, pre-date Old Irish and it is reasonable to suppose
that these accommodations were an immediate reaction at the phonetic
level at that period.

3.2.4 Raising, lowering and paradigmatic variation

There are two types of raising and lowering which are detectable (for
the historical origin of vowel affection, see 2.2.3.2). Both types are

TABLE 3.4   Epenthesis in clusters of resonant + stop

	/b/	/v/, /u̯/	/f/
/l/	[aləbən]	[s'el'əv']	
	Albain 'Scotland'	*seilbh* 'possessions'	
/n/	[banəbə]	[ban'əv']	[konəfə]
	Banba 'Ireland'	*bainbh* 'piglets'	*confadh* 'anger'
/r/	[bar'əb'ər'ə]	[s'er'əv'i:s']	
	Bairbre PN	*seirbhís* 'service'	
	/m/	/χ/	/g/
/l/	[f'iləm]		[boləg]
	film 'film'		*bolg* 'belly'
/n/	[an'əm']	[s'anəχi:]	
	ainm 'name'	*seanchaí* 'story teller'	
/r/	[gorəm]	[dorəχə]	[d'arəg]
	gorm 'blue'	*dorcha* 'dark'	*dearg* 'red'

TABLE 3.5   Paradigmatic raising and lowering

Raising
   fear 'man' /fʹar/ : nom. pl. *fir* 'men' /fʹirʹ/
   nead 'nest' /Nʹad/ : gen. sg. *neide* /Nʹedʹə/
   ceart 'right' (adj.) /kʹart/ : comparative *ceirte* /kʹertʹə/

Lowering
   droim 'back' /dremʹ/ : gen. sg. *drama* /dramə/

caused by the same factors, namely consonant quality (broad/slender or
non-palatal/palatal), the presence of nasals, or sometimes by long vowels in following syllables (Ó Siadhail 1989: 37–48). The first type,
which is of less concern at this point, is not synchronically noticeable
since there is no paradigmatic variation; for example, in Connacht /a/ is
raised to /ɯ/ when there is /a:/ in the following syllable and there is no
intervening morpheme boundary, e.g. *gabáiste* 'cabbage' /ˈguba:sʹtʹə/
(cf. Mun /gəˈbaisʹtʹə/ with stress shift, Don /ˈkaba:sʹtʹə/), *anáil* 'breath'
/ɯNa:lʹ/. The presence of nasals can also cause raising, e.g. *gloine*
'glass' /glinʹə/, *goimh* 'sting' /givʹ/, etc.

   Of greater significance in synchronic terms is the perceptible alternation between different case forms or between grammatical forms of the
same base (e.g. comparative adjectives, etc.). The alternation is caused
by the presence or absence of a palatal consonant which can often be
the sole marker of case differentiation (with or without a following /ə/)
(see Table 3.5 for examples). In some dialects cases like *nead* and *ceart*
can be raised even further, e.g. Mun /Nʹidʹə/ and /kʹirtʹə/ respectively.

3.2.5   Palatalization
The historical background to the synchronic alternation has been discussed above (2.2.3.3). The traditional terms used in Irish grammar are
'slender' (= palatal) and 'broad' (= non-palatal). From a synchronic
perspective two interesting features emerge. First, broad consonants
before front vowels are often heavily labialized or velarized; for example, /biLʹ/ may well be realized phonetically as [bʷiLʹ]. Secondly,
slender labials, i.e. /pʹ bʹ mʹ/ are hardly ever phonetically palatal. In
connection with this, it is noticeable that in initial slender clusters of /s/
+ labial the /s/ is not palatal, i.e. [spʹ], not [sʹpʹ], e.g. *speal* 'scythe'
/spʹal/; presumably the /pʹ/ is not phonetically palatalized sufficiently to
assimilate the /s/. From the historical standpoint, it may be recalled that
labials were particularly resistant to the spread of palatalization in the
early stages of the language (see 2.2.3.3 above).[5] In some dialects /s/
before a slender velar is not assimilated, e.g. /skʹe:l/ *scél* 'story'
(Ó Siadhail 1989: 84).

   There is considerable variation in the dialects between broad and slender quality in particular environments. For example, initial /t/ or /f/ tends to vary its quality, e.g. *tuigim* 'I understand' Mun, Don /tig'əm'/ but Conn /t'ig'əm'/, *faoi* 'under' Conn, Don /fi:/ (often phonetically [fʷi:]) but Mun /f'e:/. Ó Siadhail 1989: 87 suggests that the variation in *tuigim* can be explained by the fact that /h/, lenited /t/, does not distinguish between broad and slender quality and so the negative form, *ní thuigim* /N'i: hig'əm'/, could generate both /tig'əm'/ or /t'ig'əm'/. Another area of variation concerns medial liquids or nasals, e.g. *dúnaim* 'I close' Mun /du:nəm'/ but Conn /du:n'əm'/, *amáireach/ amárach* 'tomorrow' /a'ma:r'əχ/ or /a'ma:rəχ/, etc. (see Ó Siadhail 1989: 88). For *dúnaim*, in those dialects where the slender quality develops, it occurs in all parts of the verb except the verbal noun *dunadh* /du:nə/, and this suggests that the slender quality may have arisen in the verbal stem under a similar rule as that outlined by Ó Siadhail 1989: 137–8 for *oscail* 'open'.

3.3 The nominal system

3.3.1 Gender

Irish nouns are traditionally divided by gender into masculine and feminine. Apart from certain suffixes noted below, nouns are not otherwise marked for gender, but it can be marked by mutation in certain types of phrase (see Table 3.6).

Apart from certain notorious examples, e.g. *stail* (f.) 'stallion', *cailín* (m.) 'girl', there is a close correlation between sex and gender, i.e. *tarbh* (m.) 'bull', *cearc* (f.) 'hen', etc. In nominal derivatives, the gender of the base noun is usually overridden by the gender carried by the nominal suffix, e.g. *cruth* (m.) 'shape' : *cruithaíocht* (f.) 'shape, appearance'. Exceptionally, when the suffix -*ín* is used as a diminutive, the gender of the derivative follows that of the base noun, e.g. *fear* (m.) 'man' : *feairín* (m.) 'little man', *bean* (f.) 'woman' : *beainín* (f.) 'little woman'. But when the suffix is not specifically diminutive, it forms masculine nouns, e.g. *paidir* (f.) 'prayer' : *paidrín* (m.) 'rosary', etc. (de Bhaldraithe 1990).

Apart from where a suffix determines gender, there has been rela-

TABLE 3.6   Gender marking by mutation in Modern Irish

(a) Mutation after the article in a feminine noun, e.g. *an bhean* 'the woman' : *bean* 'woman'

(b) Mutation of an adjective after a feminine noun, e.g. *bean mhaith* 'a good woman' : *maith* 'good'

(c) Mutation after the article in a masculine genitive singular noun, e.g. *leabhar an fhir* 'the man's book' : *fear* 'man'

---

tively little predictability. However, there is a growing tendency for masculine nouns to end in a broad consonant and feminine nouns in a slender one. Historically, there has been a long-term development in this direction. Old Irish *o*-stem and *u*-stem nouns were usually masculine and had a final broad consonant. Feminine *a*-stems also had a broad final consonant but there was a tendency even in Middle Irish to conflate *a*-stems with *i*-stems and also to generalize the slender accusative/dative singular stem as the nominative (see 2.2.3.3 above). This pattern has, therefore, been developing for many centuries. Ó Siadhail 1989: 145 notes some examples of shifts to this pattern in Connacht, e.g. *fuinneoig* (f.) for *fuinneog* 'window', *muic* (f.) for *muc* 'pig', etc. There is also considerable variation in gender among the dialects. Wagner 1958–69: I, 69 demonstrates the variation in the genitive singular of *loch* 'lake' as *na locha* (f.), *na loiche* (f.), *an locha* (m.). We may note also *mí* 'month' (f. in Connacht and Donegal, but m. in Munster), *ainm* 'name' (f. in Munster, m. in Connacht and Donegal); these nouns, along with *loch*, were neuter in Old Irish, and in late Old Irish, as the neuter gender disappeared, they were re-assigned to the masculine or feminine genders. It could well be that such dialectal hesitation still reflects that re-assignment which may have varied in different parts of Ireland.

3.3.2   The case system

We have seen (2.2.4 above) that Old Irish had a fully fledged case system which succeeded in surviving the loss of final syllables. What remains of that system in the modern language is effectively an unmarked singular form, a genitive singular and a general plural form (see Ó Siadhail 1989: 148–59). It is possible to find genitive and dative plurals fossilized in particular phrases, but they are no longer productive case forms. Essentially, the case forms vary according to the presence or absence of three markers, slender/broad final consonants, a vocalic extension or a consonantal extension, or combinations of them (see Table 3.7 for a conspectus of possible combinations). On the basis of these three features it would appear that the singular/plural distinction is more heavily marked than the singular nominative/genitive distinction; the plural is frequently double marked with both a vowel and a consonant extension or both a vowel and a slender consonant (see 3.3.3 below). It is a system in flux with different generalizations and simplifications operating in different dialects. It has been in flux from late Old Irish onwards (see 2.2.4) often with a tendency towards clear plural marking at the expense of other distinctions. The type under considerable pressure, particularly in Conamara, seems to be the vowel extension pattern which acquires a slender consonant with or without loss of the vowel, e.g. *fuacht* 'cold' : gen. sg. Mun *fuachta*, Conn *fuaicht*. On the other hand, in Donegal and North Mayo the opposite

TABLE 3.7 Noun declension in Modern Irish

	Nom. sg.	Gen. sg.	Nom. pl.
	fear 'man'	*fir*	*fir*
± slender	−	+	+
± vowel	−	−	−
± consonant	−	−	−
	focal 'word'	*focail*	*focla*
± slender	−	+	−
± vowel	−	−	+
± consonant	−	−	−
	tamall 'spell of time'	*tamaill*	*tamlacha*
± slender	−	+	−
± vowel	−	−	−
± consonant	−	−	+
	solus 'light'	*solais*	*soilse*
± slender	−	+	+
± vowel	−	−	+
± consonant	−	−	−
	tobar 'well'	*tobair*	*toibreacha*
± slender	−	+	+
± vowel	−	−	−
± consonant	−	−	+
	máthair 'mother'	*máthar*	*máthaireacha*
± slender	+	−	+
± vowel	−	−	−
± consonant	−	−	+
	muc 'pig'	*muice*	*muca*
± slender	−	+	−
± vowel	−	+	−
± consonant	−	−	−
	binn 'gable'	*binne*	*beanna*
± slender	+	+	−
± vowel	−	+	+
± consonant	−	−	−
	Gaeltacht	*Gaeltachta*	*Gaeltachtaí*
± slender	−	−	−
± vowel	−	+	+
± consonant	−	−	−
	am 'time'	*ama*	*amanna(í)*
± slender	−	−	−
± vowel	−	+	+
± consonant	−	−	+

TABLE 3.7   *Continued*

	Nom. sg.	Gen. sg.	Nom. pl.
	greim 'grip'	*greama*	*greamanna(í)*
± slender	+	−	−
± vowel	_	+	+
± consonant	−	−	+
	bádóir 'boatman'	*bádora*	*bádoirí*
± slender	+	−	+
± vowel	−	+	+
± consonant	−	−	−
	cathair 'city'	*cathrach*	*cathracha(í)*
± slender	+	−	−
± vowel	−	−	+
± consonant	−	+	+
	coróin 'crown'	*corónach*	*corónacha(í)*
± slender	+	−	−
± vowel	−	−	+
± consonant	−	+	+
	lacha 'duck'	*lachan*	*lachain*
± slender	−	−	+
± vowel	−	−	−
± consonant	−	+	+
	caora 'sheep'	*caorach*	*caoire*
± slender	−	−	+
± vowel	−	−	+
± consonant	−	+	−

tendency seems to operate, e.g. *athair* 'father' : gen. sg. Mun/Conn *athar*, Don *athara*, etc. (Ó Siadhail 1989: 157).

Other case forms do survive in fossilized phrases, e.g. *mil bheach* 'bee honey' (lit. 'honey of bees'; *beach* gen. pl.), *radharc mo shúl* 'my eyesight' (lit. 'the seeing of my eyes'). The dative plural, marked by final /v′/, also survives in Munster, e.g. *péire do bhrogaibh* 'pair of shoes', *in áitennaibh* 'in places'; even in Middle Irish the *-aibh* ending seems to have become an all-purpose prepositional phrase marker. There are even some examples in Modern Irish of it being used as a nominative, e.g. *fearaibh* 'men' (Ó Cuív 1951: 63).

3.3.3   Number

One clear message of the preceding section is the importance of clear plural marking, which most obviously involves the generalization of consonantal markers with or without further vowel markers, e.g. *-acha(í)* and *-anna(í)*. The upshot is that many nouns in dialects outside

Munster have a 'short' and 'long' plural; Munster dialects are more conservative and tend not to go in for long elaborate plural formations, e.g. *bád* 'boat' : pl. Mun *báid*, CF *báideachaí* /'ba:d'əχi:/ and GD *bádaí*. In Connacht especially, the most productive pattern is consonantal extension + vowel extension (usually *-í* /i:/); the consonantal extension is usually *-ch-* /χ/ but *-nn-* /N/ is also widespread, particularly as the extension to monosyllables (Ó Siadhail 1989: 160), e.g. *busannaí* 'buses', *uibheachaí* 'eggs', etc. Another Connacht type involves the addition of *-áil* /a:l'/, e.g. *múr* 'shower' : pl. *múráil, plump* 'bang' : pl. *plumpáil*; even here, further plural markers can be added, e.g. *múraíolacha* /'mu:ri:ləχə/ 'showers' (Ó Siadhail 1989: 164).

Where the choice between a 'short' and a 'long' plural form is available, i.e. not in Munster, the 'short' form is used with numerals, e.g. *troigh* 'foot' : pl. *troigheannaí* : *sé troighthe* 'six feet', *scór* 'score (i.e. 20)' : pl. *scórtha* : *trí scóir* 'three score', etc.

3.3.4 Determination and definiteness

There is no indefinite article in Irish; thus, *fear* 'man', *bean* 'woman' can mean 'a man', 'a woman' respectively. Nouns can, however, be specified in a number of other ways.

3.3.4.1 The article

The forms of the article are set out in Table 3.8 with the mutations which follow them. Its phonetic realization is determined by its environment (for the details in Cois Fhairrge, see de Bhaldraithe 1953: 169–74).

The article is not used where another form of qualification occurs; for example, if a noun is made definite by a genitive singular, the article is omitted, e.g. *teach m'athar* 'the house of my father', *barr an chrainn* 'the tip of the tree'.

3.3.4.2 Demonstratives

The article also features as part of the demonstrative syntagm. The forms *-s(e)o* /s'o/ or /so/ 'this' and *-sin* /s'in/ are unaccented units which are attached to nouns to mark deixis (the noun is always preceded by

TABLE 3.8 The definite article in Modern Irish

	Singular		Plural
	m.	f.	
Nom.	*an* /əN/	*an*L /əN/	*na* /Nə/
Gen.	*an*L /əN/	*na* /Nə/	*na*N /Nə/

L = lenition, N = nasalization.

the article), e.g. *an fear seo* 'this man', *na fir sin* 'those men', *an bhean sin* 'that woman', etc.; the demonstrative particles are not marked for number, gender or case. As independent accented pronouns, they can also be governed by prepositions, be the subject or object of verbs, etc., e.g. *thairis sin* 'in addition to that', *seo (é) an lampa* 'this is the lamp', *á dhéanamh seo* 'to do that'. In addition, there is a third demonstrative *úd* (OIr *ucut* lit. 'over by you'), which functions similarly to the other two more common types. There are also forms which seem to have arisen as compounds of the above, e.g. *siúd* /sʹuːd/, *seod* /sʹod/, though they tend to be pronominal rather than adjectival (see de Bhaldraithe 1953: 163–5).

3.3.4.3 Possessive adjectives and pronouns

Nouns can also be modified by a series of possessive adjectives, presented in Table 3.9 (for emphatic forms, see 3.3.6 below). The 3rd person forms are distinguished by mutation alone. In Cois Fhairrge, there is a single plural possessive form *a*^{N} /ə/; the specific person is marked elsewhere in the sentence with a conjugated preposition, e.g. *a mbéilí againn* 'our meal' (lit. '(our) meal with us') (cf. in other dialects *ar mbéilí*), *bhfuil a ndóthain airgid agaibh?* 'have you enough money?' (lit. 'is there (your) sufficiency of money with you?') (see de Bhaldraithe 1953: 154; for similar strategies in Breton, see 7.6 below). An emphatic variant uses the demonstrative with the conjugated pronoun, e.g. *an teach seo againne* 'our house' (lit. 'this house with us'). Another strategy is simply to affix the emphatic personal pronoun, e.g. *a gcosa* 'our/your/their feet' → *a gcosa muide* 'our feet', *a gcosa sibhse* 'your (pl.) feet', *a gcosa siadsan* 'their feet'.

Possession can be marked in a number of other ways (see Mac Eoin 1993: 121–2). The use of different conjugated prepositions is frequent, e.g. *mac liom* 'a son of mine' (lit. 'a son with me'). For divisible items

TABLE 3.9   Possessive adjectives in Modern Irish

Singular			
1st		*mo*^{L} /mə/ (*m'* /mʹ/, /m/, *mh* /ɰ/)	
2nd		*do*^{L} /də/ (*t'* /tʹ/, /t/, *th* /h/)	
3rd	m.	*a*^{L} /ə/	
	f.	*a* /ə/ (+ *h* before vowel)	
Plural			
1st	*ar*^{N} /ar/ [CF *a*^{N} /ə/]		
2nd	*bhúr*^{N} /vuːr/, /uːr/ [CF *a*^{N} /ə/]		
3rd	*a*^{N} /ə/		

Forms in ( ) occur before initial vowels.

cuid 'share, part' can be used, e.g. *mo chuid airgid* 'my money' (lit. 'my share of money').

Possessive pronouns, i.e. 'mine', 'yours', etc. are formed by attaching possessive adjectives to a neutral meaning noun, either *cuid* 'share' or *ceann* 'thing', e.g. *mo chuid* (*sa*) 'mine', *a cheann* (*san*) 'his' (for the emphasizing particles, see 3.3.6 below).

3.3.5 Adjectives

Adjectives can be used both attributively, i.e. with a noun, or predicatively, i.e. 'The [noun] is [adjective]'.[6] In Old Irish, adjectives declined fully in both usages. But even within Middle Irish, declension was reduced in predicative usage, and in the modern language, declension is rare except in fixed phrases; in such cases plurals are marked by the addition of *-a/-e* /ə/ but cases are rarely marked. Generally predicative usage is becoming more common; Wagner 1959: 178 notes several devices used to avoid having an attributive adjective, e.g. *is olc an scéal é* 'that's bad news' (lit. 'the news is bad'), *is beag duine* 'it's a small man . . .' (lit. 'a man is small'), etc.

In Old Irish there were three degrees of comparison: comparative, marked by *-u* /u/, equative ('as . . . as'), marked by *-ithir* /iθ'ər'/, and a superlative *-am/-em* /əv/. Even in Old Irish the equative was being replaced by a syntagm of *com* + adjective + preposition *fri*, e.g. *duibithir : comdub fri* 'as black as' (see Meid 1967a, Charles-Edwards 1971); in Modern Irish the latter pattern is maintained but with *le* instead of *fri*. The superlative disappeared in Middle Irish and the comparative ending /ə/ (< OIr *-u*) does duty for both comparative and superlative in the modern language (see Table 3.10). The functions are distinguished by two different predicative patterns.

As in most languages, the common adjectives have irregular forms, e.g. *maith* 'good' : *fearr* 'better/best', *beag* 'small' : *lú* 'smaller/smallest', *mór* 'big' : *mó* 'bigger/biggest'.

TABLE 3.10   Comparative, superlative and equative in Modern Irish

Basic form	*bán* 'white'	*deacair* 'difficult'
Comparative/superlative	*báine*	*deacra*
Equative	*comh bán le*	*comh deacair le*

Comparative syntax
  níos báine ná 'whiter than' (lit. 'a thing which is whiter')
  níos deacra ná 'more difficult than'
Superlative syntax
  is báine 'whitest' (lit. 'which is whitest')
  is deacra 'most difficult'

3.3.6 Pronouns

The independent pronouns are presented in Table 3.11 (a). In Old Irish object pronouns were infixed into the verbal complex (see 2.2.6.2) but from Middle Irish onwards they were replaced by independent object pronouns. Moreover, the reduction of final vowels tended to break down the distinctions between the different persons of the verb, hence the increase in the use of subject pronouns. In the modern language they are standard and are particularly necessary in dialects where the verb form is not marked for person at all (see 3.4.1 below). The subject and object pronouns are distinguished mainly in the 3rd person by the presence or absence of initial /s/-. Elsewhere, only the lenition of *thusa* reveals its function as the object. In practice, word order is the key factor; compare *chonnaic mé sibh* 'I saw you' with *chonnaic sibh mé* 'you saw me'. Dialect variation is minimal except for the 1st pl. forms *sinn* /s'iN/ and *muid* /mud'/. The former is found in Munster and parts of South Donegal and North Mayo, while the latter is found in the rest of Donegal and in Connacht (Wagner 1958–69: I, 297).

The independent pronouns set out in Table 3.11 (a) are the unmarked, regular forms; the emphatic forms are presented in Table 3.11 (b). Essentially they are formed by the addition of the particles presented in Table 3.11 (c) to the basic forms. They occur in contexts where contrast or focus is implied, e.g. *ní thúsa bhí me a rádh* /N'i: hu:sə v'i: me: ra:/ 'It wasn't you I was talking to' (*sc.* but someone else).

In close conjunction with prepositions, pronouns form a single accentual unit which is generally known as a conjugated preposition. The basic endings and examples are set out in Table 3.12. The alternations in the 3rd plural ending reflect the different cases which the prepositions originally governed; the *-o/-u* ending is accusative, the *-bh* ending dative. But it is clear that endings tended to be generalized; for example, in Cois Fhairrge the *-b* is found in 3rd pl. *leób* /l'o:b/ and in Donegal *leofa* /l'ofə/ is found, when in Old Irish *la* took the accusative and we would expect modern *leó*. Even within Old Irish various dental elements crept into the conjugation in order to keep the pronoun distinct from a preposition ending in a vowel. The *-th-* in forms of *faoi* 'under' are probably late insertions to mark a hiatus (see Ó Cuív 1990, and 2.3.1 below). The 3rd singular masculine form is frequently indistinguishable from the basic form. This has to do less with the 3rd singular form being some sort of unmarked form than with the fact that the basic form of the preposition has changed. In Old Irish there was also a preposition conjugated with the neuter 3rd singular pronoun. With the demise of the neuter gender, such forms were often taken over as a more marked variant of the basic unconjugated preposition; compare, for example, OIr *fo* 'under' with MnIr *faoi*, OIr *re*^{N} : MnIr *roimh* /riv'/, etc.

TABLE 3.11   Personal pronouns in Modern Irish

(a) Independent subject and object pronouns

Singular

		Subject	Object
1st		*mé*	*mé*
2nd		*tú* /tu:/	*thú* /hu:/, /u:/
3rd	m.	*sé*	*é*
	f.	*sí*	*í*

Plural

	Subject	Object
1st	*sinn/muid*	*sinn/muid*
2nd	*sib*(*h*)	*sib*(*h*)
3rd	*siad*	*iad*

(b) Emphatic subject and object pronouns

Singular

		Subject	Object
1st		*mise*	*mise*
2nd		*túsa* /tu:sə/	*thúsa* /hu:sə/, /u:sə/
3rd	m.	*seisean*	*eisean*
	f.	*sise*	*ise*

Plural

	Subject	Object
1st	*sinne/muide*	*sinne/muide*
2nd	*sib*(*h*)*se*	*sib*(*h*)*se*
3rd	*siadsan*	*iadsan*

(c) Emphasizing particles used with other pronouns

		Singular	Plural
1st		*-sa/-se*	*-ne*
2nd		*-sa/-se*	*-sa/-se*
3rd	m.	*-san/-sean*	*-san/-sean*
	f.	*-se*	

The emphasizing particles can be added to any element containing a pronominal form, whether possessive, independent or conjugated, e.g. *mo chat* 'my cat' : *mo chat sa* 'my cat', *a bróg bheag* 'her small shoe' : *a bróg bheag sa* 'her small shoe', etc. The particle attaches itself to the final element of the phrase.

A reflexive sense of 'own' or 'self' can be marked by the addition of

TABLE 3.12   Conjugated prepositions in Modern Irish

(a) Endings

	Singular	Plural
1st	-*m*	-(*a*)*inn*
2nd	-(*i*)*t*	-(*a*)*ibh*
3rd m.	-*e*/Ø	-*u*/-*o*, -*bh*
f.	-*i*	

(b) Examples

	ag 'at'	*do* 'to'	*faoi* 'under'
1st sg.	*agam*	*dom*	*fúm*
2nd sg.	*agat*	*duit*	*fút*
3rd sg. m.	*aige*	*dó*	*faoi*
f.	*aice*	*dí*	*fúithe*
1st pl.	*againn*	*dúinn*	*fúinn*
2nd pl.	*agaibh*	*doíbh*	*fúithaibh*
3rd pl.	*acu*	*dóibh*	*fúthaib*

féin /fʹeːnʹ/ or /heːnʹ/ after the pronoun or phrase, e.g. *mé féin* 'my self', *mo theach féin* 'my own house'. The use of the lenited or unlenited form is dialectally determined. The unlenited /fʹeːnʹ/ occurs in South Munster and also in parts of South Mayo; elsewhere /heːnʹ/ is regular (Wagner 1958–69: I, 297). In Munster there are examples of an extended form /fʹeːnʹigʹ/ or /heːnəχ/.

3.3.7 Numerals

The cardinal and ordinal forms are presented in Table 3.13. There has been some simplification since the Old Irish period (Thurneysen 1946: 242–50; for the historical background, see Greene 1992, McCone 1993a). At that stage, forms for 2, 3 and 4 declined and were marked for gender. In Old Irish the regular pattern was decimal, i.e. counting in tens, but there is a widespread pattern of vigesimal counting in spoken Modern Irish, using either the native *fiche* 'twenty' or the loanword *scór* 'score'. There is dialectal variation between Conn, Don *deichead* (lit. 'two twenties') and Mun *dathad*; in addition *dáscor* is widespread (Wagner 1958–69: I, 222). There are traces of a vigesimal system in Old Irish beside the decimal, and given that there is an identical pattern in Welsh and, to judge from French, also in Gaulish, it is probably that the original Celtic system was vigesimal.

At all stages, there is for some numbers a different form used for independent numerals beside the adjectival form used with nouns, e.g. *cethair* 'four' : *ceithre cinn* 'four things', *dó* 'two' : *dhá cheann* 'two

TABLE 3.13   Numerals in Modern Irish

	Cardinals	Ordinals
1	aon (N amháin)	chéad, aonú
2	dó, dhá + N	dara, tarna
3	trí^L	treas, triú
4	ceathar^L, ceithre + N	ceathrú
5	cúig^L	cúigiú
6	sé^L	séú
7	seacht^N	seachtú
8	ocht^N	ochtú
9	naoi^N	naomhú
10	deich^N	deichiú
11	aon déag	aonú . . . déag
12	dhá + N déag	dóú . . . déag
13	trí + N déag	triú . . . déag
20	fiche	fichiú
30	tríocha	tríochadú
	deich + N as fiche	
	deich + N ar fichead	
40	daichead	daicheadú
	dathad, dáscór	
50	caoga, lethchéad	caogadú
60	seasca, trí fichead	seascadú
100	céad	céadú
1000	míle	miliú

things'. For the teens, the numeral brackets the noun it qualifies and uses a different form for 'ten', *déag*, beside *deich*. For the numerals 3–10 the following noun can be singular or plural; compare Welsh, where only singular nouns occur after numerals.

The ordinal numerals are marked by the suffix -*ú* /u:/ (< OIr -*mad* /ṽəð/) which has replaced the irregular forms which were used for the low numbers; thus, *oenú* for OIr *cét-*, *cétnae*, *dar(n)a*, *tar(n)a* for OIr *aile*, *tanaise* (the modern forms are derived from OIr *indala* (MIr *indara*), the form used with nouns in larger numbers, e.g. MIr *indara apstal déc* 'the twelfth apostle').

In addition to cardinal and ordinal numerals, Irish has a set of 'personal' numbers which refer to numbers of people; the forms are presented in Table 3.14. Most of them are traditionally etymologized as containing a reduced form of *fear* 'man', though there have been some dissenters (Tovar 1972–3, Lambert 1978). The Old Irish forms for one person and a pair have been replaced by *duine amháin* and *beirt* (lit.

TABLE 3.14   The 'personal' numerals in Modern Irish

1	*duine (amháin)* (OIr *oenur* = MnIr 'alone')
2	*beirt* (OIr *dias*) 'two people'
3	*triúr* 'three people'
4	*ceathrar*
5	*cúigear*
6	*seisear*
7	*móir-fheasear/seachtar*
8	*ochtar*
9	*naonmhar*
10	*deichneabhar*

'bundle') respectively. The earlier form *móir-fheisear* /moːrˈisˈər/ 'seven people' (lit. 'a big six') is retained in many dialects though it has in some been regularized to *seachtar*.

3.4   The verbal system

3.4.1 The forms of the verb

The complexities of the Old Irish verbal system and some of its simplifications in Middle Irish have been discussed above (2.2.6). By Modern Irish many of the complexities have been ironed out; for example, the absolute/conjunct active/deponent alternations no longer exist and the inconsistent stem patterns of strong verbs are only vestigially retained in the small group of irregular verbs. The degree of retention of the older patterns varies from dialect to dialect; for example, virtually the full range of personal endings of the synthetic verb has been retained in Munster dialects, while in Connacht and Donegal there has generally been a shift to a single verbal element which is marked for person by the addition of independent subject pronouns (see 3.1.1 and below). A sample paradigm for some tenses is given in Table 3.15 (for a full list, see Mac Eoin 1993: 127–8, Ó Dochartaigh 1992: 70–1).

The distribution of synthetic and analytic forms is not quite as clear-cut as the above description would suggest. All dialects show some synthetic forms; the smallest number is found in Donegal, the most in Munster. Even in the latter, there is a higher incidence of synthetic forms in Muskerry than in Kerry or Clare. Ó Siadhail 1989: 182–3 offers a gradation of possibilities:

(a)   synthetic and analytic forms in free variation
(b)   synthetic form used more frequently in echo forms (responsives and tag questions; see 3.5.2.2)

TABLE 3.15   The forms of the verb in Modern Irish

	tógaim 'raise'	*foilsím* 'reveal'
Present		
1 sg.	*tógaim*	*foilsím/foilsíonn mé*
2 sg.	*tógair/tógann tú*	*foilsír/foilsíonn tú*
3 sg.	*tógann sé/sí*	*foilsíonn sé/sí*
1 pl.	*tógaimid/tógann muid*	*foilsímid/foilsíonn muid*
2 pl.	*tógann (sibh)*	*foilsíonn sibh*
3 pl.	*tógaid/tógann siad*	*foilsíd/foilsíonn siad*
rel.	*thógas*	*foilsíos*
Future		
1 sg.	*tógfad/tógfaidh mé*	*foilseod/foilseoidh mé*
2 sg.	*tógfair/tógfaidh tú*	*foilseoir/foilseoidh tú*
3 sg.	*tógfaidh sé/sí*	*foilseoidh sé/sí*
1 pl.	*tógfaimid/tógfaidh muid*	*foilseoimid/foilseoidh muid*
2 pl.	*tógfaidh (sibh)*	*foilseoidh sibh*
3 pl.	*tógfaid/tógfaidh siad*	*foilseoid/foilseoidh siad*
rel.	*thógfas*	*foilseos*
Conditional		
1 sg.	*thógfainn*	*d'fhoilseoinn/d'fhoilseodh mé*
2 sg.	*thógfá*	*d'fhoilseofá/d'fhoilseodh tú*
3 sg.	*thógfadh sé/sí*	*d'fhoilseodh sé/sí*
1 pl	*thógfaimis/thógfadh muid*	*d'fhoilseoimis/d'fhoilseodh muid*
2 pl.	*thógfadh (sibh)*	*d'fhoilseodh sibh*
3 pl	*thógfaidis/thógfadh siad*	*d'fhoilseoidís/d'fhoilseodh siad*
Preterite		
1 sg.	*thógas/thóg mé*	*d'fhoilsíos/d'fhoilsígh mé*
2 sg.	*thógais/thóg tú*	*d'fhoilsís/d'fhoilsígh tú*
3 sg.	*thóg sé/sí*	*d'fhoilsígh sé/sí*
1 pl.	*thógamar/thóg muid*	*d'fhoilsíomar/d'fhoilsígh muid*
2 pl.	*thóg sibh*	*d'fhoilsígh sibh*
3 pl.	*thógadar/thóg siad*	*d'fhoilsíodar/d'fhoilsígh siad*
rel.	*thógadh*	*d'fhoilsíodh*
Imperfect		
1 sg.	*thógainn*	*d'fhoilsínn/d'fhoilsíodh mé*
2 sg.	*thógthá*	*d'fhoilsíteá/d'fhoilsíodh tú*
3 sg.	*thógadh sé/sí*	*d'fhoilsíodh sé/sí*
1 pl.	*thógaimis/thógadh muid*	*d'fhoilsímis/d'fhoilsíodh muid*
2 pl.	*thógadh (sibh)*	*d'fhoilsíodh sibh*
3 pl.	*thógaidis/thógadh siad*	*d'fhoilsídís/d'fhoilsíodh siad*

(c) synthetic form used solely in echo forms
(d) synthetic form in a restricted sense or register.

For an example of (b)/(c), see Conn *ar bhris tú an chaothaoir?*
Bhriseas 'did you break (analytic) the chair? Yes, I did (synthetic)'. In
Donegal, such echo forms are restricted entirely to irregular verbs (see
below), e.g. *an dtug tú? Thugas* 'did you give (analytic)? Yes, I did
(synthetic)'. The usage is also likely to vary from speaker to speaker;
the less frequently a speaker uses a form, the more likely it will be analytic when he or she does use it.

The Modern Irish verb has three tenses, present, future and past; the
future is marked by one of two suffixes, *-f-* (/h/ or /f/; see below) or
-eo- (/oi̯/), and the past by a prefix *do*ᴸ. This prefix has been lost in
most forms, leaving lenition as the only marker, but it is preserved
before an initial vowel, or a vowel resulting from a lenited consonant,
e.g. *d'fh-*, *d'sh-*, etc. The past tense marker is used for the preterite and
the imperfect, the future marker for the future and conditional tenses;
the latter is distinguished by having the same set of endings as the
imperfect.

Irish verbs are divided into two conjugations, largely on the basis of
their different future formations. There are, however, more fundamental
differences. The *tógaim*-type typically has a monosyllabic verbal stem,
either TVT- or TV:T-, while the *foilsím*-type has a disyllabic stem
TV(:)TVT- or TVTV:T-, or a final double consonant TVTT-.

The latter type derives mainly from the Old Irish *-(a)ig*-denominative
verbs; the *-igh-* syllable became /i:/ but it is still written as *-igh* in final
position, since in some dialects it is pronounced /ig'/ rather than /i:/.
The *f*-marker of the future seems to derive from the Old Irish *f*-future
although the details are unclear (see below), while the *-eo-* marker is
related to the Old Irish *-é-* future (see 2.2.6.1 and McCone 1987:
242–50). The *do-* past tense marker goes back to OIr *ro*, which distinguished prefects from preterites; its origin is still detectable in
negatives, e.g. *phós sé* /fo:s/ 'he married' : *nír phós* /N'i:rfo:s/ 'he did
not marry', *d'ól* /do:l/ 'he drank' : *nír ól* 'he did not drink' /N'i:ro:l/.

The addition of suffixes, particularly in the future, has brought about a
number of phonological adjustments. The *f*-future marker, usually realized as /h/, devoices a preceding voiced consonant, thus *leag-* /L'ag/-
'lay' : *leagfaidh* /L'akəi̯/ 'will lay', *nigh-* /N'ii̯/- 'wash' : *nigfidh* /N'iχəi̯/
'will wash' (compare also the behaviour of the passive marker /hə/ *-tha*
(Ó Siadhail 1989: 171)). Moreover, there is considerable variation
between the two future suffixes, orthographically *-f-* or *-eo-*. The future
endings are realized as /həi̯/ *-faidh* and /o:i̯/ *-óidh*/*-eoidh*. In parts of
Donegal a combined suffix has been created of /oi̯/ + /həi̯/ to produce
/aχəi̯/ or in Gweedore at least /ahəi̯/ (for merging conjugations in Ulster
Irish, see M. McKenna 1992). In several Cork dialects /f/ occurs for /h/

(Ó Cuív 1951: 49, Wagner 1958–69: I, 123, 282, 294), and in Cois Fhairrge /f/ can be found in impersonal forms, e.g. *brisfear* /b′r′is′f′ər/ or /b′r′is′hər/. The origin of the Modern Irish *f*-suffix has been the subject of considerable debate.[7] What emerges clearly is that the surviving realizations of the suffix as /f/ do not in most cases continue the /f/ of the Old Irish suffix (see 2.2.6.1). Old Irish /f/ seems to have been reduced to /h/ certainly by late Middle Irish if not earlier, although remarkably it has been preserved in the orthography to the modern day. It has been argued that the Modern Irish /f/, as realized in some Munster and Donegal dialects, has arisen from clusters of -*bhth*-, originally /vθ/ where /θ/ devoiced the preceding voiced fricative (Ó Buachalla 1985). A further factor should also be taken into account, namely the extent to which it was possible to use the present in place of the future in early Irish. Ó Buachalla 1977: 101–31 has discussed the continuation of this phenomenon in Ulster Irish; it occurs particularly in negative verbs where the futurity is marked elsewhere (see also Ó Corráin 1992). This is another feature shared by northern dialects of Irish and Scottish Gaelic and it is possible that it may have arisen partly in response to the complicated and confusing range of future markers available (Gleasure 1990).

The process of levelling and re-adjustment between categories is not restricted to the future. The second conjugation (the *foilsím*-type) contains a number of stem types (see above), not all of which derive from the old -(*a*)*ig*-type, and they seem to have been subject to analogical pressure (see Ó Siadhail 1989: 170); for example, the stem *seachn*-/s′axn/- has acquired an /əi̯/ syllable in the present characteristic of the old -(*a*)*ig*- type, e.g. /s′axni:N/ *seachníonn* (older orthography *seachnaigheann*) 'he follows'. The process seems to be ongoing with variation evident in the dialects, e.g. CF /Lauri:m′/ (< /Laurəi̯əm′/) : /Laurəm′/ *labhraim* 'I speak'. Generally, there seems to be an expansion in the range of the more marked present /əi̯/ and future /o:i̯/ (Donegal /axəi̯/). There are two aspects to this spread: an extension to other verbs of the same category which do not show these features, and a further extension to verbs of the first conjugation (*tógaim*-type).

In addition to the tenses discussed so far, Modern Irish also has a

TABLE 3.16   Irregular verbs in Modern Irish

'carry'	: *beir*- : *béar*- : *rug*-	= OIr *beirid*
'do'	: *ní*- : *déan*- : *díon*- : *rinn*-	= OIr (*do*)·*tgní*
'see'	: *cí*-/*tí*-, *feic*- : *chonaic*-	= OIr (*ad*)·*cí*, *feacaid*
'go'	: *tei*(*gh*) : *ragh*- : *chuaigh*-	= OIr *téit*
'say'	: *deir*- : *abr*- : *dúr*-	= OIr *as*·*tbeir*

For the Old Irish paradigms, see Thurneysen 1946: 461–74.

series of aspectually distinct periphrastic forms which are discussed below (3.4.3).

It was observed above that Modern Irish has almost entirely dispensed with the complex alternations of verbal stem and accentual patterns which occurred in Old Irish. However, there remain some eleven of the commonest verbs in the language (including the substantive verb (see 3.4.2)) where traces of these alternations are preserved (see Table 3.16 for examples). There is still some independent/dependent (= absolute/conjunct) alternation, e.g. *ní-* : *déan-* 'do', *bheir-* : *tobhr-* 'give', etc. The level of predictability is variable (see Ó Siadhail 1989: 185–95); for example, *beir-*'carry' : future *béar-* seems to have a level of predictability which is not apparent in *teigh-* : future *ragh-*. More generally, these verbs do not seem to have been significantly affected by some of the wholesale developments to the verbal system; for example, the ubiquitous *-(e)ann* ending is at best optional and generally the 3rd singular present form tends to be endingless, e.g. Don *tí* 'sees' /t'i:/, *deir* 'says' /d'er'/, *cluin* 'hears' /klun'/, etc.

3.4.2 The verbs 'to be'

Aspects of their usage have already been discussed above (2.2.6.5).[8] The Modern Irish forms are presented in Table 3.17. The discussion here focuses in particular on the forms and uses which are specific to the modern language.

Ó Siadhail 1983 and 1989: 251–2 has shown that considerable inroads have been made into the domain of the copula by forms of the substantive verb. This process is most fully advanced in Donegal and least so in Kerry.

TABLE 3.17   The Modern Irish forms of the copula and substantive verb

Copula	Present	Past	
Affirmative	*is*	*ba*	
Negative	*ní*	*níor(bh)*	
Interrogative	*an*	*ar(bh)*	
Negative interrogative	*nach*	*nár(bh)*	
Substantive verb	Present	Future	Past
Affirmative	*tá*	*beidh* /b'e:/	*bhí* /v'i:/
Negative	*níl*	*ní bheidh*	*ní raibh*
Inerrogative	*an bhfuil*	*an mbeidh*	*an raibh*
Negative interrogative	*nach bhfuil*	*nach mbeidh*	*nach raibh*

In Old Irish the copula had a full paradigm of forms (Table 2.22) but these have been subject to considerable erosion in Modern Irish (Ó Siadhail 1989: 220).

As we have seen (2.2.6.5), the copula is used in two types of sentence, classificatory and identificatory, e.g. in English 'I am a scholar' and 'I am the teacher' respectively. The former seems to have been more vulnerable to influence and invasion by the substantive verb. Some examples are set out in Table 3.18 (a). The basic order is [copula + classificatory indefinite noun + pronoun]. But when the pronoun slot is filled by a definite noun, i.e. a proper name or one marked by the article or a possessive, in Munster and Connacht dialects a pronoun is inserted before it (see Table 3.18 (a) Type 1 (ii-iii)). Alternatively, on the assumption that the pronoun-type is the most common type, it could be described as the addition of a definite noun in apposition to the pronoun. In Donegal no pronoun is required in this structure; thus we may contrast Mun, Conn *is múinteoir í Cáit* with Don *is múinteoir Cáit* 'C. is a teacher'. However, the same sense can be expressed by the two types of substantive verb construction set out in Table 3.18 (a) Types 2 and 3, essentially [substantive verb + pronoun/definite noun + preposition *i* 'in' + possessive adjective (referring to the pronoun/definite noun) + classificatory noun] or [classificatory noun + relative of the substantive verb + preposition *i* 'in' + pronoun/indefinite noun]. The latter seems to be a fronted version of the former, with the copula deleted. The substantive verb pattern often has a more dynamic sense of 'becoming' beside the simple sense 'being' (Ó Siadhail 1989: 226). The dialectal distribution is set out in Table 3.18 (b). Type 3 seems to be a northern feature but it is clear that the substantive verb has made significant inroads into the domain of the copula.

The identificatory copula sentence has fared rather better. The basic pattern is [copula + pronoun/definite noun + pronoun/definite noun], e.g. Conn *is mé an múinteoir* 'I am the teacher', where *mé* is identified

TABLE 3.18 Copula usage in Modern Irish

(a) Examples

Type 1: (i) *is scoláire mé* 'I am a scholar'

      (ii) *is múinteoir (í) Cáit* 'C. is a teacher'

      (iii) *is múinteoir (é) m'uncail* 'my uncle is a teacher'

Type 2: *tá me i mo scholáire* 'I am a scholar' (lit. 'I am in my scholar')

Type 3: *Scoláire atá ionam* 'I am/have become a scholar' (lit. 'a scholar is in me')

(b) Dialectal distribution

	Type 1	Type 2	Type 3
Munster	(–)	+	–
Connacht	(–)	+	±
Donegal	+	+	+

TABLE 3.19   The usage of the substantive verb in Modern Irish

---

+ prepositional phrase:
  tá an carr sa gharáiste 'the car is in the garage'
+ adverb:
  tá an leabhar go maith 'the book is good'
Expression of time:
  tá sé a trí a chlog 'it is three o'clock'
Existence:
  bhí rí ann fadó 'there was a king long ago'

---

with *an múinteoir*. As with the classificatory type, the rule of pronoun insertion applies, e.g. Conn, Mun *is é Sean an múinteoir* 'S. is the teacher', but with an extra refinement: where the pronoun in second position is 3rd person, it has to be repeated after the second definite noun or pronoun, i.e. *is é an múinteoir é* 'he is the teacher', *is í an scólaire í* 'she is the scholar', etc. The only intrusion of the substantive verb into this area of copula usage involves expressions of order of preference where [*tá* 'is' + preposition *ar* 'on/among' + definite noun] can replace the copula sentence; for example, compare *is é an duine as sine acu* (lit. 'he is the man who is oldest . . .') with *tá sé ar an duine is sine acu* 'he is the oldest among them' (lit. 'he is among the man who is oldest . . .').

It is common to find that the unmarked form of the copula, namely *is*, is deleted at the beginning of an utterance, but not when the copula is marked for tense, negation or interrogation, etc.; we may contrast, therefore, *múinteoir é an fear sin* 'that man is a teacher' with *ba múinteoir é* 'he was a teacher', *ní múinteoir é* 'he is not a teacher', etc.

The substantive verb is primarily used to indicate existence, position or state (its use in periphrastic formations is discussed below, 3.4.3; for its forms, see Table 3.17). The regular order is [verb + subject + complement]. The complement slot can be filled by an adjective, adverb or prepositional phrase, but only rarely by a noun in certain restricted categories, e.g. age, weight, time, etc. The substantive verb expresses existence in conjunction with the conjugated pronoun *and* 'in it'. The examples in Table 3.19 illustrate the range of usage.

3.4.3   Tenses, aspect and auxiliary verbs
The tenses discussed so far work on a threefold distinction of future/present/past. Among these tenses only in the past is any other distinction apart from the tense indicated; beside the preterite, which refers to single completed actions, the imperfect tends to refer to habitual activities, e.g. *d'fhásadh* /da:sə(χ)/ 'he used to grow', *phógadh* /fo:ga(χ)/ 'he used to kiss', etc. (Ó Siadhail 1989: 177–8). Elsewhere,

in the tenses considered above there is no other form marked for habitual action. In the whole verbal paradigm there is apart from the imperfect only one other habitual form, namely *bíonn* /b'i:N/ 'usually is' : *tá* 'is'. As regards the future, the so-called 'conditional' is essentially a future stem marked for the past (*do* + lenition) and with the habitual set of endings, e.g. *phógfadh* /fo:kə(χ)/ 'would kiss', but its syntactical function is far removed from any sense of habituality.

However, other aspectual distinctions, such as continual, prospective or perfective aspect, are marked by the use of periphrastic formations with parts of the substantive verb *tá* 'is' and a verbal noun (Ó Siadhail 1989: 293–302).[9] Continuous aspect, i.e. 'he is doing' in contrast to 'he does', is marked for all tenses by a form of the substantive verb + preposition *ag* /ə/ (or /g'/) before vowels) + VN; see Table 3.20. The preposition is subject to variation when the object of the verb is a pronoun; in Conamara *do* 'to, for' /gə/ or /ɤə/ is used in this context, e.g. *tá sé do mo thóraíocht* 'he is searching for me' (for constructions involving verbal nouns, see 8.3 below). When the object is fronted, *a*^L /ə/ replaces *ag*, e.g. *sin í an bhean atá sé a phosadh* 'that is the woman he is marrying' beside unmarked *tá sé ag posadh . . .* 'he is marrying . . .'. Not all verbs can semantically have a form marked for continuous aspect; one such category is that of stative verbs, e.g. sleeping, living, standing, sitting, etc. In this case, when we are referring to a particular state, *i* 'in' is used, e.g. *tá sé ina chodladh* 'he is sleeping' (lit. 'he is in his sleeping'), *tá sé ina shuí* 'he is sitting', *tá mé i mo chónaí* 'I am living', etc. (Ó Siadhail 1989: 295).

To refer to actions in the immediate past which are relevant to the present, i.e. 'he has done', etc. in contrast to 'he did' or 'he had done', Irish uses a similar prepositional pattern using Mun. Conn *t(h)ar éis* /tər'es'/, Don *i ndéidh* /ə'n'e:/ 'after' (for the construction in Welsh, see

TABLE 3.20   The periphrastic forms of the Modern Irish verb

(a) Continuous aspect

Present	*tá*	'he is . . .	
Habitual present	*bíonn*	'he usually is . . .	
Past	*bhí*	'he was . . .	*sé ag péinteáil*
Imperfect	*bhíodh*	'he used to be . . .	painting'
Future	*beidh*	'he will be . . .	
Conditional	*bheadh*	'he would be ..	

(b) Other aspects

Stative	Substantive verb + *i* + VN
Perfect	Substantive verb + *t(h)ar éis/i ndéidh* + VN
Prospective	Substantive verb + *le* (*chun*) + VN

IRISH

5.4.3), e.g. Mun, Conn *tá sé thar éis imeacht* 'he has gone off' (lit. 'he is after going off'), Don *tá mé i ndéidh leabhar a léamh* 'I have read a book'.

A third periphrastic formation of this type refers forward prospectively to refer to an event in the immediate future with some implication of obligation in regard to it (Ó Siadhail 1989: 296–7). The construction uses the preposition *le*, e.g. *bhí sé le leabhar a léamh* 'he was to read a book' (lit. 'he was with reading a book'). The above example does not hold good for Munster, where there is a distinction between obligation using *le* and intention using *chu(i)n* 'towards'; we may contrast, therefore, the above example, which in Munster would mean 'he was to/had to read a book', and *bhí se chun leabhar a léamh* 'he intended to read a book'. Generally, however, in Connacht and Donegal a construction with *goil* 'go' is more common, e.g. *níl sé ag goil ag déanamh leas* 'it is not going to do any good'. This looks very much like a calque on the English contruction 'going to . . .'.

The substantive verb can also be used in conjunction with other prepositions in a range of senses, e.g. Conn *ar thoib*, Mun *ar tí*, e.g. *bhí mé ar thoib/ar tí imeacht* 'I was on the point of going off', Don *ar obair*, e.g. *tá sé ar obair ag foghlaim Gaeilig* 'he has started to learn Irish'.

Apart from the substantive verb some other verbs also operate as 'auxiliaries', notably *déanamh* 'do' (see Ó Siadhail 1989: 302–8 for this and other examples). The point about an 'auxiliary' is that it should not strictly have any semantic load of its own but should be a neutral carrier of tense and person markers for a non-finite verbal element elsewhere. There are aspects of the usage of *déanamh* which fit this description but it is also very easy in some usages for it to slide over into a fuller semantic sense.

In its use in responsives, it does behave like an auxiliary, e.g. Mun *ar ólais an tae? Dheineas* 'did you drink the tea? Yes, I did', *ól ceann eile! Ní dheanfad* 'drink another one! No, I won't'. The range of usage here varies considerably from dialect to dialect (see Ó Siadhail 1973: 147). In Connacht *déanamh*-responsives are confined to futures and conditionals and there are traces of a similar usage in Donegal, but the most widespread usage is in Munster and in particular in Dunquin where it is by far the most common reponsive.

The construction can also be used to provide verbal inflection for a verbal noun which does not have a full set of finite inflections, e.g. *báisteach* 'to rain' : *rinne sé báisteach mhór* 'it rained heavily' (lit. 'it made much raining'), or as an alternative to inflection for the finite verb, e.g. Mun *dheinemair rudaí a cheannach* 'we bought things' (lit. 'we did a buying of things'). A verbal noun and object can also be fronted and parts of *déanamh* then used to carry the tense and person markers, particularly in complement clauses; we may contrast the following two clauses after *b'fheidir* 'perhaps': *b'fheidir gur chaith sibh amach é* 'perhaps you threw it out' (lit. 'perhaps that you threw out it') beside *b'fheidir gurb é a chaitheamh amach a rinne sibh* (lit. 'perhaps that it is its throwing out that you did').

3.4.4 Impersonals and passives

In addition to the six persons of the verb in each tense, Irish has an impersonal form (see Table 3.21). The earlier forms are discussed above (2.2.6.3). For convenience, *bristear an fhuinneog* is usually translated as a passive, i.e. 'the window is broken'. However, the corresponding pronominal form is *bristear í* 'it is broken', where the pronoun takes the object form rather than the subject form *sí*; a literal

TABLE 3.21   Impersonal forms of the regular verb in Modern Irish

	tógaim 'I raise'	*foilsím* 'I reveal'
Present	*tógtar*	*foilsítear*
Future	*tógfar*	*foilseofar*
Conditional	*thógfaí*	*d'fhoilseofaí*
Preterite	*tógadh*	*foilsíodh*
Imperfect	*thógtaí*	*d'fhoilsítí*

TABLE 3.22   Examples of passive forms of periphrastic verbs in Modern Irish

Progressive

Active
tá mé ag péinteáil an dorais
'I am painting the door'

Passive
tá an doras (dh)á phéinteáil agam
'the door is being painted by me'
(lit. 'the door is at its painting with me')

Prospective

Active
tá mé leis an leabhar a léamh
'I am to read the book'

Passive
tá an leabhar le léamh agam
'the book is to be read by me'
(lit. 'the book is with reading with me')

Perfective

Active
tá mé thar éis an leabhar a léamh
'I have read the book'

Passive
tá an leabhar léite agam
'The book has been read by me'
(lit. 'the book is read with me')

translation would, therefore, be '(*sc.* someone) breaks the window' or perhaps better 'there is a breaking the window'. Moreover, an agent can be marked by the preposition *le* 'by', e.g. *bristear í liom* 'it is broken by me' (see Müller 1990).

Genuine passive forms have, however, developed in Modern Irish among the periphrastic forms with the substantive verb (see 3.4.3). They are passives in that they reflect the standard shift of the object phrase to subject position. Examples of the patterns for different tenses are set out in Table 3.22. The relation between the active and passive versions is reasonably clear. The perfective passives are formed with the verbal adjective in -*te* /t'ə/. The choice of active or passive variants differs from dialect to dialect. The passive variant has a far higher frequency in Munster and usually replaces the active variant; we may compare Mun *cad atá á dhéanamh agat?* 'what are you doing?' (lit. 'what is its doing with you?') with Conn, Don *céard atá tú a dheanamh?* (lit. 'what are you at doing?') (Ó Siadhail 1989: 298).

3.5 Syntax

3.5.1 Word order

It will have emerged from the examples scattered through the above discussion that the standard word order is [verb + subject + object] (VSO). Other elements, such as adverbs and prepositional phrases, tend to follow the VSO nexus though their order can be variable (Ó Siadhail 1989: 206–7). The one major exception to this statement is the rule that unmarked object pronouns, e.g. *mé, é, í, iad*, etc., and conjugated prepositions are relegated to the end of the sentence; we may compare *bhris sé an chathaoir leis an ord aréir* 'he broke the chair with the hammer last night' (the English and Irish word orders correspond) with *bhris sé aréir leis an ord í* 'he broke it with the hammer last night' (lit. 'he broke last night with the hammer it').

The word order in copula sentences has been discussed above (see 2.2.6.5 and 3.4.2). The general question of Celtic word order is considered in Chapter 9.

3.5.2 Pre-sentential particles

Although the verb is generally assumed to be initial, it is frequently preceded by unaccented particles marking tense or type of sentence, whether negative or interrogative, etc.

3.5.2.1 Negatives

The negative in indicative main clauses is regularly marked by the preverbal particle *ní*[L]. In subordinate clauses the form is *nach*[L] (*nar* with preterite tenses). The only significant divergence from this pattern is in Donegal Irish, where *cha* is frequently found beside *ní*. The negative particle *cha* is the regular negative in Scottish Gaelic and Manx and derives from MIr *nocha*, a variant of OIr *nícon* (see 2.3.2). Ó Buachalla 1977 has argued that the use of *cha* is another linguistic feature which northern Irish dialects share with Scottish Gaelic. Moreover, it has nothing to do with Scottish Gaelic influence (cf. T. F. O'Rahilly 1932: 165–8) but is a native dialectal feature. However, even up to the modern day *cha* has remained a marker of inferior social status, and so does not figure in literary texts:

> *Ní* and *cha*, then, though free variants in the strict linguistic sense, were, initially at any rate, socially conditioned variants. And although it seems that *cha* spread in usage and incidence throughout the 18th and 19th centuries, it never succeeded in completely ousting *ní* from any variety of Ulster Irish (apart from Rathlin Island); on the other hand, *cha* has never completely shed its inferior status: even to the present day literate native speakers of Donegal Irish consider *ní* to be stylistically more prestigious (Ó Buachalla 1977: 137–8).

3.5.2.2 Interrogatives

Interrogative pronouns, e.g. *cé* 'who?', *conas* 'how?', tend to be followed by relative forms of the verb, e.g. *cé a rinne é?* 'who did it?' (lit. 'who (is it) who did it?'), *cé atá ag caint?* 'who is talking?'. When the interrogative is in a prepositional relationship to the verb, it is followed by the conjugated preposition, e.g. *cé uaidh a bhfuair tú an leabhar?* 'from whom did you get the book?' (lit. 'who from him that you got the book?').

Questions which do not have the interrogative pronoun are marked by *an*^{N} (*ar*^{L} before a preterite) and negative questions are marked by *ná* or *nach*^{N} (*nár*^{L} before a preterite), e.g. *an dtugann sibh?* 'do you give?', *nach dtugann sibh?* 'do you not give?', *nár dtug sibh?* 'did you not give?', etc. (Mac Eoin 1993: 123).

Questions can also be marked by questions tagged onto the end of a declarative sentence. Tag questions repeat the tense of the main verb but with the polarity reversed and the pronoun deleted, i.e. positive sentence + negative tag, and negative sentence + positive tag, e.g. *thug se leis é, nár thug?* 'he brought it with him, didn't he?', *ní thug sé leis é, ar thug?* 'he didn't bring it with him, did he?' (Ó Dochartaigh 1992: 38).

The answers to questions are not framed as simple 'yes/no'. The standard form of the responsive is to repeat the verb in the question in the same tense but with the appropriate change of person, e.g. *an dtiocfaidh tú? Tiocfad/ní thiocfad* 'will you come? I will come/I will not come (= Yes/no)' (see Ó Siadhail 1973). The synthetic forms or the general 3rd person form can be used here and, as was noted above (3.4.3), synthetic forms can occur in responsives even when they are not found elsewhere in the dialect. It is also possible in Munster dialects to use a part of *déanamh* 'do' instead of repeating the verb of the question (see 3.4.3 above and Ó Siadhail 1989: 303). In Connacht and Donegal this usage is restricted to future and conditional tenses. Matters are, however, more complicated in responsives involving copula forms (Ó Siadhail 1989: 245–9). The same general pattern operates, namely that the verb is repeated. But being unaccented the copula never stands alone and requires another element with it. Usually the second element in the copula question is also repeated, e.g. *is é an múinteoir é? Is é/Ní é* 'is he the teacher? Yes/no' (lit. 'he is/he is not'), *ní leis an leabhar seo? Is leis/ní leis* 'doesn't he have this book? Yes/no' (lit. 'it is with him/it is not with him'). But when the second element in the question is an indefinite noun, an adverbial phrase or an unstressed prepositional phrase, the pronoun *ea* is inserted after the copula, e.g. *is múinteoir é? Is ea/ní hea* 'is he a teacher? Yes/no' (lit. 'he is/he is not'), *inné a bhí sé anseo? Is ea/ní hea* 'was he here yesterday? Yes/no'. In the latter example, note the lack of tense marking.

3.5.2.3 Declaratives

Declarative sentences are not usually marked by any proclitic particles. However, it may be worth pointing out the past tense marker *do*[L] which occurs in some forms. It derives from the standard Old Irish *ro*-perfective marker (Thurneysen 1946: 339–48). Generally, the particle has disappeared leaving lenition as the only marker, but it is preserved before an initial vowel, e.g. *d'ól sé* /do:ls'e:/ 'he drank', *d'fhás sé* /da:s'e:/ 'he grew'.

3.5.3 Subordination

It is not intended to present a full listing of all patterns of subordination. The two constructions considered here are reported speech and relative clauses.

3.5.3.1 Reported speech

Reported speech constructions come under the more general heading of complementation, where there is usually a choice to be made between a finite verb construction following *go* (negative *nach*) or a verbal noun construction (see Table 3.23; for verbal nouns, see Chapter 8).

Following verbs of saying, thinking, perceiving, etc. there is an object complement. The choice of finite complement or verbal noun complement largely depends on the main verb. The majority of verbs take a finite verb complement but with *rá* 'say' and *síleachtáil/sílstean* 'think' a finite construction is used in reporting a statement, while a verbal noun complement is found in reporting a command ('goal oriented' Ó Siadhail 1989: 262), e.g. *dúirt sé go raibh sé go maith* 'he said he was well' : *dúirt sé an doras a phéinteáil* 'he said to paint the door'.

TABLE 3.23   Complement constructions in Modern Irish

(a) Subject complements

	go bhfuil mé ann	Finite
	'that I am there'	
is maith leis		
'he likes'	mé a bheith anseo	Verbal noun
(lit. 'it is good with him')	'me to be here'	

(b) Object complements

Direct statement: *tá/níl an chathaoir anseo*
                             'the chair is (not) here'
Indirect statement:
  Finite   *Sílim go/nach bhfuil an chathaoir anseo*
  Verbal noun   *Sílim (gan) an chathaoir a bheith anseo*
                             'I think that the chair is (not) here'

A similar alternation operates in a range of adverbial clauses. However, the finite type is more capable of marking all the nuances of mood and tense. Furthermore, in verbal noun clauses negation is marked prepositionally with *gan* 'without' (see 8.3.1.3), e.g. *gan an doras a phéinteáil* '... not to paint the door', while in finite clauses the negative *nach* can replace *go* without any other disruption to the clause.

3.5.3.2 Relative clauses
The system of relative marking in early Irish has been discussed above (2.2.6.4). Modern Irish has two types of relative clause, known as the direct and indirect relative (see McCloskey 1977, 1979: 5–50, 1990). They are marked by one of a pair of particles a^L or a^N (negative *nach*). The direct relative occurs when the antecedent is the subject or object of the verb in the relative clause, while the indirect pattern is used where the antecedent is the object of a preposition or a possessive adjective in the relative clause; in these cases a 'resumptive' pronoun occurs in the relative clause itself (see Table 3.24 for examples).

There is no overlap in the constructions; they use different particles, a^L for the direct type and a^N for the indirect type. However, the indirect type can be used to disambiguate the direct type. The example given in Table 3.24 (b) is ambiguous; it is offered as an example of an object antecedent but it could equally well be interpreted as 'the writer who praises the students'. The ambiguity arises from the indeterminacy of *na mic léinn* which could be subject or object together with the basic verbal form which is not marked for number. But if a pronoun was used in place of *na mic léinn*, there would be no difficulty as Modern Irish distinguishes subject and object pronoun in the 3rd person, i.e. subject

TABLE 3.24   Relative clauses in Modern Irish

(a) Direct (subject antecedent)
an fear a dhíol an domhan 'the man who sold the world'

(b) Direct (object antecedent)
an scríbhneoir a mholann na mic léinn 'the writer whom the students praise'

(c) Indirect (prepositional)
an fear a dtabarann tú an t-airgead dó 'the man you give the money to' (lit. 'the man who you give the money to him')

(d) Indirect (possessive adjective)
an fear a bhfuil a mháthair san otharlann 'the man whose mother is in the hospital' (lit. 'the man who his mother is in the hospital')

siad 'they' : object *iad* 'them'; thus, *an scríbhneoir a mholann siad* 'the writer whom they praise' : *an scríbhneoir a mholann iad* 'the writer who praises them'. However, the ambiguity of . . . *a mholann na mic léinn* can be resolved by the use of a resumptive object pronoun, i.e. *an scríbhneoir a molann na mic léinn é* 'the writer whom the students praise' (lit. '. . . whom the students praise him'); note that the full indirect pattern is used with the nasalizing particle as well as the resumptive pronoun.

In Connacht and Donegal the special relative forms of the verb can still be used (see Table 3.15), though they seem to have disappeared from Munster Irish (McCloskey 1979: 9). In Donegal they are optional, hence such variants as *an t-iascaire a dhíolas a bhád* and *an t-iascaire a dhíolann a bhád* 'the fisherman who sells his boat'. The special relative forms are only found after a^L, in other words, only in direct relative constructions.

3.5.4   Theoretical treatments of Irish syntax

Irish syntax has been the subject of a number of syntactical analyses in recent years, though they have tended to focus on particular topics, such as relative clauses, the complementizer system, etc.[10] The only attempt to set the whole Modern Irish syntactical system into a theoretical framework is Wigger 1972. This section is not intended as a survey but rather it focuses on one particular topic, namely relative clauses. The basic features have been set out in the preceding section (3.5.3.2) and the aim here is to consider the material from a more theoretical standpoint.

McCloskey 1985 has considered the problem from the standpoint of a theory of syntactic binding in which a close connection is established between the antecedent outside the relative clause and the gap it leaves behind within the relative clause (see also Deprez and Hale 1985). In the example *the drink$_j$ which Assumpta likes* $-_j$, the gap marks the phonologically null space usually filled by the direct object of the verb (the subscript letters are used to indicate the word which would be expected to fill the gap in a non-relative sentence, i.e. *Assumpta likes the drink*).

It has been argued more generally that 'gaps' are important syntactic entities (McCloskey 1985: 57 and references), and it seems that in many respects they behave like pronouns in that a similar relationship holds between an antecedent and a gap bound to it as between an antecedent and a pronoun; it will emerge that this is an important factor in Irish where pronouns do figure in indirect relative constructions.

The binding between the antecedent and the gap may extend over a number of embedded relative clauses, e.g. *the man$_j$ that Owen told me he thinks Assumpta wants to marry* $-_j$. However, there is a constraint on this property of 'unboundedness', namely a set of conditions known as 'island constraints'. For example, in the sentence *I know someone that wants to marry him, him* cannot be replaced by a gap bound to an antecedent outside the relative clause, e.g. **that's the man$_j$, that I know someone that wants to marry* $-_j$. Its unacceptability is based on the syntactical fact that many languages have a constraint that noun phrases modified by relative clauses are 'islands' and a gap on an island cannot be bound to an antecedent 'off the island'; in this example *someone that wants to marry* $-_j$ is an island and the antecedent *the man$_j$* is off it (see McCloskey 1985: 58–9).

Modern Irish generally follows these patterns in direct relative clauses; Table 3.25 presents some of the examples used in Table 3.24 rewritten in the present format. However, in the indirect type there is a resumptive pronoun where a gap would be expected. It should also be recalled that the two types are marked by a different relative particle, a^L (direct) and a^N (indirect). The differences can be schematized as in

TABLE 3.25: Direct relative clauses in Modern Irish presented in the format of syntactic binding

---

(a) Direct (subject antecedent)
   an fear$_j$ a dhíol $-_j$ *an domhan* 'the man who sold the world'

(b) Direct (object antecedent)
   (i)   *an scríbhneoir$_j$ a mholann na mic léinn* $-_j$ 'the writer whom the students praise'
   (ii) *an scríbhneoir$_j$ a mholann* $-_j$ *na mic léinn* 'the writer who praises the students'

TABLE 3.26   Schematization of direct and indirect relative clause usage in
Modern Irish

Direct	$NP_j \left(_{clause} a^L \ldots -_j \ldots \right)$
Indirect	$NP_j \left(_{clause} a^N \ldots Pro_j \ldots \right)$

Pro = pronoun.
After McCloskey 1985: 63.

Table 3.26. The task is essentially to formulate the rule for the differences between a^L + gap and a^N + pronoun. The choice between them is
free in cases such as Table 3.24 (b) but elsewhere one or the other is
determined in some way.

McCloskey 1985: 64 argues the point that in direct object relatives
the choice is actually free. It was claimed in 3.5.3 that the choice of a^N
+ pronoun was a disambiguating device but it is frequently used where
no ambiguity would result from the use of a^L + gap (see McCloskey
1985: 64 for examples). The explanation offered is that clarity and effi-
ciency of communication will favour the choice of the latter.

The question of examples such as Table 3.24 (d) takes us back to the
question of 'islands'. It emerges that, while the binding of a gap to an
antecedent is not permitted across an island boundary, it is permitted to
bind a pronoun to an antecedent. McCloskey 1985: 66–7 demonstrates
that those environments where a^N + pronoun occurs can on other
grounds be considered as islands in Irish, namely noun phrases, prepositional phrases and interrogative clauses. Thus, the first example in
Table 3.27 (a) is unacceptable because the gap is embedded in a noun
phrase with the antecedent outside it, in this case two removes outside
it. Likewise the example in Table 3.27 (b), where the gap is in a prepositional phrase, is unacceptable. In both cases the pattern of a^N +

TABLE 3.27   Examples of acceptable and unacceptable relative clause usage in
Modern Irish

(a) ** *seanchasóg*$_j$ . . . [*is docha* [*atá* (= a^L) *an tailliúir* [*a dhein* -$_j$ *sa chré*
       fadó]]]
   seanchasóg$_j$ . . . [*is docha* [*a bhfuil* (= a^N) *an tailliúir* [*a dhein é*$_j$ *sa chré*
       fadó]]]
   'an old jacket, . . . the tailor who made it has probably been dead for a
   long time'
(b) ** *an fear*$_j$ [*a bhí mé ag caint* [*le* -$_j$]]
   an fear$_j$ [*a raibh* (= a^N) *mé ag caint* [*leis*$_j$]]
   'the man to whom I was talking'

pronoun is acceptable. The example in Table 3.27 (b) has some important implications. As we have seen, the continuous aspect is marked by a pattern of [substantive verb + preposition + verbal noun] and is an extremely common construction; it would appear then that the prepositional phrase is an 'island' for the purpose outlined above. Such a conclusion is significant for the lengthy discussions as to whether continuous aspect constructions have nominal or verbal patterns (see 8.4 for further argumentation); the present evidence indicates a nominal interpretation.

McCloskey 1979: 35 relates the patterns discussed above to a more general view of Irish relative clauses in which he sees a rule of Relative Deletion applying in some cases but not others. In terms of the above discussion, *an t-iascaire a dhíolann a bhád* 'the fisherman who sells his boat', schematically *an t-iascaire_i [a dhíolann -_i a bhád]*, is to be derived from **an t-iascaire_i [a^L dhíolann sé_i a bhád]* by a process of deletion of *sé*. Deletion occurs when it is not subject to the island constraint. But where the island constraint applies (i.e. where the antecedent would be bound across an island boundary), then the deletion docs not apply and the pronoun remains. The advantage of this account is that it can incorporate both direct and indirect relative constructions under one rule and, as McCloskey 1985 has demonstrated, applies equally well to more complex relative constructions.

Notes

1. For other studies of Irish, see Ó Murchú 1985, 1992, Ó Dochartaigh 1992, Mac Eoin 1993.
2. For general studies, see T. F. O'Rahilly 1932, Ó Cuív 1951 and Ó Siadhail 1989; the last makes full use of a wide range of dialect material. The basis of Irish dialect studies is the magisterial survey by Wagner 1958–69. It has been supplemented and supported by numerous studies of individual dialects; see, for example, de Bhaldraithe 1945, 1953 (Cois Fhairrge, Co. Galway), de Búrca 1958 (Tourmakeady, Co. Mayo), Hamilton 1974 (Tory Island), Holmer 1962–5 (Co. Clare), Lucas 1979 (Ros Goill, Co. Donegal), Mhac an Fhailligh 1968 (Erris, Co. Mayo), Ó Cuív 1944 (West Muskerry, Co. Cork), Ó Dochartaigh 1987 (Ulster), Quiggin 1906 (Co. Donegal), Sjoestedt 1931, Sjoestedt-Jonval 1931, 1938 (Co. Kerry), Sommerfelt 1922 (Torr, Co. Donegal), Stockman 1974 (Aichill, Co. Mayo), Wagner 1959 (Teilinn). Word lists are provided by de Bhaldraithe 1985 (Galway), Lucas 1986 (Ros Goill), Nic Phaidín 1987 (Uí Rathach), Ó hAirt 1988 (Déise), Ó hOgáin 1984 (Corca Dhuibhne), T. S. Ó Máille 1974 (Ros Muc), Uí Bheirn 1989 (Teilinn).
3. See most recently Ó Murchú 1993, which was clearly written before the appearance of Hindley 1990, which paints the most pessimistic picture (for a review of Hindley, see Dorian 1991); see also L. Mac Mathúna 1990, Ó Riagáin 1992.
4. For a detailed discussion, see Ó Siadhail 1989: 15–109 (for reviews, see

A. J. Hughes 1992 and Stenson 1991). For a more complex and abstract discussion, see Ó Siadhail and Wigger 1975.

5. On the palatalization of labials, especially in Scottish Gaelic, see Oftedal 1963, MacAulay 1966, Jackson 1967b.
6. On adjectives generally, see Ó Dochartaigh 1992: 73–5, Mac Eoin 1993: 115–17; for detailed evidence from Cois Fhairrge, see de Bhaldraithe 1953: 117–32.
7. See Bergin 1902, Gleasure 1968, Quin 1969, and most recently with the fullest documentation Ó Buachalla 1985.
8. See Mac Eoin 1993: 135–7, Ó Dochartaigh 1992: 39–48, Ó Siadhail 1983, 1989: 219–52 (copula), 294–306 (substantive verb).
9. The following discussion attempts to present the facts without taking any specific theoretical stance. A surface analysis takes the pattern as [substantive verb + preposition + verbal noun], but other analyses would claim that the substantive verb is simply an auxiliary verb carrying tense, aspect and person markers while the verb as such is the verbal noun. For the former, see Stenson 1981: 137–45, for the latter Wigger 1972: 170–80; for similar discussion of Welsh material, see 5.5.4 below. For passive versions of these constructions, see 3.4.4.
10. See, for example, McCloskey 1979, 1980, 1985, etc., Stenson 1981.

Chapter 4

The Brittonic languages

4.0 Introduction

This chapter largely follows the pattern of Chapter 2 with an examination of the general features of Brittonic languages followed by consideration of the specific features of the individual languages and their inter-relationship. In the latter section, more emphasis is placed on Cornish and Breton, since Welsh forms the subject of Chapter 5.

4.1 The sources

The earliest evidence for the differentiated Brittonic languages of Welsh, Cornish and Breton only begins to emerge in around the 8th or 9th centuries AD. However, it is clear that some of the features which distinguish Welsh from Cornish and Breton arose at least as early as the 6th century. Jackson 1953, as part of what has been the standard work on the subject, established a complex relative and absolute chronology of the sound changes involved. It was based on the form of British names found in inscriptions and in Anglo-Saxon sources;[1] it relies heavily, therefore, on evidence from other disciplines, such as epigraphy and archaeology. Although Jackson's work has held the field for many years, his chronology has recently been subject to considerable critical attention, notably by Sims-Williams 1990. His conclusion (1990: 260) is that the changes which led to the emergence of the 'neo-Brittonic' languages could well have been completed by the early 6th century rather than just beginning then.[2] The following sections survey the sources of evidence for the individual languages (for Cumbric, see 1.3.1).

4.1.1 Welsh

There has been considerable debate as to when Welsh was first written down but that is rather different from the questions about the

112 THE BRITTONIC LANGUAGES

evidence we have.[3] Much of the Old Welsh material is in the form of names or single words or phrases written as glosses on Latin texts. Some of this material, particularly names in early charters in the *Book of Llandaf*, can be dated as early as the first half of the 7th century (Sims-Williams 1991: 28–9) though the glosses are probably no earlier than the 9th century and some are later (Jackson 1953: 47–56). But the earliest continuous texts in Welsh are a series of marginalia in the Lichfield Gospels claiming possession of the manuscript, recording a court action and listing names (Jenkins and Owen 1983, 1984). The longest of these, the 'Surexit' memorandum, records the outcome of a dispute between *Tutbulc* and the son-in-law of *Tutri* about the possession of *Tir Telih*; it is largely in Old Welsh with some Latin words. The first few lines may serve as an example of Old Welsh:

> Surexit Tutbulc filius Liuit ha gener Tutri di erchim Tir Telih hai oid i lau Elcu filius Gelhig ha luidt Iuguret. Amgucant pel amtanndi; ho diwed diprotant gener Tutri o guir.
> 'Tudfwlch, son of Llywyd and the son-in-law of Tudri arose to claim 'Tir Telych', which was in the hands of Elgu son of Gelli and the tribe of Idwared. They disputed long about it; in the end they disjudge Tudri's son-in-law by law' (Jenkins and Owen 1983: 51; punctuation added. For the manuscript, see lines 5–7 of the cover illustration).

Many of the differences between this and Modern Welsh are orthographical; for example, *Tutbulc* /tɨdvulχ/ would be pronounced the same in Modern Welsh but spelt *Tudfwlch*. Some changes, however, have occurred; *di erchim* /ði erχɪ̃/ 'to claim' corresponds to MnW *i erchi* /i erχɪ/ with the loss of the fricatives /ð/ and /ṽ/. Despite the Latin words the passage also shows a Welsh word order of verb–subject–object, with only an adverbial element preceding the verb (see 9.1.2.2).

There are also two poems in Old Welsh containing twelve verses in total; they are known as the Juvencus poems after the manuscript in which they are found (Bromwich 1972: 89–121). The longest passage of Old Welsh is the Computus fragment, twenty-three lines on the calendar, entirely in Old Welsh (I. Williams 1926–7). The *Book of Llandaf* (J. G. Evans and Rhŷs 1893) is an amalgam of charters and other material from about the seventh century onwards which was put together in the first half of the twelfth century. Sims-Williams 1991 has demonstrated the value of a detailed analysis of the orthography of the personal names, but for our present purposes such analysis is also important for a series of boundary clauses appended to the charters (translated in J. G. Evans and Rhŷs 1893: 363–84). They are in a form of Old Welsh which is rather later than the other material but is of sufficient bulk to be able to establish stylistic patterns (W. Davies 1979: 143–4).

The Old Welsh material presents particular difficulties to the linguist. Much of it is onomastic or single-word glosses. This type can be interesting orthographically and phonologically but provides little morphological or syntactical evidence. The few continuous passages assume particular importance but, as most of them are marginalia in Latin manuscripts, it is impossible to know when or where they were written, except in so far as the date of the manuscript itself provides a *terminus post quem*. It is, therefore, difficult to control the inevitable variation among these texts; is it due to chronological changes, regional differences or merely stylistic variation (Russell forthcoming)?

In contrast, the evidence for Middle Welsh is enormous and usually datable, even if not all the manuscripts can be located geographically. It also covers a wide range of styles and types of literature, including verse, law, tales, etc.[4] In addition to the literary material, with its own systematic orthographies and stylistic features, access to the spoken language of the period can be gained through the administrative documents and surveys compiled in the late 13th and early 14th centuries after the Norman conquest of Wales. Although they are in Latin and the Welsh evidence consists entirely of personal and local names, the names were written down by scribes untrained in the literary orthographies of the day. They may, therefore, in certain respects give us a clearer view of the pronunciation than we gain from the literary sources (Russell 1992a).

The impact of the Renaissance on Welsh literature and language, as Gruffydd 1990 has pointed out, was restricted to specific areas; in the fields of grammar and lexicography enormous progress was made but it was the first Welsh translation of the Bible in 1588, an event of great importance for the language, which was perhaps the crowning glory of the period. The language of the Welsh Bible was to affect both literary and spoken forms of the language for centuries to come (D. S. Evans 1988, D. Ll. Morgan 1988).

The use of Welsh, in both its spoken and literary form, has been maintained to the present day.[5] This century has seen a considerable growth in dialectal studies in an attempt to record those dialects which are in danger of disappearing and to understand the inter-relationships between them.[6] Further information can be gained from the study of local names; here the evidence is lexical but also has a historical and socio-linguistic dimension.[7]

4.1.2 Cornish

Cornish is far less well attested than any other Brittonic language, in part because despite the success of Revived Cornish there is no continuity of development from the earlier stages of the language.[8] The records of Old Cornish are particularly sparse (Jackson 1953: 59–62). Apart from some glosses, there is a list of saints' names (Olsen and Padel 1986) and a series of personal and local names dating from the early 10th century known as the Bodmin Manumissions (Förster 1930). The largest document is the *Vocabularium Cornicum* (c. 1100) which is an Old Cornish glossary based on a Latin - Old English glossary with the Old Cornish words substituted for the Old English (Campanile 1961 and 1974, E. Graves 1962). Again our knowledge extends only so far as the lexicon and phonology of this stage of the language (for the orthography see 6.3.2.4). Our understanding of the morphology and syntax is acquired from continuous verse texts in Middle and Late Cornish. Apart from the late-14th-century Middle Cornish Charter Endorsement, which is a brief poem on marriage, all the texts are verse translations of biblical stories intended probably for dramatic performance. There are three major works written in Middle Cornish, *Pascon agan Arluth* 'The Passion of our Lord' (Stokes 1860–1), the *Ordinalia* (Norris 1859) and *Beunans Meriasek* 'The Life of St Meriasek' (Stokes 1872), written in 1504. The last of these religious poems, *Gwreans an Bys* 'The Creation of the World' (Stokes 1864), was written in a later stage of the language in 1611.

The other important source of linguistic material is the evidence of local names. Not only do they provide lexemes which are not attested in literary texts but they offer important evidence for the gradual extinction of Cornish through the peninsula.[9]

4.1.3 Breton

The evidence for Old Breton is substantial but almost entirely in the form of short glosses on 9th- and 10th-century Latin manuscripts (Jackson 1953: 62–7).[10] In addition there are a large number of personal and local names in cartularies, the most important being the *Cartulary of Redon* (de Courson 1863) known in an 11th-century copy but largely containing 9th-century charters; it contains over 6,000 personal names and some 1,000 local names (W. Davies 1988: 1–2). This document also contains four lines of text largely in Old Breton (de Courson 1863: 112–13 (cart. cxlvi)) which is a boundary clause similar to those in the *Book of Llandaf*:

'. . . finem habens a fine Rannmelan don roch do fos Matuuor, cohiton fos do imhoir, ultra imhoir per lannam, do fois fin Randofhion, do fin Ranhaelmorin cohiton hi fosan do rud fos per lannam do fin Ranloudinoc pont imhoir.'
. . . having a boundary from the boundary of Rannmelan to the rock to the ditch of Matuuor, along the ditch to the bank, across the bank through the land to the ditch of the territory of Randofhion, to the boundary of Ranhaelmorin, along the small ditch to the red ditch through the land to the territory of Ranloudinoc, the bridge on the bank (a Latin translation of this charter is appended to charter cxlviii (de Courson 1863: 113)).

Both *fos* and *fin* are borrowed from Latin, from *fossa* and *fines* respectively, but the diminutive *fosan* (= *fossatellum* in the Latin version) has the Brittonic diminutive suffix *-an*. The structure, however, is entirely

Breton in form with the prepositions *do* 'to(wards)' (cf. OW *di*, MW *dy* /ði/, *y*) and *cohiton* 'along' (cf. OW *cihutun, cihitan*).

Apart from the names in charters of the 12th–15th centuries (Loth 1890: 181–236), the first continuous Breton texts are not attested until the 15th century.[11] From then on, Breton literature has continued to be produced and to grow despite the pressure on the language by French and the gradual but persistent reduction in the number of speakers (Hemon 1947: 43–113, R. Williams 1992). As with Welsh, the dialects of Breton, and particularly those of Modern Breton, have been an important object of study.[12]

4.2 General features of the Brittonic languages

In 1.5 two features were noted which distinguished Goidelic from Brittonic languages, the *p/q* distinction and the difference in word accent. Others were mentioned but not discussed. The aim of this section is to discuss a number of aspects which are common to all the Brittonic languages, such as lenition, accentuation and the loss of endings; features by which the separate Brittonic languages may be distinguished are discussed in 4.3.

Some care needs to be observed here since the changes discussed must be distinguished from independent but parallel changes which occurred later in all three languages. Jackson 1953: 24–5 considers that Brittonic can be safely regarded as a single language up to the end of the 6th century, but after that any common changes should be seen as independent though probably resulting from 'phonetic situations already existing in the parent language' (Jackson 1953: 23). Clear examples of the latter are the loss of intervocalic /ɤ/- (Jackson 1953: 469–70), the change of initial /u̯/- to /gu̯/- (Jackson 1953: 389–94) and the accent shift from final to penultimate position (see 1.5.2 and 4.2.3).

4.2.1 Lenition and mutations

To a large extent the Brittonic languages share the same system of lenition and mutations which must in its basics go back to the period of unity. A parallel but different series of changes took place in Goidelic (see 2.2.1 above). Over the years the standard view of Jackson 1953 has been challenged not only in terms of dating but also in regard to the processes themselves (see C. Watkins 1954 and Sims-Williams 1990). These matters are discussed in detail in Chapter 7 since they involve consideration of Irish material as well as Brittonic. At this point it may be useful to summarize the facts.

In the Brittonic period there was a shift in the pronunciation of intervocalic consonants which can be characterized – essentially, and at this point conveniently – as the spirantization of voiced consonants and the voicing of unvoiced stops, i.e. /g d b/ > /ɤ ð v/ beside /k t p/ > /g d b/

TABLE 4.1   Examples of the effects of lenition

Spirantization of voiced stops

W *afon* 'river', OCo *auon*, B (*Pont*)*aven* < **abona* (cf. Continental Celtic
    Abona, Lat *amnis*)
W *medd* 'mead', B *mez* < **medu*- (cf. Gk *méthu*, Skt *mádhu*)
W *draen* 'blackthorn', MCo *dreyn*, B *drean* < **dragen*- (cf. Ir *draigen*)

Voicing of unvoiced stops

W *cad* 'battle', Co *cas* < **catu*- (cf. Gaul *Catu*-, Ir *cath*)
W *llugorn* 'lantern', OCo *lugarn*, B *lugern* < **leuk*- 'light' cf. Ir *lócharn*, Lat
    lucerna)
W *pobi* 'cook', Co *pobas*, B *pibi* < **pop*- < **kʷokʷ*- (cf. Lat *coquō*, etc.; see
    1.7)

---

respectively (see Table 4.1 for examples).[13] Subsequent changes in the
individual languages has sometimes masked the close relationship
between the Brittonic languages; for example, in Middle Cornish a final
-/d/ became a sibilant as in Co *cas* 'battle' (see Table 4.1), and uniquely
to Breton there was a second shift which voiced certain unvoiced consonants (see 4.3.1).

The same changes affected initial consonants when the preceding
word ended in a vowel. The subsequent grammaticalization of the latter
changes led to the system of initial mutations in all the Celtic languages
(see Chapter 7).

In certain other environments, e.g. following a resonant or as part of
a consonantal cluster, the unvoiced consonants /k t p/ were spirantized
to /χ θ f/ respectively, e.g. W *march* 'horse', B *marc'h* < **marko*- (cf.
OIr *marc*), W *arth* 'bear' < **arto*- (cf. OIr *art*), W *corff* 'body' < Lat
corpus. This could have occurred either before or after the loss of final
syllables.

It is clear that the basic shifts belong to the period of Brittonic and,
perhaps apart from spirantization, must pre-date the loss of final syllables (see 4.2.3 below) which had a fundamental effect on the status of
these changes.

4.2.2   Other sound changes

It may be useful to gather a number of the more significant sound
changes which seem to belong to the Brittonic period in that they are
common to all the Brittonic languages.

4.2.2.1   *Long vowels and diphthongs*

In 1.4.1.1, it was shown that /oː/ and /aː/ fell together in Proto-Celtic as
/aː/ and that subsequently in Brittonic /aː/ was rounded to /ǫː/. The rep-

TABLE 4.2   Examples of the changes in Brittonic long vowels and diphthongs

(a) Changes to Proto-Celtic /a:/
  W *llawn*, Co *lluen, leun, len*, B *leun* 'full' < **lāno-* (cf. Ir *lán*)
  W *brawd* 'judgement', Co *bres*, B *breut* 'pleader' < **brātu-* (cf. Ir *bráth*,
    Gaul *Bratu-*)
  MW *marchawc*, MnW *marchog* 'horseman', B *marc'hek* < **mark- āko-* (cf.
    Ir *marcach*)

(b) Changes to Proto-Celtic /e:/ (from /ei/)
  W *gŵydd* 'presence', B *ar gouez* 'openly' < **ụeid-* (cf. OIr *fíad*, Gk *eîdos*)
  W *bwyd* 'food', OCo *buit*, MCo *boys*, OB *boitolion*, MB *boed* < **gʷei-* (cf.
    OIr *biad*)

(c) Changes to Proto-Celtic /o:/ and /u:/
  (i) /u:/ > /i:/
       W *rhin* 'secret' < **rūn-* (cf. Ir *rún*, OE *rūn*)
       W *din-* 'fortress' < **dūnon* (cf. Ir *dún*, Gaul *-dunum*)
  (ii) /o:/ > /ü:/
       W,B *tud*, Co *tus* 'people' < **toutā* (cf. Ir *túath*)
       W *rhudd*, OCo *rud*, MCo *ruth*, B *ruz* 'red' < **roudo-* (cf. Ir *rúadh*)
       W *llafur* < Lat *labōrem*, W,Co,B *un* 'one' < **oino-* (cf. Ir *oen*)

resentation of the vowel is partially masked by independent developments in the individual languages. In Welsh /ǫ:/ was diphthongized to /aʊ/, written as MW *au, aw*, MnW *aw*, but reduced to /ɔ/ in unaccented syllables (see 4.2.3). In Cornish and Breton, however, it gave /œ:/ variously written as *u, e, ue* and *eu* in accented syllables and as *e* in unaccented environments (Jackson 1953: 288; see Table 4.2 (a) for examples).

In Proto-Celtic, original /e:/ merged with /i:/, while /ei/ was monophthongized to /e:/. In Brittonic, /e:/ gave /ʉɨ/, W *wy*, OCo *ui*, MCo *oy*, B /ue/ *oue, oe, oa* (see Table 4.2 (b) for examples).

In 1.4.1.1 we left the development of diphthongs at a point where /eu/ and /ou/ had become /o:/ and /ei/ had become /e:/. Within Brittonic further changes occurred. First, Proto-Celtic /u:/ was centralized to give first /ü:/ and then /i:/ (see Table 4.2 (c) (i) for examples). Secondly, and after the change of /u:/ to /ü:/, /o:/, /oi/ and Latin /o:/ and /u:/ all fell together as /u:/, and this was subsequently centralized to /ü:/ and remained as such in all the Brittonic languages (see Table 4.2 (c) (ii) for examples). Traditional accounts, e.g. Jackson 1953: 312–17, include /aʊ/ in this development, but Lambert 1990 has recently argued that it fell together with /ǫ:/ and was then diphthongized in Welsh to /aʊ/. Table 4.3 contains a summary of the changes discussed in this section.

TABLE 4.3 Summary of the development of Brittonic long vowels and diphthongs

IE	Proto-Celtic	Common Brittonic	Brittonic languages
/au/	> /au/		
		> /ǫ:/	> W /au/, CoB /œ:/
/o:/, /a:/	> /a:/		
/ei/	> /e:/ > /e:/ >	/ui/
/u:/			
	> /u:/ > /ü:/		
final /o:/)			
		> /i:/	
/i:/			
	> /i:/ > /i:/		
/e:/			
/eu/, /ou/	> /o:/		
		> /u:/ > /ü:/	
/oi/	> /oi/		

4.2.2.2 Vowel affection

Another change which occurred in the Brittonic period is 'final *i*-affection', whereby /i:/ and /i̯/ in the final syllable affected the vowel of the preceding syllable (see Table 4.4 for examples; for further discussion of vowel affection and Irish examples, see 2.2.3.2). With the loss of final syllables, this final *i*-affection was to become an important marker of grammatical categories, especially the plural but also 3rd singular present tenses of the verb. A similar phenomenon affected internal syllables with /i/ or /i:/ in the following syllable, e.g. MW *Custennhin*, OCo, OB *Custentin* < Lat *Constantīnus*, but it is usually regarded as a slightly later independent development in the separate languages.

4.2.2.3 Brittonic /s/ and /i̯/

There are two important consonantal developments. Brittonic languages show a distinctive treatment of initial /s/ in contrast to Goidelic, where it was preserved; in all Brittonic languages initial /s/ deriving

TABLE 4.4 Examples of vowel affection in Brittonic languages

W *meirch*, Co *meirgh* 'horses' < *markī: sg. W *march*, etc.
MW *gureic*, MnW *gwraig*, Co *gurek*, B *grek* 'old woman' < *u̯raki-
W *cyrn*, B *kern* 'horns' < *kornī: sg. W *corn*, etc.

TABLE 4.5   Examples of the changes affecting /s/ and /i̯/

(a) Celtic /s/ > /h/
W,Co *haf*, B *hañv* 'summer' < **sam-* (cf. Ir *samh*, Gaul *Samoni*)
W *hysb*, B *hesp* 'dry' < **sisku̯o-* (cf. Ir *sesc*)
W *Hafren* 'Severn' < British *Sabrina* (cf. OE *Saefern*, MnE *Severn*)

(b) Latin /s/ > /s/ or /h/
Lat *sagitta* > W *saeth*, MCo *sêth*, MnB *seaz*
Lat *sextarius* > OW *hestaur* (Jackson 1953: 514)

(c) Celtic /i̯/ > /ð/ or /∅/
W *defnydd* 'material', MB *daffnez*, MnB *danvez* < **damníi̯o-* (cf. OIr *damnae*)
W *newydd*, Co *nowyth, newyth*, OB *nouuid*, MnB *nevez* 'new' < **nou̯íi̯o-* (cf. Ir *núae*, Gaul *Novio-*)
MW *eil*, MnW *ail* 'other' < **ali̯o-* (cf. Lat *alius*, etc.)

from Proto-Celtic and Indo-European /s/ gave /h/ (see Table 4.5 (a) for examples; see Zimmer 1994). On the other hand, Latin initial /s/ generally remained, though there are some examples of *h-* (see Table 4.5 (b) for examples). Internally, /s/ was lost and the hiatus between vowels was filled by /i̯/.

Treatment of /i̯/ in Brittonic is very complex (see Vendryes 1951, Jackson 1953: 347–63). In particular environments, particularly following the stress accent, it was strengthened to /ð/ (see Table 4.5 (c) for examples). The development may be compared with the strengthening of Latin initial /i̯/ to /dʒ/ in French, e.g. Lat *iugum* > French *joug*, etc. (Pope 1934: 267). This change is by no means fully understood; there are cases where /ð/ has not developed (see Table 4.5 (c)). There seems to be some sort of alternation between /i̯/ and /ii̯/ with only the latter giving /ð/ in the appropriate accentual environment, but the relevant conditioning factors are uncertain (see also Russell 1990: 56–7).

4.2.3   The penultimate accent, its shift and the consequences
In contrast to Goidelic with its initial accent, the stress in Brittonic fell on the penultimate syllable, which brought its own problems. The loss of final syllables (see 4.2.5 below) had the effect of leaving the accent on the final syllable. At a later stage in the independent Brittonic languages the accent shifted back to the new penultimate syllable. The effect of this was that Brittonic languages underwent a double accommodation to the stress accent. The process may be exemplified by following the fate of Pr-C /a:/; the Celtic noun **marko-* 'horse' at some stage, perhaps even in Proto-Celtic, formed a derivative **mark-ākos* (nom. sg.) 'horseman' with a Brittonic nom. pl. **markāki̯ónes* which after loss of endings and lenition gave OW and MW *marchawc*

/mar'χaʊg/ : *marchogyon* /marχɔg'yon/ (the reconstruction *-ónes* is uncertain but is used for purposes of illustration); in the singular /a:/ was rounded to /o̩:/ and later diphthongised to /aʊ/ under the accent but in the plural /o̩:/ was reduced to /ɔ/ in the pretonic syllable. The ortho- graphy of the vowels in Old and Middle Welsh represents that state of affairs. In about the 10th or 11th century AD the accent began to shift back to the new penultimate syllable; apart from the accent shift the plural *marchogyon* was left unaffected /mar'χɔgyon/ but the final diph- thong of *marchawc* now /'marχaʊg/ was reduced to /ɔ/, whence the modern form *marchog* /'marχɔg/. The shortening of pre-tonic long vowels did not just affect /o̩:/ but also /i:/ > /i/ and /u:/ > /u/, which then in Welsh reduced further to /ə/ at some time before the accent shift, e.g. Lat *cupidus* > Archaic Welsh /ku'bɨð/ > /kə'bɨð/ > with accent shift /'kəbɨð/ *cybydd* 'miser' (see Table 5.15 below). The pre-tonic shorten- ing of long vowels seems to have been a Welsh phenomenon; we may compare W *brawd* 'brother' : pl. *brodyr* (< */bro̩:t/- < *brāt-) with B *breur* : pl. *breudeur*, where the first syllable of the plural retains the long vowel (Jackson 1967a: 312, Sims-Williams 1990: 256).

   All the Brittonic languages independently underwent the accent shift, but exactly when it occurred has been the subject of some debate. Jackson 1953: 682–9, 1967: 79–84, 1975–6 sees the shift as occurring in about the 11th century in both Welsh and Breton (the Cornish evidence is too sparse to be of any use). On the other hand, T. A. Watkins 1972 argued on the basis of the same evidence that it occurred in Welsh at least no later than the 9th century. Jackson claimed that the shift had to post-date, among other changes, the diphthongization of /o̩:/ to /au/ in final syllables (but see Sims-Williams 1991: 69) and the development of a prosthetic /ə/-, written *y*-, which must have arisen before the accent could have shifted back onto it in original monosyllables (but see Russell 1992a: 388–9). Jackson also argued that it pre-dated the reduc- tion of /aw/ to /ɔ/ in final syllables and the change of *-nh-* to *-n-* in, for example, MW *brenhin* 'king', MnW *brenin*; in the last example the presence of *-h-* is taken to indicate a final stress, i.e. /bren'hin/ beside later /'brenin/. However the evidence is used, it is not clear what any dating conclusion signifies. Clearly accent shifts do not occur overnight. An accented word, be it verb or noun, is frequently surrounded by unac- cented enclitic or proclitic elements and the number and location of such elements could easily have retarded or speeded up the accent shift in a particular environment (for Irish parallels, see 3.2.2); for example, the occurrence of an enclitic affixed personal pronoun, which seems to have been optional in the early period (see 5.3.3.4), e.g. *fy mrenhín i* 'my king', *moláf i* 'I praise', would have automatically produced a penulti- mate accent in the accented unit without any shift. It is quite possible that the accent shift was a very long process and that the 9th century could mark the beginning of the change and the 11th century the end of it.

Whatever date or period is settled upon, any consideration is at the mercy of the orthography of the sources. For example, original *-nt-* gave pretonic *-nh-* /nh/ but post-tonic *-n(n)-* /n(n)/, hence the significance of *brenhin* beside *brenin*. However, the plural or any other derivative would have maintained the stress on the *-i-* and therefore retained the *-nh-* spelling, i.e. MW *brénin* : pl. *brenhínoedd, brenhínol* 'royal', etc. It is possible, therefore, that the *h*-spelling could have been retained in the singular to maintain a single basic spelling long after the accent had shifted to the new penultimate syllable.

One of the most important but difficult features is the *o*-spelling which could reflect an early pre-diphthongization /ǫ:/ or a post-accent shift /ɔ/ reduced from /au/. A crucial form for both Jackson and Watkins is OW *retinoc* (Chad 6, ca. 800 AD) (= MnW *rhedynnog* /rɛ'dǝnɔg/ 'brackeny, a place where bracken grows' (G. R. J. Jones 1972: 308–11)). For Watkins the *o*-spelling reflects the post-accent shift reduction of /au/, for Jackson it is the relic of the pre-diphthongized /ǫ:/. For both of them, the *o*-spellings found in the *Book of Llandaf* (see 4.1.1 above), e.g. PNN *Biuoc, Matoc, Conuonoc*, etc., reflect post-shift reductions, but Koch 1985–6 has recently argued that even these could reflect pre-diphthongization spellings which evaded modernization by later scribes. Furthermore, as part of his systematic study of the orthography of the Llandaf Charters, Sims-Williams 1991: 79–86 has demonstrated that the *-oc* spelling of *retinoc* represents original /ǫ:/; he concludes that the remaining evidence points to an 11th-century date for the accent shift.

In Breton a similar accent shift occurred in most dialects, though Breton did not go in for the type of vowel reductions seen in Welsh. The one exception is the Vannetais dialect of Breton, where the accent remained on the old penultimate with the resultant reductions in the preceding syllable, e.g. Vannetais Breton *klom* 'dove' < Lat *colúmba* (H. Lewis and Pedersen 1961: 78, Jackson 1967a: 67). However, Jackson (1967a: 79–84) has shown that the dialectal isogloss is not as clear-cut. It emerges that ultimate stress, i.e. stress on the old penultimate, now the final syllable, was retained not only in Vannetais but also as far north as Goelo on the northern coast and that further west there was an area of variation where both penultimate and ultimate stress coexisted. The most plausible explanation of the retention of the final stress is that, as proposed by Jackson, this area contained a higher proportion of Old French speakers with a strong final stress accent which prevented the extension of the new stress pattern.

4.2.4 The new quantity system
In early Brittonic vowel length was phonemic; that is, the short vowels /a/, /o/, /u/, /e/ and /i/ were contrastive with /ǫ:/, /u:/, /ę:/, /e:/ and /i:/. But in the modern Brittonic languages vowel length is allophonic,

Table 4.6   The distribution of long and short vowels in Modern Welsh

---

Long vowels
(i)   in monosyllables; finally or before a single consonant (including /f/, /θ/, /χ/, /s/)
(ii) in polysyllables:
        – in stressed penultimate syllable followed by vowel or /h/
        – (Breton only) in stressed penultimate syllable followed by a single consonant

Half long vowels
(Welsh only) in stressed penultimate syllable followed by a single consonant

Short vowels
(i)   in monosyllables: before consonant clusters
(ii) in polysyllables: in stressed penultimate syllable before consonant clusters

---

being dependent on its environment (Jackson 1953: 338–44, Sims-Williams 1990: 250–60; see 5.2.1). The modern distribution of long and short vowels is presented in Table 4.6. In short, there is an opposition in stressed monosyllables between CV:C and CVCC. In polysyllables the same contrast operates in Breton, i.e. 'CV:CVC : 'CVCCVC, but in Welsh the stressed vowel of 'CVCVC is only half long; Jackson (1953: 339–40) has demonstrated that this is a relatively late phenomenon arising after the accent shift. Prior to the accent shift the CV:C : CVCC pattern would have operated in all stressed syllables. In Modern Welsh the distinctions are more qualitative than quantitative, at least in southern dialects; in the north, quantity seems more significant (see 5.2.1). The changes in the quantity system outlined here are dated by Jackson to around 600, while Sims-Williams 1990 prefers the first half of the 5th century. It is nevertheless striking that these developments are analogous to the major re-arrangements in the Vulgar Latin vowel system whereby all unstressed vowels and stressed vowels in closed syllables were short and all stressed vowels in open syllables were long; thus Classical Latin *valēs* and *dīxī* became *vāles* and *dĭxĭ* (Jackson 1953: 269–71). The evidence suggests that it was a long drawn out change from about the 3rd to the 5th centuries spreading perhaps from south to north through the Roman Empire. It is unclear whether there was any direct influence on the Brittonic changes except in so far as it demonstrates parallel responses to penultimate stress accents.

4.2.5   Loss of final syllables

If there is any dateable change which marks the end of British and the beginning of Welsh, Cornish and Breton, it is the loss of final syllables (with the resulting break-up of the case system) which was completed about the middle of the sixth century... (Jackson 1953: 691).

Jackson saw the loss of final syllables as the great watershed between Brittonic and the individual Brittonic languages. At that point they acquired the distinguishing mark of Brittonic languages, the lack of a case system, with the same word forms, marked only for number, being used in all grammatical contexts. The implication is that up to that point Brittonic had a fully fledged and functioning case system which was suddenly snuffed out by phonological change. Furthermore, C. Lewis has seen the loss of final syllables as the cause of a radical change in the structure of Welsh:

> Welsh had recourse, therefore, to the use of prepositions, word-order or juxtaposition, and other devices to compensate for the loss of the old inflection endings which had formerly in the parent British tongue expressed the various grammatical relationships (C Lewis 1976: 26–7).

This scenario suggests that a language with case endings does not use prepositions, nor does it have a relatively fixed word order, yet a language like Latin or Russian rapidly falsifies that supposition. Hamp 1975–6 pointed out that the loss of endings would not have had the catastrophic effect on the case system envisaged by Jackson and Lewis. If we take the pre-6th-century declension of W *mab* 'son' and delete the final syllables (see Table 4.7), sufficient markers in the form of vowel affection and mutations of the following word remain to have maintained a functioning case system. Indeed, Irish did precisely that (see 2.2.4), although it had the added feature of phonetic consonant quality (see 2.2.3.3). Moreover, consonant-stem nouns, e.g. the putative preforms of W *brawd* 'brother' in Table 4.8, would have had another

TABLE 4.7   A reconstructed Brittonic *o*-stem declension

Singular

Nom	*mapos	>	**mab (+ [S] in Breton)
Acc.	*mapon	>	**mab[N]
Gen.	*mapī	>	**meib[L]
Dat.	*mapū	>	**meib[L]

Plural

Nom.	*mapī	>	**meib[L]
Acc.	*mapūs	>	**meib[S]
Gen.	*mapon	>	**mab[N]
Dat.	*mapobi(s) or *mapobos >		**mabof[S/L]

[S] = spirantization, [L] = lenition, [N] = nasalization.

See Koch 1982–3: 204.

TABLE 4.8   A reconstructed Brittonic consonantal declension

Singular			
Nom.	*brātīr	>	**brǫ:d(r)
Acc.	*brāteran	>	**brǫ:der^N
Gen.	*brātros	>	**brǫ:dr^S
Dat.	*brātri	>	**brǫ:dr^L
Plural			
Nom.	*brāteres	>	**brǫ:der^S
Acc.	*brāteras	>	**brǫ:der^S
Gen.	*brāteron	>	**brǫ:der^N
Dat.	*brātribos	>	**brǫ:dryf^S

^{S} = spirantization, ^{L} = lenition, ^{N} = nasalization.

variable, the presence or absence of the stem-final consonant. One could also envisage the spread of more marked consonant-stem endings to other declensional types, as happened in Middle Irish and early Modern Irish (see 2.2.4 and 3.3.2–3); indeed the spread of the Welsh plural suffix -(y)on from n-stems seems to be exactly that. Hamp 1975–6 takes the view that before the loss of final syllables, the fixed order of constituents, the use of prepositions to mark dative functions, etc. (Lewis' 'other functions'), had already been instituted. The outcome was that the loss of final syllables was not the morphological catastrophe portrayed by Jackson and Lewis; on the contrary, 'remarkably little grammatical information was lost' (Hamp 1975–6: 57).

Koch 1982–3 takes the argument a stage further. If declension did survive the loss of final syllables, it is clearly dead by the earliest Old Welsh and Old Breton evidence with no indication of recent expiry. In other words, the surviving declensional patterns must have been eliminated very rapidly. Moreover, as the 9th-century evidence of Old Welsh and Old Breton had been separate from the 6th century onwards and constitutes two independent witnesses, the tendency to dispose of final syllables may well have been rooted in 6th century late Brittonic. Koch argues that in fact the notion of post-apocope declension is a mirage and that declension had collapsed well before the loss of final syllables. The evidence of Late Latin inscriptions shows general confusion of case endings; they frequently employ Latin endings but have no conception of different declensional groups (Koch 1982–3: 210–11). Note, for example, the 7th century *CATACVS HIC FILIUS TEGERNACVS* (Nash-Williams 1950: 54) showing archaic phonology in *ā* for /ǫ:/ in *CATACVS* (for later MW *Catauc*, MnW *Cadog*) but the genitive *TEGERNACVS* with a Latinate nominative ending; the inscription would translate simply into Modern Welsh as *Cadog mab Teyrnog*

'C. son of T.'. Furthermore, Old Welsh genealogies, which often extend back to the 5th and 6th centuries show no understanding of genitives in patronymics. In addition, the early Welsh poetry of Aneirin and Taliesin, which historically should be placed in the 6th century, shows no evidence of case usage or even its eradication, which might still be detectable through rhyme and alliteration (Koch 1982–3: 221–2).

Nevertheless, some traces of declension have survived. OW *Cair Teim* (= MW *Caer Dyf* = Cardiff) 'fortified town on the river Taf' shows *i*-affection of the second element and therefore probably represents an old genitive. There are also a series of case forms 'frozen' in adverbs and compound prepositions, e.g. W,Co *erbyn* 'against' < **are pennū* (dat.) (cf. OIr *ar chiunn* (Hamp 1975c)), MW *erllyned*, B *warlene* 'last year' < **war/are blidníiā* (dat./acc.). Words referring to 'day', W *dydd*, etc., seem to preserve different case forms, e.g. W *heddiw*, MB *hizieu*, Co *hedhyu* 'today', W *beunydd*, B *bemdez* 'every day' (acc. with nasalization) (C. Watkins 1966c, Hamp 1975b). However, Koch would argue that such examples are very rare. In one group of forms where this argument has been used, he claims that the apparent case forms are simply plural (1982–3: 208–10); the second element of local names, such as W *Pentyrch*, B *Penterc'h*, W *Dinbrain*, *Dindyrn/Tintern*, W *Ceinmeirch*, do not, according to Koch, contain fossilized genitive singulars but rather they are plurals, thus *Pentyrch* 'hill of boars' not 'hill of the boar', *Dinbrain* 'fort of crows' not 'fort of the crow', etc. Some are debatable; for example, *Ceinmeirch* seems to be a descriptive local name comparing the ridge to the back of a horse rather than specifying a place where horses grazed, and thus to be analysed as 'back of the horse'. Even so, it is likely that such forms would have been readily interpreted as plurals, following the pattern of generalizing the nominative forms and maximizing the singular/plural distinction. The maximization often seems to have brought about the generation of new plurals, hence the spread of W -(*y*)*on*; W *mab* 'son' has a plural *meibyon* but its etymological plural *meib* is marginally attested in Middle Welsh as the form used with numerals, e.g MW *pedwar meib ar hugeint* '24 sons' (D. S. Evans 1964: 47).

4.2.6 The verbal system

The verbal system preserved in the early stages of the Brittonic languages shows clear affinities with the system of Old Irish (see 2.2.6), and there is no doubt that both reflect the system of their Proto-Celtic ancestor. But, while the Old Irish system is flourishing and we do not detect any significant breakdowns until the late Old Irish / early Middle Irish period, even the earliest Brittonic evidence indicates that the system had undergone and was undergoing severe modification. Our knowledge of the early Brittonic verb is almost entirely dependent on

Old Welsh and Old Breton, as there are no verbs in the Old Cornish evidence. The verbal patterns of Middle Cornish, however, suggest that it started from the same base as the Welsh and Breton forms.

The absolute/conjunct alternation of Old Irish, whereby the absolute form was used when the verb stood independently at the head of the sentence and the conjunct when it was preceded by a prefix or particle (see 2.2.6.2), can still be traced in Old Welsh and Old Breton. But the general system of terminations for synthetic verbal forms in Old and Middle Welsh seems to reflect a mixture of the two sets of endings; many of the endings seem to reflect the absolute conjugation but the 3rd singular ending is usually a reflex of the conjunct ending, e.g. MW 1st sg. *archaf* 'I ask' < **arkami* but 3rd sg. *eirch* 'he asks' < **arkīt* (D. S. Evans 1964: 115–19). Some traces of the absolute 3rd singular endings do survive, e.g. OW *prinit* 'he buys', *retit* 'it runs', OB *troit* 'he returns'. In particular, there are some Middle Welsh proverbial expressions where the absolute/conjunct alternation survives, e.g. *trenghit golut, ni threingk molut* 'wealth perishes, fame perishes not', *tyuit maban, ni thyf y gadachan* 'an infant grows, his swaddling clothes grow not'. Here *trenghit* and *tyuit* can in Irish terms be termed 'absolute' forms, while *threingk* and *thyf* after negatives are 'conjunct'. These are, however, only relics attested in the earliest evidence or in fossilized contexts.

Likewise, various verbal categories, such as the *s*- and *ā*-preterites, etc., find their reflexes in Brittonic. Some are marginal, like the reduplicated preterites (MW *cigleu* 'I have heard'), others, such as the *s*-preterite, became very productive in Middle Welsh though its usage has reduced in the modern language (D. S. Evans 1964: 122–4).

Infixed pronouns were clearly a standard feature of Brittonic (see 2.2.6.2). They were still common in Middle Welsh, e.g. *dy-m-kyueirch* 'he greets me', *yd yth geissaf* 'that I shall seek thee' (D. S. Evans 1964: 55–6) and are also still found in the formal registers of Modern Welsh (S. J. Williams 1980: 49–50, Thorne 1993: 161–4) though they have long disappeared from the spoken language, where independent forms are used (see 5.3.5). Likewise in Breton infixed pronouns were common in Middle Breton, e.g. *me-z benig* 'I bless you' (H. Lewis and Piette 1966: 24–5), and early Modern Breton and are still found in the literary language; they have been replaced in the modern language by fuller forms which may still precede the verb (Hemon 1954, 1976: 76–84). The Vannes dialect largely preserves the Middle Breton system but the other dialects have developed another system whereby a pronominal object is marked by the conjugated forms of the preposition *a* 'of' (Hemon 1954: 240–1; for conjugated pronouns see 5.3.5). The pattern is comparable to the Welsh use of forms of *o* 'of, from' after a negative (see 5.5.2.1).

The loss of final syllables had almost as much effect on the verbal system as on the declensional system (see 4.2.5) since it would have eroded but not eradicated the markers of person. Presumably the selection of 'absolute' forms with their extra syllable in Brittonic paradigms is partly determined by the fact that they would have been more marked. Nevertheless, it is clear that from a very early stage Brittonic re-marked personal endings with affixed pronouns, some of which became attached to the ends of the verb form to become person markers themselves (see 5.4.1).

It is difficult to detect any significant differences between the Brittonic system, in so far as it can be reconstructed, and the Goidelic system. As in other areas of morphology, Brittonic seems to have developed more rapidly towards simplification. Differences have emerged in the individual languages, e.g. the acquisition of a pluperfect tense, but generally the starting point seems to have been the same.

4.2.7 Compound prepositions

It has been claimed that a distinguishing feature of Brittonic languages is the tendency to compound prepositions, notably in the conjugated forms (see D. S. Evans 1964: Fleuriot 1964: 290–7), e.g. W *am* 'around' : conjugated stem *amdan-*, *o* 'from' : *ohono-*, *oddi wrth* 'away from', OB *diguar* 'from', etc. At the same time, this pattern has been claimed to have arisen through the influence of Latin, and particularly of Vulgar Latin, e.g. *de contra*, *de intus*, *de ex*, *in ante*, etc. (Väänänen 1981: 95). There have been a number of throwaway remarks to this effect (see Sommerfelt 1957: 158–9, Mac Cana 1976: 195), but the matter has yet to be investigated properly.

Compound prepositions are only one way of generating prepositions and refining the meaning of the pre-existing simple forms. For example, the use of prepositional phrases which have become fixed forms is common to all Celtic languages, e.g. OIr *ar chiunn*, W *erbyn* 'against, towards', etc. (Hamp 1975c: 169–70). There may be cases of reduplicated prepositions in Irish, e.g. OIr *cucu* 'to' : simple *co* (but see McCone 1993b). Moreover, there are a number of mysterious forms which occur in Irish conjugated forms which may upon further investigation reflect compounding of prepositions. Furthermore, it remains uncertain whether the Brittonic compound forms are genuine reflections of Vulgar Latin forms or whether they have arisen independently.

4.3   The inter-relationships of the Brittonic languages

The traditional view of the inter-relationship of the Brittonic languages was given in Figure 1.5, the Brittonic section of which is repeated in Figure 4.1 for convenience. As was discussed above (1.3.1), a form of Common Brittonic, usually known as British, was spoken throughout southern Britain in the pre-Roman and Roman periods. To some

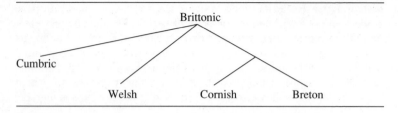

FIGURE 4.1   The traditional inter-relationship of the Brittonic languages

unquantifiable degree its extent was reduced by the impact of Latin and all the social advantages which went with it. But it is clear that in the west and north, forms of British survived and flourished. The establishment of Saxon kingdoms in southern England in the 5th-6th centuries and the subsequent incursions westwards seem to have been partially responsible for the migrations from the south-west peninsula to the Armorican peninsula of Brittany. There is no doubt that Breton is closely related to Cornish and that they form a 'south-west' group. By the end of the 6th century the Saxons had probably reached the Severn and effectively had broken the land route between the south-west peninsula and Wales, though it is not clear what degree of settlement would have been necessary to break the line of communication. Moreover, it is probable that the sea route continued to be an important link for centuries to come. The migrations to Brittany had been going on for the preceding century but from this point on the south-west group was more isolated from the Brittonic dialects further to the north.

The distinctions between Welsh on the one hand and Cornish and Breton on the other would seem then to belong to the 5th and 6th centuries, while features separating Cornish and Breton occur rather later. The evidence can be discussed under the headings of phonology (4.3.1) and morphology (4.3.2).

It may, however, be helpful first to mention one other theory about the origin of Breton which has received some support over the years. There is no doubt that when the migrants arrived in Brittany the peninsula was occupied by natives who would have spoken some kind of Gallo-Romance. The evidence of local names in -ac, a Gallo-Romance usage, which are more dense in the east of the region, suggests that the more remote, less fertile western areas of Brittany were sparsely populated (Jackson 1967a: 25–9, Russell 1988a). None of this is surprising and indeed some of the differences in the Vannetais dialect and other eastern dialects may be due to Romance influence (see 4.2.3 on accent). However, Falc'hun 1963 went so far as to suggest that at the period of the migrations the natives of Armorica still spoke Gaulish and that Breton should be seen as a modern form of Gaulish. But in every significant respect it is clear that Breton is a Brittonic language related to Cornish and Welsh and not descended from Gaulish (Jackson 1967a: 32). Falc'hun did not deny the existence of British features in Breton but he envisaged them spreading from Tréguier in the north to the south coast and largely avoiding the Vannetais dialect. But, as Jackson 1967a: 35 has pointed out, it is impossible to demonstrate that any of the distinguishing features of individual Breton dialects arose before the 10th–11th centuries; most seem to have arisen much later.

4.3.1 Phonology[14]

The Brittonic cluster *-iiá-, often from *-isá-, gave OW -aia- but OCo, OB -oia- (see Table 4.9 (a) for examples). Similarly, Brittonic /ǫ:/ was diphthongized in Welsh to /au/ but gave CB /œ:/ (unstressed /e/), e.g. MW maur, MB mur, meuur 'big'. In these cases both groups have developed divergently. But in others one group has innovated and the other preserves the original situation. For example, there are a series of vowel reductions in the pre-accent shift unaccented syllable which are unique to Welsh, namely /i/ and /u/ > /ə/ but in Cornish and Breton they continue as /e/ and /o/ respectively and the quality of the vowels is preserved (see Table 4.9 (b) for examples). Similarly, inherited clusters of -ntr- and -ntl- gave -thr and -thl in Welsh but were retained in Cornish and Breton (see Table 4.9 (c) for examples).

Table 4.9: Examples of sound changes which distinguish one Brittonic language from another

---

(a) *-iiá- > OW -aia-, OCo, OB -oia-
MW gaeaf, OCo goyf, OB gaoñv 'winter' < *giiámo- (Gaul Giamon-, etc.)
MnW haearn, OCo hoern, OB hoiarn 'iron' < *isárno- (Gaul Isarnus)

(b) /i/ and /u/ > W /ə/, Co, B /e/ and /o/
W ynyd /'ənɪd/, Co enes, B ened 'beginning of Lent' < Lat inítium
W ychen /'əχɛn/, Co ohan, MB ouhen, oc'hen 'oxen' < *uksénes.

(c) -ntr-, -ntl- > only in W -thr, -thl
W cethr, Co center, B kentr 'point, goad' < Lat centrum
OW ithr, Co yntre, B entre 'betwe͜en' < *inter

(d) *-rg-, *-lg- > Co, B /rχ lχ/, W /rɣ lɣ/
OW helgha ti 'you hunt', MW helya 'hunt', OCo helhiat 'hunter', B di-elc'hat 'lose breath' < *selg-
W llwry, MCo lergh, MnB lerc'h 'track' < *lorgo-

(e) MCo -/d/ to -/z/
OCo dauat, MC daves, W dafad, B dañvad 'sheep'
Co cas, W cad 'battle' < *catu-

On the other hand, Welsh can preserve inherited features, while Cornish and Breton innovate; for example, Brittonic clusters of *-rg- and *-lg- gave /rɣ/ and /lɣ/ after spirantization (Russell 1985a) and by the 6th century had developed towards /rχ/ and /lχ/ in Cornish and Breton. But Welsh seems to have preserved the /ɣ/ until around the 12th century when it was reduced to /i̯/, hence the Old Welsh spellings with -g and the Middle and Modern Welsh with -y (see Table 4.9 (d) for examples).

At a later stage, probably around the 11th century, Middle Cornish independently assibilated final /d/ to /z/, written s (see Table 4.9 (e) for examples). Likewise, perhaps at a slightly later stage (Jackson 1953: 507–8), -nt and -lt gave MCo -ns and -ls, e.g. argans : MW ariant 'silver', guins : MW gwynt 'wind', etc.

Breton also shows a series of distinct innovations. Clusters of /tt/ from various origins regularly gave /θ/ in late Brittonic and it was preserved in Welsh and Cornish but in Breton it first became /s/ in the 12th century and subsequently /z/, e.g. Lat littera > W llyther, Co lither, B lizer. At around the same period, /ð/ gave /z/, e.g. barz 'poet' < /barðo/ (cf. W bardd /barð/). The change of /s/ to /z/ is a forerunner of a general shift in about the 15th–16th centuries affecting /f/, /χ/ and /s/ which is conventionally called 'new lenition' (Jackson 1967a: 360–75; see 7.4.4 below). 'New lenition' effectively caused the voicing of these continuants in intervocalic position, i.e. /f/ > /v/, /χ/ > /ɦ/ and /s/ > /z/ (/θ/ had already gone to /s/ by this stage). It occurred in all the contexts where the old Brittonic lenition had operated, i.e. where the unvoiced sound stood between voiced sounds, at this stage usually vowels or /m/, /n/, /l/ or /r/. This caused some re-arrangement of categories; for example, he 'her' caused new lenition because it ended in a vowel, thus he venn 'her head', but it had not caused old lenition because at that stage it had not ended in a vowel; compare W ei phenn 'her head'. The dialectal evidence for 'new lenition' is patchy, partly due to its haphazard marking in the orthography, and also partly because it did not develop fully in all the dialects (Jackson 1967a: 371–5).

4.3.2 Morphology

As was indicated in 4.2.6, the verbal systems of the individual languages have preserved substantial elements of the original Proto-Celtic system. Interest at this point lies in those areas where the languages have innovated. In the verbal system this largely consists of replacing synthetic forms with analytic constructs and filling out the inventory of tenses often in response to external stimuli such as the verbal systems of Latin and French.

Welsh has probably gone furthest in replacing synthetic forms with periphrastic analytic constructs; the modern spoken language regularly uses a periphrastic present consisting of part of the verb 'to be' + yn +

verbal noun, e.g. *mae e'n chwarae* 'he is playing/he plays'. The synthetic forms remain as more formal alternatives, or in some tenses as modals (see 5.4.3 for details). Similarly, it has developed a periphrastic perfect consisting of the verb 'to be' + *wedi* (lit. 'after') + verbal noun, e.g. *mae e wedi chwarae* 'he has played'; it has replaced the inherited form using the particle *ry* (= OIr *ro*) + preterite which is still found in Middle Welsh, e.g. *ry welsom* 'we have seen' (D. S. Evans 1964: 106–9) and also in Cornish and Middle Breton, e.g. MCo *re gollas* 'it has lost', MB *ra-z remedo* 'he has healed you'. The periphrasis with *wedi* is comparable to Modern Irish forms using *thar éis* (Munster/Connacht) or *i ndéidh* (Donegal) 'after' (see 3.4.3). In Middle Cornish a periphrasis was constructed out of the verb 'to be' + past participle, e.g. *ancow sur yw dyuythys* 'certain death has come', *govy pan vef genys* 'alas that I have been born' (H. Lewis 1946: 49–50). This pattern can be paralleled from Latin and Romance languages and may well have been influenced by them.

Periphrastic forms have also been developed in Breton for perfect and pluperfect and seem to be modelled on the French pattern of 'to have' + past participle, e.g. perfect *kavet am eus* 'I have found', *kavet en deus* 'he has found', pluperfect *kavet am boa* 'I had found', *kavet en doa* 'he had found'. Note that the verb 'to have' is itself periphrastic in Breton (see 1.4.2.3). Its French model is made clear by the use of the verb 'to be' as the auxiliary with certain intransitive verbs, e.g. *kouezet eo* 'he has fallen', *kouezet e oa* 'he had fallen'. While the Breton perfect and pluperfect can be put down to French influence, Mac Cana 1976 has argued that the Welsh synthetic pluperfect which consists of the preterite stem + imperfect endings was modelled on the Latin pluperfect, e.g. MW *carassei* = Lat *amaverat*. The Modern Welsh periphrastic pluperfect uses the *wedi* + verbal noun construction with the imperfect of the verb 'to be'.

So far we have been concerned with aspects of the verbal system where the innovation is restricted to a single language but it is probable that innovations began at an earlier period. Cornish and Breton share a tendency to prepose pronominal subjects in unmarked sentences, e.g. MCo *my a kyrgh a gwas* 'I attack the boy', *ty a wra a les* 'you cause his death', B *te a welo* 'you will see', *me a had* 'I sow', *e vreudeur a hades* 'his brother sowed'. Irrespective of the number or person or the subject the verb is always 3rd singular. However, there is agreement when the verb is negative, e.g. *me ne hadan ket* 'I do not sow', *e vreudeur ne hadjont ket* 'his brothers did not sow'. This may not be a south-west Brittonic innovation; in Welsh a similar pattern is used emphatically, e.g. *mi a wnaeth ef* 'I did it', and preposed subjects were quite common in Old Welsh. Relics may survive in the Modern Welsh particles *mi* and *fe* which precede declarative verbs (see 5.5.2) and which are probably pronouns in origin. It is, moreover, striking that in south-eastern dialects of Welsh a subject pronoun precedes the verb, e.g. *nw welan* 'they see' (Mac Cana 1973: 117–8, C. H. Thomas 1975–6; see 9.1.2.2 below for further discussion).

Another periphrastic formation which may be of Brittonic age is the pattern of verbal noun + verb 'to do' (MW *gwnaeth/oruc*, MCo *ra*, *wruk*, B *ra*, etc.). They are very common in Middle Welsh narrative prose as an unmarked form, e.g. *kyuodi a oruc* 'he arose' (lit. 'rising he did'), and a similar construction is used in modern northern dialects for emphasis (Fife 1986a; see also 5.4.3 and 8.3.1.5). A similar construction is very common both in Cornish and Breton, e.g. MCo *my a ra y dybry* 'I eat it', *pan wruk an bara terry* 'when he broke the bread', *sevel war tyr veneges a wreth* 'you are standing on blessed land' (H. Lewis 1946: 49 = Zimmer 1990a: 46), MB *monet a raf* 'I go', *coll poen a ret* 'you are wasting your labour', MnB *c'hoarzhin a ra ar baotred* 'the boys laugh', *lenn ul levr a ran* 'I read a book'. Although emphasis may be placed on the initial phrase, it looks very much like another way of avoiding conjugation of every verb by using conjugated auxiliaries to carry the grammatical markers. There is a difference in the usage between the languages but it is possible that the seeds of this construction can be traced back to the Brittonic period; a similar pattern can be used in Irish but it is not nearly so widespread (3.4.3). In passing, we may also note the wide development of auxiliary usage in English as against other Germanic languages.

Independent innovations in nominal morphology are less common. One area of interest is the development of plurals. With the loss of final syllables we have seen that there was a tendency to re-mark the singular/plural distinction. All the Brittonic languages also create singulatives to refer to single occurrences of things which naturally occur in the plural, e.g. W *sêr* 'stars' : *seren* 'star', etc. Welsh operates with a relatively simple system with only a few productive plural markers, such as *-au/-eu* and *-(y)on*. But in Breton a very complex system has developed. Trépos 1957 has discussed them in detail. Figure 4.2 gives some idea of the complexities involved. The interplay of singulatives based on plurals which are then themselves pluralized is particularly striking. The patterns are not only created by suffixation but also by prefixation to mark duals (*daou-*) and singulatives (*penn-*).

4.3.3   The Brittonic family tree revisited

The traditional view, as outlined in 4.3 above and presented in Jackson 1953, has a south-west Brittonic group separating from west Brittonic in about the 6th century. Despite the uncertainty as to when the land link between Wales and the south-west was broken, there is no doubt that there was considerable contact if only across the Bristol Channel after this period and particularly between Wales and Brittany, well documented in the early saints' lives (W. Davies 1982: 141–68). Jackson's

Examples: *ed* 'wheat', *to* 'roof', *ster* 'stars', *bugel* 'child', *glin* 'knee', *pesk* 'fish', *daou-* 'two . . .', *penn-* 'a single . . .'

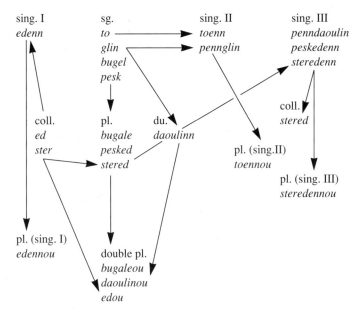

sg. = singular; sing. = singulative; pl. = plural; coll. = collective; du. = dual; sing. I = based on a coll.; sing. II = based on a sg.; sing. III = based on a pl.

FIGURE 4.2   Plural formation in Breton (based on Trépos 1957: 277).

thesis assumes a single Welsh language with later explicable dialect differences within it (though they do not figure greatly in his main discussion of the subject (Jackson 1953)). However, it is beginning to emerge from recent work that the fundamental dialect boundaries of Modern Welsh may well reflect very old linguistic divisions (P. W. Thomas 1989 and 1993). What also emerges is that the some early features of southern Welsh dialects have similarities with Cornish and Breton. Much of this is as yet uncertain but three examples may prove helpful. We have already noted that south-east dialects of Welsh in Glamorgan have an initial subject pronoun similar to that in Cornish and Breton (Mac Cana 1973: 119, C. H. Thomas 1975–6; see 5.5.2.3 below). It is not clear whether this is a relic of a pattern which has disappeared elsewhere in Welsh or a late independent innovation in this dialect (see 9.1.2.2). Part of the problem is that it is difficult to locate the Old Welsh texts where this pattern occurs; it may turn out, for example, that they originate in this area anyway, which perhaps would indicate a local innovation.

Secondly, Russell 1990: 39–60 has discussed the alternation of Welsh suffixes with and without /į/ (see also P. W. Thomas 1989: 292–4). It seems that the modern distribution of northern suffixes with /į/ and southern forms without /į/ can be traced at least as early as Middle Welsh (see 5.1.2). Moreover, in a significant number of cases the evidence of *i*-affection indicates that the southern dialects have lost /į/ rather than simply opting for a suffix without /į/ at all. Parallel treatments of -C*į*- can be found in Breton and again it is possible that we are not dealing with independent parallel developments.

Finally, the treatment of final consonantal clusters in southern Welsh resembles that of Cornish and Breton (Russell 1984); for example, final -*dl* tends to be simplified to -/dəl/ or -/dal/ in northern Welsh but in the south there is an assimilation to the following continuant, thus -/ðəl/, e.g. SW *anal* 'breath' < *anaðl* : B *alazn* < *anazl* (by metathesis), SW /hweðel/ 'tale, news' : OCo *chwethlow*, MB *hoazl*, etc. (Russell 1984: 105).

If these cases are taken seriously, then various possibilities present themselves. They could be explained away as contact features rather than representatives of a genetic affinity. Alternatively, if we accept them as hinting at a genetic link, the family tree may need rewriting along the lines of Figure 4.3. On the other hand, it would be possible to move away from an arboreal view of the situation and see a single continuum of Brittonic from Scotland to Cornwall (and subsequently to Brittany) with the central dialects of Wales sharing some features with northern dialects and others with southern dialects. In Welsh terms, it is hardly surprising that such features are difficult to detect since the literary language in the modern period has been heavily influenced and dominated by a northern standard. In geographical terms the Bristol Channel would not have been any more of an obstacle than the mountains of Central Wales and certainly easier to cross.

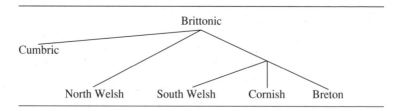

FIGURE 4.3　An alternative Brittonic family tree

Notes

1. For the post-Roman inscriptions from Britain, see the basic collection in Nash-Williams 1950. See now Okasha 1993 for a corpus of inscriptions from south-west Britain. For a wide ranging, interpretative study, see C. Thomas 1994.
2. Sims-Williams' revision of Jackson also involves a new analysis of the process of lenition (see this volume, 4.2.1 and Chapter 6). Whether his views will be generally accepted remains to be seen; for reviews, see Charles-Edwards 1992: 148–53, Russell 1991–2: 266–8 and Harvey 1992.
3. For the early stages of the debate, see Greene 1971 and Jackson 1973–4. The matter gained fresh momentum following the work of Wendy Davies 1979 on the *Book of Llandaf* (J. G. Evans and Rhŷs 1893); see Koch 1985–6 and Sims-Williams 1991.

   For a general survey on the sources of Old Welsh, see Jackson 1953: 42–59; the dating of the texts should be treated with care. He is more dismissive of the *Book of Llandaf* than more recent writers and dates the 'Surexit' memorandum too early; see Jenkins and Owen 1983: 56–61. Loth 1884 contains all the Old Welsh, Old Cornish and Old Breton material found up until the date of publication; it should be used with care as explanations are often outdated and have been superseded. In particular, note that for Loth 'breton' means 'Brittonic', while 'armoricain' refers to Breton.

   Morris-Jones 1913 remains the best historically directed grammar of Welsh despite weaknesses in certain areas. The Brittonic and Celtic background is presented in Pedersen 1909–13 and H. Lewis and Pedersen 1961. For Middle Welsh, D. S. Evans 1964 is by far the best, though Strachan 1908 and Baudiš 1924 remain useful. For the modern language, S. J. Williams 1980 gives the clearest account of the formal and literary register of the language; see also the introductions to the language by Thorne 1985 and J. Davies 1993. Two grammars of Welsh have recently appeared, Thorne 1993 and King 1993, both claiming in their titles to be 'comprehensive'; King, however, concentrates exclusively on the modern colloquial language in its written form (see Andrews 1994 for a less than favourable review), while Thorne also considers more literary registers. The main dictionary, though as yet unfinished, is *Geiriadur Prifysgol Cymru* (R. J. Thomas *et al.* 1950– (up to *O*–)). The best shorter dictionary is H. H. Evans and Thomas 1968. The only two reverse dictionaries of a Celtic language, R Stephens 1978 and Zimmer 1987, have to do with Welsh; for reviews of the latter see Russell 1988d and R Stephens 1989–90 (see also Zimmer 1992 and Russell 1993c).
4. For a survey of the medieval literature, see Jarman and Hughes 1976 and 1979. For a history of Welsh literature, see Parry 1962, while J. Stephens 1986 provides all the necessary background detail. Translations of early Welsh poetry can be found in Clancy 1965, 1970, Conran 1986, C. A. McKenna 1991 and Loomis and Johnston 1992.
5. The 1991 Census figures and the general statistical trends are now discussed by Aitchison and Carter 1994. For a survey of 19th–20th-century Welsh literature, see Parry 1962: 292–373 (with an appendix on the 20th century by H. I. Bell at pp. 374–498); see also Johnson 1992.
6. For a general discussion, see B. Thomas and Thomas 1989. A. R. Thomas 1973 provides a series of maps for individual words and phrases. Most

work on individual dialects remains in thesis form; a full list can be found in B. Thomas and Thomas 1989: 157–69. Among modern studies in print, note Awbery 1986a. *Cardiff Working Papers in Welsh Linguistics* offers a useful forum for discussion of specific questions. Note also the collections of articles in Ball and Jones 1984 and Ball 1988a.

7. There is no full-scale study of Welsh place names; I. Williams 1945 is a brief survey. There are regional studies by Pierce 1968 (Dinas Powys), Lloyd-Jones 1928 (Caernarfon), Charles 1993 (Pembrokeshire), etc. Gazetteers are provided by E. Davies 1967 and Richards 1969. There is a bibliography of Welsh local name studies in J. E. C. Williams and Hughes 1988: 131–44. The Melville Richards Archive of Place Names is held at University College, Bangor.

8. The best grammar for the early form of the language remains Lewis 1946 (= Zimmer 1990a). For a more general, though old, study, see Jenner 1904. There are two dictionaries now available: Nance 1978, which should, how-ever, be used with care as it contains modernized versions of Old Cornish forms and reconstructions from Welsh and Breton, and George 1993b (in the new orthography known as *Kernewek Kemmyn* 'Common Cornish'). For further bibliography, see J. E. C. Williams and Hughes 1988: 49–53, H. Lewis 1946: 1–6 and Wakelin 1975: 78–82. For general discussions of the language, see A. R. Thomas 1992b, George 1993a, Price 1992d (which also considers literature written in Cornish).

9. See Padel 1985 and 1988. For the spread of English, see Wakelin 1975.

10. For the glosses, see C. Evans and Fleuriot 1985 (with the comments of Lambert 1986) and the grammar largely based upon them, Fleuriot 1964. See also Loth 1884 with the reservations expressed above, n. 3. Loth 1890 contains a still useful collection of texts from all periods. For a bibliogra-phy on the early period, see J. E. C. Williams and Hughes 1988: 53–66. As for grammars, for Modern Breton see Hemon 1941, Kervella 1947, Press 1986. A historical overview is provided by Hemon 1975. For Middle Breton, see Lewis and Piette 1966. Hemon 1976– is the best dictionary for the whole language; see also Delaporte 1979 and Hemon 1978. Ernault 1895–6 is still useful for Middle Breton. For general discussions of the lan-guage, see Ternes 1992, Humphreys 1992, J. Stephens 1993.

11. Loth 1890: 267–319 contains a collection of texts extracted from journals, though he prints only texts, even when the original publication also had a translation. More accessible texts are the *Christmas Hymns* (Hemon 1956), the *Fall of Jerusalem* (Hemon and Le Menn 1969) and three Middle Breton poems (Hemon 1962). For bibliographies of Breton literature, see Hemon 1947; Le Bihan 1957, which is in origin an exhibition catalogue, is also very useful. See also J. E. C. Williams and Hughes 1988: 53–4.

12. For the raw dialect material, see Le Roux 1924–63. For a detailed phono-logical study based on it, Jackson 1967a is unsurpassable. There are many individual studies; see Le Clerc 1911 (Tréguier), Fleuriot 1967 (Vannetais), Sommerfelt 1978 (St Pol-de-Léon), Ternes 1970 (Île de Groix), M McKenna 1988 (Guémené-sur-Scoff), Jackson 1960–1 (Plougrescant).

13. There may be intermediate stages between, for example, /k/ and its lenited counterpart /g/ depending on which theory of lenition one espouses; see Koch 1990: 199–202, and 7.4.4 below.

14. For a full list of features, see Jackson 1953: 19–22.

Chapter 5

Welsh

5.0 Introduction

The linguistic situation of Welsh differs from that of Irish in that there are in Wales several registers of standard language beside the regional dialects.[1] In Ireland, as we have seen in Chapter 3, there is no widely accepted standard form. But, while for Irish numerous dialect descriptions are available, for Welsh there are few thorough descriptions of a single dialect in print.[2] The following description, therefore, attempts to provide an account which does justice to the variation in the language. The phonology must necessarily concentrate on the spoken forms but in other sections attention is paid to the literary language. The description considers the language from the point of view of the traditional categories of phonology, morphology and syntax. It does not take a strong theoretical stance to the evidence but opportunity is taken, where appropriate, to consider studies of Welsh which have used specific theoretical viewpoints.

5.1 Types of Welsh

It is a commonplace of language that native speakers have a wide range of registers at their disposal which they deploy in the appropriate contexts, and conversely that second language speakers find it difficult to distinguish registers and use them effectively. In any language a more formal register is likely to be used in talking to the bank manager than to one's best friend. The medium of communication can also have an effect; a written communication of any kind is likely to take up more time and therefore give more room for thought than a spoken conversation, but it can still take place in different registers. Native speakers are also adept at style-switching; Ball, Griffiths *et al.* 1988: 187 discuss a sermon broadcast on Radio Cymru (Radio Wales) in which the minister deliberately changed the register when the subjects of his sermon, a father and two sons, were 'speaking'. It is, therefore, hardly surprising that native speakers of Welsh have available to them a wide range of registers of both spoken and written Welsh and that any kind of classification will hardly do justice to their complexity. The point was well made by S Lewis 1968: 6:

> The truth of the matter is that every monoglot Welsh speaker, up to 1914 and in some degree up to 1938, was a bilingual person. He had the language of his locality, the language of the street and the quarry and the pit and the rugby field and the shop. He also had the language of the *seiat* and the prayer meeting and the meeting of the brethren and the literary meeting. . . And the ordinary Welsh speaker . . . never got them confused. He knew which language to use wherever he might be (my translation).

To a large extent he was talking about different registers of the spoken language but the same can apply to the written language. Roberts and Jones 1974 argued that Welsh can be seen as having a tripartite distinction of the literary language, the common standard spoken language and the local dialects, each with its variety of registers and each having both a written and a spoken realization. It is a crude distinction in so far as no set of distinctions can do justice to the complexities involved but it forms a useful starting point.

5.1.1   Modern literary Welsh
The literary language has been considered in this light by D. G. Jones 1988, who in trying to define his subject points up the significant differences between it and other forms of Welsh; he observes that differences have arisen 'the like of which English, for all its world-wide distribution, has never seen' (1988: 147). The differences, which are considered in detail below, tend to arise from the conservative nature of the literary language. For example, in its phonology it preserves final unstressed diphthongs which were monophthongized in speech centuries before, e.g. LW *trafodaeth* 'discussion': Powys and south-west -/ɛθ/ : south-east and north-west -/aθ/. It preserves final -/t/ in 3rd plural verbs and final -/v/, even though they were probably not pronounced after the 9th or 10th centuries, e.g. LW *cyntaf* 'first', *ydynt* 'they are' : SpW *cynta* /'kənta/, *ydyn* /'ədɨn/. But it is in the morphology, and particularly verb formation, that the greatest gulf lies between the two types. One example will suffice at present: LW *bûm* 'I was' (preterite) only rarely occurs in the spoken language where it has been overtaken variously by *bues i*, *buis i*, *buo i*, *buom i* (the stem being either /bi/- or /bɨ/- depending on the dialect). Moreover, just as there is no single form of spoken Welsh, so given the range of material which is written in Welsh there is no single form of literary Welsh. Features which may be acceptable in a 'high' literary style would be regarded as far too rar-

efied in another; D. G. Jones 1988: 144 and 147 gives the examples of some bare-stem 3rd singular forms, such as *etyb* 'he answers' : VN *ateb*, *ceidw* 'he keeps' : VN *cadw*, where there are complex vowel changes, and *pioedd*, the past tense to *piau* 'whose is?', as examples of 'high' literary language. It must also be remembered that literary Welsh can also have a spoken manifestation and is not simply a written form of the language. Ball, Griffiths, *et al.* 1988: 186, in a discussion of broadcast Welsh, make a useful set of distinctions between radio material which is

(a) written: read as if written, e.g. news broadcast
(b) written: read as if spontaneous, e.g. broadcast of religious service
(c) spontaneous, e.g. general entertainment.

Type (a) is a good example of the spoken version of literary Welsh and would be characterized by formal features such as the plural markers /aɨ/ as against a more informal /a/ or /ɛ/, the use of the interrogative particle *a* (see 5.5.2.2), and impersonal verbs. On the other hand, the type (b) example, as noted above, contained some formal language but also much more style-switching, especially in the sermon.

5.1.2 Modern Welsh dialects

At the other end of the continuum there are the local dialects of Welsh. A glance through the bibliography of B. Thomas and Thomas 1989 shows that the detailed survey and study of Welsh dialects has been under way for just over a century. This highlights one problem that any dialect survey has; full surveys are extremely time-consuming and become out of date very quickly. For many areas of Wales the most recent full survey, especially in the north, dates from early this century (see B. Thomas and Thomas 1989:85). In that time considerable headway has been made in establishing the main dialect boundaries.[3] There is no doubt that the main dialect distinction is between North and South Wales, but within these areas finer distinctions can be drawn (see Map 5.1 overleaf with illustrative examples in Table 5.1). These distinctions are based on the dialectal usage of different lexical items and are, therefore, relatively easy to trace (see A. R. Thomas 1973). The examples in Table 5.1 exemplify the relatively crude dialect divisions on the basis of lexical differences; Map 5.2 on p. 142, still largely based on lexical material, indicates some of the finer divisions and shows that the situation is very much more complex.

The isoglosses rarely coincide and there are some areas, notably between the rivers Dyfi and the Ystwyth in mid-Wales (marked A in Map 5.1), which show a mixture of forms associating it both with the south and the midland area just to its north (see Table 5.2). Similarly, G. E. Jones 1988 has shown that Breconshire (area B in Map 5.1) is an important linking area between south-east Wales and mid-Wales; while

MAP 5.1   The major dialect divisions of Welsh. See B. Thomas and Thomas
1989: 28, and A. R. Thomas 1973: Figure 5.

KEY
1 North-west   5 South-west
2 North-east   6 South-east
3 West Midlands   A and B Areas of transition between dialects
4 East Midlands

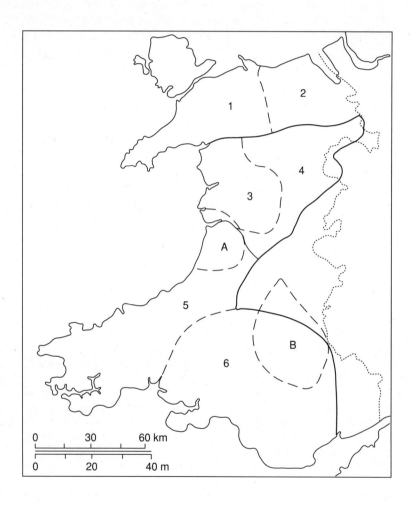

TABLE 5.1   Lexical items illustrating Maps 5.1 and 5.2

(a) South (5 and 6)	: North (1–4)	
march	*stalwyn*	'stallion'
mamgu, tadcu	*nain, taid*	'grandmother/father'
(b) South-west (5)	: South-east (6)	
(*lla(e)th*) *sgim*	*la(e)th glas*	'skimmed milk'
claw	*perth*	'hedge'
(c) Midlands (3–4)	: North (1–2) : South (5–6)	
bwtri	*tŷ llaeth* *lla(e)thdy*	'dairy'
	dêri	
(d) West midlands (3) :	East midlands (4)	
shetin	*g(w)rych*	'hedge'
torion	*pe(i)swyn/brot*	'chaff'
(e) North-west (1)	: North-east (2)	
crysmas/gwasgod	*syrcyn*	'vest'
morgrug	*mawion*	'ants'
(and elsewhere in Wales)		
(f) North (1–2)	: rest of Wales (3–6)	
gwana	*ystod*	'swath'
grisia(u)	*sta(e)r*	'stairs'
(g) North-east and	: rest of Wales (1, 3, 5–6)	
east midlands (2, 4)		
cocyn	*mwdwl*	'mound of hay'
gw(r)thban	*blanced*	'blanket'

southern parts of the region are closely related in dialect to parts of Glamorgan and Gwent, features of the dialect of north Breconshire, e.g. the presence of the close central vowel /ɨ/ (see below), connect it with northern dialects. Exploration further north is, however, ruled out by the major inroads made by English into Radnorshire.

When one turns to the phonology and morphology of Welsh, it is far harder to make the fine distinctions which are extractable from the lexical evidence and there is a tendency to regard features as being generally 'northern' or 'southern' unless they have specific regional characteristics. B. Thomas and Thomas 1989: 30–81 devote two chapters to a discussion of various features. At this point the following examples will not require too detailed an understanding of Welsh phonology or morphology.

A major north/south dialect distinction concerns the central vowels (see below 5.2.1–2). Historically Welsh had two central vowels

MAP 5.2   The minor dialect divisions of Welsh. See A. R. Thomas 1973:
Figure 6

KEY

1 Anglesey	8 Lower midlands
2 Lleyn	9 Teifi valley
3 North-west mainland	10, 11, 12 Pembrokeshire
4 Conway-Clwyd	13 Tywi valley
5 Dyfi	14 Llwchwr-Nedd
6 Tanat-Fyrnwy	15 Tywi-Usk highland
7 South-east midlands	16 East Glamorgan

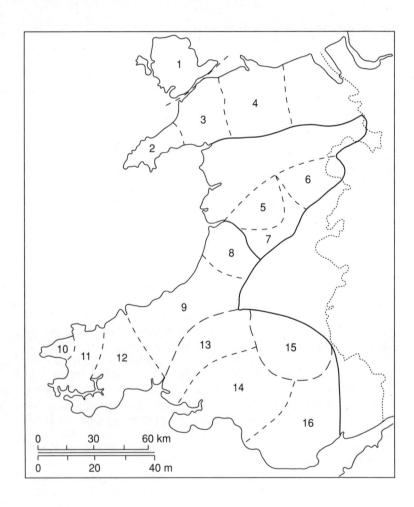

TABLE 5.2   Examples illustrating the intermediate status of area A

North	South	Area A	
allan	*mâs*	*allan/mâs*	'out'
i fyny	*lan*	*i fyny/lan*	'up'

See A. R. Thomas 1973: 16–19.

rounded /ʉ/ and unrounded /ɨ/, which were orthographically distinguished by *u* and *y* respectively in the more standard forms of Middle
Welsh orthography, e.g. MW *ty* /tɨ/ 'house' : *tu* /tʉ/ 'side', and both
were distinct from /i/, e.g. *ti* 'you' (sg.). The distinction was still identifiable in the 16th century but was clearly fast disappearing (G. E.
Jones 1982) though the distinction has remained fixed in the spelling to the
present day. In Modern Welsh dialects the merger is almost complete:
in the north /ʉ/ and /ɨ/ have merged to give /ɨ/, while in the south the
remaining single central vowel went on to merge with /i/ (for remaining
traces of the distinction, see 5.2.5 below). The upshot is that in northern
Welsh the examples in Table 5.3 (a) are minimal contrastive pairs. But
in southern Welsh all four forms would contain the vowel /i/. To put it
another way, *tu* 'side', *tŷ* 'house' and *ti* 'you' (sg.) are indistinguishable
in southern Welsh but in northern Welsh the first two are indistinguishable from each other but they are distinct from the last (see Table 5.3
(b)). The same situation operated whether the vowels were phonetically
long or short. The above examples involve phonetically long vowels
(see 5.2.1 below). The short vowels are qualitatively different but the
same mergers occur (see Table 5.3 (c)). The occurrence of /ɨ/ in
Llanwrtyd in north Breconshire is part of the argument claiming that
the traditional north/south line for this feature is drawn too far north (G.
E. Jones 1989–90, B. Thomas and Thomas 1989: 32).

TABLE 5.3   Examples illustrating distinctions among the central vowels in
Welsh

(a) *gwir* /gwir/ 'true' : *gwŷr* /gwɨr/ 'men'
     ti /ti/ 'you' (sg.) : *tŷ* /tɨ/ 'house'

(b)		*tu* 'side'	*tŷ* 'house'	*ti* 'you' (sg.)
	NW	/tɨ/	/tɨ/	/tɨ/
	SW	/ti/	/ti/	/ti/

(c)		*pump* 'five'	*gwynt* 'wind'	*print* 'print'
	NW	/pɨmp/	/gwɨnt/	/prɪnt/
	SW	/pɪmp/	/gwɪnt/	/prɪnt/

TABLE 5.4 Examples illustrating the dialect variation in the realization of
vowels in final syllables

	NW/SE	NE/SW
hanner 'half'	/'(h)annar/ .	/'hannɛr/
gafael 'take'	/'gaval/	/'gavɛl/
pethau 'things'	/'pɛθa/	/'pɛθɛ/
cadair 'chair'	/'kadar/	/'kadɛr/

B. Thomas and Thomas 1989: 40–1.

It is well known that south-east dialects lack /h/ (C. H. Thomas
1975–6: 353–4). This has a number of knock-on effects such as the lack
of the voiceless alveolar trill /r̥/ written *rh* and the voiceless nasals [m̥]
and [n̥] which occur in the mutation systems of other dialects. It also
affects the articulation elsewhere found as /hw/ in the south and /χw/ in
the north; initial *chw-*, as in *chwarae* 'play', *chwech* 'six', is usually
realized as /hw/ in the south, e.g. /'hwarɛ/ and /hwɛχ/, though both
forms occur in the area between the Dyfi and the Aeron. However, in
the south-east they are realized as /'wara/ and /wɛχ/.

The example of *chwarae*, SW /'hwarɛ/, S-EW /'wara/, NW /'χwarɛ/,
points up another dialectal feature. When the diphthong /ai̯/ (SW /aɪ/),
variously written *au*, *ae*, *ai* or *e*, occurred in the final unaccented syllable of a dissyllable, it was reduced to a monophthong. But there is a
curious dialectal split whereby the north-west and south-east realize
this vowel as /a/, but elsewhere, i.e. the north-east and south-west, it is
realized as /ɛ/ (see Table 5.4).

A feature which is restricted entirely to the south-east is 'provection'
(W *calediad* lit. 'hardening'). Essentially it amounts to the devoicing of
voiced stops which close the accented syllable, e.g. /'bikal/ : non-
provected /'bigal/ : *bugail* 'shepherd'; /dəχ'məki/ : non-provected
/dəχ'məgi/ : *dychmygu* 'imagine' (for details see C. H. Thomas
1975–6: 360–4). S. E. Thomas 1988 studied the phenomenon in
Ystalyfera in 1981–3 and concludes 'dialect is becoming less and less a
part of the speech of the area, and *calediad*, as a variation of dialect, is
quickly disappearing too' (S. E. Thomas 1988: 94).

A final case concerns patterns of word formation. Welsh makes use
of a series of suffixes to form plurals, adjectives, verbal nouns, agent
nouns, etc. Most of these suffixes begin with a vowel, e.g. *-og* (adj.),
-on, *-au* (realized as -/a/ or -/ɛ/) (pl.), etc. There is a general but not
absolute distinction, which can be traced back to Middle Welsh,
between northern and southern usage; in the north the suffix is regularly preceded by *i* /i/ but not in the south, e.g. NW *corddiad* : SW
corddad 'churning', NW *blewiach* : SW *blewach* 'hairs'.[4]

In the following discussion further dialectal material will be used to supplement the discussion.

5.1.3 *Cymraeg Byw* and standard spoken Welsh

The controversy which arose over *Cymraeg Byw* 'Living Welsh' in the 1960s and 1970s is of direct significance for the discussion of different types of Welsh (see C. Davies 1988). Between 1964 and 1970 three booklets entitled *Cymraeg Byw* appeared. Their aim was to define the main features of standard spoken Welsh, the middle area of the continuum defined above. While it attempted to define a pre-existing form of the language, as used by broadcasters, preachers, etc. throughout the country, it was accused by its detractors of creating an artificial dialect. A second focus for attack was the relationship between using *Cymraeg Byw* to teach Welsh as a second language and its use by native speakers. R. M. Jones 1965 in his own language course *Cymraeg i'r Oedolion* 'Welsh for Adults' was clear that standard spoken Welsh was not an end in itself but a bridgehead into literary and dialectal forms of the language. But elsewhere *Cymraeg Byw* was being used by the Schools Broadcasting Council for Wales in TV and radio programmes for first and second language pupils, and in children's magazines. A further criticism voiced notably by C. H. Thomas 1966, 1967 and 1979 is the dialectal mixture which emerges in *Cymraeg Byw* (see also D. G. Jones 1988: 147–9) with its eclectic mixture of features from different, largely southern, dialects, such as lack of /h/ from the south-east and lack of /s/ in past tenses. The point made by Thomas is that there is no need for a new standard spoken language as one already existed and that it is not even necessary for second language learners. However, as a bridgehead to the real language for learners, a simpler tidied-up form of the language is often very welcome, as C. Davies explains:

> The overriding concern of every successful language teacher is to establish a language 'platform' in the shortest possible time, thus enabling the learner to put his acquired language to practical use within the linguistic group he is seeking to join. . . Whereas it is conceded that every learner will eventually have to understand *euthum*, *i/ethym*, *i/etho i* and *es i* (differing forms of the 1st person past tense of *mynd* 'to go') it is maintained that only the last form is necessary in the initial stages (1988: 206–7).

The conclusion would be, then, that *Cymraeg Byw* has its place as a way into the language for learners. It is not a replacement for any notional standard spoken Welsh. Perceptions of the latter vary. It is clear that there are levels of spoken language intended for public consumption; they do contain general dialectal features, i.e. southern or northern, but not to the extent that it would make comprehension difficult for any part of the Welsh speaking population.

5.2 Phonology

5.2.1 The framework of the phonology

The Welsh of South Wales has a set of eleven vowel phonemes, while
northern Welsh, with two extra central vowels (see 5.1.2 above), has
thirteen (see Table 5.5). All dialects have a set of diphthongs based on
/ɪ/ and /ʊ/ (see Table 5.6).[5] In addition, northern dialects have sets of
combinations based on /ɨ/ and /ɨ/. It emerges that there are significant
differences in the pronunciation of diphthongs in northern and southern
Welsh. The full range of consonantal phonemes is presented in Table
5.7 on p. 148. This system is common to all dialects except for the loss
of /h/ in south-east dialects (C. H. Thomas 1975–6: 353–4).

Table 5.5   Welsh vowel phonemes

Southern Welsh		Northern Welsh	
Phoneme	*Grapheme(s)*	*Phoneme*	*Grapheme(s)*
/i/	i î	/i/	i î
	u û	/ɪ/	i
	y ŷ	/e/	e ê
/ɪ/	i u y	/ɛ/	e
/e/	e ê	/ɑ/	a â
/ɛ/	e	/a/	a
/ɑ/	a â	/o/	o ô
/a/	a	/ɔ/	o
/o/	o ô	/u/	w ŵ
/ɔ/	o	/ʊ/	w
/u/	w ŵ	/ɨ/	u û
/ʊ/	w		y ŷ
/ə/	y	/ɨ/	u y
		/ə/	y

The vowels listed in Table 5.5 for southern Welsh may, with the
exception of the central vowel, be grouped into five pairs, as in Figure
5.1. In qualitative terms, the first of the pair is closer than the second;
quantitatively the closer series is longer. Length, however, is only dis-

/i, ɪ/			/u, ʊ/
/e, ɛ/	/ə/	/o, ɔ/	
	/ɑ, a/		

FIGURE 5.1   Welsh vowel pairings. See G. E. Jones 1984: 53.

TABLE 5.6   Welsh diphthongs

Southern Welsh		Northern Welsh	
Diphthong	*Grapheme(s)*	*Diphthong*	*Grapheme(s)*
/aɪ/	*ae ai au*	/aɨ/	*ae*
/aʊ/	*aw*	/aɪ/	*ai*
/eɪ/	*ei eu*	/ɑɨ/	*au*
/ɛʊ/	*ew*	/aʊ/	*aw*
/ɪʊ/	*iw yw*	/əɪ/	*ei*
/ɔɪ/	*oe oi*	/əɨ/	*eu*
/ʊɪ/	*wy*	/ɛʊ/	*ew*
/əʊ/	*yw ow*	/ɪʊ/	*iw*
		/ɔɨ/	*oe*
		/ɔɪ/	*oi*
		/ʊɨ/	*wy*
		/əʊ/	*yw ow*

Examples

	South	North
aer 'slaughter'	/aɪr/	/ɑɨr/
aur 'gold'	/aɪr/	/a+r/
gair 'word'	/gaɪr/	/gaɪr/
oer 'cold'	/ɔɪr/	/əɨr/
troi 'turn'	/trɔɪ/	/trɔɪ/

tinctive in accented syllables; in unaccented syllables where there is no length distinction both sets of vowels tend to be in free variation. In northern Welsh, which has two more phonemes, /i/ and /ɪ/, there seems to be less qualitative difference between the vowels in each pair and more quantitative difference to the extent that it could be argued that length is phonemic in northern Welsh (G. E. Jones 1984: 57); in southern Welsh, on the other hand, it can be argued that length is an associated feature of the close series of vowels. In absolute terms the length in the close vowels is at its longest in monosyllables and stressed final syllables, and much reduced in penultimate syllables which largely carry the accent; hence the concept of 'half long' penultimate syllables in Welsh (see 4.2.4).

There are, however, wide-ranging restrictions on the possible combinations of phonemes, particularly in relation to the close/open, long/short distinction.[6] In what follows the central vowel /ə/ is ignored and will be considered below (5.2.2). In southern Welsh the quality of the accented vowel in monosyllables and the accented syllable (usually

TABLE 5.7   Welsh consonant phonemes

Voiceless stops	/p/ p
	/t/ t
	/k/ c
Voiced stops	/b/ b
	/d/ d
	/g/ g
Voiceless fricatives	/f/ ff
	/θ/ th
	/χ/ ch
	/s/ s
	/ɬ/ ll
	/r̥/ rh
	/ʃ/ s si sh
	/tʃ/ tsi tsh ts
	/h/ h
Voiced fricatives	/v/ f
	/ð/ dd
	/ʤ/ j
Nasals	/m/ m
	/n/ n
	/ŋ/ ng
Liquids	/l/ l
	/r/ r

penultimate) of polysyllables was largely determined by the following consonants (see Table 5.8). There is, thus, only one environment where open and close vowels are in opposition, namely before a single nasal or liquid (see Table 5.8 (c)).

The only difference between the behaviour of vowels in monosyllables and polysyllables concerns vowels before /s/ and /ɬ/ in polysyllables. Though close vowels are found in that environment in monosyllables, e.g. /mɑs/ *mâs* 'out' (cf. *llall* in Table 5.8), only open vowels occur in polysyllables, e.g. /'mɛsɪr/ *mesur* 'measure', /'dɪɬad/ *dillad* 'clothes'. The situation in southern Welsh is summarized in the flow diagram in Figure 5.2.

We have seen that northern Welsh differs from southern in having thirteen vowel phonemes. Generally vowels in monosyllables behave as they do in the south, with two exceptions. First, before /ɬ/ we find closed vowels in the south, i.e. it is treated as a fricative under Table 5.8 (b), but in the north the vowel is open and long, i.e. it behaves like a voiceless stop or a cluster under Table 5.8 (a), e.g. SW /gweɬ/ : NW /gwɛɬ/ *gwell* 'better', SW /ɬɑɬ/ : NW /ɬaɬ/ *llall* 'other'. Secondly, in southern Welsh, vowels preceding clusters are open and likewise in

TABLE 5.8   Conditions affecting vowel quality in Welsh

(a) Before a single voiceless stop, and any cluster, only open, and thus short, vowels occur, e.g. /at/ *at* 'to', /krʊt/ *crwt* 'boy', /gwɛrθ/ *gwerth* 'value', /plant/ *plant* 'children', /'atɛb/ *ateb* 'answer', etc.

(b) Before a single stop (other than a voiceless stop) and zero, only close, and thus long, vowels occur, e.g. /ki/ *ci* 'dog', /bid/ *byd* 'world', /moχ/ *moch* 'pig', /ɬaɬ/ *llall* 'other', /'iχɛl/ *uchel* 'high', etc.

(c) Before a single nasal or liquid, both open and close vowels occur, e.g. /din/ *dyn* 'man' : /gwɪn/ *gwyn* 'white'; /son/ *sôn* 'sound' : /brɔn/ *bron* 'breast'; /'enʊ/ *enw* 'name' : /'ɛnɬ/ *enill* 'win'; etc.

northern Welsh except where the cluster is fricative + stop; in this case the vowel is closed, and long, e.g. SW, NW /kant/ *cant* 'hundred' but SW /kʊsk/, NW /kusk/ *cwsg* 'sleep'.

The main difference between the distribution of vowels concerns polysyllables. In southern Welsh all accented syllables behave alike; thus, close and open vowels are only contrastive before liquids and nasals, and elsewhere the quality of the vowel is determined by the following segment. In northern Welsh, however, no close and therefore long vowels occur in penultimate syllables, which amounts to saying

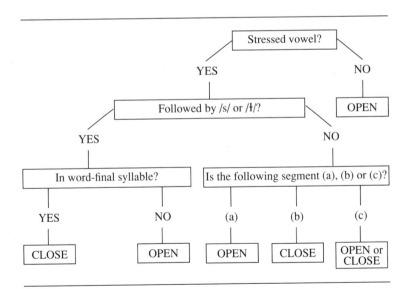

FIGURE 5.2   Factors determining vowel quality in southern Welsh. Adapted from Awbery 1984: 71; for the categories (a), (b) and (c), see Table 5.8.

TABLE 5.9 Examples illustrating the behaviour of vowels in polysyllables in southern and northern Welsh

---

SW, NW /'atɛb/ *ateb* 'answer'

BUT

SW /'ɑraɫ/ : NW /'araɫ/ *arall* 'other'
SW /'kɑdɛr/ :NW /'kadɛr/ *cadair* 'chair'

---

that in polysyllables there are very few accented close vowels (they could only occur in cases where the accent is not penultimate) (see Table 5.9 for examples). Figure 5.3 can, therefore, be contrasted with Figure 5.2 above.

The above situation operates in the north-west (area 1 in Map 5.1) but in north-east and midlands including area A (i.e. areas 2, 3 and 4 in Map 5.1) close and open vowels are in free variation in penultimate syllables though the same system operates in monosyllables. In other words, it shows all the signs of a mixed intermediate area between the two systems.

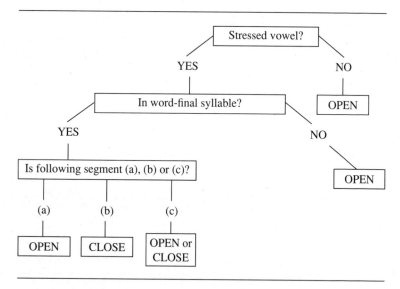

FIGURE 5.3 Factors determining vowel quality in northern Welsh. Adapted from Awbery 1984: 75; for the categories (a), (b) and (c), see Table 5.8 above.

NOTE: (a) includes /s/ and cluster of fricatives + stop.
        (b) includes /ɫ/

TABLE 5.10   Examples illustrating the distribution of diphthongs in Welsh

---

(a) /aɪ/
/ɬaɪ/ *llai* 'less'
/gwaɪθ/ *gwaith* 'work'
/'damwaɪn/ *damwain* 'accident'
/glan'haɪ/ *glanhau* 'to clean'

(b) /əʊ/
SW   /'təʊɪð/ *tywydd* 'weather'
     /təʊ'haɪ/ *tywhau* 'to fatten

The restrictions on diphthongs are far less complex and tend to affect individual cases rather than groups. For example, /aɪ/ occurs in monosyllables and final syllables (see Table 5.10 (a) for examples), but not in non-final syllables, though other front vowel diphthongs do have a wider range. Here then the crucial factor seems to be whether it is in the word-final syllable not whether it is accented or not. Similar factors affect /əʊ/ in the converse; it occurs in non-final syllables irrespective of accent but nowhere else (see Table 5.10 (b) for examples). Here the governing factor is the presence of /ə/, which itself follows a similar pattern of distribution (see 5.2.2 below). So far these comments on diphthongs may be taken to apply to all dialects of Welsh. However, in one area there is a difference between northern and southern Welsh. In one pair of diphthongs in northern Welsh there is an alternation between a close and an open (perhaps long and short) first element, namely /aɨ/ : /aɪ/, orthographically *au* : *ae*, e.g. /aɨr/ *aur* 'gold' : /aɪr/ *aer* 'slaughter'; they are indistinguishable in southern Welsh (see Table 5.6).

5.2.2   The central vowel /ə/
The central vowel /ə/, written *y*, is not involved in the opposition noted above between close and open (long or short) vowels (Awbery 1984: 76–81). However, its range is severely restricted; it only appears in non-final syllables (see Table 5.11 overleaf for examples), but irrespective of accent position. It never occurs in word-final position and not generally in monosyllables. There is one group of exceptions, /ə, ər/ *y*, *yr* 'the', /ən/ *yn* 'in', /də/ *dy* 'your' (sg.), /və, ən/ *fy* 'my'. But in many respects they should not be considered monosyllables or word final; they never carry an accent but are proclitic upon the following lexical item. It also occurs in series of alternations where there is an accent shift in related derivatives (see Table 5.11 for examples).

This pattern operates throughout Wales except for a very interesting area of south Cardiganshire and north Pembrokeshire (Awbery 1986a:

TABLE 5.11   Examples illustrating the distribution of the central vowel /ə/

/'əskavən/ *ysgafn* 'light' (adj.)
/'kənar/ *cynnar* 'early'
SW /'kətɪn/ *cytun* 'to agree'
SW /din/ : pl. /'dənɪɔn/ *dyn* : *dynyon* 'man : men' /durn/ : pl. /'dərnɛ/ *dwrn* :
   dyrnau 'fist(s)'

52–85). In south Cardiganshire and adjacent areas of north Pembrokeshire /ə/ can occur in accented monosyllables where other southern dialects have /ɪ/ and northern dialects have /ɨ/ (see Table 5.12 (a) for examples). But further to the south in the rest of Welsh-speaking Pembrokeshire the central vowel has virtually disappeared to be replaced by /ɪ/ or /ʊ/ (see Table 5.12 (b) for examples).

One problem is the alternation of /ə/ : /i/ and /u/. Usually phonological variation of this type is predictable but it is less obviously so in this instance. The difficulty is more or less the same in all dialects. In northern Welsh /ɨ/ can alternate with /ə/ or /ɨ/ in plurals. In southern Welsh the alternations are between plurals in /ɪ/ or /ə/ (see Table 5.13 for examples). The point is that phonologically conditioned variation of this type ought to be predictable. A. R. Thomas 1966: 106, also 1977, proposes a solution which involves rewriting /din/ or /dɨn/ as /dən/ beside /'dənɪɔn/ but retaining /ɬin/ or /ɬɨn/. But as there is no close allophone of /ə/ it would be realized as /ɨ/ or /i/ (see also B. Williams 1982–3: 240–1). The alternative, as he sees it, is to list every instance of /ɨ/ or /i/ which is potentially mutable. As it is, it is going to be necessary to reassign every example of /ɨ/ or /i/ which is mutable to /ə/, which seems no more economical. Thomas later offered another more abstract solution (A. R. Thomas 1984) which is discussed below (5.2.5).

The central vowel is a curiosity within the phonological system in view of its restricted range of occurrence and its failure to fit into the quantity system. For that reason a historical digression may be helpful

TABLE 5.12   Examples illustrating the behaviour of the central vowel /ə/ in different parts of Pembrokeshire

(a)
/bəθ/ : SW /bɪθ/ : NW /bɨθ/ *byth* 'ever'
/mənd/ : SW /mɪnd/ : NW /mɨnd/ *mynd* 'to go'

(b)
/'kɪvan/ : standard /'kəvan/ *cyfan* 'whole'
/'ɪskɔl/ : /'əskɔl/ *ysgol* 'school'
/'durnɪ/ : /'dərnɪ/ *dyrnu* 'to thresh'

TABLE 5.13   Examples illustrating the alternation of /ə/ with /i/ and /u/

Northern Welsh
/din/ *dyn* 'man' : pl. /ˈdəni̯ɔn/ *dynyon*
BESIDE
/ɬin/ *llun* 'picture' : pl. /ˈɬɨni̯ɛ/ or /ɬɨni̯a/ *lluniau*

Southern Welsh
/din/ : /ˈdəni̯ɔn/
BESIDE
/ɬin/ : /ˈɬɪnɛ/ or /ˈɬɪna/.

---

to fill in some of the background. The central vowel is not found in
Breton or Cornish but arose in Archaic Welsh before the accent shifted
back to the present penultimate syllable, in other words at some stage
before the 10th–11th centuries (see 4.2.3 above). Essentially it may be
characterized as a reduction of short high vowels in unaccented syllables. Its sources were /i/ and /u/ in original pretonic syllables which in
part were original and in part had developed from /o/ and /e/ before
nasals, as set out in Table 5.14. The subsequent retraction of the accent
brought about the present situation. In this historical development lies
the reason for the restrictions on the position of /ə/. In the period when
it arose final syllables were accented; it could only, therefore, have only
arisen in non-final syllables. Since monosyllables necessarily carried
the accent, /ə/ is not found there either.

TABLE 5.14   Sources of the central vowel /ə/

High back vowels		
PrW	Lat *cupidus*	/moˈnɪð/
	/kuˈbɪð/	/muˈnɪð/
Pre-shift	/kəˈbɪð/	/məˈnɪð/
Post shift	/ˈkəbɪð/	/ˈmənɪð/
Graph	MnW *cybydd*	MnW *mynydd*
Meaning	'miser'	'mountain'
High front vowels		
PrW	Lat *piscātus*	Lat *tenerum*
	/pisˈgaʊd/	/tiˈnɛr/
Pre-shift	/pəsˈgaʊd/	/təˈnɛr/
Post shift	/ˈpəsgaʊd/	/ˈtənɛr/
Graph	MW *pysgaut*	MnW *tyner*
	MnW *pysgod*	
Meaning	'fish'	'tender'

See Jackson 1953: 664–81.

5.2.3   Final consonantal clusters

Consonantal clusters are subject to different sets of restraints depending on where they occur in the words (Awbery 1984: 86–90, 1986a: 86–117). Internally any combination of obstruent and sonorant is acceptable but in clusters of nasal + stop the two elements must be homorganic (see Table 5.15 for examples). Exceptions, such as /'amgɪlχ/ *amgylch* 'around', are rare but are probably morphologically motivated and explicable by assuming a morpheme boundary in the cluster. Internal clusters are in articulatory terms easier to handle as a syllable boundary usually intervenes. But initial and final clusters present other problems.

TABLE 5.15   Examples of internal consonant clusters in Welsh

/'gʊmpas/ *gwmpas* 'around'
/'kənta/ *cynta(f)* 'first'
/'daŋgɔs/ *dangos* 'show'

As regards initial clusters, it is clear that within the history of Welsh the situation has not always been the same. In late Old Welsh initial clusters of /s/ + consonant were unacceptable and a prothetic vowel /ə/, or perhaps originally /i/, arose, e.g. /'əstrad/ *ystrad* < Lat * *strat-*, /'əsbrɪd/ *yspryd* 'spirit' < Lat *spiritus*, etc. (Jackson: 1953: 270–8). To what extent this is related to similar developments in Late Latin and Romance is unclear; it occurs in Welsh but not in Cornish or Breton, and is therefore unlikely to be the outcome of direct contact with speakers of Vulgar Latin, since it occurred at a much later date, around the 8th–10th centuries. However, it is clear that in the modern language, /s/ + consonant is acceptable despite the standard orthography, e.g. /'skadan/ *ysgaden* 'herring' (see Russell 1992a: 388–9).

Final clusters are particularly interesting in that the language inherited internal clusters which became final after the loss of final syllables. Now what was acceptable internally, with syllable and morpheme boundaries, was not always going to be acceptable in final position; the interesting aspect is the means the language devised to avoid awkward final clusters. Furthermore, it seems that there was no single wholesale solution but rather it depended on the syllable count of the word, the consonants involved and the dialect. The examples in Table 5.16, in their orthographical forms, will be used to exemplify the processes involved.

Two types can be distinguished, monosyllables where the syllable containing the cluster is accented and those polysyllables where it is not accented. As Awbery 1984: 89 has suggested, two main tactics are adopted, epenthesis (insertion of a vowel to break up the cluster) or

TABLE 5.16   Examples illustrating final consonant clusters in Welsh

anadl 'breath' : *anadlu* 'to breathe'
sg. *gwadn* : pl. *gwadnau* 'sole(s)'
ofn 'fear'
sg. *aradr* : pl. *erydr* 'plough(s)'
sg. *cefn* : pl. *cefnau* 'back(s)'
sg. *llyfr* : pl. *llyfrau* 'book(s)
sg. *ffenestr* : pl. *ffenestri* 'window(s)'

deletion of one element of the cluster. Where the form is polysyllabic, the latter usually occurs; /'arad/ (pl. /'ɛrɪd/), /'fɛnɛst/ are attested in most dialects, though the full form is maintained in derivatives, where the cluster is not final, e.g. pl. /fɛn'ɛstrɪ/. This phenomenon is not recent; MW *trawst* (pl. *trostreu*) 'beam', *brawd* 'brother' < *brawdr* are early examples (Russell 1985: 170, n.5). Monosyllables, on the other hand, because they presumably have less to lose, seem to prefer epenthesis; thus, NW /'gu̯adan/, /'kɛvɛn/, SW /'ovɔn/, etc. beside the derivatives where the cluster is preserved, e.g. /'gu̯adnɛ/, /'kɛvnɛ/, etc.

In southern Welsh there is an additional factor; as well as epenthesis, there is evidence for an early assimilation of the stop to the continuant, e.g. -/dl/ > /ðəl/ as in Cardiganshire /'gu̯aðan/, pl. /'gu̯adnɛ/, 'hu̯ɛðɛl/ *chwedl* 'news, story' (beside NW /'χu̯adal/) (Russell 1984: 106). It is probable that SW /'anal/ *anadl* arose not simply through the loss of /d/ (Awbery 1984: 89) but by a general shift of -/dl/ to -/ðl/ and subsequently to -/l/ in unaccented syllables. It is striking that the derivative even of /'anal/ retains /d/, e.g. /an'adlɪ/.

Awbery 1986a: 95–6 notes an alternative but similar strategy in Pembrokeshire Welsh: final clusters of -/vn/ and -/vl/ usually undergo epenthesis, e.g. /'kɛvɛn/, /'sɔvɔl/ *sofl* 'stubble', but some speakers reduce the /v/ to /u/ to produce a diphthong, e.g. /'keun/, /'sɔul/, /'əskaun/ *ysgafn* 'light' (adj.). This strategy does not affect all items, though it appears to be more common in western parts of Pembrokeshire than further east (Awbery 1986a: 98 (Table 15)).

Northern Welsh seems to be more tolerant of final clusters (Awbery 1984: 89–90); there is apparently evidence to suggest that /ovn/, /ɬ̩vr/, etc. are acceptable. However, such evidence needs careful scrutiny. It is impossible to articulate these clusters without some kind of vocalic glide, and whether it is recorded or not probably depends on its quality. In many cases the vowel takes on the colouring of the vowel of the accented syllable, thus /'gu̯adan/, /'χu̯adal/, but in other cases it may well simply be /ə/ and perhaps avoid detection. The quality of the epenthetic vowel seems to have been variable and has been problematic throughout the history of Welsh. In Middle Welsh the vowel was usually written y, which could otherwise represent /i/, /ɨ/, /ɪ/, /ɨ/ or /ə/. The epenthetic vowel was not recognized for metrical purposes. However, the evidence of less competent scribes who occasionally wrote *ouon* /'ovɔn/ (MnW *ofn*) suggests that the *y*-spelling may simply be orthographical conservatism and that assimilation had already taken place (see Charles-Edwards and Russell, forthcoming).

The history of these clusters is very complicated (Russell 1984, 1985a: 55–6, 1985b) but it is tempting to suggest that the assimilations found in southern Welsh may be related to similar changes which are regular in Cornish and Breton (see 4.3.3).

5.2.4 Phonology and grammatical alternations

So far the discussion has focused on the phonology itself, but there are important areas where it is significantly affected by the grammatical categories, and it is clear that many of the phonological rules have a grammatical component. There are two areas of particular interest, grammatically motivated changes in initial consonants, the so-called mutations, and similar changes in internal vowels (see A. R. Thomas 1966). For the purposes of this section we will consider only the latter type; the former is the subject of Chapter 7.

Alternations of vowels are an important part of the derivational sys-

TABLE 5.17   Examples of phonological changes determined by grammatical categories

---

(a) Examples
  gwlad 'country' : *gwledig* 'rural'
  sg. *mab* : pl. *meibyon* 'son(s)'
  (1)   /ɑ/ is raised to /ɛ/ in the environment of /ɪ/ and /i̯/:
  /'gu̯lɑd/ : /'gu̯lɛdɪg/
  /mɑb/ : /mɛbi̯ɔn/
  (2)   /ɛ/ is diphthongized to /əɪ/ in the environment of /i̯/:
  /mɛbi̯ɔn/ > /məɪbi̯ɔn/.

(b) Suffixes where changes occur
The plural suffixes -/ɪ/, SW -/ɪð/, -/i̯ɔn/:
  /garð/ 'garden' : pl. /'gɛrðɪ/ *gerddi*
  /nant/ *nant* 'valley' : pl. /nɛntɪð/ *nentydd*
The singulative suffix -/ɪn/:
  /plant/ *plant* : sg. /'plɛntɪn/ *plentyn*.

(c) Suffixes where changes do not occur
The nominal suffix -/i̯ad/:
  /'kari̯ad/ *cariad* 'love' : /karɪ/ *caru* 'to love'
The verbal noun suffix -/i̯ɔ/:
  /'tani̯ɔ/ *tanio* 'to set fire to' : /tɑn/ *tân* 'fire'

---

tem of the language, that is, the addition of morphemes can condition vowel changes in the base. For example, the alternations in *gwlad* 'country' : *gwledig* 'rural', sg. *mab* : pl. *meibyon* 'son(s)' can be described by means of two consecutively applied rules (see Table 5.17 (a)). These rules are presented by A. R. Thomas 1966: 103 and are based on his description of northern Welsh of Dyffryn Alun. He is, therefore, not concerned with southern developments. Both these rules would apply in southern dialects with the addition of a /i̯/-deletion rule; southern Welsh tends not to have /i̯/ in these suffixes but still has the vowel change indicating an underlying /i̯/ (see 4.3.3).

These are not, however, phonological rules operating blindly; the grammatical environment, particularly inflectional and derivational suffixes, is significant since some suffixes condition the application of these rules and some do not; Table 5.17 (b and c) present examples of both types. Similarly, when the suffixed element is another lexical item, to form a compound, no vowel change occurs, e.g. /kəv'andɪr/ *cyfandir* 'mainland, continent' (*cyfan* 'whole' + *tir* 'land'), /'kanrɪv/ *canrif* 'century' (*can(t)* 'hundred' + *rhif* 'number'). In these cases the vowel change is grammatically motivated by certain suffixes but not by others.

5.2.5 Theoretical treatments of Welsh phonology
The account given above has deliberately avoided any theoretical stance more controversial than basic phonemic description. But it may be useful to conclude this section by considering a case where this material has been examined from a different theoretical standpoint.[7]

In the discussion of the central vowel /ə/ (5.2.2), A. R. Thomas 1966: 106 (see also A. R. Thomas 1977) attempted to provide an adequate description of the different behaviours of /dɪn/ *dyn* 'man' and /'ɬin/ *llun* 'picture' which have the plurals /'dəni̯ɔn/ *dynyon* and /'ɬini̯ɛ/ or /'ɬini̯a/ *lluniau* respectively (the examples are taken from A. R. Thomas 1966 and reflect the situation in northern dialects; see Table 5.13 above). The problem centres on the lowering of /ə/ in the former but not the latter. The lowering feature is shared with /u/ but not with /i/, e.g. sg. /kum/ *cwm* : pl. /'kəmɔɨð/ *cymoedd* 'valley(s)' . The difference runs deeper; some adjectives in /i/ have a feminine form in /e/, e.g. m. /krɪv/ : f. /krev/ *cryf* : *cref* 'strong', m. /sɨχ/ : f. /seχ/ *sych* : *sech* 'dry', while for others there is no separate feminine form, e.g. /pɨr/ *pur* 'pure'. To judge from their orthography, i.e. *dyn* : *llun*, *cryf* : *pur*, the vowels may be historically distinct but they seem to be identical in synchronic terms and any description should be able to cope with the difference in their behaviour in non-final syllables. It is clear, then, irrespective of orthography or history, that /i/ has a complex phonology and any adequate description ought to be able to represent that complexity. It ought also to be able to cope with the similarities between /u/ and some

/i/	/ɨ₁/	/ɨ₂/	/u/
$\begin{bmatrix} + \text{high} \\ - \text{back} \\ - \text{round} \end{bmatrix}$	$\begin{bmatrix} + \text{high} \\ - \text{back} \\ + \text{round} \end{bmatrix}$	$\begin{bmatrix} + \text{high} \\ + \text{back} \\ - \text{round} \end{bmatrix}$	$\begin{bmatrix} + \text{high} \\ + \text{back} \\ + \text{round} \end{bmatrix}$
i	*y*	*u*	*w*

FIGURE 5.4   Distinctive features of high vowels in northern Welsh. A. R. Thomas 1984: 109.

instances of /ɨ/ which share lowering but at the same time distinguish those instances of /ɨ/ which have feminines in /e/ beside forms in /u/ with feminines in /ɔ/. This is essentially the task A. R. Thomas 1984 set himself within a theory of distinctive feature matrices. He specified four underlying vowels to represent /i/, /ɨ/ and /u/ with two sources for /ɨ/, as set out in Figure 5.4 (A. R. Thomas 1984: 109). His distinction between /ɨ₁/ and /ɨ₂/ is purely abstract and is retained in the grammar as long as it is necessary to prevent /ɨ₂/ from undergoing lowering. After that point it merged with /ɨ₁/. There is a difficulty with his original specification which is not made clear; he distinguishes /ɨ₁/ as [... − back, + round] beside /ɨ₂/ as [... + back, - round] and notes that this is the reverse of the accepted historical analysis which takes the orthographical *u* (= /ɨ₂/) as the more rounded vowel. A further difficulty has to do with this type of notation; it is very difficult to describe the fine gradations of front and back vowels in northern Welsh with what is essentially a binary notation. B. Williams 1982–3: 246 adopted a more detailed approach whereby she specifies the features more precisely and avoids the problem of rounded and unrounded vowels.

5.3 The nominal system[8]

5.3.1 Gender
There are two classes of Welsh nouns traditionally distinguished by gender as masculine and feminine. The distinction is marked in a number of ways – by mutation, pronoun reference and different adjectival forms (see Table 5.18). The distribution of gender among inanimate objects (i.e. neither male nor female) seems largely arbitrary. In derivatives, however, suffixes are often marked for gender, though they are prone to exceptions; for example, among abstract noun suffixes -*aint*, -*dod*, -*edd*, -*ioni*, -*ni*, -*rwydd* tend to form masculine nouns, while -*ach*, -*aeth*, -*ed* form feminines (S. J. Williams 1980: 19–26, Thorne 1993: 115–25, King 1993: 44–7). On the other hand, other suffixes, where the meaning is closely related to that of the base, take the same gender as

TABLE 5.18   Gender marking in Modern Welsh

(a) Mutation after the article
/ə 'baχgɛn/ *y bachgen* 'the boy' : /ə vɛrχ/ *y ferch* 'the girl' : *merch*

(b) Mutation of the following adjective
/'baχgɛn tɛʊ/ *bachgen tew* 'a fat boy' : /mɛrχ dɛʊ/ *merch dew* 'a fat girl'

(c) Different number forms
/daɪ, tri, pɛdᵤar 'baχgɛn/ *dau, tri, pedwar bachgen* 'two, three, four boys' :
/dʊɪ, taɪr, pɛdaɪr mɛrχ/ *dwy, tair, pedair merch* 'two, three, four girls'

(d) Demonstrative pronouns
/ə 'baχgɛn hun/ *y bachgen hwn* 'this boy' : /ə vɛrχ hɔn/ *y ferch hon* 'this girl'

(e) Pronouns
/ve, vo/ *fe, fo* → *bachgen* : /(h)i/ *hi* → *merch*

that of the base, e.g. -*aid* '-ful', *llwyaid* f. 'spoonful' : *llwy* f. 'spoon', *crochanaid* m. 'potful' : *crochan* m. 'pot'; -*od* 'blow', *dyrnod* m. 'punch': *dwrn* m. 'fist'; *ffonod* f. 'blow from a stick' : *ffon* f. 'stick'.

5.3.2   Number
The usual pattern of plural formation is noun (sg.) : noun + suffix (pl.) but there is also a widespread pattern of singulative formation of noun (pl.) : noun + suffix (sg.) especially among those count nouns which naturally occur in large numbers (S. J. Williams 1980: 9–19, M. Jones and Thomas 1977: 157–63; for Breton see 4.3.2). For the usual range of count nouns there is a range of plural suffixes, e.g. *dyn* 'man' : *dynyon*; *ton* 'wave' : *tonnau*; *merch* 'girl' : *merched*; etc. Selection of the plural suffix seems arbitrary but there are some groupings; for example, animal names form a plural in -*od*, e.g. *lleod* 'lions', *cathod* 'cats', *llwynogod* 'foxes', etc. Curiously, it also occurs in *Gwyddelod* 'Irishmen' and *Ffrancod* 'Frenchmen'. Plurals can also be formed by vowel change, as in English *men* : *men*; *mouse* : *mice*; etc., e.g. *bardd* 'poet' : pl. *beirdd*, *castell* 'castle' : pl. *cestyll*; *gŵr* 'man' : pl. *gwyr*.

On the other hand, nouns such as *pysgod* 'fish', *sêr* 'stars', *plant* 'children', *coed* 'trees, wood' are felt as plural and form a singulative by suffixation, thus *pysgodyn* 'a fish', *seren* 'a star', *plentyn* 'a child', *coeden* 'a tree'. English plurals borrowed into Welsh, which fit into this semantic group, can also undergo this process, e.g. *brics* 'bricks' : sg. *bricsen*; *pys* 'peas' : sg. *pysen*.[9] There is also a mixed group which have suffixation in both singular and plural, e.g. sg. *cwningen* 'rabbit' : pl. *cwningod*, sg. *cerdyn* 'card' : pl. *cardiau*. Beside these there are mass nouns, e.g. *mêl* 'honey', *glo* 'coal', which do not have plurals at all, and nouns which only occur in the plural; usually they are marked as plurals by suffixation, e.g. *rhieni* 'parents', *telerau* 'terms', but the

singular simply does not occur. In a few cases there is no overt plural
marker, e.g. *gwartheg* 'cattle'. These two types behave normally in
terms of concord, etc., that is, mass nouns are referred to by singular
pronouns, and the plurals by plural pronouns. However, collective
nouns, which are singular in form but refer to groups of people or
things, e.g. *pobl* 'people', *llywodraeth* 'government', tend to be
referred to by plural pronouns, e.g.:

Beth   mae'r   pobl   yn meddwl?   Maen nhw'n meddwl bod...
what   is   the people think   are   they think   that...
'What are the people thinking? They are thinking that . . .'

5.3.3 Determination
There is no indefinite article in Welsh, so that *dyn* can mean 'a man' as
well as 'man'. The noun can be further specified in a number of ways.

5.3.3.1   The article
The article /ə/ *y* (with variants /ər/ before vowels, e.g. *yr afal* 'the
apple', and /r/ *'r* after vowels, e.g. *i'r dre* 'to the town') is the most
obvious way to provide definiteness; it also, as we have seen (5.3.1),
marks gender by the presence or absence of mutation.

5.3.3.2   Demonstratives
Demonstratives add further specificity in cases of uncertainty. Two systems of demonstrative operate at different levels of the language. In

TABLE 5.19   Welsh demonstratives

Formal

	m.	f.	inanimate	
'this'	*hwn*	*hon*	*hyn*	
'that'	*hwnnw*	*honno*	*hynny*	
'these'		*hyn*		
'those'		*hynny*		

Colloquial

'this'	*yma*
'that'	SW *yna* / NW *acw*

Pronouns

	m.	f.	indefinite	pl.
'this'	*hwn*	*hon*	*hyn*	*rhain*
'that'	*hwnna*	*honna*	*hynny*	*rheina*

See M. Jones and Thomas 1977: 202, Thorne 1993: 191–7, King 1993: 85–6,
98–9.

more formal levels, the forms distinguish gender and animateness, as set out in Table 5.19, e.g. *y dyn hwn* 'this man' : *y dyn hwnnw* 'that man', *y ferch hon* 'this girl' : *y ferch honno* 'that girl'. In the spoken language these forms are used pronominally but not as adjectives, e.g. *beth oedd hynny?* 'what was that?'. For modifying nouns, the spoken language tends to use /əma/ *yma* 'here, this', SW /əna/ *yna*, NW /akʊ/ *acw* 'that', which are neutral as to gender, e.g. /ə ti ma/ *y tŷ yma* 'this house' (lit. 'the house here'), /ə ti na/ *y tŷ yna* 'that house' (lit. 'the house there').

5.3.3.3 The 'genitive' construction
The expression of possession is a further way of determining a noun; that is, while *a hat* is indefinite, *the hat* is definite and then further specified in *this/that hat* or *John's hat* or *my/his/her hat*. In Welsh, possession is marked simply by the ordering of nouns, and additionally after a feminine singular noun by mutation; using the terminology of M. Jones and Thomas 1977: 192–4, the POSSESSOR follows the POSSESSUM, the thing possessed, e.g. *car Ieuan* 'Ieuan's car', *het merch* 'a girl's hat', and with mutation after a feminine singular noun *maneg ddyn* 'a man's glove'. The POSSESSUM is never definite though it can be further determined by an adjective; for example, *het y ferch* 'the girl's hat' or *het coch y ferch* 'the girl's red hat' is acceptable but not **y het y ferch* 'the girl's the hat'. The 'genitive' construction seems already to provide the requisite level of definiteness.

As M. Jones and Thomas 1977: 194 point out, Welsh clearly distinguishes the 'genitive' construction from the partitive construction, where possession is not at issue but rather emphasis on *part* of something. In Welsh the latter is marked by the preposition *o* 'from, of', i.e. (ART) NOUN$_1$ *o* (ART) NOUN$_2$, e.g. *darn o fara* 'a piece of bread'. In contrast to the 'genitive' construction, the first noun can be determined by the article; we may contrast, for example, /ə ran vʊia or tɪdal/ *y ran fwyaf o'r tudal* 'the majority of the pages' (lit. 'the biggest part') and /tɪdaˈlenɛ ə ɬɪvər/ *tudalennau y llyfr* 'the pages of the book'.

5.3.3.4 Possessive adjectives and pronouns
Closely related to the 'genitive' construction is the use of adjectives to specify pronominal possession, i.e. 'my', 'your', etc. There is considerable variation between the forms used in more formal registers of the language and those used in the spoken language, as is indicated in Table 5.20 overleaf. The spoken 1st person forms are only distinguishable by the presence or absence of the nasal mutation, e.g. /ə ˈmraʊd/ *fy mrawd* 'my brother' : /ən ˈbraʊd/ *ein brawd* 'our brother'. The formal *ein* and *eich* are forms created artificially in the 16th century but they have acquired a phonetic reality in formal spoken Welsh. The distinction between 2nd singular and plural is rarely one of number; as in

TABLE 5.20   Possessive adjectives in Welsh

	1st	2nd	3rd
Formal			
Sg.	/və/ *fy* + NM	/də/ *dy* + SM	m. /əɪ/ *ei* + SM
	(/m/ '*m*)	(/θ/ '*th*)	f. /əɪ *ei* + SpM
			(/i/ '*i*, /ʊ/ '*w*)
Pl.	/əɪn/ /aɪn/	/əɪχ/	/əɪ/ *eu*
	ein (/n/ '*n*)	/aɪχ/ *eich*	
		(/χ/ '*ch*)	
Colloquial			
Sg.	/ən/ *fy* + NM	/də/ *dy* + SM	m. /i/ *ei* + SM
			f. /i/ *ei* + SpM/SM
Pl.	/ən/ *ein*	/əχ/ *eich*	/i/ *eu*

( ) = forms after vowels.

French *tu/vous*, Welsh 2nd person pronouns are distinguished on an intimate/formal axis as well as on the basis of number (King 1993: 93–4). The distinctions of gender in the 3rd singular are marked by mutations, though in the spoken language the spirant mutation after *ei* (3rd f.) is disappearing (see 7.6). However, the weight of reference does not hang on these forms alone. In the spoken language further marking is supplied by affixed pronouns, as in Table 5.21, which are identical to those used after verbs, e.g. /əŋ'haθ i/ *fy nghath i*, /i gaθ ev/ *ei gath ef* 'his cat', /i kaθ (h)i/ *ei chath hi* 'her cat', /i kaθ ɳu/ *eu cath nhw* 'their cat', etc. This is the standard spoken usage and is not emphatic.[10]

Emphasis can be supplied by the use of a reflexive pronoun /hin/, /hinan/ or /hinaɪn/ (NW /hɨn) etc.) *hun, hunan* or *hunain* (Thorne 1993: 198–200, King 1993: 96–8). They seem to function as nouns in that they take the same possessive pronoun, e.g. /ə mraʊd ə hin/ *fy mrawd fy hun* 'my own brother'. They are reflexive and so share the same refer-

TABLE 5.21   Affixed pronouns in Welsh

		Singular	Plural	
1st		/i/, /vi/ *i, fi*	1pl.	/ni/ *ni*
2nd		/di/, /ti/ *di, ti*	2pl.	/χi/ *chi*
3rd	m.	SW /ev/, /ve/ *ef, fe*	3pl.	/ɳu/ *nhw*
		NW /evo/, /vo/ *efo, fo*		Formal *hwy(nt)*
	f.	/(h)i/ *hi*		

See Thorne 1993: 160–1, King 1993: 80–3.

TABLE 5.22   The patterns of reflexive pronouns in Welsh

	Singular	Plural
(a)	*hun*	*hun*
(b)	*hunan*	*hunain*
(c)	*hun*	*hunan*

ence as the subject of the sentence. They are often needed to avoid ambiguity; for example,

MaeJohn wedi colli ei lyfr e
is   John after lose his book
'John has lost his book'

is ambiguous but the expansion of *ei lyfr e* into *ei lyfr ei hun* 'his own book' makes the sentence clear. M. Jones and Thomas 1977: 200 note the interesting variation between singular and plural forms in different types of Welsh; three patterns are distinguished (see Table 5.22). Type (c) is northern, but the others seem to be in free variation elsewhere.

The possessive pronouns have been subject to considerable modification in the history of the language (see Table 5.23). Type (a) is the original pattern continued from Middle Welsh (D. S. Evans 1964: 54–5), but it has been replaced by type (b) in which the 3rd singular stem *eidd-* has been generalized in the manner of a conjugated preposition (see 5.3.5; see also Thorne 1993: 169–71). Neither pattern is found in the colloquial language where the indefinite pronouns *un/rhai* 'one/some' are used with the possessive adjectives, e.g. *fy un i* /ən in i/ 'mine', *eich rhai chi* /əχ 'ṛai χi/ 'yours' (lit. 'your things'), etc. This construction is paralleled by a similar usage with adjectives, e.g. *yr un coch* 'the red one', *yr rhai coch* 'the red ones' (King 1993: 84).

TABLE 5.23   Possessive pronouns in Welsh

	(a)	(b)
1st sg.	*mau*	*eiddof* (*i*)
2nd sg.	*tau*	*eiddot* (*ti*)
3rd sg. m.	*eiddo*	*eiddo* (*fe*)
f.	*eiddi*	*eiddi* (*hi*)
1st pl.	*einym*	*eiddom* (*ni*)
2nd pl.	*einwch*	*eiddoch* (*chi*)
3rd pl.	*eiddynt*	*eiddynt* (*nhw*)

( ) show affixed pronouns

5.3.4 Adjectives

In the formal language many adjectives have plural forms (S. J. Williams 1980: 26–31, Thorne 1993: 125–31, King 1993: 74–5), usually in *-ion*, e.g. /kɔχ/ *coch* 'red' : pl. *cochion*. There are also examples of vowel change in the plural, e.g. /'bəχan/ *bychan* 'small' : pl. *bychain*, etc. At the same time many adjectival types, particularly those with derivative suffixes, have no plural form. Some adjectives, usually monosyllables with a vowel /ʊ/ or /i/ (NW /ɨ/), have a feminine form in /o/ or /e/ respectively, e.g. m. /duvʊn/ *dwfn* 'deep' : f. /dovɔn/ *dofn*, m. /gɨin/ (NW /gɨin/) *gwyn* 'white' : f. /gɨen/ *gwen* (Thorne 1993: 131–3, King 1993: 73–4). Feminine forms of the adjective usually show the soft mutation as they generally follow the noun, e.g. *het wen* 'a white hat'.

However, the dialectal evidence suggests that the retention of plural and feminine forms is more dialect-specific than the standard grammars would suggest. B. Thomas and Thomas 1989: 52–3 show that feminine forms seem to be maintained in northern dialects but in the south the alternation is found only in *gwyn* : *gwen* 'white'. It also emerges from the survey of Ceinewydd (Newquay) in Cardiganshire carried out in 1934 that the use of feminine adjectives was greatly reduced in the younger speakers. If that was true in 1934, it is probable that the reduction will have become more general since then.

Despite long lists of plural adjectives in S. J. Williams 1980: 26–9 and Thorne 1993: 125–31, according to B. Thomas and Thomas 1989: 53–5 they are as restricted in the spoken dialects as feminine forms. Few are widespread; /ɛrɨɬ/ *eraill* (: sg. *arall* 'other') is common, and plurals of /'ɪvank/ *ifanc* 'young' : /'ɪvɪnk'/, /'ɪvɛnk/, etc. with a vowel change are found in many areas. That apart, they seem to occur, particularly in the south, in colour terms, e.g. /krəʃɛ dɪɔn/ *crysau duon* 'black shirts' (used to refer to the All Blacks), /'kərans cɔχɔn/ *curans cochon* 'red currants', etc., but only sporadically in other semantic fields. Dialect evidence again suggests that they are more frequent in northern dialects (B. Thomas and Thomas 1989: 54–5).

There is a similar gap between the formal and spoken language with regard to the degrees of comparison. Welsh, along with all the Celtic languages, has an equative ('as … as') beside comparative and superlative forms (for Irish, see 3.3.5). We may begin with the formal grammar's statements (e.g. S. J. Williams 1980: 31–4, Thorne 1993: 136–46). For regular adjectives the degrees of comparison are marked by suffixation: equative *-ed*, comparison *-ach*, superlative *-af*; all three cause devoicing (a form of grammatically motivated provection) of a preceding voiced stop (see Table 5.24 (a)). There are a number of irregular forms (see Table 5.24 (b)). In addition to the synthetic, suffixed forms there is a series of analytic, periphrastic forms which in some cases are required but are otherwise optional. The markers in this type

TABLE 5.24 Degrees of comparison in Welsh

(a) Regular patterns
/kɑs/ *cas* 'hateful': *cased* : *casach* : *casaf*
/teg/ *teg* 'fair': *teced* : *tecach* : *tecaf*

(b) Irregular patterns
da 'good' : *cystal* 'as good as' : *gwell* 'better' : *gorau* 'best'
mawr 'big' : *cymaint* 'as big as': *mwy* 'bigger, more': *mwyaf* 'biggest, most'
See Thorne 1993: 137 for a full list.

(c) Periphrastic patterns
cryf 'strong' : *mor gryf* 'as strong as' : *mwy cryf* 'stronger' (lit. 'more strong') : *mwyaf cryf* 'strongest'
gobeithiol 'hopeful' : *mor gobeithiol* 'as hopeful as' : *mwy gobeithiol* 'more hopeful' : *mwyaf gobeithiol* 'most hopeful'

(d) Regularization of irregular patterns
Standard:
isel 'low' : *ised* 'as low as' : *is* 'lower' : *isaf* 'lowest'
Southern Welsh:
/'ɪʃel/ : /ɪʃ'ɛlɛd/ : /ɪʃ'ɛlaχ/ : /ɪʃ'ɛla/
Standard:
hawdd 'easy' : *hawsed* 'as easy as' : *haws* 'easier' : *hawsaf* 'easiest'
Southern Welsh:
/'hauð/ : /'hauðɛd/ : /'hauðaχ/ : /'hauða/

---

are parts of *mawr* 'big' (see Table 5.24 (c)). For most polysyllabic adjectives, and especially derivative adjectives in -*ol*, the periphrastic forms are regular, e.g. *mwy gobeithiol* 'more hopeful', not **gobeithio-lach* vel sim.

The syntax of the standard language requires the regular equative to be bracketed by *cyn . . . â/ag* 'as . . . as', e.g.:

Y mae 'r dillad cyn wynned ag eira
is the clothes as white as snow
'The clothes are as white as snow'

The comparative occurs with *na(g)* 'than', e.g.:

Y mae 'r afal yn felynach nag aur
is the apple yellower than gold
'The apple is yellower than gold'.

It can also be used as a simple adjective, e.g. *dyn cryfach* 'a stronger man'.

The spoken dialects, however, show a much more complex and fluid situation. There is a tendency to simplify the irregular comparatives and superlatives, usually by generalizing the form of the positive adjective (see Table 5.24(d) for examples). There is also variation in the syntactic patterns of the equative (B. Thomas and Thomas 1989: 55–6); in the north there is variation between the standard pattern of *cyn* + equative + *â/ag* and the periphrastic *mor* + positive adjective + *â/ag*. In the southeast the standard form occurs but with a tendency to elide *cyn* before a consonant, e.g. /kəsɪred ɑ/ *cysured â* 'as sour as' beside /kɪn ɔɪrɛd ɑ/ *cyn oered â* 'as cold as'. But in Pembrokeshire a conflation of the two types occurs, i.e. *mor* + equative + *â/ag*, e.g. /mor dɛu̯ɛd ɑ/ *mor dewed â* 'as fat as'.

5.3.5 Personal pronouns

Welsh personal pronouns take a range of forms depending on their position in relation to other accented words and on the degree of emphasis or contrast they are to carry. They occur as accented units in their own right as 'independent' pronouns and also as 'dependent' pronouns, where their form is often reduced in unaccented position.

The independent pronouns have three forms depending on the degree and type of emphasis implied (see Table 5.25; cf. Thorne 1993: 154–69). A three-way distinction is not maintained in the spoken language, where the only continuation of the reduplicated type is an initial /ə/ in some dialects. S. J. Williams 1980: 46 remarks that for the

Table 5.25 Independent personal pronouns

	Simple		Reduplicated		Conjunctive	
1st sg.	*mi*	/(m)i/	*myfi*	/(ə)vi/	*minnau*	/(m)innɛ/
		/vi/				/(m)inna/
2nd sg.	*ti*	/ti/	*tydi*	/(ə)di/	*tithau*	/tiθɛ/
						/tiθa/
3rd sg.	*ef*	/(v)ɔ/	*efe*	/(ə)vɔ/	*ynteu*	/(v)əntɛ/
		/(v)ɛ/		/(ə)vɛ/		/(v)ənta/
	hi	/(h)i/	*hyhi*	/(ə)hi/	*hitheu*	/(h)iθɛ/
						/(h)iθa/
1st pl.	*ni*	/ni/	*nyni*	/(ə)ni/	*ninneu*	/ninnɛ/
						/ninna/
2nd pl.	*chwi*	/χi/	*chwychwi*	/(ə)χi/	*chwithau*	/χiθɛ/
						/χiθa/
3rd pl.	*hwy(nt)*	/ṇhu/	*hwynt(h)wy*	/(ə)ṇhu/	*hwythau*	/ṇuθɛ/
		/nu/		/(ə)nu/		/ṇuθa/
						/nuθɛ/
						/nuθa/
						/ṇu(ɨ)ntɛ/

literary language 'the reduplicated forms are somewhat more emphatic than the simple', but in the modern literary language the reduplicated forms are now optional. The conjunctive forms tend to be more adversative than simply emphatic and imply relationship with another pronoun (King 1993: 95–6), e.g.:

Daeth ef i'r   tŷ   a   minnau newydd mynd allan
Came he to the house and I   just   going out
'He came to the house, and *I* had just gone out.'

It can also be used in apposition to a noun, e.g.

Daeth Dafydd ynteu i'r   dre
came D.   to the town
'Dafydd too came to town'

In the spoken language the distinction is essentially between the simple and the conjunctive forms. There is a range of forms attested in dialects. The main difference is in the 3rd plural where spoken /n̥hu/ or /nu/, written as *nhw*, is found beside formal *hwy*; they seem to have arisen by a resegmentation of the 3rd plural ending + pronoun, i.e. *-n hwy* (< *-n(t) wy*), followed by the reduction of the final unaccented diphthong to -/u/. The conjunctive pronouns also show a wide range of forms, either in the 3rd plural by the generalization of the -/θɛ/ ending from other forms, e.g. /n̥huθɛ/, etc. (Russell 1982–3: 38, n. 3) or by the influence of the simple pronoun, e.g. /vəntɛ/ beside /əntɛ/ and the simple /vɛ/.[11]

The conjunctive pronouns still tend to occur in adversative contexts, while emphasis is more likely to be marked by word order, e.g.:

Ti   sy   'n dweud hynny
you who is in say   that
'It is you who is saying that'

as opposed to the less emphatic version:

Wyt ti'n   dweud hynny
are you in saying that
'You're saying that'

The dependent and affixed pronouns are listed in Tables 5.20 and 5.21 respectively. Aspects of the possessive and affixed forms are discussed in 5.3.3.4. It may simply be worth repeating that in the spoken language pronouns are usual and are not emphatic unless particularly stressed.

There is one class of pronoun which does not occur in the spoken language at all but is a feature of high-level formal language, the so-called infixed object pronouns. They have a long pedigree in Celtic but have disappeared from the colloquial language. They are unaccented and require a preceding sentence particle to 'lean' against. The forms

TABLE 5.26   Infixed object pronouns in formal Welsh

1st sg.	-m	1st pl.	-n
2nd sg.	-th	2nd pl.	-ch
3rd sg.	-i, -s	3rd pl.	-u, -s

are set out in Table 5.26. The following examples are taken from the formal written language but could be paralleled many times over from the earlier language and particularly from Middle Welsh:

> *Pwy a   'm gwelodd i?*   'Who saw me?'
> who rel. me saw   me

> *Nith   gosba*   'He will not punish you (sg.)'
> neg. you punish

The -*s* forms are found for 3rd person verbs after the negatives *ni, na, oni* 'unless', *pe* 'if', e.g. *nis gwelsoch (ef)* 'you did not see him'. There is frequently an affixed pronoun picking up and re-marking the infixed form.

There is one other area where personal pronouns occur, in conjugated prepositions. There are two forms of preposition, the simple form before the noun, e.g. *o'r tŷ* 'from the house', *dan y pont* 'under the bridge', etc., and the conjugated form, which essentially consists of preposition + personal pronoun (see Table 5.27). Some of the patterns thus created resemble verb endings and have indeed been influenced by them, e.g. the 3rd pl. ending -*ynt* taken over from the verbal conjugation; the original ending preserved in Middle Welsh was -*uv* /-ʉv/, later -*ud* /ʉð/ (D. S. Evans 1964: 59). In some cases the stem of the conjugated preposition differs from the basic preposition, e.g. *o* 'from' : *ohono-*, and most prepositions have an additional dental element in the 3rd person. Traditionally the prepositions have been divided into three conjugations, depending on the singular stem vowel (see Table 5.27

TABLE 5.27   Welsh conjugated prepositions

		First *ar* 'on'	Second *tros/dros* 'over'	Third *gan* 'with'
1st sg.		*arna(f)*	*troso(f)*	*genny(f)*
2nd sg.		*arnat*	*trosot*	*gennyt*
3rd sg.	m.	*arno*	*trosto*	*ganddo*
	f.	*arni*	*trosti*	*ganddi*
1st pl.		*arnom*	*trosom*	*gennym*
2nd pl.		*arnoch*	*trosoch*	*gennych*
3rd pl.		*arnynt*	*trostynt*	*ganddynt*

and S. J. Williams 1980: 127–9, Thorne 1993: 386–90, King 1993: 268–9). The dialects have tended to level out the differences in stem vowel in favour of one of them (see Ball 1987 and Hamp 1991b); B. Thomas and Thomas 1989: 58 show that the northern dialects tend to favour *a* while in the south *o* is more popular. Midland dialects, predictably enough, tend to show a mixture of forms. In the spoken language they are regularly used with the affixed pronouns, e.g. /arnɔ vɛ/ *arno fe* 'on him', /gennɪvi/ *gennyf i* 'with me'. The only exception is when the conjugated preposition is used resumptively in a relative clause (see 5.5.3.2 below), e.g.:

> '*dwy wedi colli'r   papur yr oeddwn i'n edrych arno*
> am   after lose the paper was I   in look   at (it)
> 'I have lost the paper I was looking at'.

5.3.6 Numerals

The cardinal numerals 1–20 are presented in Table 5.28(a)(i) overleaf (for the historial background, see Greene 1992). Three and four have feminine forms (for the mutations, see 7.2.2). The 'teens' are based on two base forms *deg* '10' and *pymtheg* '15'; the only exception is *deunaw* '18' (lit. 'two nines'). The numbers beyond twenty are traditionally counted by a vigesimal system (in twenties) and the system is still found in the literary language, but the spoken, colloquial system operates with a decimal system (see Table 5.28 (a) (ii); see also Thorne 1993: 146–52, King 1993: 111–14). The ordinals have special forms for 1st to 5th but after that they are simply formed by the addition of *-fed* -/vɛd/ to the cardinal form (see Table 5.28 (b)).

All the numerals are followed by a singular noun; in earlier stages of the language plural nouns could follow numerals and this usage has been fossilized with the original plural of *blwyddyn* 'year', *blynedd*, e.g. *pum mlynedd* 'five years', etc. beside the regular plural *blynyddoedd*. Singular nouns are now the rule, even if a singulative noun has to be used (see 5.3.2), e.g. *saith wythnos* 'seven weeks' : pl. *wythnosau*; *wyth plentyn* 'eight children' : pl. *plant*; *dau dudalen* 'two pages' : pl. *tudal*.

5.4   The verbal system

The verbal system of Modern Welsh is the area of the grammar which probably shows the greatest divergence between the literary and colloquial forms of the language. The divergence is not just at a phonological level but also at both the morphological and the semantic levels. The following discussion makes no claim to exhaustiveness but focuses on a number of important areas.[12]

TABLE 5.28   Welsh numerals

(a) Cardinals

(i) 1–20

1	*un*	11	*un ar ddeg*
2	*dau* (m.) *dwy* (f.)	12	*deudeg*
3	*tri* (m.) *tair* (f.)	13	*tri ar ddeg*
4	*pedwar* (m.) *pedair* (f.)	14	*pedwar ar ddeg*
5	*pum(p)*	15	*pymtheg*
6	*chwe(ch)*	16	*un ar bymtheg*
7	*saith*	17	*dau ar bymtheg*
8	*wyth*	18	*deunaw*
9	*naw*	19	*pedwar ar bymtheg*
10	*deg*	20	*ugain*

(ii) 20 onwards

	Vigesimal	Decimal
30	*deg ar ugain*	*tri deg*
32	*deuddeg ar ugain*	*tri deg dau*
40	*deugain*	*pedwar deg*
50	*hanner cant*	*pum deg*
58	*deunaw a deugain*	*pum deg wyth*
80	*pedwar ugain*	*wyth deg*

(b) Ordinals

1st	*cynta(f)*	8th	*wythfed*
2nd	*ail*	9th	*nawfed*
3rd	*trydydd* (f. *trydedd*)	10th	*degfed*
4th	*pedwerydd* (f. *pedweredd*)	11th	*unfed ar ddeg*
5th	*pumed*	20th	*ugeinfed*
6th	*chwechfed*	30th	*degfed ar hugain*
7th	*seithfed*		

5.4.1   The forms of the verb

Table 5.29 summarizes the range of verbal forms by the traditional division of tense. The inter-relationship between the two columns and the forms in them is discussed below (5.4.3). This section concentrates on formal aspects. In short, there are four inflected elements, the synthetic present/future, the conditional/imperfect, the preterite and the various parts of *bod*, the verb 'to be', which go to make up the analytic forms (see Tables 5.30 and 5.31 respectively on pp. 172 and 173). The synthetic pluperfect, which only figures in high literary language, will generally be left to one side. Table 5.30 shows the standard forms of the three sets of endings involved in the regular verbs. Traditional

TABLE 5.29   Active forms of Welsh *canu* 'sing'

	Synthetic	Analytic
Present		
'he sings'	*cân*	(*y*) *mae e yn canu*
	(*canith/caniff*)	
Future		
'he will sing'	*cân*	(a) *bydd e yn canu*
	(*canith/caniff*)	(b) *gwneith e ganu*
Conditional		
'he would sing'	*canai*	(a) *byddai/buasai e yn canu*
		(b) *gwnai yn canu*
Imperfect		
'he was singing'	*canai*	(*yr*) *oedd yn canu*
Preterite		
'he sang'	*canodd*	*gwnaeth e ganu*
Perfect		
'he has sung'	*canodd*	(*y*) *mae e wedi canu*
Pluperfect		
'he had sung'	*canasai*	(*yr*) *oedd e wedi canu*

Note: (a) and (b) refer to the forms using different auxiliary verbs

grammars also give a present and imperfect subjunctive but they rarely occur outside high literary Welsh. The first point to note at this stage is that the synthetic forms have a restricted usage in the colloquial language (see 5.4.3). It is, therefore, to be expected that they should have undergone a certain amount of remodelling. The usual lack of correspondence between written and spoken forms applies here as elsewhere; for example, *canai* is pronounced /kanɛ/ or /kana/ (see 5.2.1 above), final -*nt* is pronounced -/n/ everywhere, final -*f* is not pronounced, thus *canaf* /kana/. Such alternations will be taken as given in what follows.

There are also some general changes beside the tense-specific remodellings. First, the standard forms have stem-vowel alternations across the tenses, e.g. *cen-* : *can-*, etc.; there is a general tendency for these to be eliminated, thus *canwch, canais*, etc. beside LW *cenwch* and *cenais*. Secondly, in the colloquial forms of the language all the forms in Table 5.30 are followed by affixed pronouns, e.g. /kana i:/ *canaf i*, /kanɛ ve/ *canai fe*, etc. In some cases, this has had phonological consequences; for example, the 1st plural ending -*m* is assimilated to the form of the pronoun *ni*, i.e. *canem ni* > *canen ni*. In this respect, history

TABLE 5.30   The forms of W canu 'sing'

	Present/Future	Conditional/Imperfect	Preterite
1st sg.	*canaf*	*canwn*	*cenais*
2nd sg.	*ceni*	*canit*	*cenaist*
3rd sg.	*cân*	*canai*	*canodd*
1st pl.	*canwn*	*canem*	*canasom*
2nd pl.	*cenwch*	*canech*	*canasoch*
3rd pl.	*canant*	*canent*	*canasant*

is repeating itself in some forms; the standard 2nd plural *-wch/-ech* is the outcome of the conjunction of an original ending **-ed* (< **-ete*) and the 2nd plural pronoun *chwi* (< **su̯īs*) to give *-ech* (< **-ed-ch(wi)*) (Hamp 1975–6: 69–73).

The present/future tense forms in the standard language have a bare-stem 3rd singular; in some verbs it shows vowel alternation, e.g. *saif* 'he stands' : *saf-* /sav/-, *teifl* 'he throws' : *tafl-* /tavl/-, *ceidw* 'he keeps' : *cadw-* /kadu̯/-, *etyb* 'he answers' : *ateb-* /atɛb/-, etc. (S. J. Williams 1980: 82–4, Thorne 1993: 229–34). In addition to a general levelling and elimination of anomalous vowels, the colloquial language has acquired a new ending, north/south-west *-ith* /ɪθ/ or south-east *-iff* /ɪf/ to produce a fully marked 3rd singular, e.g. *gwelith/gweliff* : *gwêl* 'he sees', *credith/crediff* : *cred* 'he believes', etc. The origin of the ending is uncertain but it is perhaps to be derived from a resegmentation of *caiff* /kaif/ where the *-ff* is original (Hamp 1954). The original forms without this ending are still to be found, particularly in proverbs and sayings, more so in the north than the south (B. Thomas and Thomas 1989: 63–4).

The standard form of the conditional/imperfect shows a wide range of vowel alternation in its endings, *-wn*, *-it*, *-ai*, *-em*, etc., which does not survive into the colloquial language (B. Thomas and Thomas 1989: 65). It was noted above that the 3rd singular, e.g. *canai*, would be subject to the regular dialect differentiation into north-west/south-east /kana/ but north-east/south-west /kanɛ/. It seems that the dialect paradigms which generalize either *a* or *e* as the stem vowel may well be based on the 3rd singular, which is the only person where the *e/a* could have arisen. There is also a tendency for *-s-* to appear in these forms, e.g. *welsech* beside *welech*, etc. In terms of the standard language, they look like pluperfects, though there is no difference in meaning between the dialectal forms with and without *-s-* (see Mac Cana 1976: 200–1).

The simple past tense or preterite shows the same kind of reduction of the diphthong in 1st sg. *-ais* and 2nd sg. *-aist* as elsewhere, though in the north-west *-is* and *-ist* are found. In the plural the *-s-* forms are widespread though in Ceinewydd (Newquay), -s-less forms are found, e.g. *canon, canoch*, etc.; they are likely to based on the 3rd sg. *canodd*, where *-s-* is never found (B. Thomas and Thomas 1989: 67–70). The only significant dialectal variation is the presence of a 3rd singular ending -/ʊs/ *-ws* in the south-east. It was a common ending in Middle Welsh in certain forms which suggests it may have been more widespread at one time (see P. W. Thomas 1989: 295–9); in certain forms, e.g. /r̥os/ 'he gave', /tros/ 'he turned', it is even more widespread in the south.

5.4.2 The verb *bod* 'to be'

So far we have been concerned with the formal patterns of the regular verbs, where the stem form remained the same throughout. A number of areas were noted in which the standard patterns had been regularized and alternations levelled. Parts of the verb *bod* /bod/ 'to be' are a vital element of all parts of the analytic tenses of the verb (see Table 5.29) and therefore it deserves special attention. The standard forms are set out in Table 5.31. The phonological variations in the spoken language noted in the preceding section apply here too and are not discussed specifically, e.g. *byddai* /bəðɛ/ or /bəða/. Even in the standard conjugation the present tense forms show a mixture of stems. The dialects tend to preserve most of the forms but with affixed pronouns (B. Thomas and Thomas 1989: 61). Northern dialects prefer the *yd-* /əd/- forms, often with the reduction of the initial vowel, thus 1st sg. *ydw i* /ədʊ ɨ/ : *'dw i* /dʉi/. Further south, the *yd-*forms occur in the form /ɔd/-, e.g.

TABLE 5.31 The forms of W *bod* 'be'

	Present	Future	Conditional
1st sg.	(yd)wyf	byddaf	byddwn/buaswn
2nd sg.	(yd)wyt	byddi	byddit/buasit
3rd sg.	(yd)yw,	bydd	byddai/buasai
	(y)mae, oes		
1st pl.	(yd)ym	byddwn	byddem/buasem
2nd pl.	(yd)ych	byddwch	byddech/buasech
3rd pl.	(yd)ynt	byddynt	byddent/buasent
	Imperfect	Preterite	
1st sg.	oeddwn	bûm	
2nd sg.	oeddit	buost	
3rd sg.	oedd	bu	
1st pl.	oeddem	buom	
2nd pl.	oeddech	buoch	
3rd pl.	oeddynt	buant, buont	

south-east 3rd pl. /ɔdɪn/, but the shorter forms are frequent, e.g /ʊ i/ *wyf i*, etc. The standard form *oes* /ɔɪs/ tends to undergo simplification or change of diphthong in the south, e.g. south-east /os/, Pembs /os/, /ʉes/, etc. (Awbery 1986a: 144; cf. also Pembs /kʉes/ *coes* 'leg').

The imperfect, based on a stem *oedd-* /ɔɪð/-, would seem to be ripe for reduction in the colloquial forms. B. Thomas and Thomas 1989: 66 show how the standard form is essentially maintained in the north-west but further south the diphthong is reduced to /o/ and internal /ð/ is lost. In Cyfeiliog Welsh both forms still co-exist, i.e. 1st sg. /ɔɪðʊn/ : /on/, etc., but in south-east Welsh only the reduced forms are found, i.e. /on/, /oð/, etc. In south Cards/Pembs the characteristic treatment of /o/ is found, i.e. 1st sg. /ʉen/, 3rd sg. /ʉeð/, etc.

Preterite forms tend to retain the standard forms for the most part (B. Thomas and Thomas 1989: 69). Two tendencies are found which tidy up the paradigm. First, the regularization of the 3rd sg. /bi/ *bu* by the addition of the regular ending -/ɔð/, thus /biɔð ɛ/ *buodd e*, and of the 1st sg. by using the regular ending -/es/, thus /bies i/ *bues i*. Secondly, in the north and south-east, the -*o*- of the plural and 2nd singular spread to the other forms, thus 1st sg. /biɔm/ and 3rd singular /biɔ/.

The present tense of *bod* has three different forms for the 3rd singular, (*yd*)*yw*, (*y*)*mae* and *oes* (S. J. Williams 1980: 99). All three forms are found in the colloquial language and continue the same function (see Table 5.32 for examples). The form (*y*)*mae* is used in the simple declarative statement (see Table 5.32 (a)). If the complement is brought to the front for emphasis or contrast, the form of the verb is (*yd*)*yw* (see Table 5.32 (b)). But where the fronted element is adverbial, (y)*mae* is used (see Table 5.32 (a)). The (*yd*)*yw* form is used in negatives and questions (see Table 5.32 (b)). *Oes* has a much more restricted use in negatives and questions with indefinite subjects (see Table 5.32 (c); on the historical background, see H. Lewis 1967).

5.4.3   Tenses, aspect and auxiliary verbs
Table 5.29 above gives all the possible 'tenses' of the verb *canu* 'sing' according to the traditional listing of the tenses; for convenience they are listed in the 3rd singular form. The two columns are distinguished in purely descriptive terms as 'synthetic' and 'analytic' (= periphrastic) but it will emerge in due course that the system is rather more complex than that (see M. Jones and Thomas 1977, Fife 1990).

At first sight, a plausible relabelling of the two columns might be 'non-continuous' : 'continuous/progressive', analogous to English 'he goes' : 'he is going'. The implication is that both versions of each tense are available to all speakers on all occasions. However, as is clear from any consideration of the more colloquial levels of Welsh, the analytic forms are extremely widespread and carry much of the load of the

TABLE 5.32   The uses of the different 3rd sg. forms of bod

(a)   (y)mae
Simple declarative statement:
  mae Ieuan yn athro 'I. is a teacher'
  mae'r ferch yn bert 'the girl is pretty'
  mae Ieuan yn y siop 'I. is in the shop'
Fronted adverbial element:
  Yn y siop y mae Ieuan 'I. is in the shop (*sc.* not in the garage)'

(b)   (yd)yw
Fronted complement:
  Athro yw Ieuan 'I. is a teacher (*sc.* as opposed to a mechanic)'
  pert yw'r ferch 'the girl is pretty (*sc.* not ugly)'
Negatives and questions:
  a ydyw Ieuan yn athro? 'is I. a teacher?' (colloquial *ydy Ieuan yn athro?*)
  nid ydyw Ieuan yn athro 'I. is not a teacher' (colloquial *dydy Ieuan ddim yn athro*)

(c)   oes
Questions and negatives involving indefinites:
  mae plant yn yr ysgol 'children are in the school'
    : question (*a*) *oes plant . . .?*
    : negative (literary) *nid oes plant . . .*
        (colloquial) *does dim plant . . .*

---

synthetic forms; thus, *mae e'n canu* means 'he sings' as much as 'he is singing' (B. Thomas and Thomas 1989: 61). The effect of this is to rule out any simplistic terminological distinction of continuous/non-continuous and more significantly to permit a wider range of temporal and modal usage among the synthetic forms.

The synthetic present should more realistically be termed a future or present/future (Fife 1990: 94–5). In colloquial Welsh it tends to refer to the future, e.g. *ceisiwn ni* 'we shall try', *gwela i chi* 'I'll see you', etc. The analytic future *bydd e'n . . .* can also carry the same sense; for example, it is not clear that there is any significant difference in meaning between (*mi*) *ganith Mair heno* and (*mi*) *fydd Mair yn canu heno* 'M. will (be) sing(ing) tonight' (for *mi* see 5.5.2.3 below). B. Thomas and Thomas 1989: 63–4 suggest that the synthetic forms (and especially those without *-ith/-iff*) may be more common in the north.

The most common of the synthetic tenses in colloquial Welsh is the preterite. It seems to have maintained its status by virtue of there being no direct analytic replacement (see below for *gwnaeth*). It refers to completed actions in the past and is therefore to be distinguished from the analytic 'perfect' tense, e.g. *canodd e* 'he sang' : *mae e wedi canu* 'he has sung'. The latter does not refer to an action completed in the past but to one which began in the past but has some closer link to the present (see Fife 1990: 158).

So far we have been dealing with 'factual' tenses which deal with reality. The use of the analytic present left the synthetic form free to move into a future tense. The analytic imperfect, *oedd e' n canu* 'he was singing', was also preferred to the synthetic *canai*, etc. The *oedd*-type of imperfect of *bod* (see Table 5.31) is, as Fife 1990: 155 observes, unique in being the only synthetic imperfect form which has retained a temporal, non-modal usage. All other synthetic 'imperfects' have a modal sense, e.g. *synnwn i ddim* 'I wouldn't be surprised'. The reason for this may well be that *bod* has another 'imperfect' form which is modal, namely *byddwn, byddai*, etc. The semantic range of imperfects and conditionals also includes the 'habitual' usage. In some northern dialects the conditional forms can imply a stronger sense of habit than the simple present form, e.g. *yr wyf i' n mynd i'r gwely yn gynnar* 'I am going (or 'I go') to bed early', which can be understood habitually, as against *byddwn i' n mynd . . . ,* where the habitual sense is to the fore-front (Fife 1990: 187–8).

It emerges, then, that there is no simple terminological or functional distinction between the two columns of Table 5.29. The bulk of the temporal distinctions in colloquial Welsh are carried by the second col-umn but not all of them; the synthetic preterite still thrives. In the literary language, however, the second column forms barely exist except in specifically continuous contexts. One upshot of this is that the spoken dialects operate with a very different set of modal forms, since some of the synthetic tense forms have become modals.

One aspect is yet to be considered, the use of 'auxiliary' verbs. Clearly, *bod* is the auxiliary *par excellence*. But, as can be seen from the second column of Table 5.29, tense forms of *gwneud* 'do' also fig-ure, namely present/future *gwneith*, preterite *gwnaeth*, and in restricted contexts the imperfect/modal *gwnai*, e.g. *'neith mêl ddim cadw* 'honey won't keep', *mi wnaeth Mair ganu neithiwr* 'M. sang last night', *wnewch chi roi benthyg arian i fi?* 'would you lend me some money?', etc. (examples, from Fife 1990: 235–6; see also Fife 1986a).[13] Parts of *gwneud* in such constructions have generally been taken as 'meaning-less' auxiliaries analogous to English *do* which simply carry the tense markers (M. Jones and Thomas 1977: 72–95). But, as Fife 1990: 235–52 argues, its distribution does not suggest a meaningless carrier; for example, it is not restricted to certain sentence types (as is Eng *do*) nor is it found in every dialect, but only occurs in northern dialects. The latter does not in itself mean that it is more than a meaningless auxil-iary; a single dialect could easily have developed the usage independently of other dialects. Moreover, it is easy to see how it could

Table 5.33: *Gwneud* forms in requests

'lend!'	→	'will you lend' (polite)	→	would you . . . lend?' (more polite)
benthyca!		*fenthycwch?* → *wnewch fenthyg?*		*fenthycech?* → *wnaech fenthyg?*

be interpreted as a meaningless auxiliary. In its basic sense of 'do, make' it is often the neutral way of describing an action, e.g. *fe wnaeth Gareth groesair* 'G. did the crossword' (vs. 'solved'), *fe wnaeth Gareth fara brith* 'G. made *bara brith*' (vs. 'cooked'), etc., and relies on other elements to fill the semantic gap. Moreover, its use as a responsive (see below 5.5.2.2 below), e.g. *ganith Mair heno? Gweith* 'is M. singing tonight? Yes' (lit. 'she does'), does suggest a carrier of tense and person. However, in one area *gwneud*-forms seems to carry a different force from other similar constructions. Requests can range from the less polite commands to very polite requests, i.e. in English from 'lend me a pound' to 'would you be so kind as to lend me a pound?'; or more schematically 'lend' → 'will you lend?' → 'would you . . . lend?'. In Welsh the polite end of the spectrum involves *gwneud*-forms, as in Table 5.33. Here, at least, there is some force carried by the *gwneud*-variant as the more polite alternative in each case. Ellis 1972: 469 has argued that the *gwneud*-forms convey a greater sense of volition. In some areas of their use this may be true, but the dialect evidence seems to suggest that some speakers in North Wales may be moving towards a complete replacement of the inflectional patterns by constructions involving *gwneud* + verbal noun.

   Another 'auxiliary' is also in use in north Welsh dialects, namely /ðarɨ/ *ddaru*, but only as a variant of synthetic preterites or *gwnaeth*-preterites, e.g. *ddaru nhw roi* 'they gave', *ddaru chi ddechrau* 'you began' (Fife 1990: 268–74). There is no doubt that historically it is a reduced form of the preterite of *darfod* 'happen', i.e. /darvɨ/ *darfu*, but synchronically there are significant differences in form and construction. *Ddaru* is an indeclinable fixed form. On the other hand, the pronominal forms used with it are non-subject, e.g. *ddaru mi gweithio* 'I worked' (the subject pronoun would be *i* or *fi*), which might be paralleled by *darfu i mi weithio* lit. 'it happened to me to work'. Here, unlike *gwneud*, *ddaru* seems to be in a stage of transition away from *darfod* towards being a separate auxiliary.

5.4.4 Passives
Traditional grammars state that Welsh has no passive (S. J. Williams 1980: 79, Thorne 1993: 312–14) and strictly speaking with reference to

TABLE 5.34 Impersonals and passives in Welsh

(a) Synthetic forms

Present	*cenir*	lit. 'there is a singing'
Imperfect	*cenid*	lit. 'there was being a singing'
Preterite	*canwyd*	lit. 'there was a singing'

(b) Periphrastic forms

cael + verbal noun, e.g.:

cafodd yr ffermwr ei laddu 'the farmer was killed' (lit. 'the farmer got his killing')

mae'r gwaith wedi cael ei orffen 'the work has been finished' (lit. the work has got its finishing')

(c) Stative passive

bod + *wedi* + verbal noun, e.g.:

mae'r gwaith wedi ei orffen 'the work is finished'

---

the literary language it is true, but it does not tell the whole story. Literary Welsh has a series of impersonal forms differentiated by tense (see Table 5.34 (a)). Grammatically speaking, these forms are active, and transitive verbs can take an object which is interpretable as the subject of a passive with the agent marked by *gan* 'by', e.g. *lladdwyd y ffermwr gan y tarw* 'the farmer was killed by the bull' (lit. 'there was a killing of the farmer by the bull'), *gwelir y môr* 'the sea is seen' (lit. 'there is a seeing of the sea'). B. Thomas and Thomas 1989: 73 note that in Pwllheli in the early 1970s it was recorded that younger speakers were not using the impersonal forms, though they were still common among the older generation. Nevertheless, the dialectal evidence does show examples of impersonals (B. Thomas and Thomas 1989: 74), though the findings from Pwllheli suggest that they might be disappearing.

The common passive construction in colloquial Welsh is one with the auxiliary verb, *cael* 'get' (see Table 5.32 (b) and Fife 1990: 458–82). To repeat the example used above, the passive would be *cafodd y ffermwr ei laddu (fe) gan y tarw* (lit. 'the farmer got his killing by the bull'). This construction is widespread and is taking over from the impersonal pattern, certainly in Pwllheli and probably everywhere. Its advantage within the patterns of colloquial Welsh is that it can mirror the tense and aspectual distinctions of the active constructions better than the impersonals (for theoretical discussions, see 5.5.4 below).

There is another type of pattern which can be described as 'stative' passive as opposed to the more 'dynamic' *cael*-construction (see Table 5.34 (c)). We may contrast *mae'r gwaith wedi cael ei orffen heddiw* 'the work has been finished today' (lit. '. . . has got its finishing today') and *mae'r gwaith wedi (ei) orffen (e)* 'the work has been finished' or equally 'the work is finished'. The latter represents the state of completion while the former with *cael* refers to the action of completion. *Wedi* is not the only marker used in this construction; compare *mae'r gwaith heb ei orffen (e)* 'the work has not been finished' (lit. '. . . without its finishing') and *mae'r gwaith newydd ei orffen (e)* 'the work has just been finished' (lit. '. . . newly its finishing'). In all three types the emphasis is on the state of completion not on the action. In colloquial usage the possessive preceding the verbal noun is usually dropped leaving the mutation and the affixed pronoun to carry the semantic load. In standard traditional terminology such constructions are equivalent to 'past participle passive', and indeed seem to be the colloquial Welsh equivalents of verbal adjectives in *-edig*; the above examples would equate with a notional *gorffenedig* (Williams 1980: 120).

5.5 Syntax

5.5.1 Word order[14]

It will have emerged from the range of sentences quoted above that, apart from some initial particles which are the subject of 5.5.2, the usual order of constituents in both modern colloquial and literary Welsh is verb + subject + object (VSO), e.g.:

Collodd Ieuan y llyfr
lost I. the book
'I. lost the book'

Even if the semantic load of the verb does not appear until later in the sentence in the form of a verbal noun, the tense and person markers are carried by a verbal element in initial position, e.g.:

Mae Mair yn mynd i 'r pentre
is M. in go to the village
'M. is going/goes to the village'

In sentences involving the verb 'to be', the verb comes first in unemphatic, unmarked sentences in predicative, descriptive types, e.g. *mae Ieuan yn ddoniol* 'I. is funny', *mae Ieuan yn athro* 'I. is a teacher'; here *yn* functions as a predicate marker. But in identificatory copula sentences the word order is SVO, e.g. *Ieuan (yd)yw'r athro* 'I. is the teacher' (for the difference in form of the verb, see 5.4.2 and Table 5.32). The relationship is one of identification, i.e. the teacher is identified as Ieuan or vice versa. The latter sentence is unemphatic and unmarked and in that form is distinct from the preceding predicative sentence. But the former, *mae Ieuan yn athro*, can undergo 'inversion' (M. Jones and Thomas 1977: 48) or fronting in contrastive or emphatic contexts, typically in response to questions, e.g.:

TABLE 5.35   Fronting in Modern Welsh periphrastic tenses

(a)	Basic and unmarked

(a) Basic and unmarked
    (Yr) Oedd Ieuan yn eistedd yn yr   ardd
        was I.   in sit   in the garden
    'I. was sitting in the garden'
(b) *Eistedd yn yr ardd yr oedd Ieuan*
    sitting in the garden was I.
    'I. was sitting in the garden (as opposed to cutting the grass)
(c) *Ieuan a oedd yn eistedd yn yr   ardd*
    I.   was in sit   in the garden.
    'I. was sitting in the garden (in contrast to Mair who was cutting the grass)
(d) *Yn yr   ardd yr oedd Ieuan yn eistedd*
    in the garden was I.   in sit.
    'I. was sitting in the garden (as opposed to on the beach)

    Beth ydy Ieuan? Athro   ydy e
    what is   I.?   teacher is he
    'What is I.? He is a teacher

A different question can produce a different fronted element, e.g.:

    Pwy yma sydd yn athro?   Ieuan sydd yn athro
    who here is (rel.) teacher   I.   is (rel.) teacher
    'Who here is a teacher? I. is a teacher.'

There are, then, cases where the order of constituents in predicative statements gets very close to the order in identificatory statements. There are still differences, notably in the presence or absence of the definite article.

The phenomenon of fronting is not unique to copula-type sentences, but is widespread in the language. It is possible to front almost any element of the sentence for contrast or emphasis. The variations on one sentence, set out in Table 5.35, show the range of possibilities and implications (see T. A. Watkins 1991). The written forms cannot possibly do justice to the intonation and stress which the spoken forms would have. Note that in Table 5.35 (b) the 'aspect' marker *yn* is deleted when the phrase is fronted. However, other aspect markers are preserved in that position, e.g. *mae Ieuan wedi eistedd* . . . 'I. has been sitting' and *mae Ieuan newydd eistedd* . . . 'I. has just been sitting', are shifted to *wedi eistedd y mae Ieuan* . . . '. . . but is now getting up' and *newydd eistedd y mae Ieuan* . . . '. . . but has to get up already'. The use of the imperfect makes the example very easy to construct. Matters are, however, more complex with a synthetic verb (see Table 5.36). Fronting the subject or object causes no difficulties (see Table 5.36 (b) and (c)) but the verb cannot be emphasized by fronting. In this case the

TABLE 5.36   Fronting in Modern Welsh synthetic verbs

(a) Basic and unmarked:
     Torrodd Ieuan y   glaswellt
     cut   I.   the grass
     'I. cut the grass'
(b) *Ieuan (a)   dorrodd y   glaswellt*
     I.   rel. cut   the grass
     'I. cut the grass' (as opposed to Mary)
(c) *Y   glaswellt (a)   dorrodd Ieuan*
     the grass   rel. cut   I.
     'I. cut the grass' (as opposed to the prize daffodils)
(d) *Torri y   glaswellt (a)   wnaeth/ddaru Ieuan*
     cut   the grass   rel. did   I.
     'I. cut the grass' (as opposed to pruning the roses)

auxiliary *gwnaeth/ddaru* has to be used (see Table 5.36 (d)). In fronting, the verb is preceded by a relative pronoun in more formal and literary styles of the language but in colloquial Welsh the relative particle rarely occurs and the only marking is the remaining mutation which is only found after the fronted subjects or objects.

5.5.2 Pre-sentential particles
In literary Welsh there are a number of particles which regularly appear before the verb (see M. Jones and Thomas 1977: 356–63). They function as markers of sentence type as declarative, negative or interrogative. This is yet another area where there is a significant difference between the literary and the spoken language; to a large extent, though not entirely, they do not exist in the spoken language, since the information is conveyed differently.

5.5.2.1 Negatives
Negation in Welsh is marked both by pre-sentential particles and/or by medial negative particles. The former is regular in literary Welsh. The form of the negative is determined partly by the type of clause following it. Preceding a main clause the negative is *ni* (*nid* before a vowel) (see Table 5.37 (a) overleaf). When an element is fronted, i.e. where the initial of the sentence is not a verb, the negative is *nid* irrespective of the following phonetic context (see Table 5.37 (b)). *Oni(d)* occurs in negative questions (see Table 5.37 (c)). The form *na(c)* is used in negative imperatives (see Table 5.37 (d)). Subordinate clause negation is usually marked by *na(d)* (see Table 5.37 (e); see also 5.5.3 below).
    None of these negatives occurs in its full form in the spoken language. Frequently, the only sign of its original presence is the soft

182

TABLE 5.37 Negatives in Literary Welsh

(a) Preverbal negative *ni(d)*
  mae Mair yn aros 'M. is waiting' : neg. *nid ydy Mair yn aros*
  rhedodd Ieuan i ffwrdd 'I. ran away' : neg. *ni redodd ...*

(b) Negative *nid* before fronted elements
  Ieuan sy'n torri y glaswellt 'I. cuts the grass' (*sc.* as opposed to Mary) :
    neg. *nid Ieuan . . .*

(c) *Oni(d)* in negative questions
  mae Mair yn mynd 'M. is going' : *onid yw mair yn mynd* 'isn't M. going?'

(d) Negative imperatives *na(c)*
  canwch! 'sing!' : neg. *na chanwch!* 'don't sing!'

(e) Negative in subordinate clauses *na(d)*
  yr wyf yn gwybod bod Ieuan yn dôd 'I know that I. is coming' : neg. . . .
    nad ydy Ieuan yn dôd

---

mutation of the initial of the verb. The negative function has largely
been taken over by the medial negative *d(d)im*. Its basic meaning was
'thing' but it developed into a negative much as the second element of
French *ne . . . pas* and Breton *ne . . . ket* (Hemon 1975: 284–6); originally it had no negative sense but has tended to carry more and more of
the functional load. In the spoken language the functional shift has now
gone so far that the initial negative has been lost (see Table 5.38(a)).
The final *-d* of the negative is preserved in *dydy* and only mutation
marks the passing of the initial negative in *redodd*. In fronted sentences
nid tends to be maintained though it can be replaced by *ddim* (see Table
5.38 (b)). The spoken form of the negative imperative is entirely different in that it uses another verb to mark the negation (see Table 5.38 (c)).
  However, in transitive sentences with synthetic verbs the original
sense of *dim* '(any)thing' leads to a slightly different pattern where the
object is treated partitively with the preposition *o* 'from', and in the
pronominal form the conjugated form of the preposition is used (see
5.3.5; see Table 5.38 (d) for examples). The high frequency of the pattern has led to a common reduction of *ddim o* to /mɔ/.
  Generally these patterns are found in most dialects. However, in
Pembrokeshire some interesting variants are found (Awbery 1988,
1990; also B. Thomas and Thomas 1989: 79–80; see Table 5.39 for
examples). The explanation is to be found in a reworking of the *ddim
ohono fe* type construction discussed above. Beside the usual position
of *dim*, i.e. verb + subject + *ddim*, in the Welsh of Pembrokeshire the
negative with *bod* 'to be' can occur between the verb and the subject,
i.e. verb + *ddim* + subject, and seems to carry the preposition *o* with it,

TABLE 5.38   Negatives in spoken Welsh

(a)   Spoken variants of Table 5.37(a)
    nid ydy Mair yn aros → *dydy Mair ddim yn aros*
    ni rhedodd Ieuan i ffwrdd → *redodd Ieuan ddim i ffwrdd*

(b)   Spoken variants of Table 5.37(b)
    nid/ddim Ieuan yn torri' r glaswellt
    'it is not I. who is cutting the grass'

(c)   Spoken variants of Table 5.37(d)
    na chanwch → *peidiwch â chanu* (lit. 'stop at singing')

(d)   Partitive negatives
    torrodd Ieuan y glaswellt 'I. cut the grass' : neg. *dorrodd Ieuan ddim*
    o' r glaswellt (lit. '. . . nothing of the grass')
Pronominal version:
    torrodd Ieuan e 'I. cut it' : *dorrodd Ieuan ddim ohono fe* (lit. 'none of it')

---

which will conjugate with a pronominal object. Another factor seems to have conspired with this construction, namely the spread of /os/ (see 5.4.2 = literary Welsh *oes*) in a reduced form *s*, from being a 3rd singular present form to the general negative present form. Out of this has emerged such forms as *s dim ono i'n gwbod* 'I don't know', etc. Beside these Awbery 1988: 43 treats the *sana i'n gwbod* type as reflecting the deletion of *ddim*, e.g. *sana i'n cofio* < *s oni'n cofio* 'I don't remember'. Similarly, the past tense forms are based on /ɥeð/, the dialectal treatment of *oedd* (see 5.4.2) with loss of /ð/, e.g. *weno fe* . . . < **we(dd)*
ono fe . . . . Two further variants show further truncation; *sa i'n cofio* seems to show the unconjugated form of *o*, while *eno'n cofio* has dropped the initial *w-*, leaving the *e* as the sole remaining indicator of the verb. Effectively, the close parallel, noted above (5.3.5), between

---

TABLE 5.39   Pembrokeshire negatives

Standard
(dy)dwy i ddim yn gwybod 'I don't know'
(dy)dy e ddim yn gwybod 'he doesn't know'

Pembrokeshire

Present	1st sg.	*simo i'n gwbod* (Morgan 1987)
		sana i'yn gwbod
	3rd sg.	*sano fe'n gwbod*
Past	1st sg.	*wena i'n gwbod*
	3rd sg.	*weno fe'n gwbod*

---

the verbal endings and the conjugated prepositions has permitted the easy shift from the latter to the former to create a fully fledged negative conjugation of *bod* unique to Pembrokeshire Welsh.

Another dialectal development is found in some southern dialects, where instead of the standard pattern of negation, *nag* occurs before the verb without a following *ddim*, e.g. *nag wi'n lico mynd i'r ysgol* 'I don't like going to school' (B. Thomas and Thomas 1989: 78).

5.5.2.2   Interrogatives

Apart from the negative question marker *onid* noted above and interrogative pronouns, e.g. *pwy?* 'who?', *ble?* 'where?', *pam?* 'why?', the basic interrogative particle in literary Welsh is *a* before a verb and *ai* before any other element, e.g. *a welaist ti ef?* 'did you see him?', *ai cysgu y mae hi?* 'is she sleeping?' (lit. 'sleeping is she?'). In the spoken language there are no interrogative particles; the only trace is mutation of the initial of the verb but the burden of the interrogative rests on intonation. Only *bod* 'to be' has a separate interrogative form, *oes*, when the subject is indefinite; for example, compare *oes cathod yn yr ardd?* 'are there cats in the garden?' with *ydy'r cathod yn yr ardd?* 'are the cats in the garden?'.

As in Irish (3.5.2.2), questions can be asked by adding tag questions to the end of declarative statements. If the statement contains a part of *bod*, it is repeated following the same tense and person. It is prefixed by *on'd* in positive statements and by *na(g)* in negatives (see Table 5.40 (a), King 1993: 159–60). When a synthetic verb is used, a general *onid*

TABLE 5.40   Tag questions in Welsh

(a)   With parts of *bod*
Positive:

Present	*mae . . ., (on'd ydy?)* (definite)
	(on'd oes?) (indefinite)
Imperfect	*roedd . . ., on'd oedd?*
Future	*bydd . . ., on'd fydd?*

Negative:

Present	*dydy . . . (ddim), nag ydy?*
	does . . . (ddim), nag oes?
Imperfect	*doedd . . . (ddim), nag oedd?*
Future	*fydd . . . (ddim), na fydd?*

(b)   With synthetic verbs
Literary: *onid e?*
Colloquial: *ynte?*, *yntefe?*, etc., e.g. *aeth e i'r dre, ynte?* 'he went to town, didn't he?'

TABLE 5.41   Welsh responsives

(a) Summary	yes/no
(i) Nominal first element	*Ie/nage*
(ii) Parts of *bod*:	
Present *ydy*	*Ydy/nag ydy*
Imperfect *oedd*	*Oedd/nag oedd*
Future *fydd*	*Bydd/na fydd*
Conditional *fyddai*	*Fyddai/na fyddai*
(iii) Preterite synthetic verb	*Do/naddo*

(b) Examples (the sections correspond to (a)
- (i) *Ieuan sy'n torri y glaswellt? Ie/nage* 'is I. cutting the grass? Yes/no'
- (ii) *oes cathod yn yr ardd? Oes/nag oes* 'are there cats in the garden? Yes/no'

  ydy Ieuan yn yr ardd? Ydy/nag ydy 'is I. in the garden? Yes/no'

  oedd Ieuan yn yr ardd? Oedd/nag oedd 'was I. in the garden? Yes/no'

  ydyn ni yn Abertawe eto? Ydyn/nag ydyn 'are we in Swansea yet? Yes/no'
- (iii) *welaist ti Ieuan? Do/naddo* 'did you see I.? Yes/no'

(c) Other verbs used in responsives

ga(f) i fynd? cei/na chei (cewch/na chewch) 'may I go? Yes/no' (lit. ' you may/you may not')(variation of informal and formal forms)

ddylai hi fynd? Dylai/na ddylai 'ought she to go? Yes/no' (lit. 'she ought/she ought not')

redi di i'r siop i fi? Gwnaf/na wnaf Will you run to the shop for me? Yes/no' (lit. 'I will do/I will not do').

---

e is used as the tag irrespective of the tense or person; in the spoken language it becomes *ynte?*, *yntefe?* or *ontefe?* (see Table 5.40 (b)).

The most complex aspect of interrogatives has to do with the answers to questions (see Table 5.41 (a) for a summary and (b) for examples). Essentially, as in Irish, there are no simple 'yes/no' words, except in two specific contexts: first, after synthetic preterites and, secondly, where a non-verbal element has been fronted (see Table 5.41 (b). Elsewhere, and in particular with the periphrastic *bod* forms, the verb form (including tense, number and person) is repeated (see Table 5.41(b)) (ii) for examples). The same pattern operates for a number of other common verbs in Welsh, namely *gwneud* 'do', *cael* 'get, receive', *gallu/medru* 'can', *dylai* 'ought' (see Table 5.41 (c)). For the synthetic forms of most other verbs, the responsive forms are provided by *gwneud*.

5.5.2.3 *Declaratives*

A striking feature of both literary Welsh and colloquial Welsh is the
tendency to generalize either *mi* /mi/ or *fe* /vɛ/ before synthetic verbal
forms. They look like preposed personal pronouns (and indeed this is
probably their origin (Mac Cana 1973: 117–18; see also 9.1.2.2)) but
they show no agreement with the subject of the verb, e.g. *fe/mi ddaeth e*
'he came', *fe/mi dorrodd Ieuan* . . . 'I. cut . . .', etc. In literary Welsh
they are not used before parts of *bod* where *yr* occurs, but in the spoken
language they are relatively common, e.g. *mi oedd* /mi ɔɪð/ 'he was', *fe
fydd* /vɛ vɪð/ 'he will be'. T. A. Watkins 1977: 147–8 has claimed that
use of the particle has become more common in the literary language
where its function is to colloquialize; in other words, the implication is
that it is primarily a feature of the spoken language. However, the
dialect evidence suggests that, while these particles do occur, particle-
less verbs are very common (B. Thomas and Thomas 1989: 75–7). The
regional distribution indicates that *mi* is northern, but in the southern
dialects there is considerable variation between *mi* and *fe*. The most
striking adaption of the pattern, or perhaps a continuation of the earlier
state of affairs, is found in south-east Glamorgan where the interpretation of *mi* and *fe* as pronouns seems to have reached its logical
conclusion and the forms agree in number and gender, e.g. *fi wn* 'I
know', *ti wddet* 'you (sg./informal) know', *chi wddoch* 'you (pl./for-
mal) know', etc. (see 4.3.2).

5.5.3 Subordination

It is not intended to list here and discuss all the types of subordinate
clauses, but some general distinctions may be helpful. Essentially, they
are marked either by an initial conjunction or particle + finite verb, e.g.
in temporal clauses with *pan* 'when' and relative clauses with *a* or *y*, or
by a verbal noun construction. Reported speech and relative clauses are
used to illustrate some of the features involved.

5.5.3.1 *Reported speech*

Following main verb constructions, there are two different syntactical
devices available to mark reported speech (see Table 5.42); they are not
interchangeable but are determined by the type of verb in the subordinate clause. Where the verb in the clause is synthetic, the construction
is simply *y* + finite verb (as in Table 5.42 (a)-(c)); in the spoken language the particle usually vanishes, leaving no clear marker of
subordination beyond the ordering of the verbs. But when the verb in
the subordinate clause would be *mae* 'is' or *oedd* 'was', as it frequently
would be in periphrastic verbs, the verbal noun is used instead (as in
Table 5.42 (d)). Where the subject of the subordinate verb is pronominal, it is marked by a possessive pronoun, as befits the nominal
character of a verbal noun (as in Table 5.42 (e); see also 8.3.1.1). The

TABLE 5.42   Reported speech in Welsh

Mae Ieuan yn dweud 'I. said' / *dwedodd Ieuan* 'I. said':
(a) (*y*) *gweithiodd Tom yn Abertawe llynedd*
    'that T. worked in Swansea last year'
(b) (*y*) *bydd Tom yn gweithio yn A. y fory*
    'that T. will be working in S. tomorrow'
(c) (*y*) *dylen nhw fynd adre*
    'that they ought to go home'
(d) *bod Tom wedi gweithio yn A.*
    'that T. has/had been working in S.'
(e) (*ei*) *fod ef wedi gweithio yn A.*
    'that he has been working in S.'
(f) *na weithiodd T yn A. llynedd*
    'that T. did not work in S. last year'
(g) *na fydd Tom yn gweithio yn A. y fory*
    'that T. will not be working in S. tomorrow'
(h) *nad ydy Tom yn gweithio yn A.*
    'that T. is not working in S.'
(i) *bod Tom ddim yn gweithio yn A.*
    'that T. is not working in S.'
(j) *mai/taw Mair* (*a*) *dorrodd y glaswellt*
    'that M. cut the grass (*sc.* not Ieuan)'
(k) *nid Mair* (*a*) *dorrodd y glaswellt*
    'that it was not M. who cut the grass'

---

possessive element preceding the verbal noun is usually lost in speech, leaving *bod* (mutated where necessary) at the head of the clause. As a verbal noun, *bod* is neutral as to tense; the tense distinction between past and present is determined by the tense of the main verb. The finite verb construction is also clearer in negative constructions. In more formal levels of the language, only the finite verb type can be negated (as in Table 5.42 (f)-(g)). The *bod*-type construction is required to revert to the former construction (as in Table 5.42 (h)). However, in the spoken language the use of *ddim* with *bod* is widespread (as in Table 5.42 (i)). In some respects, then, the *bod*-construction is marginal but in view of the widespread use of the periphrastic present as the unmarked form, it is extremely common.

There is a third type of reported speech which is restricted to the non-verb initial-pattern, e.g. *Mair* (*a*) *dorrodd y glaswellt* 'M. cut the grass' (as opposed to Ieuan), etc., where there is some focus or emphasis on the initial element. In such cases, the focus cannot be maintained in the indirect forms by either of the above constructions, but rather the clause is preceded by *mai* /maɪ/ or *taw* /taʊ/ (see Table 5.42 (j) for an example). *Mai* is the standard and northern form, while *taw* is used in southern dialects. They are verbal forms in origin, marginal forms in the complex paradigm of *bod*, but they do not change and very much have the status of particles.

5.5.3.2   Relative clauses

Formal levels of Welsh have two relative particles, *a* and *y(r)* (S. J. Williams 1980: 51–4, Thorne 1993: 171–86). The former is used to refer to an antecedent which is the subject or object of the verb, e.g. *dyma'r llyfr a brynais* 'here is the book I bought', the latter when the antecedent is something other than the object or object, e.g. *dyma'r modd y clywais am y peth* 'this is how I heard about the thing'. The subject/object relative particle causes the soft mutation, while *y* is followed by the unmutated form. However, in the spoken language the relative particles have disappeared, leaving behind only the mutation associated with subject/object relatives.

An important feature of Welsh relative clauses is the use of resumptive pronouns. Periphrastic verbs, such as *mae e'n prynu* 'he is buying', etc., do not take a direct object, even though they may be semantically transitive. This arises out of the nominal nature of the verbal noun, which does not, therefore, take a grammatical object but rather a possessive, genitive construction (see 8.3.1.2); for example, *mae e'n prynu llyfr* is to be interpreted literally as 'he is in buying of a book'. The genitival nature of the phrase is made clear by the pronominal usage, i.e. *mae e'n ei brynu ef* (lit. 'he is in its buying'), where the possessive pronoun is used (5.3.3.4). When periphrastic verbs appear in relative clauses, therefore, they are preceded by *y* in the formal language. The result is a mismatch between the semantics of the relative clause and its formal realization, i.e. there is a semantic antecedent but not a formal one. The solution was to use a resumptive pronoun with the verbal noun which refers to the antecedent, e.g. *ble mae'r llyfr (yr) wy(f) i wedi ei brynu?* 'where is the book I have bought?' (lit. '. . . I am after its buying?'); the pronoun *ei* refers to *y llyfr* 'the book'. A similar pattern is found with formally intransitive verbs which are followed by a preposition, e.g. *edrych ar* 'look at', *dianc o* 'escape from', etc., e.g. *ble mae'r llyfr (yr) oeddwn i'n edrych arno?* 'where is the book I was looking at?' (lit. '. . . I was looking at it?'). In this case the 'copy' pronoun is in the conjugated preposition *arno* 'at it'. They tend to occur in the formal language only in the latter construction by virtue of the fact that periphrastic verbs are rare at that level of the language. Finally, there is one feature of resumptive pronouns which distinguishes them from full-scale possessive pronouns; namely, they never have a following affixed pronoun; thus we may compare *mae e wedi (ei) brynu ef* 'he has bought it' : *y llyfr (y) mae e wedi (ei) brynu* 'the book he has

SYNTAX   189

bought'. Even if in the spoken language the preceding possessive disappears, the mutation is then the only marker.

5.5.4 Theoretical treatments of Welsh syntax

In recent years Welsh syntax has received considerable attention from theoretical linguists keen to test their theories in a rather trickier field than some.[15] This section is not intended to survey all work on Welsh syntax but will concentrate on one area. The *cael*-passive (see 5.4.4) has received considerable attention, notably in Awbery 1976 (Transformational Grammar), Fife 1990 (Cognitive Grammar) and Borsley 1990a (Head-driven Phrase Structure Grammar). Awbery 1976 produced an account of the Welsh passive concentrating largely on the *cael*-passives; her account is couched in terms of Transformational Grammar of the late 60s and early 70s. The examples used in the following discussion are set out in Table 5.43. According to Awbery 1976: 6–12, the deep structure of Table 5.43 (a) would be that given in Figure 5.5 overleaf with a series of rules to produce the surface structure. However, the periphrastic present (Table 5.43 (b)) has a split between the tense- and aspect-carrying verb and the uninflected but semantically loaded verb. Awbery 1976: 12–31 analyses such a sentence as a complex sentence containing a matrix sentence with tense and person markers and a prepositional phrase (PP), with an uninflected verb embedded below the object NP of the prepositional (as in Figure 5.6). The obligatory application of equi-subject deletion would remove *Ifor* from S_2. Awbery's contention is that a passive sentence can be interpreted in a similar way; thus Table 5.43 (c) could have the deep structure set out in Figure 5.7. Two different rules must apply here which did not affect Table 5.43 (b); first, an agent postposing rule is needed to raise the subject of the embedded sentence (S_2) into a

TABLE 5.43   Active and passive examples.

Active
(a) Preterite: *rhybuddiodd Ifor Wyn*
                 'Ifor warned Wyn'
(b) Present: *mae Ifor yn rhybuddio Wyn*
                 'Ifor is warning Wyn'
Passive
(c) Preterite: *cafodd Wyn ei rybuddio gan Ifor*
                 'Wyn was warned by Ifor'
                 (lit. 'Wyn got his warning by Ifor')
(d) Present: *mae Wyn yn cael ei rybuddio gan Ifor*
                 'Wyn is warned by Ifor'
                 (lit. 'Wyn is in getting his warning by Ifor')

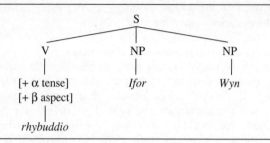

FIGURE 5.5   The deep structure of Table 5.43 (a)

matrix sentence prepositional phrase. Secondly, instead of an equi-subject deletion rule, a pronominalization rule is required to turn *Wyn* in
S_2 into a preposed pronoun (for details, see Awbery 1976: 57–68).
Thus, the deep structure of Figure 5.7 develops into the intermediate
structure of Figure 5.8. Sentence (d) in Table 5.43, the periphrastic present passive, where *cael* itself is not inflected, can be treated in a
similar way but with a double embedding. Figure 5.9 presents the deep
structure; the same rules as described above would be applied to S_3.
   The rules devised by Awbery are very similar to those required by

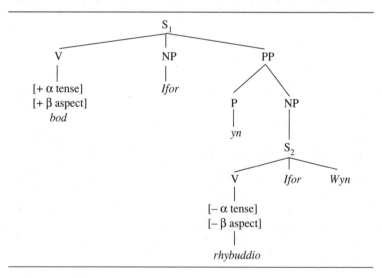

FIGURE 5.6   The deep structure of Table 5.43 (b).

PP = prepositional phrase.

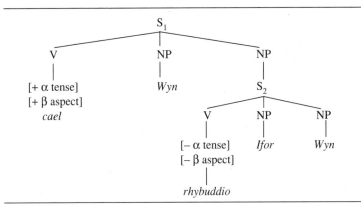

FIGURE 5.7   The deep structure of Table 5.43 (c)

other constructions in Welsh, especially those involving verbal nouns. The passive construction differs in requiring rules to identify the subject of the matrix sentence with the object of the embedded sentence. This, of course, captures a generalization about active/passive sentences, that they require the object of the active sentence to become the subject of the passive sentence.

One area where Awbery's analysis seems rather cumbersome and does not really capture the general pattern of the language is the distinction between periphrastic and synthetic verbal formation, whether active or passive. The question is approached in a different way by M. Jones and Thomas 1977. The two main differences are that they set up a large class of auxiliary verbs, such as *bod, gwneud, gallu, ddaru,* etc. (see 5.4.3), but which also includes the endings of synthetic verbs; thus, they include as auxiliaries *-ith* (present/future), *-odd* (preterite), *-ai* (modal), etc. By doing so, they can analyse synthetic verbs as auxiliaries + a verbal phrase unmarked for tense and person. Another difficulty has to do with the *yn/wedi* clauses; Awbery treats them as prepositional phrases but Jones and Thomas analyse them simply as aspect markers. Taking our sentences (a) and (b) in Table 5.43 (we will ignore the complexities of (c) and (d) here), Jones and Thomas would analyse them in very similar ways (see Figure 5.10 (a) and (b) on p. 193). The analysis of the *cael*-passive is similar to that of Awbery in that it involves the embedding of the active sentence and the subsequent deletion of certain elements in S₂, namely PT, AUX, NP-*Wyn* (M. Jones and Thomas 1977: 268–76; see Figure 5.11 on p. 194).

One significant difference between these accounts which causes some difficulty for Jones and Thomas is that they treat the verbal ele-

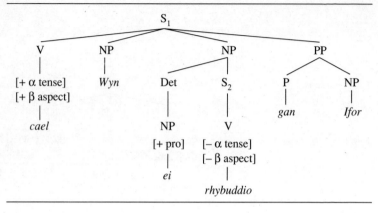

FIGURE 5.8   The intermediate structure of Figure 5.6

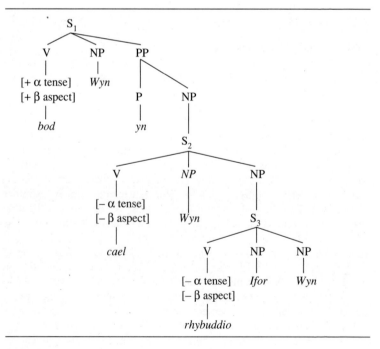

FIGURE 5.9   The deep structure of Table 5.43 (d).

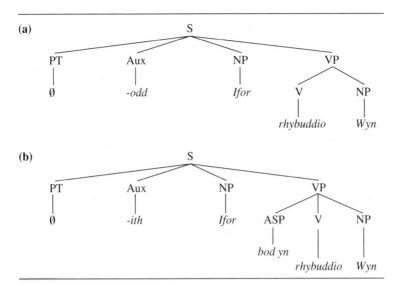

FIGURE 5.10   Deep structures of active sentences (according to M. Jones and Thomas 1977: 69)

PT = particle, ASP = aspect

ment as a VP; when in the passive construction a pronominalization rule is invoked to delete *Ifor* from S$_2$, it is not clear why the surface form is a possessive pronoun. In some ways, then, Awbery's account is more elegant for passives, but does cause difficulties in aligning all the present forms under one explanation.

Another question which arises is the level of the *gan*-phrase. Awbery, together with Jones and Thomas, locates this relatively high in the structure. But, if one is trying to extract some general principles of formation, it would seem to belong closer to the embedded sentence, especially as it can be paralleled by possessive phrases, such as *mae'r llyfr gan Mair* 'M. has the book' (lit. 'the book is with M.'). In other words, *gan* is associated with nominal elements more than with verbal elements. Awbery argues that the *gan*-phrase must be outside the NP because it cannot be preposed; i.e. we do not find **ei rybuddio gan Wyn a gafodd Ifor*. On the other hand, her approach seems to miss the generalization available by this slightly different approach.

Despite certain differences, Awbery 1976 and M. Jones and Thomas 1977 are working within the same theoretical framework. Borsley 1990a looks at the matter from the point of view of Head-driven Phrase

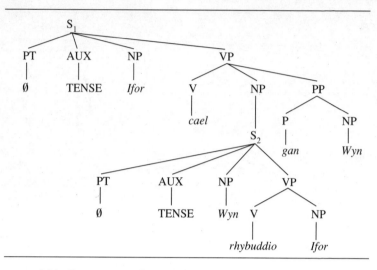

FIGURE 5.11   Deep structure for a passive sentence (according to M. Jones and Thomas 1977: 269)

Structure Grammar. He works within a theory of PSG (Phrase Structure Grammar) but where each head, i.e. V, N, incorporates information about the categories with which they combine rather than allowing the rules to be generated piecemeal. Borsley would analyse the structure of Table 5.43 (c) as in Figure 5.12. He, rightly in my view, incorporates the PP into the VP but, unlike Awbery but with Jones and Thomas, takes *ei rybuddio*, etc. as a VP and not a NP. This is a major point of difference and affects the sets of rules which have to apply subsequently to produce the right surface structure. The difficulty lies with the ambiguous status of verbal nouns which behave partly like verbs and partly like nouns (see Chapter 8). The question amounts to whether it is more satisfactory to produce an analysis which is consistent with the patterns of the passive formation in other languages, or one consistent with the behaviour of similar elements elsewhere in Welsh; for example, *cael* 'gets' occurs frequently as a transitive verb with nominal objects and *gan* occurs with nouns.

The latter approach is very much that of Fife 1990 in his use of Cognitive Grammar. In short, Cognitive Grammar recognizes a direct, symbolic relation between form and meaning. The form of the language is taken as indicative of the meaning and there is no concern with underlying deep structure or abstract entities (Fife 1990: 17–80). In other words, a language works the way it looks as if it works. Thus, for example, since *cael* means 'take, get' and regularly takes nominal

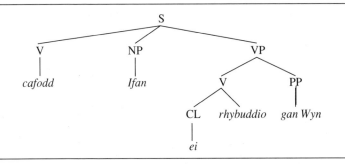

FIGURE 5.12   Deep structure of Table 5.43 (c) (according to Borsley 1990a: 97)

CL = clitic.

objects, then its use in passives is precisely that and the verbal element must be taken at face value as a verbal noun. At the level of a specific language this may seem very satisfying but it would appear to lack any idea of generalization and construction of general theories about, for example, passivization. The cognitive grammarian's concept of passivization would hardly satisfy many theoretical linguists:

> This does not mean the cognitive grammarian does not recognize a general linguistic notion of 'passive'. It does deny that all languages have precisely the same structures underlying their passives, as is plainly evidenced by the propositional diversity among the world's passive structures . . . However, all passives seem to have one thing (at least) in common: some non-agentive (usually a patient) serves as the most prominent or profiled THING in a construction with a verbal element. In other words, the most prominent nominal in construction with a verbal is equated with the 'object' (direct, or sometimes oblique) of the verbal process (Fife 1990: 454).

It is perhaps the price to be paid for closer analysis of specific features of specific languages.

Notes

1. For general discussions of Welsh, see A. R. Thomas 1992a, T. A. Watkins 1993, Thorne 1992; see also Price 1992c for the present-day language. For brief introductions, see Thorne 1985 and J. Davies 1993.
2. There are a vast number of MA and PhD theses describing dialects (see B. Thomas and Thomas 1989: 157–69) but most have yet to attract a publisher; see Sweet 1882–4, Fynes-Clinton 1913, Sommerfelt 1925a, C. H. Thomas 1993, and briefer discussions such as T. A. Watkins 1967, C. H. Thomas 1975–6, etc.

3.   See R. O. Jones 1986; for a useful introduction and background discussion to Welsh dialectology, see Ball 1988b.
4.   See A. R. Thomas 1973: 316–17, B. Thomas and Thomas 1989: 35. For a detailed discussion of the historical developments, see Russell 1990: 39–60, P. W. Thomas 1989: 292–4, 1993, and 4.3.3 above.
5.   The notation used for diphthongs shows a vocalic second element. But Awbery 1984: 90–8 interprets diphthongs as containing a consonantal glide, /u̯/ or /i̯/, as the second element. She argues that their realization as glides enables her to explain their distribution more satisfactorily. However, her account (1984: 96–8) raises more problems than it solves. It tries to show that by treating the second element as a glide the diphthongs can be aligned with the pattern of vowel + nasal/liquid. But this account only really holds good for northern Welsh. The vocalic notation has been retained here.
6.   The most useful discussions are G. E. Jones 1984 and Awbery 1984; however, their approaches differ in that Awbery regards length as phonemic while Jones sees it as connected to the closeness of one of each pair of vowels.
7.   In addition to the example discussed in detail, see Awbery 1986a, where use is made of Generative Phonology; Ball 1990 where it is suggested that Dependency Phonology is the most satisfactory way of considering /ɬ/ and its mutated forms; see also Griffen 1990.
8.   Much of the material in this section is discussed in M. Jones and Thomas 1977. A more traditional grammatical description can be found in S. J. Williams 1980; see also Thorne 1993 and King 1993.
9.   It is interesting to note that English *peas* was itself borrowed from the French singular *pois*, and that sg. *pea* is a back-formation; cf. *pease-pudding*, etc.
10· For a full survey see T. A. Watkins 1977–8a, and for usage at earlier stages of the language see Mac Cana 1975–6.
11. For suggestions about the origin of the three-way system of pronouns, see Russell 1982–3; for Middle Welsh usage see Mac Cana 1990b.
12. For full discussions, see M. Jones and Thomas 1977 and Fife 1990; see also King 1993: 135–236, Thorne 1993: 224–95.
13. For a similar usage in Irish, see 3.4.3; and for Cornish and Breton, see 8.3.1.5 where the matter is discussed from the standpoint of the verbal noun.
14. Word order in the Celtic languages is the subject of Chapter 9. The present discussion is concerned only with Modern Welsh; the historical background and especially the debate over Middle Welsh word order is disregarded at this point (see 9.1.2.2).
15. In addition to the studies considered in this section, see Sadler 1988 and Hendrick 1988, 1990b (Government Binding), and various discussions about word order and related matters, e.g. Harlow 1981, Sproat 1985, Borsley 1983, 1984, 1987, 1990b, Fife 1986b; see also Rouveret 1990, Stump 1990.

Chapter 6

The orthographies of the Celtic languages

6.1 Orthography and phonology

Some justification is probably required for a chapter on writing systems in work on the Celtic languages. Linguists are primarily concerned with the spoken form and tend to regard the written notation as of secondary importance.[1] Nevertheless, for all but the most recent stages of a language, that is, the stage since the development of sound recording devices, our only access to the language has been through the written form. If we do not fully understand the orthography of the language, if we have failed to crack the code, then our access is going to be at least restricted, if not blocked totally. Because the modern Celtic languages are written in Roman script in which many of the signs have the same values as they do in English, it is easy to be lulled into a false sense of security about our understanding of the phonology of these languages. For example, it is important that we understand that Welsh *f* represents /v/ not /f/, that Modern Irish *th* can represent /h/ or /∅/ depending on the dialect, but never /θ/. Again, in Old Welsh internal *p, t, c* represented /b d g/ respectively, not /p t k/; this is, for example, crucial for our understanding of lenition (7.4).

Writing systems are notoriously mobile. We may recall the extent of variants of the Phoenician script which have not only given us the Greek alphabet and from there the Latin alphabet via Etruscan, but also the Punic script, which developed into various Iberian scripts, and the subsequent development of the Cyrillic and Glagolithic scripts from Greek.[2] At each stage there is never a one-to-one fit of script to sound system, and accommodations have had to be made, either by re-using a sign for a different sound from the one it represented in the donor language, or by creating new signs for new sounds, or by borrowing a sign from the script of a neighbouring language. Such adaptions were carried out in fitting the Roman script to Celtic languages, as in the use of double letters in Welsh or combinations of consonants and *h* in Irish. For earlier stages of the languages, such developments offer precious insights into what distinctions speakers of the language regarded as important and in what contexts. Evidence of signs borrowed from other spelling systems also indicates cultural and linguistic contacts, notably in a Celtic context the acquisition of the Roman script itself by the Insular Celtic languages.

Some of the Celtic languages of Continental Europe did not use the Roman script at all but rather other scripts the signs of which were sometimes of uncertain value. In these cases we can feel no sense of security at all about the phonological values of the signs, and an understanding of the script is a crucial stage in establishing the sound system of the language.

Even where we have a good understanding of the orthography and feel on safe ground, the orthography itself can act as a barrier to the language. Writing systems are notoriously conservative in their notation; in English we continue to note velars in *night* and *bought*, etc. centuries after their disappearance. How, then, can we get behind the veneer of the orthography? There are occasional cases where a language is written in more than one orthographical system, and there are examples in Celtic; if so, there can be a way in for the linguist (see Russell 1992a). Beyond that, detailed understanding of the normal standard orthography can make us aware of deviations from it in the form of errors; this will often take us closer to what the perpetrator of the error really said as opposed to what he wrote. However, in societies where there is no generally recognized standard orthography, our standard may well be that of a single scribe copying a series of manuscripts or at best perhaps the orthographical practices of a particular school of scribes.

6.2   The scripts of Continental Celtic

6.2.1   Greek

When in 58 BC Julius Caesar defeated the Helvetii, a Gaulish tribe of modern western Switzerland, he records that upon entering their camp some documents were brought to him: 'they were written in Greek characters (*Graecis litteris*), and contained a register of the names of all the emigrants capable of bearing arms, and also, under separate heads, the numbers of old men, women and children' (*de Bello Gallico*, I, 29 = Handford 1951: 55). Later in his account of the campaign in Gaul he discusses the divisions of Gaulish society and notes that the druids were forbidden by their religion from committing their teaching to writing; Caesar contrasts this attitude with the practice of Gauls, who 'for most other purposes, such as public and private accounts, . . . use the Greek alphabet (*Graecis litteris*)' (*de Bello Gallico*, VI, 14 = Handford 1951:

32). On the other hand, in 54 BC, when in the territory of the Nervii
(central Belgium), Caesar 'induced one of his Gallic horsemen to convey a letter to Cicero, which he wrote in Greek characters (*Graecis
litteris*) for fear that it might be intercepted and his plan become known
to the enemy' (*de Bello Gallico*, V, 48 = Handford 1951: 155). The
apparent contradiction may be resolved not by assuming that the Nervii
were too far north to have come into contact with the Greek alphabet
(Dottin 1920: 46), since the anticipated interception would have
occurred further south, but rather by acknowledging the ambiguity of
Graecis litteris, which can mean 'in Greek' as well as 'in Greek script'.
There is no doubt that Caesar could have written to Cicero in Greek and
that would have prevented most Gauls from learning of his plans. There
is considerable doubt also whether the Helvetii knew any Greek.
Further evidence for ignorance of Greek beside knowledge of Greek
script comes from Caesar's encounter with Diviciacus, a pro-Roman
Aeduan noble (*de Bello Gallico*, I, 19 = Handford 1951: 50); because
the discussion is to be confidential, Caesar dismisses his usual inter-
preters and speaks to him with the assistance of Caius Valerius
Troucillus, a prominent man in the province of Gaul, who could presumably speak Gaulish as well as Latin. If Diviciacus could have
spoken Greek, there would have been no need for Troucillus' presence.
The point is that outside the immediate sphere of influence of Massalia
there is plenty of evidence for Gauls using Greek script to write
Gaulish, but no suggestion that they wrote Greek (see Whatmough
1970: 59–62).

The first writing system the Gauls experienced was the script of the
Greek colony of Massalia (Marseilles), which was established around
600 BC and from where settlements spread along the southern coast of
Gaul and inland up the valley of the Rhône (Cunliffe 1988: 13–32). By
the first century BC it is clear from Caesar's account that the Gauls used
Greek script. This use is confirmed by a large number of 'Gallo-Greek'
inscriptions on both stone and ceramic found in southern Gaul. The
majority have emerged around the southern stretch of the Rhône, from
Orange to the sea with a western limit of Montpellier and an eastern
limit of Marseilles, the Roman province of Gallia Narbonensis
(Lejeune 1985: 16 (map)). Sporadic finds have also been made further
north along the Loire and the upper reaches of the Seine (Lejeune 1985:
328 (map)). These inscriptions have been roughly dated by Lejeune
1985: 3 to between the late 3rd century BC and the first half of the 1st
century AD with nothing after the end of the Neronian period (– AD 68).
Of the 281 inscriptions collected by Lejeune 1985, the majority, 195,
are on ceramics and tend to be fragmentary; the most informative group
are the 73 stone inscriptions, even though none is longer than ten
words. Drawings of two ceramic and one stone inscription are presented in Figure 6.1, with transliteration and translation beneath.

G-193: MAⲅ€⊂IΛΛΛ

Transcription: *magesilla*

G-13: €⊂Κ€ⲅⲅⲨⲬΛΤΙΛΝΙΛͻ⊂ΙΜΜΙ

Transcription: *tei*
eskeggolatianiaosimmi

Analysis: *Eskeggolati aniateios immi*
Translation: 'I am the (? plate) of Eskengolatos

G-153:

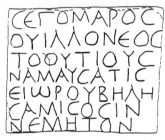

Transcription:
segomaros
ouilloneos
tooutious
namausatis
eiōroubēlē
samisosin
nemēton

Analysis: *Segomaros Ouilloneos tooutious Namausatis eiōrou bēlēsami sosin nemēton*
Translation: 'Segomaros, son of Villō, citizen of Nîmes, has dedicated this sacred place to Belesama'

FIGURE 6.1   Gallo-Greek inscriptions

(G + a number refers to the inscriptions in Lejeune 1985.)

The most common type of ceramic inscription is simply the name of the potter scratched on the base, as in *Magesilla*. The middle word of G-13 is unclear, but the last word *immi* 'I am' is cognate with Gk *eîmi*, Skt *asmi*, Eng *am*, etc. (< **esmi*), while the first word is the genitive singular of the name of the owner, *Escengolatos*. In G-153 the term *tooutious* is a derivative of the Proto-Celtic term **toutā* 'people' > Ir *túath*, W *tud*. The verb *eiōrou*, in Gallo-Latin orthography spelt *ieuru*, pl. *ieurus*, is problematical and much debated but it clearly means something like 'dedicated' (Lambert 1979b). The final phrase contains the term *nemēton* found in Galatia and in the insular languages, e.g. OIr *nemed* 'sanctuary'.

The ceramic inscriptions tend to use a more cursive form of script than the stone inscriptions, where large capitals are the norm. In general terms, as far as we can tell, the Greek alphabet was relatively efficient at representing the Gaulish consonantal system but less so with regard

TABLE 6.1   The Gallo-Greek values of the Greek alphabet

Letter	Greek	Gallo-Greek	Example (translation)
ι	/i/	/i/	*litoumareos* (G-17)
		/i:/	*ourittorigou* (G-207)
		/i̯/	*iougilliakos* (G-28)
ου	/ou/	/u/	*dagolitous* (G-271)
		/u:/	*baladoui* (G-120)
		/u̯/	*ouindikos* (G-118)
οου	–	/ou/ (southern)	*taranoou* (G-27)
ωυ	–	/ou/ (northern)	*tōuti* (G-153)
η	/e:/	/e/ ?/e:/	*bēlēsami* (G-153)
ω	/o:/	? /o:/	*praitōr* (G-108)
ει	/ẹ:/	/e:/	*-reix* (G-3)
χ	/χ/	/χ/ before /t/	*anextlo-* (G-268)
θ	/tʰ/, /θ/	/ts/ /ss/	*karθi . . .* (G-1)

G + a number refers to the inscriptions in Lejeune 1985.
In the examples, the letter in question is in bold.

to the vowels; it was unable to mark all the distinctions of length and quality (Lejeune 1985: 441). Table 6.1 shows the original values of some of the Greek letters and their use in Gallo-Greek; it concentrates on those areas of the system where difficulties arose. For many of the consonants and some of the vowels there was a simple one-to-one correspondence.

There are two areas of particular interest (see Lejeune 1985: 441–6). First, Greek unlike Gaulish had no consonantal forms of /i/ and /u/, i.e. /i̯/ and /u̯/, and therefore in Gallo-Greek they had to be created. For /i̯/ ι was simply used. But Greek υ caused further difficulties in that it represented /ü/ and not /u/. Gallo-Greek had no /ü/ and therefore υ is not found, but ου is regular for /u/, /u:/ and also /u̯/; it would appear that /ü/ was felt to be sufficiently different from /u/ that υ could not be used for /u/. Since ου no longer represented a diphthong, a sign had to be created for /ou/, namely οου with omega replacing οο in the northern group of inscriptions. Generally, η and ω are rare and do not tend to represent long vowels as they did in Greek, except where a Latin word is being used, e.g. *kornēlia* (G-65) for Lat *Cornēlia*. In Hellenistic Greek ει no longer represented the diphthong but rather a closed long vowel /ẹ:/ between /e:/ and /i:/. It, therefore, came to be used for the similar vowel which had arisen from the merging of Proto-Celtic /e:/ and /i:/. Its use in *-reiks* 'king' < **rēks* suggests that the merger of /e:/ and /i:/ may not have been completed in Gaulish (Lejeune 1985: 441).

As is clear from the Insular languages, the cluster /kt/ became /χt/ at

THE ORTHOGRAPHIES OF THE CELTIC LANGUAGE

an early period, and this stage is already found in Gallo-Greek, where Gk χ is conveniently to hand. It proved so convenient that it was borrowed into the Latin script to represent the same sound, which was alien to Latin, e.g. *Atextorigi, Rextugenos* (Lejeune 1985: 445).

One of the most thorny difficulties which faced writers of Gaulish in Greek script was the representation of the dental affricates /ts/ or /st/, /ds/ or /sd/, etc. (for a full discussion, see D. E. Evans 1967: 410–20; also Lejeune 1985: 444–5). In Greek script θ or $\theta\theta$ was used, e.g. *ouri$\theta\theta$* (G-207), etc.; by this stage of Hellenistic Greek θ still represented an aspirate /tʰ/ but was probably the closest the Greek alphabet had to offer (Allen 1974: 16–24). In addition $\sigma\theta$ and $\sigma\sigma$ were also used and this perhaps gives us a better indication of the phonetic reality, e.g. *atesθas* (G-3), *kassi-* (G-206) (for further discussion in relation to the Latin spellings, see 6.2.4 below).

The adaptation of the Greek script to write Gaulish resulted in the discarding of some letters, e.g. υ /ü/ in favour of a digraph $o\upsilon$ /u/, but also the employment of letters to fill a different gap in the system, as with the use of θ for /ts/, etc.

6.2.2 Celtiberian

The form of script used for Celtiberian, the Celtic language of the Iberian peninsula, derives from the script used for other non-Celtic Iberian languages. It is largely written in a script unique to the Iberian peninsula. As shown in 1.2.3, the evidence consists principally of a large number of names on tesserae and coins, two relatively short inscriptions from Peñalba de Villastar and Luzaga, and two large inscriptions from Botorrita. A few of the brief inscriptions and the one from Peñalba de Villastar are written in a Latin script; these inscriptions together with Celtiberian names recorded in Latin inscriptions offer us a useful check on the interpretation of the Celtiberian script, in which the majority of the inscriptions are written. Table 6.2 lists the characters and their values, while Figure 6.2 is a drawing of side A of

TABLE 6.2   The conventional transcription of the Celtiberian script

a	ⅅ	e	╻	i	ⱈ	o	H	u	↑
Ta	⤬	Te	⬧	Ti	ⵗ	To	⊔	Tu	△
Ca	⋀	Ce	⺄	Ci	⅄	Co	ⴼ	Cu	◇
Pa	⎮	Pe	ⵁ	Pi	Γ	Po	⚹	Pu	◻
s	⟨	$\acute{s}$	M	r	⟡	l	ⴕ		
either		m	ⵦ	n	ⴅ	or		$\acute{m}$	ⴈ		$\acute{n}$	Y

See Eska 1989a: 7–10.

Transcription of the first three lines:

1. ticui cantam; bercunetacam: tocoitos cue: sarnicio: cue: sua: combalces nelitom

2. necueto ertaunei: litom: necue: taunei: litom: necue: masnai: tisaunei: litom: sos: aucu

3. areitaso: tamai: uta: oscues: stena: uersoniti: silabur: sleitom: conscilitom: cabiseti

FIGURE 6.2   Side A of the Botorrita inscription. After Beltrán and Tovar 1983: Figure VII, facing p. 38.

the Botorrita inscription with a transcription of the first three lines. Although the script was deciphered in 1922 (Gómez-Moreno 1922), the separating out of the different languages using versions of the Iberian script took much longer (see Tovar 1949).

It is immediately clear that this is not an alphabetic script but largely a syllabary, where each sign stands for a combination of consonant + vowel. There are a few cases where it looks as if an attempt has been made to use the script alphabetically; that is, the sign for the syllable *Ta* is followed by the sign for *a* to represent /ta/ or /da/ (Lejeune 1955: 43), e.g. *aleTuureś* (Lejeune 1955: 102 (B4)). The script has its deficiencies; there is, for example, no indication of vowel length, i.e. *a* can represent /a/ or /a:/, etc. There is no distinction of voice in the consonantal syllables; it is conventional to write them as capitals using the unvoiced set, e.g. *Ca*, *Te*, etc., but it is to be remembered that *Ce* can stand for /ke/ or /ge/. In some cases, names in Latin script can come to our aid; thus, *śeCoPiriCes* is to be read as /segobriges/ on the basis of Lat *Segobriga*. Furthermore, as the last example shows, the Celtiberian script has difficulties with clusters of consonant + liquid. Various mechanisms are adopted: the cluster can be expanded using a 'dead' vowel, e.g. *Tiri* for /tri/; or the liquid can be dropped, e.g. *ConTePaCom* for /kontrebakom/; or an 'orthographical metathesis' can occur, e.g. *ConterPia* for /kontrebia/ (cf. Lat *Contrebia*), where the vowel of the syllable /re/ is used before the /r/ (see Untermann 1975: 72).

The Iberian script from which the Celtiberian script was derived was also used for non-Celtic languages of the peninsula from about the 4th

TABLE 6.3 Other Iberian scripts

/di/ *ti*	ψ	: /ti/ *tí*	ψ	/gi/ *ki*	ς	: /ki/ *kí*	ς̄
/de/ *te*	⊖	: /te/ *té*	⊕	/ge/ *ke*	(	: /ke/ *ké*	₵
/du/ *tu*	Δ	: /tu/ *tú*	♆	/ga/ *ka*	ʌ	: /ka/ *ká*	Ѧ
/bo/ *bo*	✳	: /po/ *bó*	✱	/go/ *ko*	⧗	: /ko/ *kó*	⧗

See de Hoz 1985.

to 1st centuries BC. An interesting aspect in one group of Iberian inscriptions is the apparent development of unvoiced consonantal counterparts in the syllabary by the addition of an extra stroke to the voiced group (see Table 6.3); the values can be established by reference to the same words written in Greek or Roman script, e.g. Iberian *atin* = Roman *adin*, *tíbás* = *tibas*, *baites* = Gk *baidēs* (de Hoz 1985).

It is generally agreed that the script used for both Iberian and Celtiberian derived from a script used in the southern part of the peninsula for writing an early form of Iberian and another unknown language between the 7th and 1st centuries BC (de Hoz 1983). In origin the script was a modified version of the Phoenician script of the Phoenician and Carthaginian settlers of Tartessus and the southern coast of the peninsula (Cunliffe 1988: 16–18). Given the identity of most of the signs, this explanation is essentially correct, but the modifications have been considerable (see Table 6.4). First, being originally a script for a Semitic language like Phoenician, it has no vowel signs, and these have been developed. Secondly, Phoenician is an alphabetic script, but it has been turned into a syllabary in a rather haphazard way. For example, there does not seem to be any correlation of voice; Phoenician /p/ corresponds to Iberian /bi/, /g/ to /ka/. A shift from alphabet to syllabary is of itself curious; the usual line of development tends to be from a syllabary to an alphabet. Moreover, there is no correlation with Phoenician alphabetical order in the Iberian ordering of syllables, i.e. /be/, /ka/, /tu/, /te/, /ti/, /ke/, etc. It has been suggested that Greek influence may explain the vowel signs and the shape of certain letters, e.g. Iberian /ś/ beside Greek sigma, but if the dating of the earliest Iberian material to the 7th century BC is correct, it is rather early to expect Greek influence of that type. Justeson and Stephens 1991–3: 21–30 have recently argued that the shift to a syllabic analysis may be based on the names of the Phoenician letters. There is, they claim, a significant correlation between the syllabic combinations of consonant + vowel and the names for those signs in Phoenician.

6.2.3 The Lugano script of northern Italy

The Lugano alphabet was used to write a series of inscriptions in

TABLE 6.4 The Iberian and Phoenician scripts

Phoenician Sign	Phoenician Value	Iberian Sign	Iberian Value
	/ʼ/		/a/
	/b/		/be/
	/g/		/ka/
	/d/		/tu/
	/h/		?
	/u̯/		/u/
	/z/		/o/
	/ḥ/		? /te/
	/ṭ/		/ti/
	/i̯/		/i/
	/k/		/ke/
	/l/		/l/
	/m/		/ba/
	/n/		/n/
	/s/		/ś/
	?		/e/
	/p/		/bi/
	/ṣ/		/ś/
	/q/		/ki/
	/r/		/r/
	/š/		/ś/
	/t/		/ta/

Lepontic, a Celtic language of northern Italy (see Table 6.5 overleaf).[3] The inscriptions date from the 6th to the 1st centuries BC. There is no doubt that the script derives from the north Etruscan script. The form of the Etruscan script adopted is extremely archaic since it still has *o*. The Etruscans borrowed their script from western versions of the Greek alphabet which contained *o*, but it rapidly disappeared from the Etruscan script as they had no use for it.[4] It is an extremely exiguous script containing only fourteen regular signs. As in Etruscan, no orthographical distinction is made between voiced and unvoiced stops, though in some inscriptions attempts have been made to use variant forms of *theta* to indicate the voiced dental /d/.

The script also has two sibilant signs conventionally transliterated by

TABLE 6.5   The Lugano alphabet

Sign	Value	Sign	Value
⋀	/a/	⋈	/m/
+	/d/	⋏	/n/
⋨	/e/	○	/o/
—	/v/	⋂	/p/, /b/
—	/z/	⊲	/r/
—	/h/	Z	/s/
⊕ ⊙	/θ/	⋈	/š/
I	/i/	X	/t/, /d/
⋊	/k/, /g/	V	/u/
⋀	/l/	V Ⴘ	/χ/

After Lejeune 1971: 370.

s and š. Some distinctions between them can be observed. The former seems to be used to represent the outcome of /ks/, e.g. *esopnos* 'blind' (< *eks-ops-), while the latter is used for the outcome of /ᵗs/, as in the accusative plural -aš (< *-āᵗs < *-āns), or the preposition aš (< *ads) (see Lejeune 1971: 356).

6.2.4   Latin

The use of the Latin script to write Continental Celtic of various types is at the same time most useful and most potentially misleading. Its usefulness lies in the fact that we think we have a reasonable idea what the signs represent, but its potential for confusion is that we only think we know. For even though we may be familiar with the script, there was never a one-to-one fit between the phonologies of Latin and Continental Celtic (see generally Lejeune 1988: 57–9). Moreover, it is not clear that the Latin alphabet is any better than the Greek when it comes to representing Gaulish sounds; similar problems arise with vowels and there is also confusion over consonantal usage.

Different types of Latin script are used, ranging from capitals in stone inscriptions to various forms of cursive script on the lead tablets of Chamalières and Larzac and on graffiti on pottery (see 1.2.1 above).[5]

The following discussion focuses on some of the problematic areas. A particular problem arises where we encounter confusion between letters which should in theory represent the voiced and unvoiced pairs, e.g. *c/g*, *t/d*. The question has arisen particularly over the alternation among the dentals *c* and *g*, *Clanum* : *Glanum*, *uercobreto-* : *vergobretos*, etc. (D. E. Evans 1967: 400). It has been argued, for example by

TABLE 6.6   Single stops in Gaulish and Latin

Latin			Gaulish		
	Fortis	Lenis		Fortis	Lenis
+ voice		+	+ voice		+
− voice	+		− voice		+

See C. Watkins 1955: 19.

Gray 1944, that the writing of *g* for an expected /k/ indicated that a form of lenition, related to that found in insular Celtic, had already taken place in Gaulish (see 6.3.2.1 below). The matter has caused considerable debate (summarized in D. E. Evans 1967: 399–404), but it is likely that the confusion arose from a fundamental incompatibility between the consonant systems of Latin and Gaulish. C. Watkins 1955 convincingly suggested that, while in Latin single intervocalic voiced stops were lenis and voiceless stops fortis, in Gaulish both were lenis (see Table 6.6). The upshot would be that native speakers of Latin might well hear Gaulish voiceless stops as voiced, or those taught to spell by native speakers of Latin would relate the sound of the voiceless stops to the signs which in Latin represented the voiced stops, because in reality the crucial distinction for a speaker of Latin was the fortis/lenis one.

Confusion might, therefore, arise from unsuspected incompatibilities between the sound systems. It also arose in a case where the Latin script could not offer an exact correspondent. As we have seen in relation to the Greek script (6.2.1), it seems that Gaulish had a dental fricative of some sort arising from combinations of dentals, perhaps /ts/ or /ds/. In the Latin script, the possible combinations were enormous, e.g. *d, dd, đ, đđ, TH, TTH, DS, TS, S, SS, SD, SS, T, TT* (for examples, see D. E. Evans 1967: 411). It was clearly a well-known phenomenon in antiquity when it was known as the *tau gallicum* 'Gaulish *t*'. Sibilants of this type caused problem not only for the Latin script (see 6.2.3 above on Lugano *ś*). The range of spellings does suggest a lack of unanimity as to its precise sound and that therefore it did not correspond to any single Latin sound.

6.3   The scripts of Insular Celtic

With one apparent exception (discussed in 6.3.1), the Insular Celtic languages were and are written in a script derived from Latin. As was pointed out above (6.1), there is a danger that our familiarity with the values of the letters in Latin can lull us into a false sense of security. To a certain extent we can be secure since in many cases the letters do more or less represent the same sounds as in Latin; thus, for example, *a* has the value /a/ or /ɑ/. Moreover, the modern languages give us access to the end product and the orthography and sound system of Latin can provide a starting point (see Allen 1978). The issue is whether we can trace the developments in between. This section begins by considering the only non-Latin script used to write an Insular Celtic language, and then goes on to examine the developments and adaptions of the Latin script used to write the Brittonic and Goidelic languages.

6.3.1   Ogam

In the early Irish epic *Táin Bó Cúailnge* 'The Cattle Raid of Cooley', Etarcomol mac Eda meets his death at the hands of the Ulster hero Cú Chulainn; his burial is described as follows: 'Then Etarcomol's grave was dug, and his headstone was planted in the ground; his name was written in Ogam and he was mourned' (C. O'Rahilly 1976: 163). On another occasion, Cú Chulainn writes an Ogam inscription on a peg of twisted withe and casts it over the top of a pillar-stone in order to delay the advance of Medb's army into Ulster (C. O'Rahilly 1976: 131). McManus 1991: 161–3 argues that in such examples from early Irish literature there is no implication of magic or secrecy but simply a reference to writing.

Dating from the 5th-6th centuries, and perhaps even from the late 4th century, Ogam inscriptions were carved mainly in southern Ireland and southern Wales to write Irish (many stones are bilingual Irish/Latin).[6] The second literary example quoted above suggests that the script was in much wider use on portable objects. The carving of Ogam on wooden sticks is also suggestive about the origin of Ogam as a method of reckoning with tally sticks (McManus 1991: 11–12; see also below).

Essentially, as can be seen from Figure 6.3 (a), the letters of Ogam were lines or notches cut in particular directions in relation to a stem line. Each group is called an *aicme* 'family', the letters *feda*, plural of 'wood', the stem line the *druim* 'ridge' and each stroke a *flesc* 'twig'. Each of the letters has a meaningful name, the initial of which corresponds to its sound (McManus 1991: 35–43), e.g. *B* = *beithe* 'birch tree', *S* = *sail* 'willow', *G* = *gort* 'field', etc. Many are names of plants and trees, which has misleadingly suggested that all the names are arboreal. The correspondence of initial letter of the name and sound has been important in confirming the original values for the signs; for example, *Q* = *cert* 'bush' (< *k^wert-*; cf. W *perth*) confirms the original value of the letter as /k^w/ and that the script had been created before /k^w/ had fallen together with /k/ (see 1.5.1). In Irish the script was often called *beith luis nin* after the first two or three letters of the script; this

(a) Basic version

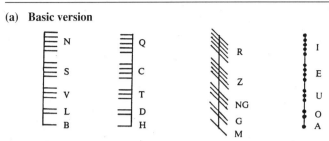

The manuscript transcription corresponds generally to their phonemic representation except for NG which probably stood for /gw/ (see McManus 1991: 37–8).

(b) *forfeda* 'additional letters'

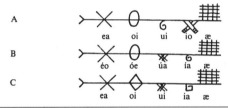

FIGURE 6.3   The Ogam script and its transcription in early Irish manuscripts

is probably modelled on the terms *alphabet* and Lat *abecedarium*, which are based on the names of the first few letters of the alphabet. In manuscript versions of the script the vowels appear as cross-strokes bisecting the stem line rather than as dots. A fifth group of symbols regularly appears in the manuscript tradition (see Figure 6.3 (b)) but did not form part of the original system; McManus 1991 has suggested they were added with the Greek and Latin alphabets in mind, but Sims-Williams 1992, 1993 has argued that they were devised to represent Irish sounds which had arisen in the later stages of the language.

There is no doubt that the script has an alphabetic origin but it has been the subject of much controversy. Two separate questions need to be addressed: the origin of the form of the script and the origin of its alphabetic use. As for the former question, one theory is that the form of the Ogam script derives from an adaption of the tally notation whereby numbers are grouped in units of five (McManus 1991: 6–18). Another origin has been suggested originally by C. Graves 1876 in the so-called *Notae S. Bonifatii*, a system of abbreviating vowels by the use of dots, whereby one dot represented *A*, up to five dots for *U* (see Sims-Williams 1993: 134–5, Bischoff 1990: 177, 255). However, it has to be pointed out that the Ogam vowels do not run in the same order (see Figure 6.3 (a)).

How the phonological values were allocated relates to the latter question. Many attempts have been made to account for the distributional pattern, whether derived from Greek, Germanic runes, or Latin (McManus 1991: 19–27), by various *ad hoc* shuffling and reshuffling of the order of the letters. It is now generally accepted that the grouping of the letters can be derived from the classification found in Latin grammarians of the 1st-4th centuries AD. The traditional classification, which can be traced to Greek models, is set out in Table 6.7. The bracketed forms were those discarded by the inventor(s) of Ogam as being unnecessary or superfluous. The details of the allocation into groups remains unclear; group 2 (*HDTCQ*) is entirely made up of *mutae*, and group 1 (*BLVSN*) contains mainly *semivocales*. It is thought that *B* may have been promoted in place of *M* in acknowledgement of the position of *B* in the alphabet sequence. *V* is also assumed to correspond to *F*. The third group was then all the rest. The occurrence of *NG* suggests that the framer of the script was also familiar with the Greek letter *agma* /ŋ/. The ordering within *aicmi* 'groups' is entirely unclear, although there may have been phonetic groupings of, for example, *D/T*, *G/NG*, and *C/Q*. A further point suggestive of a Latin origin is the invariable left to right direction of the script.

While Ogam was a highly original writing system, it did not win many prizes for practicality. On block stone monuments where there was a clear edge, that edge was taken as the stem line and signs were incised either side of it, starting at the bottom of the left-hand side and running up, across the top and down the right-hand edge. The obvious problem is that the edges have been most prone to weathering and general damage not least by cows using them as rubbing posts (McManus 1991: 47–9). On the bilingual inscriptions, the Latin is written on the flat surface of the stone and has therefore often survived better.

The Ogam inscriptions offer us a glimpse of a form of Irish which in some cases pre-dates the earliest material in Latin script by several cen-

TABLE 6.7   The traditional classification of letters in Latin grammar

Vocales	A E I O U
Semivocales	F L M N R S [X]
Mutae	B C D G H [K] [P] Q T
Graecae litterae	[Y] Z

See McManus 1991: 28.

Letters in brackets were discarded by the inventor(s) of Ogam as being superfluous.

turies. Its important linguistic contribution has been discussed above (2.1.1). The orthographical significance is considered here (McManus 1991: 123–7). The conventional view has been that the orthography of Ogam and that of manuscript Irish were totally distinct, but Harvey 1987b and 1989 has argued for continuity between Ogam and early forms of manuscript Irish orthography (see also McManus 1986: 11, and 6.3.2.5 below for further discussion).

Since Ogam was devised before the phenomenon of lenition occurred (see Chapter 7), it is hardly surprising that there is only the slightest indication that Ogam had any notation for it. For example, *T* and *C* were used to represent /t/ and /k/, but when intervocalic /t/ and /k/ lenited to /θ/ and /χ/ they continued to be marked by *T* and *C*, thus *RITTECC* = OIr *Rethech*, *CARRTTACC* = OIr *Carthach*, etc. Only in manuscript Irish was the use of *h* and other markers devised to mark lenition, though there are some example of an Ogam-type spelling in the manuscript orthography, e.g. *rígteg* = later *rígthech*, *Findubrac* = later *Findabrach* (McManus 1991: 11). The haphazard duplication of consonants is a curiosity, e.g. *BROCC/BROCCI, CATTUVVIRR/CAT-TUVIR/CATVVIR*, etc. There seems to be no real pattern, and certainly nothing which can be correlated with original geminated/non-geminated stops or lenited/non-lenited stops. Harvey 1987, however, has noted a bias towards duplication in the case of non-lenited sounds in intervocalic position but nothing more systematic than that.

Another difference is in the marking of palatal consonants (see 2.2.3.3 and 6.3.2.5). In manuscript Irish the nominative singular *macc* is distinct from the genitive *maicc* by the glide vowel *i*. The use of Ogam spans the period of the loss of syllables but there are no sure examples of palatal glide vowels in Ogam forms without final syllables, suggesting that the convention had not yet arisen, e.g. *CARRTACC* = gen. sg. *Carthaich*, *-ANN* = gen. sg. *-áin*, *CATTUVIR* = *Caither*, etc.

6.3.2 Latin

6.3.2.1 British
As was noted above (6.3.1), Ogam inscriptions are also found in Britain, particularly in Cornwall and south-west Wales. Many form part of bilingual inscriptions in Irish (written in Ogam) and Latin.[7] A number of the names in these inscriptions from Britain are British, and the parallel Ogam version can provide a useful guide to the Latin usage in the sense that the Ogam version can sometimes provide a more 'Celtic' version of the name than the Latin form; for example, Lat *MAGLOCVNI FILI CLVTORI* : Ogam *MAGLICUNAS MAQI CLU-TARI* (Macalister 1945–9, no. 446) contains the British name **Maglocū*, gen. **Maglocunos* which gave W *Meilyg* and *Maelgwn* respectively (Jackson 1953: 182, C Thomas 1994: 63–4, 81–2). The

Latin version shows a Latin genitive singular case ending -*i* replacing British -*os* (represented as -*AS* in the Ogam form). According to Jackson, this inscription dates from the mid to later 5th century AD and on his dating of lenition *MAGLOCVN*- could either reflect unlenited /maglokun/- or lenited /maʏlogun/-. According to Sims-Williams 1990, who dates lenition rather earlier (see 7.4.3), it could only represent the latter lenited form.

We encounter here an early example of the orthographical problem which affects our understanding of both early Brittonic and early Irish phonology. Essentially, the Latin script adopted to write British, Old Welsh, Old Cornish and Old Breton does not indicate the effects of lenition, i.e. it does not show that intervocalic /p t k/ were voiced to /b d g/ and that intervocalic /b d g/ were spirantized to /v ð ʏ/ (see Table 7.2 below for details). One possible but perhaps less likely explanation is that the Latin script was adopted to write British before lenition had taken place and that the inherent conservatism of orthographical habit maintained this early pre-lenition system. Jackson 1953: 70 has objected to this on the grounds that it would imply a rigidly fixed spelling system based presumably on a considerable written practice already in the 5th century, or for Sims-Williams 1990 up to a century earlier. Jackson observes that 'it is fairly certain that there was no real written language so early as that time other than Latin' (Jackson 1953: 70). However, since then, two lead tablets have been found at Bath which may contain Celtic texts (Tomlin 1988: nos. 14 and 18; see also 1.3.1). At present they remain unintelligible and cannot yet form a substantive objection to Jackson's claim even though they raise doubts. The still generally accepted explanation of this orthographical phenomenon is that presented by Jackson 1953: 70–1. For Britons of the 5th and 6th centuries Latin was as much a spoken language as British and, when the loosening of articulation which brought about lenition affected intervocalic consonants, it affected them when they spoke Latin as well as when they spoke British. Thus they pronounced Lat *caper*, *locus*, *medicus* and *agō* as /kaber, logus, meðigus, aʏo:/ even though they spelt them as before. It would follow, then, that when they wrote British, *p*, *t*, *c* would be used to represent initial /p t k/ but internal /b d g/, while *b*, *d*, *g* would stand for initial /b d g/ but internal /v ð ʏ/. Thus, for example, the native word /adanɔgion/ would be written *atanocion*, since *adanogion* would stand for */aðanɔʏion/* (Jackson 1953: 71); it is only in Middle Welsh (i.e. from about the 13th century onwards) that *adanogion* could represent /adanɔgion/.

On this basis alone, it would be reasonable to ask how we can know that lenition took place at all until the spelling changed to indicate it in the 13th century. There are other early sources which provide a clearer picture. Some of the loanwords into Irish show that British lenition had already taken place, e.g. OIr *Pátraic* /pa:drig'/ < British /padrig/- (

Patricius) (see 2.2.5). In addition, there are a few examples in Old
Welsh where the scribe has used *b* and *d* for lenited /p/ and /t/, e.g.
scribl /scribəl/ 'penny', *gubennid* /gɔbennið/ 'pillow', *hendat* /hɛndad/}
'grandfather'. Moreover, British names which occur in Latin texts other
than in Britain can be revealing; for example, a Breton bishop is named
in the Council of Braga in 572 as *Mahiloc* (var. *Mailoc*) (see Jackson
1953: 549–50, Sims-Williams 1991: 20–1). This corresponds to British
*maglākos lenited to /maxlọ:g/. Such spellings suggest that /g/ was
already lenited to /ɤ/ and perhaps had developed as far as /i̯/ as it did in
Welsh. But although the *Mailoc* spelling is tantalizingly close to what
we would expect in Old Welsh, a British name in a Galician document
can tell us nothing about the dating of the British spelling system as we
have no way of knowing who created this spelling.

The following sections consider the orthographical practices of the
individual Brittonic languages. Although their orthography developed
from the same starting point, it is interesting to trace the different influences and pressures upon them which have resulted in significantly
different orthographies.

6.3.2.2 Welsh

It has until recently been generally agreed that the written evidence for
the individual Brittonic languages does not extend back earlier than *c.*
800. However W. Davies 1979, followed by Sims-Williams 1991, has
argued that some of the charters in the *Book of Llandaf* can be dated as
early as the first half of the 7th century (see 4.1.1), and therefore we can
now fill the orthographical gap between the early inscriptions and the
earliest of the 9th century vernacular glosses. The orthographical development of Welsh now has a much longer timescale than previously
thought. It has been conventional to regard the development of Welsh
orthography as a linear progression from Old Welsh to Modern Welsh;
for the early part of this period, this view has been most clearly
expressed by I. Williams 1930: xii–xx, who claimed that there was a
single line of development from early Old Welsh to late Old Welsh into
early Middle Welsh. However, recent studies are suggesting that the
situation is far more complicated and that it is a question both of
regional developments and of scribal schools establishing particular
styles of orthography which became more or less popular.[8]

The present discussion will concentrate on how particular areas of
the sound system were represented in Welsh. Those which corresponded more or less exactly to Latin caused no real problems; thus *a*
for/a/, *o* for /o/, *m* for /m/, *s* for /s/, etc. But where Welsh developed
sounds which had no clear correspondent in Latin, orthographical deci-
sions had to be made. They were made by individual scribes or groups
of scribes and so at all periods of Welsh prior to 1928, when the orthography was fixed (University of Wales Press 1928), there was

(a) Latin

/i/		/u/	/i:/		/u:/
	/e/	/o/		/e:/	/o:/
	/a/			/a:/	

(b)Early Welsh (/closed, open/)

/i, ɨ/		/ʉ/		/u, ʊ/
		/ə/		
	/e, ɛ/		/o, ɔ/	
		/ɑ, a/		

FIGURE 6.4   The vowel systems of Latin and early Welsh

considerable variation in orthographical practice. The two areas of particular interest are the central vowels and fricatives.

The Latin alphabet was established for a language which had a vowel system as set out in Figure 6.4 (a). It is not clear that Welsh had or has any clear distinction of length (see 5.2.1) but rather distinguished an open and closed series together with two central vowels, as in Figure 6.4 (b). For the extra phonemes there were, to begin with, no extra letters; but in the 10th century one extra sign, *y*, was introduced probably from English and used more widely from the 11th century onwards (see Table 6.9 below).

The problem of central vowels was further complicated by the fricatives; in addition to the stops various sound changes resulted in a new series of fricatives, as set out in Table 6.8. Of these, /f/ was native to Latin and *th* and *ch* were used in Latin to represent Greek θ and χ, and /ɤ/ was lost in Old Welsh. The real difficulties came with /v/, because in coping with it a scribe could well encroach upon the area of the central vowels. Latin had two versions of *V*, a pointed form used in capitals for /u̯/ (> /v/) and /u/, and a round form *U* used in uncial, half-uncial and minuscule scripts. A partial solution in the early 13th

TABLE 6.8   Welsh fricatives and their orthography in Modern Welsh

	Labio-dental		Dental		Velar	
– voice	/f/	ff	/θ/	th	/χ/	ch
+ voice	/v/	f	/ð/	dd	[/ɤ/]	

The phoneme in square brackets did not survive the Modern Welsh, but disappeared in Old Welsh.

century was, therefore, to create two letter forms *v* and *u* out of *V*. But in doing so, *u* sometimes came to be used not only for /v/ but also for /ʉ/ and /u/. A subsequent development created another letter. Thirteenth-century Welsh scribes tended to write *v* in two different ways; at the beginning of a sentence or word the first stroke turned outwards, but internally it curled inwards like a *6*. In the thirteenth century, *v* and *6* remained two forms of the same letter in complimentary distribution, but by the fourteenth century *v* and *6* had developed into separate letters used at any point in a word. A third device was also gradually adopted, namely the use of double letters; thus, in Modern Welsh we find *ll* /ɬ/, *dd* /ð/, *ff* /f/, *w* (originally either double-*v* or double-*u*) /u/ or /ʉ/. The use of *6* as a separate letter did not survive the Middle Welsh period. Other attempts were also made to create new signs; for example, the scribe of the National Library of Wales (NLW) MS Peniarth 20, written around 1330, used a ligatured version of *qu* for /ð/ which never caught on elsewhere (G. J. Williams and Jones 1934: 39).

These particular areas where the Latin alphabet did not offer ready solutions caused difficulties at all periods. It may be worth considering the problem at different periods. In her fundamental study of Old Welsh orthography, Meinir Lewis 1961 distinguished two periods of Old Welsh, period A (5th–11th centuries) and period B (11th–12th cen-

TABLE 6.9   Comparison of early and late Old Welsh orthography

Chad 1 and 2 (9th century)

/ị/	/i/	/ɨ/	/ʉ/	/u/	/ʊ/	/v/	/f/	/θ/	/ð/
i	*i*	*i*	*u*	*u*	*u*	*b m*	*f*	*th*	*d*
/e/	/ə/	/o/						*ht*	
e	*i*	*o*						*dt*	

***Breint Teilo* (12th century)**

/ị/	/i/	/ɨ/	/ʉ/	/u/	/ʊ/	/v/	/f/	/θ/	/ð/
i	*i*	*y i*	*u*	*u*	*u*	*u f*	*f*	*th*	*d*
/e/	/ə/	/o/							
e	*y*	*o*							

Cf. Modern Welsh

/ị/	/i/	/ɨ/	/ʉ/	/u/	/ʊ/	/v/	/f/	/θ/	/ð/
i	*i*	*y*	*u*	*w*	*w*	*f*	*ff*	*th*	*dd*
/e/	/ə/	/o/							
e	*y*	*o*							

TABLE 6.10   The orthography of dentals in Old and Middle Welsh

	/t/-	-/t/-	/θ/	/d/-	-/d/-	/ð/
Old Welsh						
	t	tt	th d dh t ht dt	d	t	d
Middle Welsh						
(i)	t	t tt	th	d	t	d
(ii)	t	t tt	th	d	d	t
(iii)	t	t	th	d	d	qu
(iv)	t	t	th	d	d	dd
Cf. Modern Welsh						
	t	t	th	d	d	dd

Examples
 (i) *White Book of Rhydderch*, *Red Book of Hergest*, Dingestow Court MS.
 (ii) National Library of Wales (NLW) MS Peniarth 6, *Black Book of Carmarthen*, Hendregadredd MS (hand α).
 (iii) NLW MS Peniarth 20.

/n/- = phoneme in initial position; -/n/- phoneme in internal or final position

turies). Few scholars would now accept that division, partly because some of the texts have been re-dated but mainly because she included the *Book of Llandaf* in period B; as Sims-Williams 1991 has argued, many of the charters are datable to as early as the mid-7th century. Nevertheless, there are some significant differences between early and later Old Welsh. In Table 6.9 the spellings of central vowels and fricatives are given for two of the earliest texts, Chad 1 and 2 (J. G. Evans and Rhŷs 1893: xliii, Jenkins and Owen 1984: 91–2), and one of the latest, *Breint Teilo* 'The Privilege of Teilo' from the *Book of Llandaf* (J. G. Evans and Rhŷs 1893:120–1). Two points are striking: first, by the time of *Breint Teilo*, y has made an appearance and eased the phonological load on i.[9] Secondly, in early Old Welsh there is still considerable hesitation over how to represent /θ/, which has been settled in favour of *th* in *Breint Teilo*. The impression created by Old Welsh is one of gradual organization and use of extra letters to ease the phonological load on certain letters. We should not, however, be misled into thinking that everything is straightforward from then on. Even in the system of *Breint Teilo*, u is heavily overloaded, a problem which was to be solved in Middle Welsh by the development of v and w. As was noted above, Old Welsh used p, t, c within words for /b d g/ and b, d, g for /v ð ɤ/, but even in the Old Welsh period difficulties were arising because of the development of secondary internal /p t k/ from the simplification of clusters and from loanwords. The gradual resolution of this problem was to take several centuries, and Middle Welsh orthographies reflect a number of options which were adopted by different scribes. For ease of explanation we shall concentrate on the dental series /t θ d ð/. Table 6.10 sets out the various patterns of usage in Old and Middle Welsh. The pressure for innovation seems to arise from the different values assigned to *t* and *d* in initial and internal/final position, together with the problem of having two signs for three phonemes. If regularity had been sought, it would probably have resulted in the generalization of the sign used in initial position; in a system where initial mutations carry grammatical weight, any adjustment to the spelling of initial consonants could not have happened without severe disruption to grammatical structures. The generalization, then, would have operated in the reverse direction. In Middle Welsh two basic systems arose: system (i), a continuation of the Old Welsh pattern reflecting the pre-lenition situation, and system (ii) which attempted to regularize the spelling of /d/ but at the expense of producing an anomalous internal and final *t* for /ð/. System (iii) was unique to one scribe but does indicate that he had perceived the problem and was trying to solve it. Systems (i) and (ii) existed side by side in different manuscripts of the same date, and in one manuscript, the Hendregadredd MS, some of the hands use system (i), some system (ii) (Charles-Edwards and Russell 1993–4). In 14th-century 'standard' Middle Welsh, that of manuscript collections such as the *Red Book of Hergest*, system (i) seems to prevail, but even this could not cater for the rise of internal and final /t/. From the late 14th century another shift seems to occur, to system (iv), with *dd* for /ð/.

So far, the portrayal of these developments has taken on a linear appearance but, as was observed above, the temptation must be resisted to view the development in such a simplistic way. Two examples may help to demonstrate the complexity of the situation.

We have seen that *y* was adopted in late Old Welsh to reduce the load on *i*. In some Middle Welsh manuscripts the load was spread evenly between *y* and *i*, much as in Modern Welsh (see Table 6.9). But it is striking that in some manuscripts deriving from North Wales *i* is not used at all. Instead the phonological load of the front and central vowels is carried by *y* and *e*. Table 6.11 overleaf shows the orthographical system of two mid-13th-century manuscripts from North Wales. Here it looks as if *i* has been dispensed with completely. On the other hand, a detailed analysis of another manuscript from the same area and dating to about a generation earlier than the above two, the *Black Book of Chirk*, which is notorious for its orthographical peculiarities, suggests that it was copied from a manuscript which had no *y* in it at all, but which seems to have been written in an orthography very similar to

TABLE 6.11   Central vowels and fricatives in two 13th century manuscripts from North Wales.

BL Cotton MS, Caligula A.iii (see Russell 1993b)

/i̯/	/i/	/ɨ/	/ʉ/	/u/	/ʉ̯/	/v/	/f/
y	y	y e	u w v	v w u	v w u	v w u f	ff
/e/	/ə/	/o/					
e	e y	o					

BL Cotton MS, Titus D.ii

/i̯/	/i/	/ɨ/	/ʉ/	/u/	/ʉ̯/	/v/	/f/
y	y	y e	u v	u	w (g)u-	u f	f
/e/	/ə/	/o/					
e	e	o					

that of early Old Welsh (Russell, forthcoming). The *Black Book of Chirk* is a law manuscript containing a version of Welsh law associated with a lawyer whose *floruit* was about 1240. It would seem, then, that at least in Arfon in North Wales an early Old Welsh orthography was still current in the mid-13th century. Yet maybe a generation later manuscripts in the same area were being copied in an *i*-less orthography. It is clear, then, that the Old Welsh trend for introducing *y* had not reached Arfon in the early 13th century but did so with a vengeance slightly later. One difficulty in dealing with this feature is our lack of knowledge of the location and secure dating of Old Welsh manuscripts, while for Middle Welsh manuscripts we are on slightly more certain ground. Nevertheless, our picture is skewed by the absence of clearly located and dated manuscripts of this period from South Wales.

The second example concerns the development of *dd* for /ð/. It seems to arise in the late 14th and early 15th centuries (G. C. G. Thomas 1988: xviii–xxii). But although *dd* does not occur in the important 14th-century manuscripts, it does occur earlier in the 13th century, where it may be possible to see the motivation for its creation. The earliest examples occur in verse in the *Black Book of Chirk* (mid-13th century) and the Hendregadredd manuscript (1300–50) (Charles-Edwards and Russell 1993–4). The main scribe of the latter manuscript tended to use *t* for internal and final /ð/ but it is clear that in some of the exemplars he was copying, *dd* for /ð/ occurred and he adopted the practice for a particular purpose, namely to mark when /ð/ came at the beginning of the second element of a compound. Welsh verse makes much use of compounds, and lenition of the initial of the second element of the compound was often the only feature to distinguish a compound from two separate words (word division was not always clear in Welsh manuscripts). Thus it was important to have a clear and unambiguous marker for lenited /d/, and *dd* was more satisfactory than *t* in this position. It would appear, then, that *dd* was in use in the 13th century but only in a very restricted sphere of scribal activity. It was, however, adopted in the late 14th and early 15th centuries as a clearer alternative to the binary *t*/*d* alternation common in the great 14th-century manuscript collections. Indeed, it is possible that the creation of all the double letters, *dd*, *ff*, *ll*, *w*, etc., may belong to this period.

Our understanding of Middle Welsh orthography and phonology is largely based on the literary texts. There was, however, another system of orthography in use in the mass of survey documentation generated in the early stages of the English conquest of Wales from 1282 onwards. The scribes involved in the compilation of these documents were trained in an Anglo-Norman style of orthography and provide a useful corrective on our understanding of the relationship of orthography to phonology in Welsh (Russell 1992a).

It would be misleading to suggest that the orthography of Welsh became fixed and settled by the 15th century. Many of these develop-ments, like the adoption of double letters, took centuries to become widespread. The modern system of orthography derives from the 1588 translation of the Bible by William Morgan. But even in the 16th and 17th centuries orthographical experiments continued. For example, /ð/ was written as *ḏ* by Gruffudd Robert (*c.* 1532–98), as *dh* by Siôn Dafydd Rhŷs (1584– *c.* 1619), as *z* by William Owen Pughe (1759–1835), as *δ* by William Salesbury (1520–84).[10] In addition to different attempts to represent existing phonemes, the strong influence of English has brought about the creation of signs to represent English phonemes occurring in loanwords (T. A. Watkins 1993: 294); thus, /dʒ/ is written as *j* whether initial, internal or final, e.g. *jwg* 'jug', *garej* 'garage'; *tsh* or *ts* for /tʃ/, e.g. *tships* 'chips', *wats* 'watch', etc.; initial *si* and final *s* for /ʃ/, e.g. *siop* 'shop', *fres* 'fresh'. Within Welsh, initial /r̥/ is voiceless but English /r/ is voiced; thus, English loanwords with initial /r/ use *r*, e.g. *rwber* 'rubber' beside native *rh-*, e.g. *rhaw* 'shovel'.

6.3.2.3 *Breton*

The most interesting aspects of Breton orthography are not found in the early stages of the language but in the more recent period when various orthographies have been devised. In contrast to Welsh, where the orthography seems until recently to have developed without too much reference to English, Breton orthography has been subject to consider-able French influence. Furthermore, it has encountered difficulties with dialectal diversity (see 4.1.3); unlike Welsh, the dialectal differences are too great to sit comfortably with one another under the same orthography.[11]

Old Breton orthography was very similar to that of Old Welsh (see above); and Old Cornish ; it encountered the same difficulties with the mixed central vowels and with fricatives; for example, /ð/ could be represented by *d, dd, td* or *th*, and /θ/ by *d, dh, dth, t* or *th* (Jackson 1967a: 825–6). By the end of the Old Breton period, around the 11th century, French orthographical practice was having more and more influence; for example, *c* was no longer used for /k/ before front vowels, since in French this would represent /s/ or /ts/. In early Middle Breton it was no longer felt appropriate that *u* could represent /u/ as well as /ʉ/ (in French *u* stood for /ʉ/ only), so *ou* was adopted for /u/. In essence, Middle Breton was spelt virtually the same as contemporary French. Unlike Old Breton, /t/ was now spelt consistently *t* and /d/ as *d*. The problem of /ð/ did not occur since by this period /ð/ had been assibilated to /z/ and was thus usually written as *z* (Jackson 1967a: 647–8). Certain anomalies and ambiguities remained. For example, final vowel + /ṽ/, written as -V*m* in Old Breton but -V*ff* in Middle Breton, had developed into a simple nasalized vowel, e.g. MB *eff* /ẽ/ 'heaven'. The French orthography also failed to distinguish /χ/ and /ʃ/, spelling both as *ch*. In 1659 Father Julian Maunoir published a grammar in which he proposed various changes to resolve the problems outlined above (Hemon 1977: viii–ix): *-ff* was abandoned and replaced by a vowel with a circumflex accent + *-n*, e.g. MB *quemeraff* : *quemerân* /kemerã/; /χ/ was spelt *c'h* beside *ch* for /ʃ/.[12] Furthermore, the initial mutations were now to be marked more systematically than before.

The next step was made with the publication of a grammar and a dictionary by Le Gonidec (1801 and 1821 respectively) in which he presented an orthography for the Modern Breton literary language of the Léon dialect. He introduced accents to mark length and the quality of vowels. He also attempted to remove doublets, e.g. *c* and *qu* for /k/, *i* and *y* for /i/, *s* and *z* for /z/, etc., and to produce a reasonably phonetic spelling system (see Jackson 1967a: 828–9). Its main drawback, however, was that it was not always suited to representing the other dialects apart from the Léon dialect. In 1911 a group of writers calling themselves 'l'entente des écrivains breton' set out an orthography known as KLT after the initial letters of the three dialects it was to be used for. They dispensed with Le Gonidec's accents and exploited the ambiguity of final stops to mark grammatical categories. Final stops are phonetically voiced but are voiceless in many contexts and in many earlier orthographies were written *p, t, k*. In KLT they were written *b, d, g* in nouns and *p, t, k* in adjectives, verbal nouns and prepositions. Similarly, the 2nd singular verbal ending -/ez/ was written -*ez* by Le Gonidec, but in KLT it is spelt -*ez* in the present but -*es* in the imperfect and conditional.

In 1941 it was felt that some attempt should be made to produce an orthography for all four dialects; Vannetais had been deliberately omitted from KLT as being too divergent. Involving Vannetais inevitably

TABLE 6.12   The main differences between the two main orthographical systems for Modern Breton.

	Zedachek	Orthographie universitaire
/z/ (Vann. /ɦ/)	*zh*	*z*
-/z/	*-s*	*-z*
/e:/	*é*	*e*
-/ou/	*-o'u*	*-ou*
-/dʒ/	*-ch*	*-j*
-/m/	*-mp*	*-m*
/χ/-	*c'h-*	*c'h-*
/ɦ/-	*c'h-*	*h-*
/ʁ/	*c'h*	*h*
-/g/	*-k*	*-g*
-/χ/	*-c'h*	*-h*

led to compromise and non-phonetic spellings (see Table 6.12). The most notorious example was *zh*, which for a Vannetais speaker was to represent /ɦ/ but /z/ for a Léon speaker; the spelling is simply a compromise between two pronunciations, previously spelt *h* in Vannetais and *z* elsewhere, e.g. *kazh* 'cat' (= Vannetais *kah*, Léon *kaz*). This case led to the nickname 'zedachek' for this orthography. The orthography of the Vannes dialect, Vannetais, had been established by Guillenic and Le Goff 1902 and so its exclusion from later attempts was of no consequence to speakers of Vannetais.[13]

In 1955 Falc'hun proposed an 'orthographie universitaire' which gained the official approval of the French Ministry of Education and became the official orthography for textbooks and examinations (see Table 6.12). Its claim was to bring the spelling closer to pronunciation but it would have only been possible to achieve this in regard to a single dialect; in effect, 'Falc'huneg', as it became known, was modelled on Léonais and can be seen as a modification of the 1911 system, which many have seen as a retrograde step. Its main changes were to use final *b*, *d*, *g*, *z* everywhere and to discard the grammatical alternations (see Jackson 1967a: 831).

The difficulty is not simply linguistic. The 1941 'zedachek' system gained the approval of the German occupational forces and for some still retains the taint of collaboration. The 1955 system, on the other hand, is for some too closely associated with the French authorities. As Ternes puts it:

A Breton writer chooses his orthography not for linguistic reasons, but on the basis of his or her political persuasions. On the other hand, even when a person does not have the slightest political affiliation or interest, he or she cannot help immediately being classified politically through the mere choice of orthography alone (Ternes 1992: 384).[14]

6.3.2.4   Cornish

As with Old Welsh and Old Breton, Old Cornish orthography developed out of the British system (see above 6.3.2.1). However, due to the paucity of early material there is very little evidence for this stage of affairs. The only known text written in this orthography is the list of Cornish saints' names (Olsen and Padel 1986), but even here there is some doubt as to whether we can legitimately call it an Old Cornish text; it is a list of names written in an Insular script but there is no evidence that it was written in Cornwall or by a Cornishman. Moreover, at this stage Old Cornish and Old Breton would have been orthographically, and perhaps even linguistically, indistinguishable (Olsen and Padel 1986: 39). Apart from that, other Old Cornish texts have generally been distinguishable from Old Breton on the grounds that they show the influence of Old English orthographical practices, notably þ (thorn) for /ð/ and ƿ (wynn) for /u̯/; this is particularly clear in the *Vocabularium Cornicum* (Campanile 1961), e.g. *bliþen* /bliðen/ 'year' (cf. W *blwyddyn*), *heþeu* /heðeu̯/ 'today' (cf. W *heddiw*), *aƿuit* (corrected to *aƿuir*) /au̯ir/ 'air' (cf. W *awyr*), etc.[15]

Middle and Late Cornish were written down using the contemporary English orthography and since there was no consistency or standard for English, there was *a fortiori* none for Cornish. Furthermore, most writers of Late Cornish were unfamiliar with Middle Cornish texts and so were not influenced by earlier attempts to write Cornish; in other words, no literary spelling tradition had developed (see Table 6.13). In Middle Cornish vowel + *y* could be used to mark a long vowel. The vowels with the circumflex accent in Late Cornish were used by Lhuyd 1707 in his attempt to produce a phonetic spelling system for Cornish (see George 1993a: 418). In part the variation reflects the changes between Middle and Late Cornish, but it also indicates the vagaries of

TABLE 6.13   Spelling variation in Middle and Late Cornish.

	Middle Cornish	Late Cornish
/a/	*a*	*a*
/aː/	*ay*	*â a*
/i/	*i*	*i*
/iː/	*y*	*i î ee*
/v/	*v f u ff*	*v f*
/ð/	*th 3*	*dh th*

For further details, see George 1993a: 416–17.

the English orthography with which each writer of Cornish had come into contact.

Various attempts have been made and are being made to revive Cornish, and establishing a written standard is an important element in achieving that (George and Broderick 1993: 648). The most recent attempt, *Kernewek Kemmyn* 'Common Cornish', is used in George 1993b.

6.3.2.5 Irish

Essentially, the same orthography has been in use for Irish and Scottish Gaelic from an early stage.[16] The orthography of Manx, on the other hand, has been acquired from quite different sources. This section concentrates on important aspects of Irish orthography, while the section on Scottish Gaelic (6.3.2.6) deals with developments unique to that language.

The question of early Irish orthography is closely related to that of British orthography. Until recently, it was the general view that early Irish orthography had been taken over from the British pronunciation of Latin, and thus internal *p t c* represented /b d g/, and *b*, *d*, *g* represented /v ð ɣ/, as we have seen for British and the early Brittonic languages (Jackson 1973–4: 23, and 6.3.2.1 above). In other words, the British taught the Irish to write. But the British system was not the first writing system to appear in Ireland. As we have seen (6.3.1), an earlier orthographical system had been developed, namely Ogam, which despite appearances seems to have been based on Latin. It has been recently argued that there was continuity between the Ogam system and the earliest manuscript orthographical systems (Carney 1977–9, Harvey 1987b, 1989). One of the most striking features of the Ogam system is the use of *G, D, B* for /g d b/, which would usually be written *c, t, p* in the Old Irish manuscript orthography which is derived from British, e.g. Ogam *TOGITACC* = OIr *Toicthech*, *BAIDAGNI* = OIr *Báetán*, *CORRBRI* = OIr *Coirpre*, etc. The orthography of the *prima manus* (the

Table 6.14: The spelling of internal consonants in Ogam and Old Irish.

	Ogam/*prima manus*	Old Irish	Middle Irish
/θ/	t	th	th
/χ/	c	ch	ch
/b/	b	p .	b
/d/	d	t	d
/g/	g	c	g
/v/	b	b	bh
/ð/	d	d	dh
/ɣ/	g	g	gh

earliest scribe) of the Würzburg glosses, Old Irish glosses on Latin biblical texts (see Stokes and Strachan 1901–3: I, xxiv), shows the same Ogam-like spellings, e.g. *roslogeth* (= OIr *ro·sluiced*), *adobrogart* (= OIr *atob·rogart*) with *g* for /g/ and *d* for /d/ (see Table 6.14 above). The orthography is, however, unsettled; for the same scribe also wrote *t* for /d/, and so appears to represent a transitional stage. The second and third hands in the manuscript, who between them wrote the bulk of the glosses, show none of these features. The 'British' system is used standardly in Old Irish orthography but even then was running into the same kind of difficulties as were found in Welsh. The situation was, if anything, more acute in Old Irish; in internal position four sets of sounds, /p t k/, /b d g/, /f θ χ/ and /v ð ɤ/, were to be represented by only two sets of signs, *p*, *t*, *c* and *b*, *d*, *g* (internal /p t k/ had by this stage arisen from the resolution of clusters created by syncope (see 2.2.2)). The problem was resolved partly by using *tt*, *cc*, *pp* for the voiceless stops, but the ultimately successful strategy was the use of digraphs with *h* for the fricatives, i.e. *bh*, *dh*, *gh*, *th*, *ch* and occasionally *ph*. A full *h* was in practice relatively rare in the early manuscripts, where the scribes preferred to use various versions of the Greek *spiritus asper* 'rough breathing' (ʽ) written over the letter to represent *h*. Indeed, *h* only seems to have been regularly written in full in Modern Irish spelling. A brief survey of the manuscript samples in O'Neill 1984 reveals that up to at least the 16th century there was a tendency to mark with *h* or a diacritic the spirants /θ/ and /χ/ more often than /ð/ and /ɤ/.

The origin of the use of *h* in fricatives has been considered by Harvey 1989, who is concerned with the similar use of *h* in British and also in English, where *th* replaced the runes ð and þ. His conclusion is that the practice arose first in Ireland in response to the difficulties outlined above and from there spread to the Brittonic languages and so to English. In this respect, he claims the Irish perhaps taught the British and the English to spell. However, the use of *th* for /θ/ need not derive from Irish. Names in *Theod-* /θeod-/- were very common on the Continent and are attested in the letters of Gregory the Great.

The use of clear signs for the fricatives allowed a more logical distribution of the other signs, with the result that *p*, *t*, *c* came once again to represent /p t k/, and *b*, *d*, *g* came to represent /b d g/, as in Modern Irish (see Table 6.14 above). The chronology of this development is not as clear as it might be due to the archaizing practices of scribes. They varied considerably in the extent to which they modernized the language and orthography of the manuscripts they were copying. A manuscript copied in the 14th century can show digraphs with *h*, *d* for /d/ and *t* for /t/, while a 16th-century manuscript can preserve *d* for /ð/ and *t* for /d/ with only sporadic use of *h* or a diacritic to make a fricative.

As regards the marking of fricatives, Irish encountered similar problems to those found in British, but with the marking of long vowels Irish was on its own. In British many long vowels had been diphthongized and were, therefore, written as digraphs, and elsewhere long vowels were determined by their environment and so not marked orthographically (see 5.2.1), but Irish had a system of long vowels beside short vowels, thus /a/ : /a:/, /e/ : /e:/, /i/ : /i:/, etc.

Not all of these vowels were of equal antiquity; original /o:/ and /e:/ were diphthongized to /u:ə/ and /i:ə/ respectively, although very early examples of original /e:/ and /o:/ survive, e.g. *Feec* (= OIr *Fíacc*), *Boin* (= OIr *Búain*), etc. (Bieler 1979: 242). Moreover, new long vowels arose from final clusters of -VTR, e.g. Ir *cenél* < **kenetlo-* (cf. W *cenedl*) (see 2.2.3.1). In archaic Old Irish the long vowel was often marked by a doubling of the vowel, e.g. *baan* 'white' (= later *bán*), *ee* 'he' (= later *é*) (Thurneysen 1946: 20). But the usual marker of length was and has continued to be an acute accent over the vowel. The marking of long vowels was by no means consistent in the manuscripts and often obscured by scribes marking all vowels with an accent or marking them haphazardly. Rhyming patterns in verse are often helpful in identifying long vowels, since only long vowels can rhyme with long vowels (Knott 1962: 8).

Irish also had a series of palatal consonants beside the non-palatal series, i.e. /p/ : /p'/, /t/ : /t'/, etc. (see 2.2.3.3). The alternation of non-palatal and palatal consonants carried grammatical information, e.g. OIr *lám* /la:ṽ/ 'hand' (nom. sg.) : *láim* /la:ṽ'/ (acc. sg.), and so it was vital that the distinction was marked. The palatal consonant was marked by the writing of a 'glide' vowel before the consonant in question. Phonologically it does not have the status of a full vowel as it does not form a diphthong with the preceding vowel, e.g. OIr *maith* /maθ'/

TABLE 6.15   Schematized development of glide vowels in early Irish

(a) Stressed syllables

	(i)	(ii)
/TVT/	TVT'	TVT'I
archaic OIr	TV*i*T'	TVT'I
OIr	TV*i*T'	TVT'I/TV*i*T'I
late OIr	TV*i*T'	TV*i*T'I

(b) Unstressed syllables

	(i)	(ii)	(iii)
/TVT/	TVT'A	TVTI	TVTA
archaic OIr	TVT'A	TVTI	TVTA
OIr	TV*i*T'*e*A	TVT*a*I	TVTA
late OIr	TV*i*T'*e*A	TVT*a*I	TV*a*TA

T = any consonant, V = any vowel, A = back vowel, I = front vowel.

'good', OIr *slóig* /slo:ɤ′/ 'host' (gen. sg.), OIr *luid* /luð′/ 'he went', etc. (Thurneysen 1946: 55–6, and Table 6.15, type (a) (i) above). In Old Irish the palatal glide is regularly written in a stressed syllable before a final consonant, but less regularly when the palatal cluster is internal, e.g. *mathi/maithi* /maθ′i/ 'good' (pl.), *súli/súili* /su:l′i/ 'eyes', etc. (Table 6.15, type (a) (ii)). Presumably the presence of a front vowel after the consonant may have been regarded a sufficient indication of palatalization. In some of the earliest evidence, such as the spelling of names in the B version of Adomnán's *Life of Columba* (Anderson and Anderson 1991: lxxvii), the *i*-glide is not found at all, e.g. *Darmag* (= *Dairmag*), *Cannecho* (= *Cainnecho*), *Felni* (= *Feilni*), etc.

Glide vowels were not restricted to stressed syllables. It was also necessary to indicate in unstressed syllables that a non-palatal consonant was followed by a front vowel and a palatal consonant was followed by a back vowel, e.g. *cumachtai* /'kuṽəχti/ 'power' (gen. sg.), *toimseo* /'toṽ′s′o/ 'measure' (gen. sg.) (Thurneysen 1946: 61–2, and Table 6.15, types (b) (i) and (ii)). The writing of glide vowels in unaccented syllables does not usually occur in the earliest sources, e.g. Archaic OIr *colpdi* (= *colpdai*), *Mache* (= *Machae*), etc. (Bieler 1979: 243). The latest stage in writing glide vowels does not emerge until late Old Irish/early Middle Irish, when a non-palatal consonant followed by a front vowel is marked by an *a*-glide, e.g. *sleachta* (= OIr *slechta*), etc. (Thurneysen 1946: 57; see Figure 6.19, type (b) (iii)).

The more or less standardized system of orthography established in the medieval period continued in use well into the 20th century. The Insular letter forms also continued to be used until they were finally replaced by cursive letter forms as used in English. By the mid-20th century the original orthography had clearly become divorced from the phonology. The real problems lay with the fricative consonants, which had begun to disappear in pronunciation from the 13th century onwards; /ð/ and /ɤ/ became totally confused at this period and developed to /ɤ/, /i̯/ or zero in most dialects. The labial fricative /v/ tended towards /u̯/ or to create a *u*-diphthong. The loss of fricatives also brought about a compensatory lengthening or diphthongization of adja-

TABLE 6.16 Examples of diphthongs and long vowels arising from loss of fricatives in Modern Irish

leaghadh 'melting'	OIr /L′eɤəð/
	MnIr /L′aɤəɤ/ > /L′a:ɤ/ (> Conn /L′a:u̯/)
nimhe 'poison' (gen. sg.)	OIr /N′iṽ′e/
	MnIr/N′iv′ə/ (Conn /n′iɤ′ə/ > /N′i:/)

See Ó Siadhail 1989: 72, 69.

cent vowels (see Table 6.16 for examples).

In the 1950s and 1960s a concerted attempt was made to establish a standard orthography which more closely reflected the modern pronunciation; given the dialectal variation, *Caighdeán na Gaeilge* 'Standard of Irish' could not satisfy everyone. But it does have the effect of removing certain inconsistencies and simplifying or removing complex consonantal clusters, e.g. *léann* = *léigheann* 'learning', *fáim* = *fáithim* 'hem', *leafaos* = *leamhthaos* 'paste'.[17]

6.3.2.6 Scottish Gaelic

Scottish Gaelic orthography is generally a continuation of that of Classical Irish, as discussed above, and does not, therefore, in its broad outlines require further discussion. The changes in the phonology of Scottish Gaelic since the 12th and 13th centuries are not usually recorded in the orthography, but it is clear that similar changes occurred to those in Irish, notably in the reduction of fricatives. One interesting feature which is related to the loss of fricatives is the use of an inorganic *-th-* to mark hiatus (see 2.3.1). For example, Irish has two words pronounced /'fi:əχ/, *fiach* 'raven' and *fíach* 'debt. While the latter contains a diphthong arising from an original */e:/, the diphthong in the former arose from two vowels in hiatus. In Irish they are indistinguishable but in the medieval period there must have been some difference since Scottish Gaelic marked the hiatus orthographically by

TABLE 6.17   Examples of inorganic *-th-* in Scottish Gaelic

OIr *bruäch* /bruəχ/ 'bank' > MIr *brúach*, ScG *bruthach*
OIr *beüs* /beəs/ 'yet, still' > MIr *fós*, ScG *fathast*

inserting *-th-*, thus *fitheach* 'raven'. For this to happen, *th* must have become a virtually silent consonant by this period (for further examples, see Table 6.17; for examples in Irish, see Ó Cuív 1990: 103–4).

The bulk of Scottish Gaelic literature is written in the Classical Irish orthography but there is one precious example where it is written in a spelling which follows the conventions of contemporary Scots. The *Book of the Dean of Lismore* is an early-16th-century manuscript from Perthshire containing a wide range of poetry (for a selection, see Quiggin 1937). Its orthography is extremely valuable in allowing us to glimpse the pronunciation of Scottish Gaelic in 16th-century Perthshire. The most obvious area of difference is with the fricatives. The Dean's quasi-phonetic orthography to a large extent records what is said and so we find the regular loss of fricatives and the diphthongization of surrounding vowels. Examples are presented in Table 6.18.

TABLE 6.18   Examples of the orthography of the Book of the Dean of Lismore

---

wen = bhean 'woman' (voc.)
chroywe = crodh 'cattle'
will = bhfuil 'is'
avir, awir = adhbhar 'material'
hei^t = thí 'house'
corrik = comhraig 'contest'
breour = brioghmhar 'powerful'
di zoywin = do gheobhainn 'he will take'
da zawlo^t zeig = dá ghabhladh dheag 'twelve forks'
fai^{t}w = feathamh 'looking'

The examples are taken from Quiggin 1937; the orthography of the manuscript is followed by a rendering in traditional Irish orthography.

6.3.2.7   Manx

Just as the *Book of the Dean of Lismore* offers us a glimpse of a 'non-Gaelic' orthographical system for Scottish Gaelic, the orthography of Early Modern English appears to have been the basis of Manx orthography.[18] It is generally supposed that this system was devised to produce a Manx translation of the Book of Common Prayer and the Bible (Moore and Rhŷs 1893–4) by John Phillips. a native of North Wales who was Bishop of Sodor and Man between 1605 and 1633 (R. L. Thomson 1969: 178–9). However, there are hints in contemporary criticism of his work that there was an orthography already in existence although we have no trace of it (Broderick 1993: 230). To a large extent the system followed the Early Modern English system, e.g. *gh* for /χ/, etc., and thus marked distinctions which were crucial for English but not necessarily so for Manx; for example, the distinction between palatal and non-palatal consonants was marked by different spellings and so did not maintain the relationship between the palatal and non-palatal variant, e.g. *t* /t/ : *ch* /t′/; *d* /d/ : *j* /d′/; *s* /s/ : *sh* /s′/. The distinction between /g/ and /ɤ/ was not observed at all, both being written as *g*. On the other hand, the spelling of vowels seems to bear no resemblance to the orthography of Early Modern English but seems to be based on some other system where the vowels had remained pure, i.e. where *a* represented /a/, *i* /i/, etc. The radical changes undergone by the vowel system of southern English in the 15th and 16th centuries had produced a situation where the vowel orthography would have been inappropriate for a language such as Manx, particularly in the area of long vowels and diphthongs. It is clear that Phillips looked elsewhere. It is possible that he looked to the pronunciation of Italian or Spanish, but the most likely source for the vowel orthography is his own native language, Welsh. The most compelling evidence for this is

TABLE 5.19 Examples of diphthongs and long vowels arising from loss of fricatives in Manx

thalloo 'land' (gen. sg. *thallooin*) = ScG *talmhan*   *sheeloghe* 'generation' = ScG *síolbhach*   *buirroogh* 'roar' = ScG *búirfeadhach*   *breeoil* 'effective' = ScG *bríoghamhail*

See R. L. Thomson 1992a: 131.

the regular use of *y* or final *-ey* for /ə/, a usage unique to Welsh among the languages he could have considered, e.g. *dooinney* /dunʹə/ 'man', *dorrys* /dorəs/ 'door', *follaghey* /folaχə/ 'hiding', *jirrym* /dʹirəm/ 'I shall say', etc. If this is the source of the Manx vowel orthography, Phillips has abstracted the spellings from the phonological context of Welsh; in Welsh, /ə/ does not occur in final position except in some monosyllables, but in Manx its use is widespread (see 5.2.2).

The advantage of Manx orthography for the linguist is that it allows us access to the pronunciation of the language in a way that the standard 'Gaelic' orthography does not, particularly with regard to the vocalization and diphthongization associated with the loss of fricatives (see Table 6.19 for examples).

Notes

1. Such an attitude is revealed in the scant attention paid to orthography in recent surveys of the Celtic languages, such as MacAulay 1992a, Price 1992a and Ball and Fife 1993.
2. On early writing systems, see Gelb 1963, Diringer 1968, Hooker 1990.
3. The basic work is Lejeune 1971; the script is discussed in detail at pp. 345–64; see also Lejeune 1988: 3–8.
4. The earlier view of Lejeune 1971: 349 was that the Lugano script was borrowed from a later form of the Etruscan script and subsequently *o* was borrowed from the Greek script of Massalia. Similary, his theory of spelling reforms in later inscriptions (Lejeune 1971: 357–60) has been called into question by new theories about the dating of certain inscriptions; it now appears that the so-called reforms are largely archaic features in early texts (see Gambari and Colonna 1988: 130–64 and Pandolfini and Prosdocimi 1990: 289).
5. For a summary of the script on the Chamalières tablet, see Lejeune and Marichal 1976–7: 158; for Larzac, see Lejeune et al. 1985: 114–18. For a more general discussion of orthography, see D. E. Evans 1967: 390–420.
6. The fullest discussions and analyses of Ogam are McManus 1991 (with full bibliography) and Ziegler 1994; the original collections of material were Macalister 1945–9 and Nash-Williams 1950. See also the work of Harvey 1987a, 1987b, Uhlich 1989, and Sims-Williams 1992, 1993. For British

Ogams, see now Okasha 1993 (south-west Britain) and C. Thomas 1994. Transliterated Ogam examples are conventionally written in capitals.

7. For a full collection, see Nash-Williams 1950; see also Okasha 1993 for inscriptions from south-west Britain. Jackson 1953: 149–93 offers a detailed discussion; see also C. Thomas 1994.

8. See Russell 1993b and forthcoming, and Charles-Edwards and Russell 1993–4.

9. The first appearance of *y* for /ə/ and /ɨ/ seems to be in the *englyn* on Padarn's staff, dated to the second half of the 11th century (I. Williams 1941).

10. See T. A. Watkins 1993: 294–5. For further details, see M. Stephens 1986: s.nn. For the peculiarities of the orthography of William Salesbury, see Fisher 1931: xxxvi–xl.

11. For a detailed discussion of all stages of Breton orthography, see Jackson 1967a: 825–33; see also Ternes 1992: 381–5, J Stephens 1993: 352–3.

12. Hemon 1977 edits two versions of the same text written before and after Maunoir's reforms respectively.

13. For the fundamental dialectal differences between Vannetais and other dialects, see Jackson 1967a: 66–77, Fleuriot 1967, and for a brief grammar of Vannetais, see Hemon 1956: xii–lxxii.

14. See also Jackson 1967a: 832. For more recent attempts to set up new orthographies, see Ternes 1992: 383–5, Humphreys 1993: 618.

15. On Old Cornish orthography, see Haywood 1982. For a general discussion, see George 1993a: 415–18.

16. For very brief discussions, see Ó Dochartaigh 1992: 28–9, Mac Eoin 1993: 104–5.

17. See Ó Murchú 1985: 64–7. Ó Dónaill 1977 is the fullest dictionary written in the new orthography. De Bhaldraithe 1981 provides a useful index between it and the *Dictionary of the Irish Language* (Quin *et al.* 1913–76); see also Wigger 1979.

18. For Manx orthography, see R. L. Thomson 1969: 178–82, Broderick 1993: 230.

Chapter 7

Lenition and mutations: phonetics, phonology and morphology

7.0 Introduction

All the Insular Celtic languages display a regular, grammatically motivated set of consonant alternations at the beginning of words. Although these alternations, termed mutations, are triggered by more or less the same grammatical categories in each language, there is considerable variation in their phonological realization.

7.1 The phonological data

Goidelic languages operate with two mutations of the basic consonant, termed lenition and nasalization (the latter is otherwise known as eclipsis in Irish grammars). Table 7.1 overleaf shows the mutations and their usual spellings in Modern Irish. This seems to be the general picture although there are dialectal variations particularly with regard to the palatal and non-palatal forms (Ó Siadhail 1989: 67–69). Scottish Gaelic has a similar set of alternatives with a certain amount of dialectal variation; for example, in Arran palatal /χ/ tends to become /ç/ or /h/, e.g. *cheana* /ç'eNə/ or /h'eNə/ (Holmer 1957: 80). Moreover, it is important to note that many of these sounds, especially /ɣ/, were preserved initially even though they were prone to disappear in other positions (Holmer 1957: 74.). The mutations in Manx are more difficult to ascertain because the language did not inherit the same orthographical system as the other Goidelic languages; the spelling of Manx tends to reflect actual pronunciation (R. L. Thomson 1969: 179–82; see also 6.3.2.7 above), and so does not usually display the systematic spelling alternations between the mutated and unmutated form of a word. R. L. Thomson 1969: 190–202 (see also J. Kelly 1804: 6–8) discusses the evidence for mutations in 18th-century texts and shows that mutations occur in contexts similar to those discussed below for Irish. The

TABLE 7.1   Initial mutations in Modern Irish

Basic consonant		Lenited consonant		Nasalized consonant	
/k/	c-	/χ/	ch-	/g/	gc-
/g/	g-	/ɣ/, /i̯/	gh-	/ŋ/	ng-
/t/	t-	/h/	th-	/d/	dt-
/d/	d-	/ɣ/, /i̯/	dh-	/N/	nd-
/p/	p-	/f/	ph-	/b/	bp-
/b/	b-	/u̯/, /v/	bh-	/m/	mb-
/s/	s-	/h/	sh-		
/f/	f-	/∅/	fh-	/u̯/	bhf-
/N/	n-	/n/	n-		
/m/	m-	/ũ̯/, /v/	mh-		

The second realization in the second column is the realization of the palatal variant; see Ó Siadhail 1989: 112.

changes themselves are almost identical to those listed for Irish in Table 7.1. Broderick 1984–6: I, 7–24 (also III, 64–7) discusses the mutations in the language of the last few native speakers. He concludes that 'at an earlier stage of the language these forms would have functioned as a complete system, but in LSM [late spoken Manx] this system has to a great extent broken down, and in the use of nasalization has practically ceased functioning' (Broderick 1984–6: III, 67).

Brittonic languages differ from Goidelic in that the shifts are different and they use three mutations of the basic consonant, conventionally termed lenition, spirantization (or spirant mutation) and nasalization. Table 7.2 shows the mutations and their usual spellings in Modern Welsh, Modern Breton and Middle Cornish. Though there are isolated cases of assimilation, e.g. B *an nor* 'the door' : *dor*, etc., nasalization does not figure as a major grammatical marker in Breton or Cornish (Hemon 1975: 24–5), hence the lack of data.

7.2   The grammatical function of the initial mutations

Despite some difference in the phonology of the mutations, the languages show a high degree of uniformity in the grammatical categories marked by them. The following list of categories which take mutations is by no means exhaustive but serves to show the heavy grammatical load carried by the initial consonants of words in Celtic.[1]

7.2.1   Nouns

7.2.1.1   Feminine nouns
(i) Preceded by the article a feminine noun is lenited, e.g. MnIr *an*

TABLE 7.2   Initial mutations in Modern Welsh, Modern Breton and Middle Cornish.

Modern Welsh

Phonology:

Basic	/k/	/g/	/t/	/d/	/p/	/b/	/m/
Lenited	/g/		/d/	/ð/	/b/	/v/	/v/
Spirantized	/χ/		/θ/		/f/		
Nasalized	/ŋh/	/ŋ/	/nh/	/n/	/mh/	/m/	

Orthography:

Basic	c	g	t	d	p	b	m
Lenited	g		d	dd	b	f	f
Spirantized	ch		th		ff		
Nasalized	ngh	ng	nh	n	mh	m	

Modern Breton

Phonology:

Basic	/k/	/g/	/t/	/d/	/p/	/b/	/m/
Lenited	/g/	/ɣ/	/d/	/z/	/b/	/v/	/v/
Spirantized	/χ/		/z/		/f/		
Nasalized				/n/			

Orthography:[†]

Basic	c k	g	t	d	p	b	m
Lenited	g	c'h	d	z	b	v	v
Spirantized	c'h		z		f		
Nasalized				n			

Middle Cornish

Phonology:

Basic	/k/	/g/	/t/	/d/	/p/	/b/	/m/
Lenited	/g/		/d/	/ð/	/b/	/v/	/v/
Spirantized	/χ/		/θ/		/f/		

Orthography:

Basic	c k	g	t	d	p	b	m
Lenited	g		d	th	b	v	v
Spirantized	gh, h		th		f		

[†]See Jackson 1967a: 825–33.

bhean 'the wife': *bean*, W *y ferch* : *merch*, B *ar vamm* 'the mother' : *mamm*.

(ii) A feminine noun causes lenition of a following adjective, e.g. MnIr *bean mhaith* 'a good woman' : *maith*, W *merch dda* 'a good girl'

: *da*, MC *benen vras* 'a strong woman' : *bras*, B *ur vamm baour* 'a poor woman' : *paour*. This type is rare in Breton (Hemon 1975: 17).

7.2.1.2 Masculine nouns
Breton is unique in having the spirant mutation after the masculine singular definite and indefinite articles. Its effects are, however, restricted to initial *k-*, e.g. *ar c'hloc'h* 'the bell' : *cloc'h*; *er hy* 'the dog' : *ky*; *ur c'horf* 'a body' : *corf*; *eur c'hastell* 'a castle' : *castell* (Hemon 1975: 10–11; see also M. McKenna 1988: 193)

7.2.1.3 Case forms in Goidelic
(i) Genitive singular masculine preceded by the article, e.g. MnIr *an fhir* /əN ir'/ 'of the man' : *fear*, ScG *an dhuirn* 'of the fist' : *dorn*.
(ii) Dative singular masculine preceded by the article, e.g. MnIr *san fhómhar* 'in the autumn' : *fómhar* (northern dialects only; southern dialects have nasalization (Ó Siadhail 1989: 127–9)), ScG *don chnoc* 'to the hill' : *cnoc*.

7.2.2 Numerals
Many numerals cause some kind of mutation but it varies between the languages.

'Two' lenites in all languages, e.g. MnIr *dhá bhád* 'two boats' : *bád*, W *dwy fis* 'two months' : *mis*, MC *dew then* 'two men' : *den*, B *daou baotr* 'two boys' : *paotr*.

'Three' causes the spirant mutation in Brittonic, e.g. W *tri chath* 'three cats' : *cath*, B *tri c'hant* 'three hundred' : *cant*. In Welsh *chwech* 'six' also causes spirantization, e.g. *chwe(ch) plentyn* 'six children' : *plentyn*. In Breton, however, 'four' and 'nine' used to take the spirant mutation, e.g. *pevar c'hrouader* 'four children' : *crouader*, *nao c'hant* 'nine hundred', but as early as the 18th century spirantization tended to be replaced by lenition, e.g. *tri baotr* 'three boys', *pevar bost* 'four posts' : *post*; *nao dest* 'nine witnesses' : *test* (Hemon 1975: 8–9). On the other hand, Welsh shows a historical development towards using the basic form. In Middle Welsh, the numerals 'seven', 'nine', 'ten', 'twelve', 'fifteen' and 'hundred' caused nasalization especially with particular nouns, e.g. *seith mlyned* 'seven years' : *blyned*; *naw nieu* 'nine days' : *dieu*; *dec mrenhin* 'ten kings' : *brenhin*; *can mu* 'a hundred oxen' : *bu* (D. S. Evans 1964: 22). Nasalization also spread to *pym(p)* 'five', *wyth* 'eight', and occasionally to *tri* 'three' and *chech* 'six'. However, in Modern Welsh most of these numerals are followed by the basic form except for certain phrases, e.g. *blynedd/blwydd* 'years' and *diwrnod* 'day', where the nasal mutation remains (S. J. Williams 1980: 43–5). In Irish, the numerals 'seven' to 'ten', MnIr *seacht*, *ocht*, *naoi*, *deich*, are all followed by nasalization, e.g. *seacht mbád* 'seven boats' : *bád*.

7.2.3 Possessive pronouns and adjectives

(i) First singular 'my' causes lenition in Irish, e.g. MnIr *mo chatt* 'my cat' : *catt*; *mo mháthair* 'my mother': *máthair*. However, the Brittonic evidence is more varied; in Welsh *fy* /və/ or /ə/ causes nasalization, e.g. *fy nhad* 'my father' : *tad*; *fy machgen* 'my boy' : *bachgen*, etc.; but in Cornish and Breton it is followed by the spirant mutation, e.g. MC *ow thy* 'my house' : *ty*, B *va zi* 'my house' : *ti*, etc.

(ii) Second singular 'your' is followed by lenition in all languages, e.g. MnIr *do thech* 'your house' : *tech*, W *dy dŷ* 'your house' : *tŷ*, MC *the vroder* 'your brother' : *broder*, B *da di* 'your house'.

(iii) The third singular masculine and feminine possessive adjectives are very similar in form in each language but are differentiated by the following mutation. The masculine form causes lenition as in 'his house': Ir *a thech*, W *ei dŷ*, MC *i/y dy*, B *e di*. But the feminine form is followed by the basic form in Goidelic and the spirant mutation in Brittonic, e.g. 'her house': Ir *a tech*, W *ei thŷ*, MC *i/y/hy thy*, B *he zi*. In both Welsh and Breton the possessive pronouns can be re-marked in speech by auxiliary affixed pronouns which are identical in form to the independent pronouns, e.g. W *ei dŷ ef* 'his house' : *ei thŷ hi* 'her house', B *e di ean* 'his house' : *he zi hy* 'her house' (S. J. Williams 1980: 50, Hemon 1975: 75–6).

7.2.4 The negative particle

The negative prefix causes lenition of the initial of the verb, e.g. MnIr *ní thuigeann sé* 'he does not understand': *tuigeann*, ScG *cha ghlan mi* 'I shall not clean': *glanaidh mi*, B *ne gomprenan ket* 'I do not understand' : *comprenan* (Hemon 1975: 281–6), MC *ny glowys* 'I did not hear': *clowys*. In Old Irish, however, *ní* was not followed by a mutation, e.g. *ní·beir* /niː'berʲ/ 'he does not carry'. In Welsh negation is more complicated; voiced consonants are apparently lenited, e.g. *ni ddaw ef* 'he does not come' : *daw*, *ni ddywedais* (*i*) *ddim* 'I did not say' : *dywedais*, but unvoiced consonants are spirantized, e.g. *ni phrynodd e ddim* 'he did not buy' : *prynodd*, etc.[2] In passing, it is worth noting that both Welsh and Breton have developed a negative system analogous to French *ne . . . pas*. In spoken Welsh the *ni* has disappeared and the negative force rests on *ddim*. Likewise, Breton *quet/ket* plays a similar role. In origin neither is a negative but both mean 'thing' (see 5.5.2.1 above).

7.2.5 Provection

In addition to the mutations discussed above, another type called 'provection' also occurs. It involves the devoicing of voiced consonants, i.e. /b d g/ > /p t k/.[3] It only has any grammatical significance in a few places in Cornish and Breton. In Middle Cornish it occurs after the verbal particle *ow* before verbal nouns, e.g. *ow pewe* 'living' : *bewe*; *ow tos* 'coming' : *dos*; and also after *mar* 'if', e.g. *mar pyth* 'if he is' : *byth*; *mar qura* 'if he does' : *gura*, etc. In some cases it seems to occur after lenition as it apparently devoices the outcome of that mutation, e.g. *yn fras* 'great' devoiced from *vras*, the lenited form of *bras* (Lewis 1946: 9–10). In Breton it is less common, only occurring regularly after *ho* 'your' (2nd pl.), e.g. *ho tillad* 'your clothes' : *dillad*; *ho quelet* 'to see you' : *guelet* (Hemon 1975: 11–12).

7.2.6 Initial vowels
The system of mutations discussed above affects consonants but not vowels. However, words beginning with a vowel were in some categories marked in a similar way. In Irish certain elements which affect initial consonants produce a prefixed *h-* on initial vowels, e.g. *a haois* 'her age' : *aois*, *na héin* (nom. pl.) 'the birds' : *éin*. Similarly in Welsh *ei* 'her' was followed by the spirant mutation but an initial vowel was prefixed by *h-*, e.g. *ei hanifail* 'her animal' : *anifail*. In Irish nouns with initial vowel preceded by the article were affected differently; masculine nouns prefixed *t-*, e.g. *an t-éan* 'the bird' : *éan*. Likewise, initial *s-*, which when lenited gave /h/-, prefixed *t-*, e.g. *an t-súil* /ən'tu:l'/ 'the eye' (nom. sg. f.), etc.

7.3 Mutations in the consonantal system
The series of alternations described above mark grammatical categories and grammatical relationships. However, it is clear that it was not only the initial consonants which were affected in this way but the whole consonantal system, even though the changes only eventually had grammatical significance for initial consonants. The kind of changes involved can be best illustrated by examining loanwords where the original form of the word has survived in the donor language; for Celtic that leads us to consider the fate of Latin loanwords, and especially those borrowed into Welsh (see Table 7.3 for examples). Leaving aside questions about the vowel changes, it is clear that the Latin words underwent wholesale changes in their consonant structure, changes which are identical to those outlined in Table 7.2 for the initial mutation called lenition, i.e. /p t k/ > /b d g/, /b d m/ > /v ð v/. Moreover, there is also evidence that geminate consonants in Latin were spirantized in Welsh, as in *pechod* 'sin'. Similar systematic changes can be detected in Latin loanwords in early Irish. However, the problem here is that many of these words were borrowed into Irish from British or British Latin and had, therefore, undergone British rather than Irish changes (McManus 1983, and 2.2.5 above).

Although the initial mutations of the modern languages are grammatically motivated, their origin lies in phonological changes in about the 4th or 5th century AD which affected all consonants in intervocalic

TABLE 7.3   Examples of Latin loanwords in Welsh

abostol < Lat *apostolus*	*disgybl* < *discipulus*
Addaf < *Adam*	*pechod* < *peccātum*
cardod < *caritātem*	*ysblennydd* < *splendidus*
corff < *corpus*	*tafel* < *tabella*
diffyg < *dēficio*	*ufyl* < *humilis*

See H. Lewis 1943.

position; even a word boundary was no barrier to the changes. Thus where within one accented group one word ended in a vowel and the next began with a consonant, i.e. schematically -V # TV-, the consonant was as vulnerable to change as if it had been in intervocalic position in the middle of a word. In general terms, single intervocalic consonants were affected differently from double consonants and clusters of resonant + consonant. The latter type was immune from the effects of these changes (Russell 1985a).

So far the description of the process has been deliberately vague so as to be equally applicable to both Goidelic and Brittonic. However, the outcome of these changes was different in the two language groups (see Table 7.4 for a summary). In Brittonic single intervocalic stops were 'lenited'; more specifically unvoiced stops were voiced and voiced stops were spirantized, thus /p t k/ > /b d g/, /b d g m/ > /v ð ɣ v/, e.g. W *maneg* 'glove' < Lat *manica*, *modd* 'way' < *modus*, *escob* 'bishop' < *episcopus*, *Padrig* < *Patricius*, *profi* < *probō*. Subsequently, /ɣ/ was lost, e.g. W *pla* 'plague' < Lat *plaga*. On the other hand, double consonants seem to have been simplified, i.e. /pp tt kk/ > /p t k/, and subsequently in Welsh spirantized, e.g. *cath* /kaθ/ 'cat' < *cattus*, *achub* /aχʉb/ 'save' < *occupo*, *boch* /bɔχ/ 'cheek' < *bucca*, etc. A single consonant which had been protected from lenition by a preceding resonant was also spirantized, e.g. *corff* < *corpus*, *gwrdd* < *gurdus*, *diserth* < *desertum* (Russell 1985a). However, it is clear that these changes

TABLE 7.4   Summary of consonantal changes in Celtic

Brittonic

Lenition	/p t k/ > /b d g/
	/b d g m/ > /v ð ɣ v/
Spirantization	unlenited /p t k/ > /f θ χ/

Goidelic

Lenition	/p t k/ > /f θ χ/	
	/b d g m/ > /v ð ɣ v/	
Geminates	/pp tt kk bb dd gg/ > /p t k b d g/	

took place in Brittonic and not in Proto-Celtic; for, although a similar range of changes took place in Goidelic, the outcomes were not the same. The voiced stops were spirantized, i.e. /b d g/ > /v ð ɣ/, e.g. OIr *suide* 'seat' /suð'e/ < **sod-i̯o-*, *tige* /tiɣ'e/ 'house' (gen. sg.) < **tegesos*, etc., but in contrast to Brittonic the unvoiced stops were also spirantized, thus /p t k/ > /f θ χ/, e.g. OIr *athair* /aθər'/ 'father' < **pater*, *deich* /deχ'/ 'ten' < **dekm̥*. Unlike Brittonic, geminates did not spirantize but were simplified to the single unvoiced and voiced consonant, e.g. MnIr *atach*, OIr *attach* 'entreaty' < **ad-tech-*, OIr *ruccae* 'shame' (lit. 'redness') < **rud-k-* (Thurneysen 1946: 92). The same environmental rules seem to have applied in Goidelic to the effect that clusters of resonant + consonant were immune from lenition, e.g. OIr *corp* /korp/ < Lat *corpus*, etc., but such clusters were not spirantized as in Brittonic.

From a historical point of view it emerges, then, that those categories which were listed above in 7.2 as causing lenition of the following item were originally forms which ended in a vowel, e.g. a feminine singular noun, and thus the initial consonant of the following word was lenited, as being in intervocalic position, e.g. W *ei gath* 'his cat' < **esi̯o cattos* : *ei chath* 'her cat' < **esi̯ās cattos*. It would follow, therefore, that lenition in both Celtic sub-groups pre-dated the loss of final syllables. Likewise, spirantization in Brittonic, as for example in the conjunction *a(g)*, may well have arisen because a geminate was formed by the assimilation of the final consonant to the initial consonant of the following word, e.g. W *cwn a chathod* 'dogs and cats' < **ak katt-*. Similarly, nasalization reflects the presence of a nasal at the end of a word which has survived in the mutation at the beginning of the next.

7.4   Theories of lenition and spirantization[4]

It is generally accepted that the stop system of early Brittonic developed into Old Welsh as presented in Table 7.5. In Irish the system differed in a number of respects (see Table 7.5). In Proto-Celtic, /p/ had been lost (see 1.4.1.2), hence its absence at the Goidelic stage; but, while in Brittonic /kʷ/ was labialized to produce a new /p/, in early Irish /p/ re-entered the system in loanwords from Latin. The labiovelars remained distinct from the velar stops at least until Archaic Irish, since they are distinguished in the Ogam inscriptions (*Q* = labiovelar /kʷ/, *C* = velar /k/). Otherwise, the basic distinction between Goidelic and Brittonic is in their geminates; Goidelic had a voiced set which arose from clusters of resonant + consonant, e.g. /nt/ > /dd/, /ŋk/ > /gg/, etc.

Recent discussion has centred on how the changes are to be characterized and their precise chronology, both relative and absolute. The shift of the geminates to spirants has probably caused the greatest debate.

TABLE 7.5   The consonant systems of Brittonic and Goidelic.

Brittonic			Early Old Welsh		
p($< k^w$)	t	k	p	t	k
pp	tt	kk	b	d	g
b	d	g	f	θ	χ
			v	ð	ɣ
Goidelic			**Early Old Irish**		
t	k	k^w	p	t	k
tt	kk	k^wk^w			
b d	g	g^w	b	d	k
dd	gg	g^wg^w			
			f	θ	χ
			v	ð	ɣ

7.4.1   Jackson and Greene
Jackson described lenition as follows:

> It evidently arose from a loosening and slackening of the articulation of the
> C[ommon] C[eltic] consonants in certain positions. There are analogies in
> the history of the Romance languages in their development from Vulgar
> Latin, and one may compare also the regular change of intervocal *t* to *d* in
> colloquial American English. That this loosening should have taken a
> different form for the voiceless stops in Irish, namely *ph*, *th*, *ch*, is not
> surprising when we consider that the Goidelic and Brittonic groups had
> been separate for centuries before true lenition occurred (Jackson 1953:
> 544).

The first sentence is all he has to say about the phonetic processes
involved in lenition and, though he acknowledges the different treatment in Irish, he does not treat it in detail. Only Martinet 1952, 1955
(followed by Koch 1990) has taken any serious notice of the Romance
evidence (see 7.4.4 below). In terms of relative chronology Jackson
placed lenition before the loss of final syllables and before the break-up
of Brittonic into its constituent languages but after the Roman period
since loanwords underwent the same changes (Jackson 1953: 548). As
regards the relative chronology of Irish and Brittonic lenition, on the
basis of Latin loanwords into Irish via Brittonic he regarded lenition as
simultaneous in the two language groups (see 2.2.5 for Latin loanwords). In his absolute chronology he places lenition in the second half
of the 5th century (Jackson 1953: 560–1, 695). Later Jackson added
some further remarks, largely in response to subsequent work by
Martinet 1952, 1955 and Sommerfelt 1925b (= 1962: 325–8), 1954
(= 1962: 349–59) on fortis and lenis consonants:

The origins of the Brittonic and Goidelic consonant systems are best understood on the assumption that in primitive insular Celtic, if not already in Common Celtic, most consonant phonemes existed in two allophones, a fortis (tense and probably comparatively long) and a lenis (lax and probably comparatively short). The fortes occurred in absolute initial, initially after certain consonants in external sandhi, and internally and finally in certain consonant groups; and the lenes were found initially after vowels and after certain *other* consonants in external sandhi, and internally between and finally after vowels or in certain *other* consonants. Further, most consonants groups could occur as geminates, in which case they were fortes. This system is not Indo-European and may possibly be the result of speech-habits of substrate populations affecting the make-up of the superimposed Celtic languages (Jackson 1967a: 307).

The remarks about substrate influence are tantalizing but are never pursued (see 7.4.4 below).

We now need to consider the theory in greater detail. Jackson 1953, 1960 (more detailed) and 1967a presented a theory of a three-way system whereby, for example, the phoneme /t/ had three realizations:

[t] short lenis –   intervocalic position
[T] long fortis – absolute initial position
[TT] geminate – intervocalic and after resonants

Only [t] was vulnerable to lenition to Irish [θ] and Brittonic [d]. In Brittonic [TT] was later spirantized, while in Irish it was simplified and fell together with [T]. In short, after lenition in both Goidelic and Brittonic and spirantization in Brittonic, [t], [T] and [TT] gave Brittonic [d], [t] and [θ] and Goidelic [θ], [t] and [t] respectively, e.g. in Jackson's notation, *Toutā* > Ir *túath*, W *tud* 'tribe', *arTTos* > Ir *art*, W *arth* 'bear'.[5]

Jackson's theory was based on experimental work carried out by Falc'hun 1951 on the articulation of consonants in Breton. Falc'hun showed that Breton has a system in which there is a series of consonants with a long articulation in positions which correspond to those where lenition did not occur and a series with a shorter (roughly half) articulation in lenitable positions. Jackson projected this state of affairs back into Proto-Celtic but also added a third variable. Falc'hun's work would suggest a binary opposition which would work very well for Goidelic but Jackson needed a three-way opposition to account for the difference in outcome in Brittonic between initial stops which remained and geminates which gave spirants, hence his distinction between [T] and [TT]. Jackson also supported his view by reference to the tendency in Old Irish to write unlenited consonants as geminates, e.g. *du·bber* 'he gives', *a ccú* 'her dog', but as Greene 1956: 286–8 pointed out this is more likely to be a spelling device to clarify the opposition between lenited and unlenited forms; *a ccú* could be contrasted with *a chú* 'his dog', and *du·bber* clarifies the ambiguity of *do·ber,* which could stand for /do'b'er'/ 'he gives' or /do'v'er'/ 'which he gives'. It was a way of marking non-lenition at a period when lenition was not always regularly marked.

The main criticism by Greene 1956, 1966, however, was structural; partly because he viewed the evidence from the Irish standpoint he objected to the three-way distinction of lenis, fortis and geminate and argued that a binary opposition was sufficient. Essentially the problems are in Brittonic; how to account for the spirantization of voiceless stops. He envisaged a system after lenition where Brittonic had two sets of voiced stops, fortis /B D G/ and lenis /b d g/ (< lenited /p t k/), but only one set of unvoiced stops, fortis /P T K/, and one set of voiced fricatives /v ð ɤ/ (< lenited /b d g/) (see Table 7.6 for a summary). He argued that fortis /P T K/, through lack of lenis counterparts, were reduced to /p t k/. The subsequent rise of a new set of unvoiced geminates in intervocalic position, from the devoicing of clusters which had arisen through syncope, was the key development; for it brought about an opposition of /P T K/ : /p t k/ and led subsequently to the maximization of the distinction through the spirantization of /p t k/ to /f θ χ/. This shift only occurred in intervocalic position and left initial unvoiced stops untouched, e.g. Lat *cattus* > /KaTTus/ > /KaTus/ > /Kaθus/ > /kaθ/ W *cath* beside */kaledðuvr/ > /kalettur/ > /kaleTur/ RN *Calettwr*. According to Greene, no new voiced geminates arose, and so no spirantization of voiced stops was provoked. But it is also the case that a voiced spirant already existed (from lenited /b d g/). For Greene, as for Jackson, the final stages of spirantization occurred after the loss of final syllables.

Greene's account does not, however, explain why there should be spirantization after resonants, as in W *corff*, *arth*, *bardd*, etc., since in that position no new geminates had arisen. Russell 1985a has argued that spirantization in that position should be separated from the general process discussed above. It is clear from the Irish evidence that stops in clusters of -RT were protected from lenition, e.g. OIr *art*, *corp*, *bard*, etc. The discussion of Jackson 1953: 565–73 attributes the change of

TABLE 7.6   Consonantal development (according to Greene 1956, 1966)

Post lenition
/P T K; B D G; b d g; v ð ɤ/

Loss of final syllables
/p t k; B D G; b d g; v ð ɤ/

New unvoiced geminates
/P T K; p t k; f θ χ; B D G; b d g; v ð ɤ/
(initial /p t k/ but intervocalic /P T K/ and /f θ χ/)

-/Rt/ > /Rθ/ to spirantization but that of /Rd/ > /rð/ to lenition. Russell 1985a: 54–6 has argued that spirantization affected all stops after a resonant, both voiced and unvoiced, and that this spirantization which is widespread in all the Brittonic languages can be characterized as part of the assimilation of the stop to the preceding continuant which is effectively what lenition as a whole amounts to. As such, it is to be kept separate from the processes discussed above.

7.4.2 Harvey
The debate between Jackson and Greene ended in 1966 and was not re-opened until Harvey 1984 reconsidered the material. His approach to Jackson's threefold distinction was to re-analyse it in terms of those developments which are relevant at any given time, in other words 'to slice the diachronic development into synchronic cross-sections, and to take note of only the distinctive features present at that particular point in time' (Ball and Müller 1992: 65). In doing so, it emerges that at any given point there is only a binary opposition. Following Greene, he distinguishes at the pre-lenition stage simply between lenitable and non-lenitable stops, e.g. [To:ta:], [KaTəs], which gave after lenition Brittonic [tu:da:] and [KatəΣ] and Goidelic [to:θa:] and [katəs].[6]

Unlike Greene, Harvey sees the rise of unvoiced spirants in Brittonic as due to the non-existence of voiceless fricatives causing asymmetry in the system. Thus, Harvey claims, there was 'the opportunity, without disturbing the distribution of phonemes, for the voiceless stops to become spirantized *at a purely realizational level* [my italics], as prompted by the phonetic environment' (Harvey 1984: 98). Like Greene, he sees the rise of new intervocalic stops resulting from syncope as decisive in bringing about the phonemicization of the former fricative allophones.

7.4.3 P. W. Thomas and Sims-Williams
The recent contributions of P. W. Thomas and Sims-Williams may be considered together as they reach similar conclusions from rather different starting points. In essence, they conclude that the process of lenition, seen by Jackson and others as a single change, is to be broken up into discrete segments occurring at different times: the lenition of voiced stops to /v ð ɤ/ occurred more or less simultaneously in Goidelic and Brittonic but preceded the changes to unvoiced stops. At this point we encounter a terminological tangle where spirantization is used in more than one sense by different authors writing about similar features; see Table 7.7 for clarification.

The first three stages correspond to the traditional idea of lenition, while the fourth is spirantization. There is nothing new in such proposals; Loth 1892: 87 and Förster 1942: 162 both suggested for Brittonic that the lenition of /b d g/ must be older than that of /p t k/ on the

TABLE 7.7   The terminology of P. W. Thomas 1990 and Sims-Williams 1990

Example	Thomas	Sims-Williams
Britt. /d/ > /ð/	Voiced spirantization	First spirantization
Britt. /t/ > /d/	Voicing	Voicing
Irish /t/ > /θ/	†	Second spirantization
Britt. /t/ > /θ/	Voiceless spirantization	Spirantization

†P W Thomas 1990 is not concerned with Goidelic, hence no discussion of Irish lenition.

grounds that otherwise /p t k/ would have gone through both changes and all the stops would have ended up as /v ð ɤ/. P. W. Thomas 1990: 5 produces a similar argument; he claims that the Jacksonian view that 'as *p t c* moved towards *b d g* so original *b d g* were advanced towards *v ð ɤ*, and the two series were phonemically distinct the whole time' (Jackson, 1953: 545) is simply not tenable when dealing with discrete consonantal segments. He argues that these changes could not have occurred simultaneously as 'a certain amount of phonemic interference would have been inevitable and . . . would have been highly likely to lead to a certain amount of inappropriate feeding and bleeding' (1990: 5). He acknowledges that there is no clear evidence for such interference and concludes that the two processes were temporally distinct. One could equally well conclude that he has overestimated the inevitability and likelihood of such interference and that it simply does not happen. Moreover, it is difficult to believe that this 'inappropriate feeding and bleeding' could happen on a small scale; if it happened at all, it would surely have led to lexical chaos. In pragmatic terms, speakers would have kept and do keep words distinct from one another, hence minimal pairs of the *bat : pat, bat : bad* type (see Bynon 1977: 87–9). It is significant that in all his relative chronologies he finds no change that could have occurred after 'Voiced spirantization' but before 'Voicing'.

From this starting point (uncertain though it may be) he presents an analysis in terms of four phases of lenition (see Table 7.7) with the prime motivation being the asymmetry of a Brittonic system rich in stops and poor in fricatives. Thomas works by internal reconstruction with no concern for absolute chronology or the details of the evidence which is actually available. Yet this does cause difficulties which he is unable to resolve within his framework. Unlike all previous analyses he sees all the changes subsumed under lenition as occurring before the loss of final syllables. But, if we operate with the absolute chronology of Jackson 1953, which has the loss of final syllables completed by the mid-6th century, and we associate *Cothriche*, the early form of

Patrick's name (see 2.2.5), with the Patrician mission, at best the last three phases of Thomas' system would have to be completed in little over half a century (Charles-Edwards 1992: 152). In terms of linguistic change it would be easy to claim that those three phases were contemporaneous.

By contrast, Sims-Williams 1990 presents a meticulous discussion of the available sources. His main argument presents a major re-assessment of Jackson's relative and absolute chronologies of sound changes in Brittonic. Jackson's absolute chronology depended 'on correlations with the absolute chronology of other languages which interacted with British and on evidence from ancillary disciplines for the dates of inscriptions, texts and population movements' (Sims-Williams 1990: 221). As Sims-Williams points out, scholarly advances since 1953 in all these fields are capable of affecting his chronology and probably 'would blur the precision of Jackson's absolute chronology rather than produce an equally precise, but preferable, alternative' (Sims-Williams 1990: 221). The latter part of the paper is concerned with these advances and he concludes that in many areas the re-dating and re-analysis of the evidence lead to the conclusion that 'the transition from British to neo-Brittonic could have been completed early in the sixth century, a century or more earlier that the generally accepted dates for these developments' (Sims-Williams 1990: 260).

A major section is concerned with the evidence of the Latin loanwords in Irish. Since the rejection by McManus 1983 of the two strata division it has been customary to regard the entry of Latin loanwords into Irish as a continuum. However, Sims-Williams points out a difficulty in the relative chronology of British and Irish lenition: if British lenition pre-dated Irish lenition then we might expect forms in which, for example, British [k] was lenited to [g] in British and then lenited again in Irish to [ɤ], i.e. to produce **Pádhraigh(e), or alternatively, if Irish lenition pre-dated British lenition we should find forms which entered Irish after Irish lenition in which, for example, [k] remained as [k], producing, for example, **Páttraicc(e). The immediate, and conventional, response would be that British and Irish lenition occurred at the same time so that there would be no 'inter-lenition' forms. Sims-Williams regards this as an extraordinary coincidence, especially as they are phonetically distinct phenomena. His solution is to suggest that there is no single phenomenon of lenition but that lenition of [b d g] to [v ð ɤ] occurred both in British and Irish before the voicing of [p t k] in British, which itself occurred before the lenition of [kʷ t k] in Irish (see Table 7.7). Note that these 'spirantizations' are not to be confused with the spirantization which took place later in British and affected stops after continuants. Sims-Williams side-steps the accusation of generating his own coincidence by claiming that the 'First Spirantization' happened 'by no means simultaneously in British and Irish' (Sims-

Williams 1990: 233); the fact is that it does not matter, as the outcome of British lenition, i.e. [v ð ɤ], would have been immune from Irish lenition since it would have been identical to the outcome of it.

On the general idea of lenition working in stages it seems easier to think of Irish lenition in those terms than British lenition. Within British both the change of voiced stops to voiced spirants and the voicing of unvoiced stops both seem to involve reduction of articulation and in some sense the assimilation of the stops to the surrounding vowels. In Irish the spirantization of voiced stops is a similar type of change but the spirantization of unvoiced stops seems to be a rather different type of change in that it involves no voicing. It is not clear, therefore, why one should want British lenition to be broken up into separate stages and indeed there seems to be no objection to allowing that, while Irish lenition might be a two stage process, British lenition should have occurred at the same time; a chronology of

(1) Irish 'first spirantization'
(2) British lenition
(3) Irish 'second spirantization'

would produce the same outcome as Sims-Williams' pattern. One objection might be that, for example, a word containing British [b] could enter Irish after (1) above but before (2) and the [b] would remain for evermore; in other words, they would generate the voiced equivalents of **Pátraicc(e) words. But it all depends on how one views the process of lenition and at this point the Koch-Martinet theory has something to recommend it (see 7.4.4 below). For we must acknowledge that it is likely that almost all of the borrowings from British Latin into Irish took place through speakers bilingual in British and Irish. Now, if a word containing British /b/ entered Irish after the 'first Irish spirantization' but before it had undergone British lenition, where would British /b/ have fitted into the Irish phonemic system? This depends not on the phonemic status of the sounds in British but on their phonetic realization as perceived by speakers of Irish, i.e. whether they were perceived as stops and going together with Irish /b/ (< /bb/), or as spirants and going together with /v/. British /b/ in intervocalic position in contrast to /bb/ may well have been moving towards an allophonic realization as [v]. In Irish the rise of /b/ from /bb/ would have phonemicized [v] when previously it would have been an allophone of /b/. Would British intervocalic /b/ (allophonically [v]) have been associated with Irish /b/ or /v/? Sims-Williams assumes that it would have been perceived as closer to Irish /b/, and thus he thinks British spirantization must already have taken place, hence his splitting of British 'lenition' into two stages. But the British allophone [v] may well have been equated with Irish /v/ before strict phonemic spirantization had taken place in British, and so no separation of British lenition need be necessary.[7]

7.4.4 Martinet and Koch

Even though Sims-Williams has argued that lenition could have occurred up to a century earlier than the absolute dating offered by Jackson 1953, all the theories considered so far assume lenition to be a change undergone by the Insular Celtic languages in or around the 4th or 5th century AD. However, Martinet 1952, 1955, followed in many respects by Koch 1990, argued that systematic lenition, grammaticalized in Celtic, was part of a wide-scale reduction in the articulatory force of consonants in western European languages. Jackson 1953: 544 (see 7.4.1) mentioned the 'analogy' of western Romance consonantal development but Martinet argued that they are to be linked. The discrepancy in dating may be in part illusory; Jackson is more concerned with when lenition became systematized and is less interested in explaining it in phonetic terms. Martinet, however, is concerned with the beginning of the process (see Jackson 1953: 710). However, Jackson 1967a: 307 (see 7.4.1 above) did suggest that the lenis/fortis opposition was due to speech habits of a substrate pre-Celtic population and thus seemed to imply that the weakening of consonants is western European languages may be more than merely analogous.

It has been claimed that lenition is detectable in Continental Celtic, and particularly in Gaulish. Gray 1944 was one of the most ardent advocates of this view; he quotes examples such as *GNATHA* : Lat *nata*; *Petrocorii* : *Petrogoricus*; *Rigotamus* : *Riotamus*. C. Watkins 1955 in his study of the Gaulish dialect of Narbonensis (modern Provence) showed that the consonantal system was similar to that of Brittonic. He also noted that there was a tendency for /k/ and /t/ to weaken to /χ/ and /θ/ respectively and also that there was some hesitation between /g/ and /∅/, e.g. *Macho* : *Maco*; *Vethonianus* : *Vetonianus*; *Maiorix* : *Magius*; *Acilius* : *Agileius*; etc. Watkins does point out, however, that other explanations are possible. For example, the use of *-ch-* and *-th-* may just be an attempt by the scribe to show a difference in pronunciation from the normal /t/ and /k/. The difference between *C* and *G* for a stone-cutter was merely a cross-cut which could easily have been forgotten. Moreover, the phonemics of Gaulish stops may have caused problems in that they differed from those of Latin; C. Watkins 1955: 18–19 has argued that, while in Latin intervocalic unvoiced stops are fortis and voiced stops lenis, in Gaulish both were lenis (see Table 6.6 above, and 6.2.4 for the orthography of Gaulish). In such circumstances confusion could easily have arisen which had nothing to do with lenition. Nevertheless, for Watkins not all the evidence can be dismissed so easily and he concludes that 'the evidence we have been able to muster points only to the beginnings of the phonetic process, the relaxing of obstruents between vowels which is a necessary precursor of systematic morphophonemic lenition' (C. Watkins 1955: 19; see also D. E. Evans 1979: 527).

There is no doubt that a similar process of consonant weakening occurred in western Romance and it is quite probable that we have to do with an areal phenomenon, whether a substratum needs to be invoked or not. If one needs a substratum for western Romance, that substratum may have been Celtic itself, although there is evidence that similar changes to intervocalic stops took place in the Latin of southern and central Italy and north Africa, e.g. *obordet* (= *oportet* (southern Italy)), *lugum* (= *locum* (North Africa)) (Tovar 1951). Martinet 1952, 1955 argued that the fortis/lenis opposition arose in Proto-Celtic. He also emphasized the importance of aspiration as a property of the fortis allophones, so that he envisaged a phonetic distinction between fortis aspirated [kʷʰ kʰ tʰ b g d] in absolute initial position and lenis unaspirated [kʷ k t b g d].[8] The shift which is labelled lenition is triggered in Martinet's scenario by the simplification of geminates (see Table 7.8). The consequences of this were different in Goidelic and Brittonic, and it is one of the strengths of Martinet's case that he is the only scholar to account for the different outcomes of lenition in the two sub-groups of Celtic. In Brittonic the simplification of unvoiced geminates (voiced geminates were so rare as to be insignificant) pushed the unvoiced stop towards its voiced realization, and thus the voiced stop towards the spirant. The main difference in Goidelic was the existence of voiced geminates. Thus, as both voiced and unvoiced geminates simplified, original intervocalic [t] which went to [d] could not weaken to [d] without risking confusion with the outcome of [dd], hence its spirantization instead in parallel to the outcome of [d].

In theoretical terms, Martinet's account incorporates a 'push-chain' whereby pressure at one point in the system produces 'knock-on' effects elsewhere. All other accounts with their emphasis on asymmetries and gaps in the system, such as the lack of fricatives, etc., are implicitly using a 'drag-chain' or 'pull-chain' mechanism (see Hock 1986: 156–8, Bynon: 1977: 82–8, Martinet 1955: 59–62). Hock 1986:

TABLE 7.8   Martinet's theory of lenition

Brittonic	[atta]	>	[aTa]	>	[ata]
	[ata]	>	[aḍa]	>	[ada]
	[ada]	>	[aða]		
Goidelic	[atta]	>	[aTa]	>	[ata]
	[ata]	>	[aḍa]	>	[aθa]
	[adda]	>	[aDa]	>	[ada]
	[ada]	>	[aða]		

After Martinet 1955: 268 and 270 respectively; see Table 7.4 above for the starting points.

157 notes that there is much more empirical evidence for drag-chains than push-chains, but Bynon 1977: 84–5 argues that it is often difficult to decide between competing accounts of a sound change when one makes use of a drag-chain and the other a push-chain. In the context of the present argument, it could be claimed that the same outcome could have been initiated by a shift towards spirantization by single intervocalic stops, that is, by a pull-chain mechanism.

Koch 1990: 198–200 argues in line with Martinet's theory that lenition represents a systemization of old allophonic alternations. Moreover, he observes that voiceless stops are still phonetically aspirated, [pʰ tʰ kʰ], in all the modern languages. He supports Martinet's view about aspiration by noting confusions in the spelling of Celtic words in Latin, e.g. *gladius* for **kladi̯os*, *Pretani/Bretanni* and *Mons Graupius* for *Craupius*, where the following liquid de-aspirated the initial stop; the lack of aspiration allowed the stop to be interpreted as voiced. His interpretation of the lenition of voiceless stops in Brittonic is more controversial. Martinet assumed that the voiceless stops went through a stage of voiceless lenis stops on their way to becoming voiced lenis stops (see Table 7.8). Koch now adds the support of Modern Welsh and Breton where such stops are still phonetically voiceless and their contrastive feature is not presence of voice but rather lack of aspiration (see Ball 1984: 14–18, Sommerfelt 1978: 85, Falc'hun 1951: 55–7). On the basis of this evidence Koch, argues that full voicing of the lenited forms of /p t k/ did not occur until rather later, for intervocalic stops in Middle Welsh and for final stops not until Modern Welsh. In part his argument is based on the orthography of Old and Middle Welsh, where *p, t, c/k* are regularly used for the lenited forms of /p t k/; this is indisputable but does not show that lenition had not yet occurred (see 6.3.2.1). Final unvoiced stops are more problematical; words borrowed into Old English, e.g. *Dinoot* < British Latin *Donatus* vs. *Caedmon* < **catumannos*, are misleading since Old English tended sporadically to devoice final voiced stops (Campbell 1959: 181 and Charles-Edwards 1992: 148). The difficulty is in part one of phonetics vs. phonology. Phonetically, as can be seen from modern studies, lack of aspiration may be a distinctive feature in internal and final stops rather than presence of voice. But in phonological terms they are more likely to be perceived as allophones of /b d g/ rather than of /p t k/.

Both Martinet and Koch see the mutations in the Insular languages as the culmination of long-term developments, the beginnings of which may be traced in Continental Celtic. It would also appear that the tendency to reduce articulation remained in the languages. The 'new lenition' in Breton has been discussed above (4.3.1) where in early Modern Breton intervocalic stops were subject to a weakening analogous to the original lenition. A similar secondary reduction is found in

TABLE 7.9   Examples of the secondary reduction in articulation in Late Manx

cappan 'cup' /'kavan/
cabbyl 'horse' /'ka:vəl/
peccah 'sin' /'pegə/
poosey 'marry' /'pu:zə/
baatey 'boat' /be:ðə/

See R. L. Thomson 1992: 129.

Manx, where single intervocalic stops and fricatives are relaxed and frequently voiced (see Table 7.9 for examples).

7.5   The grammaticalization of the mutations

The key point in the development of grammatical mutations from phonetic lenition was the loss of final syllables. As we have seen, the status of initial consonants as fortis or lenis, voiced or unvoiced, or spirantized, was conditioned by the ending of the preceding word if it was in close connection with it, for example, as in article + noun, noun + adjective, negative particle + verb, etc. It is worth noting that such juncture phenomena (*sandhi*) could have occurred between any two words. But with the loss of the automatic conditioning factors, either final vowel, final consonant (often *-s*) or final nasal, the remaining initial mutations were used to mark significant grammatical relationships. Phonologically, the mutations also changed status from mere allophonic variants to contrastive phonemes; whereas previously Brittonic [t] : [d] as reflexes of /t/, or Goidelic [t] : [θ] as reflexes of /t/, were determined by environment, i.e. [t] in absolute initial position and [d] or [θ] in intervocalic position, it was now possible for /t/ and /d/ in Brittonic and /t/ and /θ/ in Goidelic to be contrastive. Taking the example of W *tud* and Ir *túath*, prior to the loss of endings but after lenition there was an allophonic relationship in Brittonic between [-VΣ + tu:da:] and [-V + du:da:] and in Goidelic between [-Vh + to:θa:] and [-V + θo:θa:] (Σ represents the intermediate stage in the shift from /s/ to /h/ in Brittonic). But after apocope the environments would have become identical, the contrast phonemic and motivated no longer by phonetics but by grammatical considerations; thus Brittonic /-V + tʉ:d/ and /-V + dʉ:d/ beside Goidelic /-V + to:θ/ and /-V + θo:θ/ (Harvey 1984: 93–6). A more concrete example may clarify the point. In Irish *a chú* 'his dog' and *a cú* 'her dog' (: *cú* 'dog') and in Welsh *ei gi* 'his dog' and *ei chi* 'her dog' (: *ci* 'dog'), the grammatical category of possession is subdivided by gender; the sub-divisions are marked only by the mutation (we leave aside here the subsidiary marking in Welsh by affixed pronoun (see 5.3.5)). But before the loss of endings the mutations were conditioned by the form of the possessive pronoun, i.e. Proto-Celtic *esio* 'his' : *esiās* 'her'; the masculine form caused lenition but the feminine had no effect in Goidelic but ultimately gave rise to the spirant mutation in Welsh.

Once the mutations had become grammaticalized and their phonetic environments eradicated, it was possible for the mutations to be used functionally. This often entailed both expansions and contractions of their original ranges of application. Four specific examples will be discussed in detail.

It was noted above (7.2.1.2) that Breton is unique in having the spirant mutation after the masculine singular definite and indefinite article and the feminine plural. Even though the mutation only affects initial /k/, its distribution suggests that it is the relic of an older pattern. The article is conventionally reconstructed as *sindos* (m. nom. sg.) beside a feminine *sindā*, and the final /s/ of the masculine form is exactly the environment where the spirant mutation would be expected to arise; thus *sindos kattos* would regularly give B *ar c'haz*. The question is not why it is found in Breton but why it does not occur in Welsh or Cornish. Welsh does make use of the spirant mutation in certain environments, e.g. after numerals and the feminine possessive pronoun, etc., and there is some evidence that it had a wider range. The LNN *Mathafarn* and *Machynllaith* show spirantization of the second elements *-thafarn* and *-chynllaith*. *Ma-* derives from an *s*-stem *magos* 'field, plain', and the final *-s* was responsible for the spirantization (Jackson 1967a: 320). The impression is that Welsh and Cornish considerably reduced the number of grammatical categories marked by spirantization. Given the close relationship between Cornish and Breton as against Welsh (see 4.3), Welsh and Cornish may have innovated independently in this respect.

Welsh also seems to have developed a more thoroughgoing nasal mutation in environments where there is a spirant mutation in Cornish and Breton, e.g. the possessive 'my', W *fy*, MnB *va*, C *ow*. It is followed by nasalization in Welsh, e.g. *fy mhenn* 'my head' (: *penn* 'head'), but by the spirant mutation in Breton and Cornish, e.g. B *va fenn*, C *ow fen* 'my head'. Jackson 1967a: 318–20 argues that in southwest Brittonic final /-n/ lost its nasality, while it was preserved in Welsh. Jackson 1953: 635 rather vaguely states that 'it is obvious that there was much levelling out by analogy and other causes working in different ways'. However, in some respects it is possible to be more precise. For example, spirantization had one grave defect which made it unusable as a full-scale grammatical marker, namely it was only effective on unvoiced initial stops; voiced stops were unaffected since in origin the spirantized forms of /b d g/ were /v ð ɣ/, identical to the lenited forms (Russell 1985a). In other words, it is hardly surprising that the spirant mutation was on the retreat as a grammatical marker.

The third example has to do with the lenition of the direct object after a conjugated verb in Welsh, e.g. *gwelodd y dyn gi* 'the man saw a dog' (lit. 'saw the man dog') (see T. J. Morgan 1952: 182–233 for details). Direct object mutation only follows synthetic verbs; after periphrastic verbs a direct object has its basic form, e.g. *mae e'n gweld ci* 'he sees a dog' (lit. 'is he in seeing dog') (see 5.4.3). The mutation serves to distinguish subject and object of the verb; it is particularly important to disambiguate sentences where the pronominal subject may not be expressed (see Table 7.10). There is no evidence that this mutation has any historical basis. Mutation of the object is sporadic in Middle Welsh but seems not to have become established at that period (D. S. Evans 1964: 17–19). Here, then, is a clear case of grammatical mutation establishing itself as a distinguishing marker.[9] It may be worth noting as a parallel that lenition of the direct object also occurs in 9th century Irish but is not found earlier.

The last example concerns Middle Irish. As was seen above (2.2.6.2), in Old Irish, lenition was the only distinction between *fo·ceird* 'he puts' and *fo·cheird* 'he puts it' or, as a relative clause, 'which he puts'. With the decline and loss of the neuter gender in late Old Irish, neuter 3rd singular leniting infixed pronouns tended to become fixed, especially in verbs of motion, e.g. *do·théit* 'he comes' (lit. 'he comes (to it)'). This led to *fo·cheird* ousting *fo·ceird* as the simple indicative form 'he puts'. Main clause lenition of this type occurs sporadically in Old Irish but is very common in Middle Irish with all forms of the verb, e.g. *ro·chan* 'he sang', *do·choid* 'he went', *ro·chreit* 'he believed', etc. A similar expansion of lenition occurred with negatives after the blurring of the Old Irish distinction between *ní·ceil* ' he does not hide' and *ní·cheil* 'he does not hide it' leading to the disappearance of the former, e.g. *ní·chélat* 'they will not hide', *ní·chuimgem* 'we do not seek', etc. In this case, the spread of the lenition may have been supported by the regular lenition after the longer form of the negative *nicon·*, e.g. *nicon·chechrat* 'they will not love' (McCone 1987: 187–8).

TABLE 7.10 Direct object mutation in Welsh

(a) *gwelodd ci* : *gwelodd gi*
saw dog (subj.) saw dog (obj.)
'a dog saw' '(he) saw a dog'

(b) *y dyn a welodd ci* : *y dyn a welodd gi*
the man rel. saw dog (subj.) the man rel. saw dog (obj.)
'the man whom a dog saw' 'the man who saw a dog'

7.6 Modern mutations and functional load

> Perhaps the most amazing feature of the mutations, however, is the
> persistent nature of the alternations in some environments, considering their
> low information value and their marginality to the system . . . it might have
> been expected that they would have disappeared long ago (P. W. Thomas
> 1984: 234).

As Thomas points out, the functional load of mutations is variable.
After lexical items, such as numbers or prepositions, its functional load
is nil, i.e. no information would be lost by the absence of the mutation.
Towards the other end of the scale, there are cases where the mutation
is the only distinctive feature. The direct object mutation in Welsh is a
case in point. Furthermore, in Welsh the 3rd singular possessive is distinguished for gender by the mutation (see 7.5), but in the spoken
language the mutation is reinforced by affixed pronouns, e.g. /i ben ɛv/
ei ben ef 'his head' : /i fen (h)i/ *ei phen hi* 'her head'.

A similar difficulty arises in Breton where the masculine and feminine 3rd singular possessive adjectives have fallen together as /i/. The
problem is exacerbated by the gradual disappearance of the spirant
mutation as a functional marker. Just as Welsh resorts to affixed pronouns, Breton has recourse to a disambiguating periphrasis using
conjugated forms of the preposition *da* 'to' (see 5.3.5 above), a pattern
which is similar to and perhaps influenced by French *à moi, à lui*, etc.;
for example, /i lụa:/ standing both for *e loa* 'his spoon' and *hi loa* 'her
spoon' has been replaced by the unambiguous *e loa dezhañ* (lit.) 'his
spoon to him' and *hi loa dezhi* (lit.) 'her spoon to her' (Hennessey
1990: 217); French influence is not, however, a necessary assumption
since similar periphrases are also found in Modern Irish (see 3.3.4.3)
and in Middle Welsh (D. S. Evans 1964, 198).

Another case from Welsh is the distinction between the three functions of *yn* /ən/, which is formally marked only by the mutation (see
Table 7.11 for examples). As the preposition 'in' it is followed by the

TABLE 7.11   Mutation markers after Welsh yn

(a)   *yn* 'in' + nasal mutation
       ym Mangor 'in Bangor'
       yng Nghaerdydd 'in Cardiff'

(b)   *yn* as a predicative marker + lenition
       mae'r eira yn wyn 'the snow is white' (: *gwyn*)
       rhedodd ef yn gyflym 'he ran quickly' (: *cyflym*)

(c)   *yn* as an aspect marker + unmutated form
       mae Ieuan yn canu 'I. is singing'
       mae Mair yn rhedeg 'M. is running'

nasal mutation. As the marker of predication and in adverbs it lenites. Finally, as the aspect marker in periphrastic verbs it is followed by the basic form of the verbal noun. Though the only distinctive feature is the mutation, there are few cases where the context would not disambiguate irrespective of the mutation; in the second type only adjectives follow *yn*, while in the last type it is followed by a verbal noun. Cases of ambiguity which are only resolvable by reference to the mutation occur in the rare cases where adjective and verbal noun are identical, e.g. *mae'r athro yn fyw* : *mae'r athro yn byw* 'the teacher is alive/living' respectively. Moreover, a number of dialects have replaced the nasal mutation after *yn* with lenition; the risk of ambiguity cannot, therefore, be crucial (see generally Awbery 1986b).

In spoken Welsh a question is only formally marked by a soft mutation, e.g. *welodd y dyn?* 'did the man see?', etc. Here again, the mutation is not the only indicator; intonation is the main guide. In the written form the verb is preceded by a particle *a*, thus *a welodd?*, etc. (see 5.5.2.2). In Modern Irish the past tense is marked by the proclitic particle *do* which causes lenition, e.g. *do phós* 'he married'. However, in most dialects the particle has been dropped and the only marker of the past tense is the lenition, e.g. Dunquin *phós* /fo:s/, though the particle is retained where lenition cannot be indicated, e.g. *d'ól* /do:l/ 'he drank', *d'fhás* /da:s/ 'he grew' (Ó Siadhail 1989: 176–7). Likewise in Modern Irish the semantic load rests entirely on the mutation in pairs of phrases such as *ar dóigh* 'excellent' : *ar dhóigh* 'in a way', *ar fad* 'entirely' : *er fhad* 'in length' (Ó Siadhail 1989: 115). It is usual for prepositions to cause lenition but there are some fossilized adverbial expressions which have preserved an older situation; as such, they do not indicate a living alternation, but in those particular cases they demand that attention is paid to the mutation.

Despite the above examples, the functional load on the mutations across each language is relatively light, and it might be predicted that there should be some re-arrangement and perhaps eradication of distinctions within the mutation system, especially in Welsh which has the option of lenition, spirant mutation and in certain environments the nasal mutation. The other languages tend to operate with two out of the three ; Breton and Cornish with lenition and spirantization, Goidelic languages with lenition and nasalization (eclipsis).

B. Thomas and Thomas 1989: 48–50 have provided some general evidence for the reduction of mutations in Welsh dialects. For example, in the standard language there is a three-way alternation in verbs with an initial voiceless stop but a two-way alternation in verbs with an initial voiced stop (see Table 7.12 overleaf). Especially in the dialects of south Wales there is a tendency to generalize the lenited form. Again the ineptness of the spirant mutation to affect voiced stops may be a factor in this re-arrangement. In addition, it is also possible even in the

TABLE 7.12   Verb mutation in Welsh dialects.

Standard Welsh

cerddodd e	:	*a gerddodd e?*	:	*ni cherddodd e*
'he walked'		'did he walk?'		'he did not walk'

gwelodd e	:	*a welodd e?*	:	*ni welodd e*
'he saw'		'did he see?'		'he did not see'

Southern dialects

gerddodd e	:	*gerddodd e?*	:	*gerddodd e ddim*
'he walked'		'did he walk?'		'he did not walk'

welodd e	:	*welodd e?*	:	*welodd e ddim*
'he saw'		'did he see?'		'he did not see'

standard language to use a lenited form of the verb in a declarative sentence when it is preceded by *fe* or *mi* (see 5.5.2.3). Such considerations clearly favour the generalization of the lenited form. The nasal mutation, which is restricted to the preposition *yn* 'in' (see above) and the 1st singular possessive *fy* 'my' is also prone to disappear or be replaced by the soft mutation; thus, beside the standard *ym Mangor* 'in Bangor', dialects offer *yn Bangor* and *yn Fangor*, and also in some parts of South Wales /əm bel/ 'my ball' (: standard *fy mhêl* : *pêl* 'ball'), /ən dɑd/ 'my father' (: standard *fy nhad* : *tad* 'father'), etc.

In a study of speakers in South Glamorgan, P. W Thomas 1984 demonstrated that decline in the use of mutations was related to how frequently the speakers used Welsh and perhaps also to their age. His oldest group used the spirant mutation and nasal mutation more often than his other groups. There was also a tendency for the soft mutation to spread at the expense of the other mutations. Interestingly, the decline in mutation with possessive pronouns seems to be related to a significant syntactic change, whereby the affixed pronoun is gradually taking over as the main marker of possession, especially with verbal nouns, e.g. /on ɪ dɪ gu̯eld ɑ/ 'I had seen him' (: standard *oeddwn i wedi'i weld e*); here the verbal noun /gu̯eld/ is unlenited and the only pronoun marker is /ɑ/. There is a tendency, then, for possessive pronouns to behave like object pronouns with conjugated verbs and follow the verbal element. With nouns mutation occurs more often but Thomas' Group IV, who are the youngest and use Welsh least, often produce examples such as /braud vi/, /ti vi/ 'my brother', 'my house' in contrast to the mutated /əˈmraud i/, /ənˈhi i/.

Reductions and re-arrangements in the mutation system have been regarded by some as clear indications of the imminent decline and death of the language. Dorian 1977 and 1981 has studied the Gaelic dialect of East Sutherland and argued that features such as mutations

TABLE 7.13   Mutation in East Sutherland Gaelic

Environment	Fluent % failure	Non-fluent % failure
Past tense	0	10.5
Article + feminine noun	0	28.5
Adverbs and numbers	2	46
Vocative	17	74

After Dorian 1977: 103.

are most likely to remain where there is a parallel morphological marker in the dominant language, in this case English, and most likely to disappear where there is no marker. She studied a range of mutation contexts and made several working distinctions which are vital in work of this kind (Dorian 1977): the possibilities are that mutation would disappear entirely or that obligatory mutations would become optional. Secondly, the distinction between a high or a low functional level is crucial to our expectations of the survival rate of the mutation. Thirdly, she compares and contrasts the performance of fluent speakers (generally old) and non-fluent speakers who do not use Gaelic as their usual language of communication (generally younger). Four environments are considered: mutation as a marker of past tense, mutation of a feminine noun after a definite article, adverbs and numbers, and the vocative. The percentage of failure to mutate is presented in Table 7.13. It is clear that those who do not speak Gaelic regularly and fluently are less competent. However, they are not totally incompetent. In the case of past tenses, initial lenition is in regular verbs the only marker of the past; it is formed simply by lenition of the basic stem, thus /v'r'i:s'/ 'he broke' beside the unlenited /b'r'i:s'/ 'break' (2nd sg. imperative). Here, then, the mutation alone is distinctive (some dialects of Scottish Gaelic still retain the particle *dho* to mark the past). Furthermore, as Dorian points out, lenition in Gaelic corresponds to English markers such as *-ed*, etc. As regards the mutation of feminine nouns, it is less crucial to understanding, and furthermore does not correspond to any indicator in English. It emerges that even among fluent speakers there is a significant failure of mutation in those contexts where there is a light functional load. Dorian argues that this hierarchical failure of lenition is indicative of general language failure in the face of strong influence from English. However, analysis of evidence from Breton discussed below may suggest otherwise.

A parallel case from Breton has been analysed in a similar way by Dressler 1972 and 1981 who argued that the replacement or loss of the spirant mutation was a sign of decline:

Teenagers use lenition or no mutation at all after the spirantizing numerals
'3, 4, 9' and also increasingly after the spirantizing possessives *ma* 'my',
i 'her', *o* 'their', so *ma venn* 'my head', etc. is heard more often than *ma
fenn* . . . from *penn* (Dressler 1972: 450.)
(See also Timm 1985, and Falc'hun 1951: 94–6.)

Older speakers retain the spirant mutation in possessives but also use
the soft mutation after numerals. This case is put forward in terms of
decay and decline of the language. However, Hennessey 1990 has produced evidence to show that these changes date back to monolingual
speech communities and as such have nothing to do with the decline
and death of Breton. He shows that lenition after numerals is several
centuries old, with the earliest examples as early as 1710 (Hennessey
1990: 212). Change of mutation in numerals can be dated from at least
the 1870s if not earlier. The minimal functional loss in such changes
has already been discussed above. There is no doubt that Breton as a
medium of daily communication is in decline but, as Hennessey argues,
not every change in the language should be regarded as decline, especially when there is no evidence of functional loss.

Notes

1. Most grammars contain listings of the categories involved. For a general
    overview, see Pedersen 1909–13: I, 386–471 (= H. Lewis and Pedersen
    1961: 112–47), although the explanations offered are dated; on the linguis-
    tic background, see Hamp 1951, McBrearty 1976, Oftedal 1962, Pilch
    1986. For Old Irish, see Thurneysen 1946: 140–53; and for Middle Irish,
    Dottin 1913: I, 33–44, Jackson 1990: 77–8. For Modern Irish,
    Bammesberger 1983: 16–28 offers a clear survey, and see also Ó Siadhail
    1989: 114–21; the dialectal works are usually more concerned about the
    phonetics and phonology, though de Bhaldraithe 1953: 257–94 (Cois
    Fhairrge) and Lucas 1979: 3–40 (Ros Goill) provide helpful evidence. For
    Scottish Gaelic, see Calder 1923: 20–35; the dialect studies are almost
    entirely concerned with phonology (see Rogers 1992). For Manx, see the
    early grammar J. Kelly 1804: 6–8, R. L. Thomson 1969: 190–202 for a full
    discussion of the 17th-19th century evidence, Broderick 1984–6: I, 7–24,
    III, 64–7 for late spoken Manx. For Welsh, the fullest discussion is Ball and
    Müller 1992. For Middle Welsh, see D. S. Evans 1964: 19–23; and for
    Modern Welsh, S. J. Williams 1980: 174–7 (summary with cross refer-
    ences), Thorne 1993: 22–94, King 1993: 14–20, Awbery 1986c. For Middle
    Cornish, see Lewis 1946: 8–10 (= Zimmer 1990a: 7–10). For Middle
    Breton, see Hemon 1941: 5–16 and 1975: 7–25, Kervella 1947: 77–102,
    Press 1986: 38–54, Le Dû 1986; for dialectal material, see, for example, Le
    Clerc 1911: 15–28 (Tréguier), Sommerfelt 1978: 104–12 (St. Pol-de-Léon),
    Ternes 1970: 141–83 (Ile de Groix), M. McKenna 1988: 192–215
    (Guémené-sur-Scoff).
2. Russell 1985a has argued that, where such alternation occurs, the original
    pattern would have been spirantization; the apparent lenition of voiced

stops is simply the result of the fact that for voiced stops the spirantized and lenited forms are identical; hence the decline in spirantization as a distinct mutation since it was only distinctive for unvoiced stops (see below 7.5).

3. Despite the same name and essentially the same phonetic change, this process should be regarded as separate from the 'provection' which affects intervocalic voiced stops in south-eastern dialects of Modern Welsh (see 5.1.2).

4. For a recent survey of Welsh scholarship, see Ball and Müller 1992: 62–73, which omits any discussion of Sims-Williams 1991 (see 7.4.3). This section concentrates on discussions which are relatively neutral as to theory, adopting nothing more controversial than a phonemic stance or a distinctive feature analysis. However, there are a number of discussions which are more theoretically orientated, e.g. Griffen 1975 (Stratificational Grammar), 1984, 1985, 1990 (Dynamic Phonology), Willis 1986, 1987. For pre-transformational and transformational approaches, see Ball and Müller 1992: 29–45. Irish mutations do not seem to have attracted the same attention; for a general discussion, see Ó Cuív 1986.

5. For simplicity of presentation and exemplification, examples will focus on internal stops, though, as is clear from the preceding part of this chapter, the same changes affected initial stops in intervocalic and preconsonantal position.

6. There are problems of notation here. Harvey 1984 misleadingly uses *tt*, etc. to denote non-lenitable stops which all too easily implies gemination. Here T and t are used to denote non-lenitable and lenitable stops respectively.

7. Note incidentally that Sims-Williams is happy to have medial [b m d g] in Latin loanwords into British be assimilated to new British medial [v v ð ɤ] without necessarily assuming that they had already been spirantized in Latin (Sims-Williams 1990: 225); but he seems unwilling for the same phenomenon to have operated in transfers between British and Irish.

For reviews of P. W. Thomas 1990 and Sims-Williams 1990, see Charles-Edwards 1992: 148–53 and Russell 1991–2: 266–8.

8. The aspiration may simply be a concomitant of a stronger articulatory force, but in terms of scholarship it is reminiscent of the view of Pedersen 1909–13: I, 242, who considered that lenition had to do with the presence and absence of aspiration.

9. For modern theoretical approaches to direct object mutation, see Ball and Müller 1992: 136–61.

Chapter 8

Verbal nouns, verbs and nouns

8.1 Verbs, nouns and verbal adjectives

It is traditional for grammars to make a distinction between finite and non-finite parts of the verb. The former are marked for number, person, tense, mood, voice (active, passive, etc.), and aspect (progressive, stative, etc.). The latter, which are often termed infinitives, participles, verbal adjectives, etc., are not usually marked in this way. Participles can display more nominal characteristics, such as number, gender, case, declension, agreement with nouns, and they often appear to behave like adjectives. Celtic languages have neither infinitives nor present participles.[1] Moreover, it is clear that speakers of Insular Celtic languages saw no link between their verbal nouns and Latin infinitives; it is striking that the verbs 'to read' and 'to write', which are borrowed from Latin *legere* and *scrībere* respectively, use a form derived from the Latin gerund as the verbal noun, i.e. Ir *léinn, scríbend*, W *llên, ysgrifennu* < Lat *legendum, scrībendum* respectively. But, even if Celtic languages did not have infinitives, that is not to say there is a gaping hole in traditional grammars of Celtic when the finite verb has been discussed. The traditional slot in the grammar is filled by two categories, the verbal noun and the verbal adjective.[2]

The former category is the main subject of this chapter. In addition there were two types of verbal adjective in the early stages of the languages. Old Irish distinguished a past participle and a 'verbal of necessity' (Thurneysen 1946: 441–3 and 443–4 respectively). The past participle was always passive and was marked by the suffix *-t(h)e*, which declined as an adjective, e.g. *mórthae* 'praised', *bíthe* 'struck', *clithe* 'hidden', etc. The 'verbal of necessity' corresponded in usage to a Latin gerund(ive) of necessity which it often translated in the early glosses; it was marked by an indeclinable suffix *-t(h)i* or *-di* and was always used in a predicative construction with the copula, e.g. *is comal-*

nidi 'it is to be fulfilled', *is srethi* 'it is to be spread out', etc. Only the former, the past participle, has survived to the modern language. There is a great deal of dialectal variation in the outcome of this suffix when added to stem-final consonants; the basic suffixes seem to be -/t′ə/, -/hə/ and in Connacht -/hi:/, e.g. /po:ki:/ *pogtha* 'kissed', /statəhə/ *stadtha* 'stopped', /N′it′ə/ *nite* 'washed', /b′r′is′t′ə/ *briste* 'broken', etc. (Ó Siadhail 1989: 198–200; for its use in perfective passives, see 3.4.4).

The exact etymological equivalents are represented in the early stages of the Brittonic languages by respectively MW -*eit* /aɪd/, OB -*eit*, e.g. MW *honneit* 'known', OB *loscheit* 'burnt' (Fleuriot 1964: 313–14), and W -*adwy* /′adʊɪ/, OB -*atuiu*, -*atoe*, MCo -*adow*, e.g. B *aatoe* 'to be entered', MCo *ewnadow* 'desire' (lit. 'that which is to be desired'), W *moladwy* 'to be praised', etc. The former gradually disappeared during the early period and was replaced by a fuller suffix, OW, OCo, OB -*etic*, MnW -*edig* (Fleuriot 1964: 314–15). It is unclear whether it is to be analysed as an expanded version of -*eit*, etc. or as a different suffix altogether (Russell 1990: 106–8). It functions as a past participle which is regularly passive with transitive verbs but can also be active in sense especially with intransitive verbs; thus *caredig* (: *caru* 'love') can mean 'beloved' or 'loving, friendly', etc. (Russell 1990: 78–9). The -*edig* forms have been replaced in Modern Welsh by a periphrasis of *wedi* 'after' + verbal noun (see below). While verbal adjectives do seem to retain verbal features, such as voice and to a certain extent tense, verbal

TABLE 8.1 Characteristics of verbal nouns.

Nominal features
1. subject to nominal-type modification by
   (a) article
   (b) adjectives
   (c) nouns (genitive case in Goidelic) or possessive pronouns
   (d) prepositions
2. have gender (and full nominal declension in Goidelic)
3. can be the subject, object, etc. of the verb
4. neutral to formal active/passive distinctions

Verbal features
1. subject to verbal-type modification by adverbs
2. periphrastically linked to auxiliary verbs
3. marked for aspect with aspect markers
4. replace finite verbs in subordinate clauses
5. replace finite verbs in co-ordinated strings

Cf. D. S. Evans 1964: 159–61, Ball and Müller 1992: 135.

nouns are singularly devoid of verbal features in both their formal and syntactical characteristics.

As a starting point, a list of nominal and verbal characteristics, both morphological and syntactic, is presented in Table 8.1 above. The list is considered in detail and fully exemplified in 8.3. As will emerge in that section, a clear-cut distinction between nominal and verbal characteristics is extremely problematical. The consequences of that are considered in 8.4.

8.2 Formal characteristics of verbal nouns

There is no single verbal noun marker in any Celtic language. Some general patterns have developed, usually in the later stages of the languages. For example, Welsh has three main endings -u /ɪ/ or /ɨ/, -i /ɪ/, and -o /ɔ/, which are distributed according to the stem vowel (D. S. Evans 1964: 156–7, S. J. Williams 1980: 111–2); the ending -u is added to stems containing a, ae, e and y, e.g. caru 'love', helpu 'help', synnu 'be surprised', etc., -i is added to stems in o and oe, e.g. torri 'break', poeni 'worry', etc., and stems in final /u̯/, e.g. berwi 'boil', llenwi 'fill', etc. The ending -o, however, is added to stems with a final front vowel, such as /i̯/, though this is subject to dialectal variation (see 4.3.3 and 5.1.2, and Russell 1990: 39–43). Apart from these, a wide range of other suffixes are in use, most of which also have nominal functions, e.g. -aeth (also abstract suffix), -ach (also collective (see Russell 1990: 80–4)), -ael (probably generalized from caffael, etc. 'get' (Hamp 1954)).[3]

In Modern Irish there is a similar generalization of certain markers to particular types of stem (Ó Siadhail 1989: 195–7); -/t′/ is added to stems in a final palatal nasal, liquid or final /χ/, e.g. sechaint 'follow', oscailt 'open', éisteacht 'listen'. Monosyllabic stems and those ending in -áil /aːl′/ have no ending, e.g. péinteáil 'paint', fás 'grow', etc.; the latter suffix is in origin itself a verbal noun suffix which probably spread from gabáil, the etymological equivalent of W caffael above (Ó Cuív 1980). It is the most common denominative suffix. The most common verbal noun suffix across all types is -adh /ə(ɣ)/, e.g. pósadh 'marry', briseadh 'break', etc. Again as in Welsh, there are a range of other verbal noun markers, e.g. seasamh 'standing', screadach 'crying out', leanacht 'following', etc. The pattern emerges most clearly in the earlier stages of the languages, especially in Old Irish.

In general a wide range of suffixes are employed to mark verbal nouns, suffixes which are mostly indistinguishable from those which figure in the derivational system of nouns. Disterheft 1980: 16 (following Thurneysen 1946: 445–55) lists twelve suffixes used for verbal nouns in Old Irish, six of which do not occur as verbal noun/infinitive markers in other Indo-European languages. The degree of predictability

TABLE 8.2   Verbal nouns of Old Irish B IV verbs

---

benaid 'cuts' : VN *béimm*
crenaid 'buys' : VN *creicc/crith*
ernaid 'bestows' : VN *rath*
glenaid 'clings' : VN *glenamon*
renaid 'sells' : VN *reicc*
sernaid 'scatters' *: sreth*

---

between the verbal stem and verbal noun varies markedly in Old Irish depending on the verbal class. At one extreme, weak verbs generally have a verbal noun in -*ad/-ud* (m. *u*-stem), e.g. *léicid* 'he leaves' : VN *léiciud; móraid* 'he praises' : VN *mórad, suidigidir;* 'he places' : VN *suidigud*, etc. (note that verbal nouns of deponent verbs are not themselves marked as deponent). The one exception is denominative verbs, where the base noun acts as the verbal noun, e.g. *ásaid* 'he grows': VN *ás* (MnIr *fás*), *rímid* 'he counts' : VN *rím*. One point of interest is that there is a gradual but not total replacement of 'base-noun' verbal nouns by fully marked verbal nouns in Middle and Modern Irish, thus OIr *sluindid* 'signifies' : VN *slond* but also *slondud*. It is also common to find variation between simple and compound verbs, e.g. *rád* 'speech' : *rádid* 'speaks' but VN *imrádud* 'conversation' : *imm·ráidi* 'converses'. The replacement is gradual and irregular; for example, beside *cor* 'cast, throw' : *cuirethar/fo·ceird* 'puts', the compounds also have verbal nouns in -*chor*, e.g. *tochor, freccor*, etc. That this process is not regular and more complete is because towards the other end of the scale of predictability are the various classes of strong verbs where there is no regular and predictable connection between verb type and verbal noun. For example, BIV verbs (in the terminology of Thurneysen 1946; see Table 2.12) which show a reasonably coherent pattern of finite forms have a wide range of verbal noun types (see Table 8.2 for examples). There is also significant alternation between the verbal noun formations of simple and compound verbs, e.g *bongid* 'strikes' : VN *búain* but *con·boing* 'smashes' : VN *conbach, gairid* 'calls' : VN *gairm* but *ar·gair* 'forbids' : VN *ergaire*, etc. (Greene 1952–4: 334–5, Hamp 1976: 10–13). Even in this one verb class there is no predictability. In a few cases predictability is totally impossible since the verbal noun is based on a quite different root, e.g. *caraid* 'loves' : VN *serc; tongaid* 'swears' : VN *luige; fichid* 'fights' : VN *gal*.

In both Welsh and Irish, then, specific verbal noun markers seem to have arisen within the history of the languages perhaps by the specialization of more general action noun markers. They are characteristically the weak verb markers; as all new verbs tend to be either denominal or de-adjectival, they become weak verbs with a clear conjugational pattern. In such circumstances, clearly predictable verbal nouns become an ever-growing feature of the verbal system, and it is not surprising that the older verbal nouns, with more archaic patterns, are often replaced by formations showing a regular suffix. It is nevertheless important to note that in Irish at least the verbal noun is still declensionally a noun with as much of a case system as any other noun and has not become an indeclinable unit.

In addition to being marked by nominal-type morphology, verbal nouns also function like nouns in the derivational system; in other words, suffixes which can be added to nouns can also be added to verbal nouns. For example, the early Irish suffix -/əχ/ -ach/-ech was used to form adjectives from nouns, e.g. *maccach* 'having sons' : *macc* 'son', and also from verbal nouns, e.g. *osnadach* 'sighing' : *osnad* 'sigh', *marbthach* 'killing' : *marbad* 'kill', etc. (Russell 1990: 86). The formation based on verbal nouns seems to have been so productive that a separate suffix -/θəχ/ -thach/-thech was resegmented. The pattern seems to have arisen in the productive class of verbal nouns in -/əð/ -ad/-ud, to which the suffix -/əχ/ was added. A re-analysis in terms of a verbal stem + suffix would have produced a suffix -/θəχ/, which was added to verbal stems which did not have a verbal noun in -ad, e.g. *gabthach* : VN *gabáil* 'take', *focarthach* : VN *focrae* 'warn', etc. (Russell 1990: 88–90, 104–5). There are further complications in that stems such as *gabth-*, *marbth-*, etc. are identical to the stem of the past participle; the parallelism has given rise to a few forms based on the participial stem, such as *gnéthech* : *gniid* 'does' (VN *gním*) and *érrethach* : *as·ren* 'pay' (VN *éraicc/éra*) (Russell 1990: 89–90 and Thurneysen 1946: 171 for a parallel example in Old Irish agent nouns).

Similar patterns operate in Welsh but the difficulties are of a different type. While verbal nouns form derivatives in exactly the same way as nouns, there is rarely any clear formal distinction between a derivative based on a verbal noun and one based on the simple stem (Russell 1990: 34–5, 76–7); thus, W *cofiog* 'remembering' could in principle be analysed as noun *cof* + suffix -*iog*, the stem *cof-* + suffix -*iog*, or even as VN *cofio* + suffix -(*i*)*og*. Where there is a clear verbal noun base, it is sometimes used, e.g. *cadwadog* 'protecting', *galluog* 'capable, clever' : VN *gallu*; but in some cases, especially with compounds of *bod* 'be' (verbal stem *bydd-*), both formations seem to be available, though perhaps in different stylistic registers, e.g. verbal stem + suffix *gorfyddog* 'conquering', *adnabyddedig* 'well-known' : VN + suffix *gorfodog*, *adnabodedig*; there is no obvious semantic distinction between them. The point is that in Welsh the generalized verbal noun suffixes are all vocalic and so prone to disappear before a suffix with an initial vowel.

Nouns also have a role to play as the base of new denominative verbs. In Irish, at least, where verbal nouns are usually distinct from verbal stems, they too can also fulfil that function. This curious state of affairs arose out of the chaotic verbal system of Old Irish and attempts to tidy it up in Middle and early Modern Irish. As has been demonstrated (2.2.6.2), Old Irish operated with a double system of verbal conjugation, absolute and conjunct, which resulted in a vast range of forms, e.g. *con·utaing* 'he builds' : *ní·cumtaig* 'he does not build' : VN *cumtach*, *con·oí* 'he protects' : *ní·cumai* 'he does not protect' : VN *coimét*, etc. In Middle Irish it was common for new simple uncompounded verbs to be formed on the verbal noun, thus respectively MIr *cumtaigid* : MnIr *cumhdaíonn*, MIr *coimétaid* : MnIr *coimeádann*, etc. (McCone 1987: 209–10). This was an ongoing process; at a later stage within Modern Irish itself, *ibhidh* 'he drinks' (: VN *ól*) was replaced by *ólann*. As if to underline the nominal status of these stems, the productive -(*a*)*ig*- denominative suffix was sometimes used to mark such forms, e.g. OIr *for·tét* 'helps' : VN *fortacht* → MIr *fortachtaigid* (MnIr *fortachtaíonn*), *aithnid* 'entrusts' : VN *aith*(*g*)*ne* → MIr *aithnigid* (MnIr *aithníonn*), etc. (McCone 1987: 210).

8.3   Syntactical characteristics of verbal nouns

8.3.1   Nominal features
The sub-divisions follow the scheme of Table 8.1, and it will emerge that verbal nouns are subject to all the modifications applicable to other types of noun. Verbal nouns are indicated in bold.

8.3.1.1   Modification by article and adjective
Verbal nouns can be used with the article, e.g. MnW *ydych chi'n clywed y canu* 'do you hear the singing?', MB *amser an hadaff* 'the time for the sowing', MnB *ar rannañ war ar feurm* 'the dividing up of the farm' (Timm 1990: 190), MnIr *locc in crochda* 'the place of the crucifixion', etc., and modified by adjectives, e.g. MW *y gossot kyntaf* 'the first attack', MnW *rhedeg gyflym* 'swift running', OIr *a chétgabáil n-gaiscid* 'his first taking up of arms'.[4]

8.3.1.2   Modification by noun and pronoun
Verbal nouns can be modifiers of other nouns, e.g. MW *gwisc hela* 'hunting garb', MnW *cae chwarae* 'playing field', OIr *airde n-éelutha máma* 'signs of escaping the yoke', early MnIr *fear dhéanta na mbróg* 'cobbler' (lit. 'man of making shoes'), etc. Note that in Irish the verbal noun is in the genitive case, while in Brittonic languages it is in the genitival position, i.e. after the noun (see 5.3.3.3). Verbal nouns are also found as the modified element with the modifier in the genitive case or in the genitival position, if it is a noun, and as possessive adjective, if it is a pronoun, e.g. MnW *mae e'n gweld Mair* 'he is seeing M.' (lit. 'seeing of M.') beside *mae e'n ei gweld hi* 'he is seeing her' (lit.

'seeing of her'). Similarly in Irish the 'object' of the verbal noun is in
the genitive case, e.g. *tá sé ag moladh Pheadair* 'he is praising P.' (lit.
'praising of P.'), and the pronominal variant uses the possessive forms,
e.g. *tá sé dhá mhóladh* 'he is praising him' (lit. 'praising of him') (for
ag/dha, see 3.4.3 above). In Modern Irish the use of the genitive is disappearing and the above pattern tends to occur only with proper names
and definite nouns but not always. With indefinite nouns the nominative form occurs, e.g. *tá sí ag posadh fear óg* (nom.) 'she is marrying a
young man'. Moreover, Ó Siadhail 1989: 277 shows that there is a general drift away from the use of possessive adjectives towards using a
pronoun; thus, for example, *tá sé ag caint faoina dhéanamh* 'he is talking of doing it' (*faoina* = preposition *faoi* + possessive adjective) is
gradually being replaced by *tá sé ag caint faoi é a dheanamh*.
However, at earlier stages of the language the genitive was regular, e.g.
MIr *tichtu Phátraicc* 'the coming of Patrick', OIr *dénum tuile dáe*
'doing the will of God'.

  In certain complement constructions, however, an alternative
arrangement is possible. In Modern Irish there can be two types of
complementation, with a finite verb or with a verbal noun, after, for
example, *is maith leis* 'he likes' (lit. 'it is good with him'), e.g. *is maith
leis go bhfuil mé ann* ('. . .that I am here') or *mé a bheith ann* ('me to
be here') 'He likes me being here' (see 3.5.3.1). The details vary from
dialect to dialect (see Ó Siadhail 1989: 253–60) but essentially with
transitive verbs the subject or object of the verbal noun precedes it, e.g.
ba mhaith liom an doras a phéinteáil 'I would like to paint the door'
(lit. 'the door, its painting . . .'). It is also possible to have both a subject and object in such a construction, e.g. *ba mhaith liom sibh an
doras a phéinteáil* 'I would like **you** to paint the door'. Such patterns
are common in Donegal but rare in Munster where . . . *sibh a phéinteáil
an dorais* would be preferred with *dorais* in the genitive (Ó Siadhail
1989: 256). With intransitive verbs the verbal noun itself seems to
function as the subject of the verb, e.g. *ba mhaith liom teacht* 'I would
like to go off', though in Connacht and Donegal a preceding *a* (+ lenition) is still required, e.g. *ba mhaith liom a theacht*. Passives can also
be formed in this way, e.g. *Tá an doras dhá phéinteáil* 'the door is
being painted' (lit. 'the door is for its painting') (see 3.4.4).

  This type of construction can be traced back to Old Irish, e.g. *is bés
leo-sum in daim* (nom.) *do thuarcain ind orbe* 'it is a custom among
them that the oxen thresh the corn' (Thurneysen 1946: 444–5). The pattern also occurs in Welsh though very rarely, e.g. MW *dadyl dieu
agheu y eu treidu* 'it is a certain fact that death visited them' (lit. 'dying
to visit them'). Disterheft 1980: 152–5 discusses this type under the
heading of 'subject raising'; she sees them developing in cases where
the subject slot of the copula sentence is left empty and the subject of
the verbal noun is promoted or 'raised' into the subject of the copula.

She notes, following Gagnepain 1963, that this type is rare in the Old Irish glosses though very common later, However, she may have been misled by Gagnepain's treatment of the evidence; this pattern does occur with some frequency outside the glosses, particularly in legal texts.

So far we have been concerned with what may be termed 'objective' genitives, but the example above of both a subject and an object of a verbal noun raises the question of subjective genitives and how the risk of confusion between them and the objective type is avoided. The point is that the same slots could well be required for both; for example, in English 'my shooting of the hunters' and 'my shooting of them' are clear and unambiguous, but in Celtic the latter could cause difficulties in that the possessive pronoun slot would seem to have to carry two pronouns. Potential confusion can only arise with transitive verbs where both a subject and an object could occur; with intransitives there is no possibility of conflict, thus, for example, MW *dyuot Caswalawn am eu penn* 'C. fell upon them' (lit. 'the coming of C. around their heads'), and, with a pronoun, OIr *far **cretem**-si* 'your belief'. However, with transitive verbs the genitive/possessive slot is left for the objective genitive, while the subject or agent is marked by a preposition, usually *do* in Old Irish but sometimes *la*, and *o* or *y* in Welsh; for example, OIr ***toimten** dam-sa* 'that I think' (lit. 'thinking to me'). Thus in Old Irish ***serc** dé* (lit. 'love of God') does not mean the love God gives to others but someone's love for God; by contrast, *far serc-si do día* means 'God's love for you' (lit. 'your loving from God') or *far serc-si lim-sa* 'my love of you' (lit. 'your loving with me') where in the former *día*, and in the latter the 1st singular pronoun are marked as the agent by the preposition (Thurneysen 1946: 158). Within Welsh there is some change in usage between Middle and Modern Welsh. In the former the most common prepositional marker is *o*, e.g. *am **lad** ohonaf uu hun uy mab* 'because I killed my son' (lit. 'the killing from me myself of my son'); but two usages with *y* also occur: first, with the prepositional phrase following the verbal noun, e.g. MW ***emystynnu** idaw ... yn y peir* 'stretching himself out in the cauldron' (lit. 'stretching for him ...'), and secondly insubordinate clauses with the prepositional phrase before the verbal noun, e.g. *ef a dywawt wrthunt idaw **anuon** Arthur* 'he said to them that he would send A.' (lit. 'a sending of A. to him ...') (D. S. Evans 1964: 161–2). The latter construction has become the most common pattern in subordinate clauses in Modern Welsh, e.g. *wedi iddo **ddod*** 'after he came' (S. J. Williams 1980: 115–16).

It is striking that, although we are dealing with categories which seem in some senses very 'verbal' and one is forced into using verbal terminology of subjects, objects, agents, etc., the means of expression are nominal through and through.

8.3.1.3   Modification by prepositions

Another important usage of verbal nouns is their occurrence in prepositional phrases.[5] There is no space here to deal with all the types in
detail but often they correspond to full finite verb subordinate clauses in
other languages. For example, OIr *do* 'to' + verbal noun is the standard
pattern of final clause formation in Old Irish, e.g. *du dénam uilc* 'in
order to do evil' (lit. 'to doing of evil'), *dum fortacht húait-siu* 'that I
may be helped by you' (lit. 'to my helping from you'). By Modern
Irish, however, this usage is relatively rare and, as Ó Siadhail 1989:
324–5 shows, *go* + finite verb has become the usual final clause pattern.
The cognate preposition in Welsh, *i*, has remained productive, e.g.
MnW *prynodd e gar i fynd i waith* 'he bought a car to go to work'
(D. S. Evans 1964: 198, S. J. Williams 1980: 138).

The use of prepositions with verbal nouns is widespread and many
other examples can be encountered in other sections; note particularly
the use of W *wedi* 'after' to create a perfect tense (5.4.3). A particularly
interesting case is the use of the preposition 'without', Ir *cen*, W *heb*, B
hep, to negate a verbal noun, e.g. *is ingir lem cen chretim duib* 'it
grieves me that you do not believe' (lit. 'without believing to you')
(Thurneysen 1946: 545, Gagnepain 1963: 52–7), MnIr *gan an doras a
phéinteáil* 'not to paint the door' (lit. 'without the door its painting') (Ó
Siadhail 1989: 275), MW *heb allu seuyll* 'and he could not stand'
(D. S. Evans 1964: 164–5), MnB *hep marc'hata* 'without bargaining'
(Timm 1990: 191). In Middle Irish the negativizing effect of *cen* led to
its use before subordinate clauses, from which there arose a new con-
junction *cenco* 'without (the fact) that', 'although . . . not', etc., e.g.
MIr *cen co n-accatar* 'although they did not see it'.

8.3.1.4   Gender and declension

In Goidelic verbal nouns have full declension and gender like any other
noun. Thurneysen 1946: 447–55 gives a full list for Old Irish. All genders are represented, though most are *u*-stems; many are neuter, which
mostly became masculine in the later language. A full range of declensional classes occur with *o*-stems and *a*-stems, and also a range of
consonant-stem formations, e.g. *-tiu* (f.) (gen. sg. *-ten*), *-m* (gen. sg.
-men), etc. The distribution of these declensional types has undergone
the same reduction in the later language as other nouns with the corresponding growth of the weak verb verbal nouns (see 8.2).

In Brittonic there is obviously no declension, though traces remain of
a similar system to Goidelic; for example, consonantal stems can
remain fossilized in derivative personal names, e.g. *Llemenig*, where
the *n*-stem oblique stem of a verbal noun corresponding to OIr *léimm*
(*n*-stem) is preserved (Russell 1990: 117–18). In both Welsh and
Breton the masculine gender seems to have been generalized to all verbal nouns (Hemon 1975: 265, Morris-Jones 1913: 895–6); this is at

least the case with regular verbal noun formations, but with other patterns, e.g. W *-aeth*, which also have a separate existence as nominal suffixes, gender is more flexible. For example, *rhedeg* used as a noun 'course' is feminine, as in OW *trited redec* 'the third course', where the feminine form of the adjective is used, but as a verbal noun 'running' it is often masculine.

8.3.1.5   Verbal noun as subject or object of a verb

Verbal nouns also behave in a nominal fashion as subjects and objects of verbs: as subject (indicated in bold), OIr *ní airic ní* **césad crist** 'the suffering of Christ is of no use' (Gagnepain 1963: 76–7). MW *da yw gennyf dy* **welet ti** 'I am glad to see you' (lit. 'seeing you is good with me') (D. S. Evans 1964: 159), MB **aznavout Doue** . . . *so dleet* 'to know God is a duty' (Hemon 1975: 265); as object (indicated in bold), OIr *ní relic Dia doib* **orcuin** *Duaid* 'God did not let them kill David' (Gagnepain 1963: 79–92), MW *ef a uyn* **ymrwymaw** . . . 'he wishes to bind . . .', MnB *e veze d'* **ober paeañ** *al lojeiz* 'he was to pay for the lodgings' (lit. 'to make a paying'). The last example, where *paeañ* is itself the object of *ober* 'do, make' draws attention to a significant subcategory of this type. As has already been noted (see 3.4.3 for Irish and 5.4.3 for Welsh and Breton), the general verb 'do/make' + verbal noun is a common pattern as an alternative to a fully inflected verb, e.g. (verbal noun in bold) MnIr *rinn sé* **broinn** 'he broke wind (lit. 'he made a breaking of wind') (Ó Siadhail 1989: 304), MnW *mi wnes i* **atgoffa'r** *swyddogion* 'I reminded the officials' (lit. 'I made a reminding'), MnB **selaou** *a reas ar vamm* 'the mother listened' (lit. 'made a listening') (Timm 1990: 192), MCo *my a ra y* **dybry** 'I eat' (lit. 'I do eating') (Lewis 1946: 49 (= Zimmer 1990a: 46)). This pattern is particularly widespread in Middle Welsh prose, where often *oruc/wnaeth* 'did' can generate a string of verbal nouns, e.g. **bwyta** *a* **chyuedach** *ac* **ymdidan** *a wnaethont* 'they ate and caroused and conversed' (D. S. Evans 1964: 160).

The use of an object verbal noun with the verb 'do' in Celtic seems a *prima facie* case of nominal behaviour. In support of this argument for Breton, S. R. Anderson 1981 has drawn attention to the use of the particle *a* in MnB *selaou a reas*, etc. (see above), which is characteristic of nominal phrases preceding the verb rather than any other constituent where the particle is *e*. However, Timm 1990: 192–4 has suggested that the behaviour of the verbal noun in this construction seems more 'verbal' when it involves direct or indirect objects or adverbs, e.g. *kompren mat a ran* 'I understand well' (lit. 'understanding well I did'), *anazevout a walc'h a ran ac'honout* 'I know you well enough' (lit. 'knowing you well enough I do'), *he c'harout a ra kalz* 'he loved her greatly' (lit. 'loving her he did greatly'). However, in many respects the verbal noun still behaves like a noun; *mat* is adjectival agreeing with *kompren*; *he c'harout* contains a possessive pronoun, not a pronoun. Even an adverb like *kalz* could be interpreted as modifying *ra* and not the verbal noun.

8.3.1.6   Neutral to active/passive distinctions

Unlike finite or non-finite forms of the verb, verbal nouns are unmarked for tense, voice, person, mood, etc. (see 8.1). In being unmarked, they differ from the infinitive of other languages. Nevertheless, in most Celtic languages it is possible to find verbal nouns in contexts where they can be interpreted as passive. In Middle Welsh examples such as **brathu** *Bendigeiduran yn y troet* 'B. was wounded in the foot' (lit. '(there was) a wounding of B.'), its passive interpretation is very much dependent on the context. There are, however, three specific markers which indicate that a passive interpretation is required (D. S. Evans 1964: 163–4). First, MW (*g*)*wedy* (MnW *wedi*) 'after' + verbal noun, e.g. MW *gwedy* **gossot** *y vorwynn* 'after the maiden had been brought' (lit. 'after bringing of the maiden'). In Modern Welsh there are two constructions involving *wedi*; it is used to form a periphrastic active perfect tense (see 5.4.3), but it also occurs with or without a finite verb where it seems to function either as a perfect participle passive, e.g. *siop wedi* **cau** 'shop closed', or as a stative passive, e.g. *mae'r gwaith wedi ei* **orffen** 'the work is finished' (lit. 'is after finishing it') (Fife 1990: 482–512). Secondly, in Middle Welsh the verbal noun can occur with an impersonal or passive finite verb, e.g. **kyweiriaw** *y neuad a wnaethpwyt* 'the hall was made ready' (lit. 'readying of the hall was done'). Thirdly, there are already traces in Middle Welsh of the wide-spread Modern Welsh passive construction of *cael* + verbal noun (see 5.4.4), e.g. MW *ni a gawn yn* **goganu** 'we shall be defamed' (lit. 'we shall get our defaming').

In Old Irish a passive interpretation of a verbal noun is again contextually determined, though in some cases it is not always clear whether the verbal noun is to be regarded as passive or impersonal. One group, which occur in legal texts, are quasi-imperatives, e.g. *a* **mbeith** *i mbúailid fo* **íadud** *i n-aidchi* 'they are to be shut up in an enclosure at night' (lit. 'their being shut up . . .'), **córugad** *cach cúailni íar n-úachtar* 'each stake is to be fixed at the top' (lit. 'the fixing of each stake . . .') (Binchy 1978: I, 192.34–5 and 195.30 respectively). A similar type operates in Middle Breton, e.g. **ranna** *an aval aour* 'let the golden apple be divided' (Hemon 1975: 267). Another group, discussed by Disterheft 1980: 148–50, involves verbal nouns as objects. Essentially, the active/passive interpretation of the verbal noun object depends on the application or non-application of equi-deletion, the deletion of possessive pronouns referring to the subject of the main verb. For example, in OIr *arromertus-sa* **buith** *and* 'I intended to be there', a co-referent *mo* referring to the subject of *arromertus* has been deleted. But when there is no equi-deletion, a passive interpretation follows, e.g. *as·boinn a **dingbáil*** 'he demands to be removed' (lit. 'his removal'). In this case the co-referent possessive adjective *a* remains.

8.3.2 Verbal features

8.3.2.1 Modification by adverb
A verbal noun can be modified by an adverb rather than by an adjective (see above 8.3.1.1), e.g. MW *reit yw **gerdet** yn bryssur* 'it is necessary to walk quickly', MnW ***gweithio** yn galed* 'working hard'. Examples are rare in early Irish, partly because of the difficulty of identifying adverbs, but Gagnepain 1963: 17, n. 1 does give the following example, *im almsu do **beith** ind fholach* 'almsgiving in secret'. Adverbial use does occur, therefore, but is relatively rare, except where verbal nouns occur in periphrastic verbal constructions where adverb usage is mandatory (see below).

8.3.2.2 Periphrastic auxiliary verbs and aspect
The various periphrastic constructions used in Irish and Welsh have already been catalogued in the relevant sections (3.4.3 for Irish and 5.4.3 for Welsh). They all involve the use of verbal nouns, usually in the construction of auxiliary verb + preposition + verbal noun, e.g. Irish *tá sé ag* + VN (progressive), *tá sé thar éis/i ndéid* + VN (perfect), *tá sé le* + VN (prospective), *tá sé i* + possessive adjective + VN (stative) (Ó Siadhail 1989: 294–302), Welsh *mae e yn* + VN (present), *mae e wedi* + VN (perfect), Breton *emañ o* + VN (progressive) (Hewitt 1990), Cornish *ym ow* + VN (progressive) (H. Lewis 1946: 50 (= Zimmer 1990a: 46)).

At one level these constructions simply show the nominal pattern of preposition + verbal noun, but they do carry important aspectual distinctions, and aspect is a verbal rather than a nominal feature. In one case, however, Welsh *yn* + verbal noun, it has been pointed out (7.6) that it does not behave like the preposition, which causes nasalization; in the verbal noun construction, e.g. *mae e'n **canu***, there is no mutation. Fife 1990: 432–3 argues that this is analogous to the use in Latin, German, Russian or Old English of 'switch' prepositions which have different cases depending on the semantics, e.g. Latin *in* + accusative or ablative. But it is not clear whether he is suggesting anything about the etymology of the preposition by this statement.

There has been some debate as to how these periphrastic forms should be analysed. Analyses in other languages, e.g. Eng *I am going*, etc., tend to treat the second element as the aspectually marked verb with the auxiliary as the carrier of tense, person and number markers. Such an approach to Welsh is made by M. Jones and Thomas 1977: 168–76 (see 5.5.4 above); the effect is to treat the verbal noun as a verb

and the preposition as an aspect marker. A similar approach is espoused
for Irish by McCloskey 1980, 1983 and implied for Breton by Hewitt's
1990: 184 'conjunction of a lexical infinitive VP preceded by a progressive particle'. However, it has been criticized by Stenson 1981: 137–45
as follows:

> Aux + V analyses . . . have been proposed entirely on the basis of languages
> like English, whose auxiliary and main verb are contiguous. Such an
> analysis is considerably less plausible for Irish, where the relevant
> constituents are discontinuous (Stenson 1981: 138).

She recognizes that the alternative analysis as a prepositional phrase
containing a noun phrase has its drawbacks, especially that it fails to
capture the essentially verbal nature of aspect. She goes on to note, as in
Welsh, that prepositional phrases involving verbal nouns do not always
operate syntactically like simple prepositional phrases; for example, the
Irish preposition *thar éis* is followed by a genitive when it governs a
simple noun, e.g. *thar éis tamaill* 'after a while', but when followed by a
verbal noun the verbal noun is not in the genitive. She argues that this
extension of the basic positional sense of the prepositional phrase is
'typical of lexical items which have taken on more strictly grammatical
functions' (Stenson 1981: 140) Similarly, Fife 1990: 326–98 has argued
for the identity of these 'aspect' markers and prepositions.

Although aspect can be seen as something altogether verbal, Comrie
1976: 98–105 draws attention to a number of languages other than
Celtic, including Dutch, French, Georgian, Mandarin Chinese and
Yoruba, where locative, usually prepositional, expressions of aspectual
oppositions occur. He also notes the use of primarily or etymologically
locative verbs as a progressive auxiliary and in particular the case of
Spanish *estoy cantando*, Portuguese *estou cantando*, etc. 'I am
singing'; all etymologically related to Latin *stāre* 'stand'. Furthermore,
he points out that Ir *tá*, ScG *thá* is historically cognate with *stāre*. The
point needs to be made that such patterns are too widespread across the
languages of the world for the locative sense to be eradicated by linguistic analysis; there is a clear relationship between locative
expression and aspect which should be encapsulated in any analysis.

8.3.2.3   *Verbal nouns in subordinate clauses*
As has emerged from the descriptions of Irish and Welsh, verbal nouns
play a large role in subordinate clause syntax (see 3.5.3 for Irish,
5.5.3.1 for Welsh). Particularly in Irish, the verbal status of such verbal
noun usage is apparent by the fact that they can be replaced by finite
verb constructions (see Ó Siadhail 1989: 260–87, and 8.3.1.2 above).
After verbs of saying, thinking, etc., indirect statements tend to have a
finite clause, while indirect commands have a verbal noun, e.g. Ir *duirt
sé go raibh sé go maith* 'he said he was well' but *duirt sé an doras a*

phéinteáil 'he said to paint the door'. Other types of clauses show a similar range of alternatives (Ó Siadhail 1989: 268–9). In Welsh, however, most subordinate clauses have no finite construction but use various types of verbal noun construction. Patterns of indirect statement with verbal nouns are discussed above (5.5.3.1). In addition, a number of other clauses also use verbal nouns; for example, indirect commands use *am* + verbal noun, e.g. *dwedodd y fam wrth y plentyn am fod yn dawel* 'the mother told her child to be quiet', temporal clauses with *cyn* + verbal noun, e.g. *cyn i'r athro i weld e* 'before the teacher saw him' (lit. 'seeing him to the teacher'). The verbal status of these clauses is further indicated by the negative forms. Especially in indirect statements, the negative clause can be expressed by a finite verb; for example, we can compare the positive *dywedodd e bod y tŷ wedi ei godi* 'he said the house had been built' with two possible negatives: (a) *heb* + verbal noun . . . *fod y tŷ heb ei godi* or (b) *nad* + finite verb . . . *nad oedd y tŷ wedi ei godi*. In Breton, likewise, verbal nouns play a part in subordination but in many cases there would seem to be French influence in the background (Hemon 1975: 318–20). In Middle Breton there are cases of verbal noun usage parallel to Welsh, e.g. *gouzuezher bezout un mab bihan ganet* 'it will be known that a small boy will be born' (lit. 'being of a small boy born'); this pattern has been replaced by finite clauses in the modern language.

8.3.2.4 Replacement of finite verbs in co-ordinated strings
One of the most verbal characteristics of verbal nouns is their use after a fully marked verb to list a series of actions, e.g. (verbal nouns in bold) MW *y syrthawd y blew oll . . . a thorri y croen y amdanei, a syrthyaw y holl berued y'r llawr* 'all its hair fell out . . . and the skin was rent from around it and all its entrails fell to the floor' (D. S. Evans 1964: 161), MB *ma-z huesenn certen ha crenaf, ha coezaf da-ndouar* 'so that I sweated and trembled and fell to the ground' (Hemon 1975: 266). This pattern is rare in Modern Breton; and it does not occur in early Irish where the unmarked verb form was a narrative present rather than the verbal noun (Tristram 1983). In view of the absence of this pattern in early Irish, Disterheft 1980: 195–6 has made the intriguing suggestion that this Brittonic pattern may be related to the historic infinitive in Latin.[6]

8.4   Verbal noun: noun or verb?

The above discussion has highlighted the difficulties of separating nominal and verbal usage. Indeed Fife 1990: 399–402 has questioned the utility of such an exercise; he points out that verbal characteristics of verbal nouns are not on the same footing as the nominal characteristics. Apart from the use of adverbs, the other verbal characteristics are not characteristics of verbs; for example, verbs cannot be linked periphrastically with auxiliary verbs. In contrast, all the nominal characteristics are also applicable to true nouns. Fife concludes:

> It is clear that traditional grammarians had something else in mind, two different levels of analysis, when they described VNs as having nominal and 'verbal' traits. What they meant was that the 'verbal' environments, though impossible with real verbs, seem to bring out the verbal *interpretation* of the VN more clearly than do the nominal environments (Fife 1990: 401.)
> (See also Willis 1988.)

On the other hand, Borsley 1993, focusing on Welsh verbal nouns, has criticized Fife's approach on the grounds that he is comparing verbal nouns with the wrong thing. Verbal nouns, in his view, are to be compared not with finite forms of the verb but with the non-finite forms, in English grammatical terminology, infinitives, participles, etc. Borsley 1993: 36 distinguishes between an 'ordinary' verbal noun, which corresponds to English non-finite verbs, e.g. W *mae'r bachgen yn canu* 'the boy is singing', and a 'nominal' verbal noun corresponding to usage where verbal nouns clearly function as nouns, e.g. W *clywais i'r canu* 'I heard the singing'. His conclusion, which seems to follow inevitably from his own definitions, is that 'ordinary' verbal nouns are verbs and, as this is the most common pattern with verbal nouns, then verbal nouns are verbs not nouns. One difficulty which underlies this argument is the implicit parallelism with English, which is made clear in his conclusion:

> In many ways, Welsh VNs are like what we might call the ING forms in English verbs. These too are basically verbs although some can appear as nouns. When they are verbs, an object is a bare NP and they are modified by adverbs. Thus, we have phrases like *singing the anthem slowly*. When they are nouns, an object appears as a PP [prepositional phrase] of some kind and they are modified by adjectives. Hence, we have phrases like *slow singing of the anthem* (Borsley 1993: 60–1).

The danger of such an approach is that it can lead to some rather bizarre interpretations of the evidence. For example, he would argue that the use of possessive adjectives to mark pronominal objects, e.g. *ceisiodd Emrys ei weld ef* 'E. tried to see him', does not make (*g*)*weld* a noun, and that to interpret *ei . . . ef* as a possessive marker is to force 'Welsh into an English mould'. It is difficult to see what this means since English does not regularly use possessive adjectives in this way, and moreover *ei . . . ef* are clearly possessive markers in Welsh and no English model is required for a such an analysis; the closest English has to offer is the subjective possessive as, for example, in *my going upset him*, but there is nothing parallel to the regular objective use of possessives found in Welsh. Borsley 1993: 42–4 also compares and contrasts the use of the noun *disgrifiad* and the verbal noun *disgrifio* 'describe/

describing'. The argument goes something like this: since *disgrifiad* is a noun and *disgrifio* is not used in the same patterns, then *disgrifio* cannot be a noun and, therefore, must be a verb. Clearly *disgrifiad* and *disgrifio* are not used in exactly the same way but there seems to be a terminological weakness if *disgrifio* must be called a verb because *disgrifiad* is a noun. His argument does highlight not only terminological weaknesses but also this grey area of verbal noun usage. It is difficult to resist the thought that Celtic languages show more nominal tendencies in non-finite verbal forms than those languages more commonly used for linguistic analysis, such as English, but the linguistic terminology and the theory underlying it finds difficulty in coping with such usage. Hence the strained and laboured arguments to force Celtic patterns into a different mould.

Furthermore, by concentrating on Welsh it is rather easier to dismiss nominal features than it is in Irish, and particularly in earlier forms of the language, where verbal nouns are much more obviously behaving as nouns with genitival objects and clearer prepositional dependence. Even in later stages of the languages, the surface structure is nominal with prepositions, possessive adjectives, etc. In view of the remarks of Comrie 1976: 98–105 that many languages share a surface realization of progressive and stative aspect by locative prepositions (see 8.3.2.2), it may be worth pursuing the question of surface structures. The unease felt by Fife, quoted above, may lie in the fact that, although many of the constructions discussed above do have a nominal pattern, they nevertheless do refer to the same kind of thing as verbs, namely, actions. The question of whether verbal nouns are nouns or verbs is a non-question in linguistic terms, since a linguist would want to know at what level of the language the question is pitched. It is clear even in English that the famous ambiguous surface structure 'the shooting of the hunters' can be resolved by reference to a deep structure where it can be analysed as a verb with 'the hunters' as either a subject or an object. On that basis would we want to call 'shooting' a verb? It does seem that much of the criticism directed at nominal analyses of Celtic verbal nouns proceeds along such lines. However, it would be possible for Fife's 'verbal interpretation of verbal nouns' (1990: 401) to rest in the deep structure analysis but for it to be realized as a noun phrase. For example, Stenson 1981:138 has argued that MnIr *tá Mairtín ag casadh amhráin* 'M. is singing a song' can be analysed as containing a sentential complement containing a verb (see Figure 8.1 overleaf). Rules of equi-deletion and infinitivization would then apply to produce the surface structure.

Another difficulty which has been noted is one of terminology. Borsley 1993 attempts to resolve the problem by fitting Welsh into a framework of non-finite verbal forms. The outcome of this is to allow *disgrifiad* to be a noun but *disgrifio* a verb. The question is whether such a framework has any application in Celtic. It may be instructive

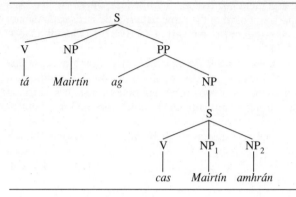

FIGURE 8.1   Deep structure (according to Stenson 1981: 138)

that Celtic lexicographers tend to give verbal nouns and verbal adjectives separate lemmata from the verb, while English lexicographers would include non-finite forms under the lemma of the verb. If this is of any significance, it may suggest that Celtic lexicographers think of these forms as having an existence independent from that of the finite verb. It is true that not all verbal nouns are immediately predictable from the form of the verb, or vice versa for that matter. But it may indicate a difference in approach. There seems to be no objection to viewing both *disgrifiad* and *disgrifio* as nominal forms which have slightly different meanings and therefore different syntactical patterns; *disgrifio* seems to refer to the act of description itself as opposed to *disgrifiad*, which refers to the outcome of the completed act of description. It is, nevertheless, of importance that the syntax of the structures with prepositions is nominal. *Disgrifio* and *disgrifiad* do both refer to verbal actions but are nominalizations of different activities. Both relate to the deep structure verb 'describe' but the difference has to do with a difference between the progressive sense of the one as against the completed sense of the other.

Finally, it is clear from the discussion in 8.3 that some usages are more verbal than others. As will emerge from the historical discussion (8.5), Celtic verbal nouns started as nouns and have gradually shifted towards verbs within the documented history of the languages. Progress seems to have been much slower in Celtic than in other Indo-European languages but a question which should be asked is to what extent verbal noun usage in Celtic is being influenced by the other language of bilingual speakers, i.e. English or French (and in the past Latin). The work has yet to be done, but it would be interesting to know, for example, to what extent the use of preposition + verbal noun is related to the *to* + infinitive in English.

8.5 Verbal nouns and infinitives: the historical background

At the beginning of the chapter we distinguished finite and non-finite parts of the verb and offered a definition of an infinitive; it was implied that a verbal noun did not share those characteristics. In Table 8.3 a clearer group of criteria is listed by which we may crudely distinguish infinitives and verbal nouns. This definition of verbal nouns is not based solely on Celtic but takes into account the types of verbal nouns which occur in other languages, often alongside infinitives, e.g. Eng verb *act* : infinitive *to act* : N *action*, Lat *amat* 'loves' : *amāre* : *amātio*, Gk *kineî* 'moves' : *kineîn* : *kinēsis*. It is noteworthy that the general definition of verbal nouns does not predict that they are used in place of finite verbs, but that is what we find in Celtic (see 8.3.2.4).

The question under consideration here is how far back in the history of the Indo-European languages that distinction can be maintained. An examination of the morphology of infinitival formations shows a series of endings added to the verbal stem or root, e.g. Latin active present *-re*, perfect active *-isse*, Greek active present *-ein*, *-nai*, middle/passive *-sthai*, Vedic *-dhyai*, *-tave*, Skt *-tum*, Hittite *-anna*, *-wanzi* (see Disterheft 1980: 12–17 for a fuller listing for Vedic and Avestan).[7] It is striking that many of the suffixes listed can also be used to form verbal nouns. The point is that many of the infinitive endings are fossilized case endings; thus, Lat *-re* < *-s-i* (locative or perhaps dative), Skt *-tum* (accusative), Hittite *-wanzi* < *-u̯ant-i* (McCone 1984: 180), etc. Disterheft 1980 argues that in most Indo-European languages there was a drift towards the verbalization of nouns based on verbal roots, i.e. towards the creation of infinitives. The characteristic infinitival pattern which has emerged is a fossilized oblique case ending, accusative (i.e. verbal) object, and forms marking tense and mood. Disterheft's claim is that, although there are archaic features in Vedic, such as occasional genitive objects, Celtic alone has preserved the archaic pattern.[8]

TABLE 8.3   Comparison of verbal noun and infinitive patterns

	Infinitive	Verbal noun
Predictable from verb	+	−
Capacity to inflect	−	+
Marked for tense and mood	+	−
Nominal word formation	−	+
Nominal behaviour:		
genitive object	−	+
adjective	−	+
Use as finite verb	+	(+)
Verbal semantics (aspect)	+	−

However, Jeffers 1978 has argued that Old Irish verbal noun usage represents a morphological and syntactical innovation conditioned by the rise of VSO (verb–subject–object) word order patterns. His claim is that VSO languages have a clear proclivity towards the widespread use of nominal complement constructions (Jeffers 1987: 8), and that Celtic eradicated all the inherited Indo-European types such as infinitives, participles and gerunds and replaced them with more nominal forms.[9] But, the development of VSO order is a relatively recent phenomenon within Celtic (see C. Watkins 1963a, McCone 1979a, and 9.2 below), and if that was the trigger for the re-arrangement of the infinitival system, it happened very late in the history of Celtic. Moreover, the morphological diversity of verbal noun patterns in Old Irish and their inherent unpredictability does not suggest an innovative pattern but something much more archaic (McCone 1984: 181). Whatever is to be made of arguments about universal patterns of VSO order going together with nominal usage (see 9.0), if that approach is accepted, then it may have provided an environment in which archaic verbal noun usage was somehow insulated from the changes towards infinitival usage which occurred independently in other Indo-European languages.

Notes

1. Traces of ancient present participles with the characteristic IE *-nt-* marker survive in Old Irish *namae* 'enemy' < **ne-amant-* and *carae* 'friend' < **karant-* (cf. W *câr*, pl. *ceraint*). Archaic feminine forms may survive in OIr *berit* 'sow' < **berṇtī*, *elit* 'hind' < **(p)elṇtī*.
2. For Irish, see Thurneysen 1946: 441–4 (verbal adjectives), 444–55 (verbal nouns), Ó Siadhail 1989: 195–8 (verbal nouns), 198–200 (verbal adjectives). The fullest treatment of the syntax of Irish verbal nouns is Gagnepain 1963; his text-based study is valuable for its vast array of material but can be misleading in that the Old Irish discussion, for example, is largely based on the glosses which are notoriously vulnerable to Latin influence. For Scottish Gaelic, see Calder 1923: 248–55; for Welsh, D. S. Evans 1964: 156–65 (verbal nouns), 165–6 (verbal adjectives), S. J. Williams 1980: 109–20 (verbal nouns), 120–1 (verbal adjectives), Thorne 1993: 314–36 (verbal nouns), 336–9 (verbal adjectives), King 1993: 130–5 (verbal nouns), 87–8 (verbal adjectives); for Breton, Hemon 1975: 264–70 (verbal nouns), Fleuriot 1964: 328–31 (verbal nouns), 313–16 (verbal adjectives).
3. See D. S. Evans 1964: 157–9, S. J. Williams 1980: 112–13. For similar patterns in Breton, see Kervella 1947: 110–11, Hemon 1941: 56 (note that in Breton and French linguistic terminology B *anv-verb* 'verbal noun' corresponds to French *infinitif*).
4. See D. S. Evans 1964: 159, S. J. Williams 1980: 113, Hemon 1975: 265, Gagnepain 1963: 17, 133, Timm 1990.
5. For a detailed discussion of the Irish evidence, see Gagnepain 1963: 43–75 (Old Irish), 134–80 (Middle Irish), 248–97 (Modern Irish) (see also Genee

1994); for Welsh, see D. S. Evans 1964: 159, S. J. Williams 1980: 113; for Breton, Timm 1990: 191, Hemon 1975: 267. For an interesting case of a misinterpreted preposition in Brittonic, see Armstrong 1987–8.

6. For a similar use of the verbal noun to add information or set the scene, see Gagnepain 1963: 119–24, Ó Siadhail 1989: 284–7, Hemon 1975: 266–7, and S. J. Williams 1980: 114.

7. On infinitives generally, see Disterheft 1980, Jeffers 1975 and 1978, Leumann 1977: 580–2, Rosén 1981.

8. One aspect which requires further investigation is the treatment of verbal noun/infinitive subjects; in a number of Indo-European languages the subject is in the dative. We may compare the use in Latin gerunds and Greek verbal adjectives. Could this be the origin of the Old Irish *do* + dative construction for marking verbal noun subjects (see McCone 1984: 181–2)?

9. Word order is discussed in Chapter 9. There is an interesting correlation in the fact that often those linguists who want to argue that Celtic verbal nouns are verbal are the very same ones who want to say that Celtic languages are not VSO.

Chapter 9

Word order in the Celtic languages

> *Ro bíth oss la Tadc macc Céin,*
> *Tadc macc Céin la oss ro bíth,*
> *la oss ro bíth Tadc macc Céin,*
> *Tadc macc Céin i rRoss na Ríg*

> 'A deer has been slain by Tadc mac Céin'
> Tadc mac Céin has by a deer been slain,
> by a deer has Tadc mac Céin been slain,
> Tadc mac Céin in Ross na Ríg' (Stokes 1902: 310)

9.0 Introduction

Throughout the preceding chapters there have been numerous comments about word order (see in particular 3.5.1, 5.5.1, 8.4). This chapter
is concerned not with the relative ordering of, for example, nouns and
adjectives but rather with the ordering of the main constituents of the
sentence, primarily subject, object and verb. It has also emerged that a
number of different word orders are possible, e.g. verb (V) + subject
(S) + object (O) in Irish and Welsh, but SVO in Breton and Cornish,
and SOV in some Continental inscriptions. The Middle Irish verse
quoted above illustrates the range of possible word orders in verse (see
Mac Cana 1991: 77–8). Copula forms, on the other hand, seem to
present all kinds of order of verb, subject and complement. In many
languages it is possible to have other elements in initial position
depending on the requirements of emphasis, focus or topicalization.
The question then arises as to what counts as the basic order from
which other word orders can be seen to have developed. A subsidiary
question concerns the matter of changes in word order and what type of
evidence can be used to demonstrate change.

As soon as we move away from the modern languages, our evidence
is textual and, for Continental Celtic, inscriptional. Moreover, textual
evidence can be in verse as well as in prose. It is clear that word order
in verse does not necessarily correspond to the order of prose from the
same period. It is frequently assumed that word order in the former is
more archaic and reflects the normal word order of an earlier period,
but that is not the only response to abnormal word order; we must allow

for stylistic licence and metrical considerations to play their part. For example, the order of OIr *túatha adortais síde* 'they used to worship the people of the fairy mound' (Stokes and Strachan 1901–3: 317.4) is object + verb + dependent genitive; in this case it is probable that the order is motivated by the need to have *síde* rhyming with *fíre* in the next line (Mac Cana 1991: 53).

Similar concerns may be expressed about the inscriptional evidence from the Continent. The longer inscriptions from Chamalières, Larzac or Botorrita (see 1.2) may perhaps be a more reliable guide to basic word order, where the bulk of material might allow common patterns to be identified, but the briefer funerary inscriptions or potters' graffiti are potentially misleading in their preoccupation with names rather than verbal elements. Though all the inscriptions may be grammatical, they may not represent all the word orders possible in the language but merely the marked variants (Mac Cana 1991: 49).

There are important methodological considerations here which have been brought out by Mac Cana 1991 in a discussion of aspects of work on word order by Koch 1985a and 1987. Koch takes the word order evidenced in the Continental material as his starting point and attempts to explain the development of Brittonic word order from that basis; he is keen, therefore, to identify 'Continental' types of word order in early Brittonic languages and inevitably he finds them in verse. Mac Cana, on the other hand, has worked backwards from the modern spoken languages (see Mac Cana 1973, 1979–80). It is hardly surprising, therefore, that there should be considerable divergences in the conclusions reached.

Even if we restrict the investigation to prose, we are immediately confronted by a number of difficulties. First, it is not always clear what we should wish to call prose. In Old Irish, for example, there are alliterative runs which do not necessarily conform to any clear metrical pattern but seem too artificial to be called prose (see Breatnach 1984: 452–9, C. Watkins 1963b).

Secondly, it is very difficult to decide how to identify a basic word order. An important aspect of recent work on word order, especially in Brittonic, is interest in the communicative effects of word order. Early work has tended to operate with the blunt tool of the presence or absence of emphasis. However, an interesting area of recent linguistic research has been what has been called 'information structuring' (see Fife and King 1991: 93–120; for the general background, see Li 1976 and Li and Thompson 1976). The basic notion is that the flow of information and its communicative function can affect the grammatical structure of the sentence. The content of a sentence can be divided into 'theme' and 'rheme', or 'topic' and 'comment'. Usually, the theme or topic will precede any comment upon it and this may have the effect of disrupting the expected or basic patterns of constituent order in the sentence. An important concept within this general field is 'focus', i.e. 'the degree to which an item is made more prominent in the communicative structure of the sentence' (Fife and King 1991: 95). Emphasis is one type of focus but the latter term also includes other more subtle distinctions involving identification or salience within the context. Another type of marked focus is what is known as 'topicalization', the explicit marking of an item as the topic of the sentence. A topic need not be emphatic since almost all sentences will have a topic and comment, but not all of them could be emphatic. Another aspect of focus and topicalization which again distinguishes them from emphasis is the general discourse principle that old (or given) information tends to precede new (or asserted) information (Bolinger 1952).

Generally, the idea of focus, or even the more specific topicalization, has a wider range of semantic and syntactical effects than emphasis and can more readily capture the subtleties of complex discourse. Languages mark focus in different ways. Japanese, for example, marks it almost entirely by the use of particles, while Russian operates with a combination of particles and changes in word order (see Fife and King 1991: 99–120 for examples). Celtic languages, however, tend to use word order to mark these distinctions.

The question which can then be legitimately asked is how we can ever hope to decide upon a basic word order when every utterance has its communicative function and its topic and comment. The response may be that there are enough neutral utterances to decide what counts as the least marked pattern. But that depends very much on being able to identify neutral utterances. A case in point is the claim that Breton has developed a basic unmarked order of SVO (see Mac Cana 1979–80: 181); but Timm 1989 and 1991 has argued that the subject-initial noun phrases mark topicalization and focus functions and she claims that at base Breton remains a VSO language (see 9.1.2.2 below).

Another approach can be made through the typology of word order patterns. Greenberg 1966 has argued that Celtic languages are prime examples of VSO languages in that they follow all the universal features predicated of VSO languages; those listed by Greenberg are that VSO languages should be prepositional rather than post-positional, have SVO as an alternative order (cf. in particular Cornish and Breton), have initial interrogative particles, place WH-words before the verb, have the main verb after the auxiliary, have post-head modification as the main format (i.e. genitives and adjectives following the noun), and have special relative forms of the verb (see Downing 1978 for the last, and generally Fife 1993: 16). These features are, however, frequently a matter of analysis and debate; on main verbs and auxiliaries, see 5.5.4, where alternative analyses are canvassed. The matter of prepositions may, however, be of significance; Comrie 1976: 98–105 has argued that there is a correlation between VSO structure and aspect marking by locative prepositions (see 8.3.2.2). But even in this case Comrie suggests that this is a surface realization and more generally it is not clear how deep these typological indicators run; some seem to be relatively trivial. One point which is of concern here and will emerge in the following discussion (especially in 9.2) has to do with the historical depth of VSO order in Celtic. It seems clear that it was a feature of Insular Celtic languages but not of Continental forms. Moreover, discussion of the rise of VSO order in Celtic tends to place it relatively late in the line of historical developments from Proto-Celtic (whether we follow the arguments of C. Watkins 1963a or those of Koch 1987 and 1991; see 9.2 below). If so, it would follow that the other typological features characteristic of VSO languages are also late. However, to take one particular example, the special relative forms of the verb can largely be explained by assuming the addition of a -*io*- particle to the end of the verb, e.g. W *sydd*, MW *yssyd* 'who is' < **esti-io*, OIr 3rd pl. *cartae* < **karont-io*, etc. (see 2.2.6.4; the OIr 3rd sg. relative -*s* remains a problem). If this is to be regarded as a typological correlate of VSO languages, we would not expect to find it in SVO or SOV languages. But the exact pre-forms of the Old Irish and Welsh forms can be found in Gaul *dugiiontiio* and *toncsiiontio*, which are to be analysed as 3rd plural verbs + the relative marker -*io*, although they are not apparently VSO languages. It is, of course, difficult to extract one feature and to discuss it out of context when clusters of features are the significant factor. Nevertheless, it gives pause for thought. In this particular case it may be the definition of a 'special' form of the relative which is the difficulty. In Gaulish the relative marker is clearly analysable. However, in the Insular languages the construction has become opaque and no longer analysable into its constituent elements. The point is when these 'special' relative forms became 'special'; it could be argued, for example, that they are not 'special' in Continental Celtic since they are a clear and perceptible part of the morphological system.

9.1   The evidence

The following sections consider the evidence of word order patterns. To avoid repetition, the categories discussed are fairly broad; for example, the Continental Celtic evidence is considered *en bloc* and not sub-divided into geographical areas. Similarly, Brittonic word order involves consideration of the patterns of Welsh, Cornish and Breton since it is difficult to discuss one without reference to the others. Within each section the evidence is presented where relevant from different stages of the language, and various approaches to it are discussed. Specifically historical aspects of the question which involve consideration of all the Celtic languages are reserved for the final section of the chapter (9.2).

9.1.1 Continental Celtic

It seems that the regular unmarked order in Gaulish was SVO; even
where an object is not expressed, the verb frequently follows the subject (see Koch 1983, 1985a: 2). The set of inscriptions containing the
formula *dede bratu dekantem* '(X) gave a tithe in gratitude' are a case
in point (see Figure 1.1 (p. 4) for an example); the standard pattern is
'PN (subj.) . . . *dede* (verb) . . . *dekantem* (obj.)'. Similarly, the *ieuru*
inscriptions show a pattern of 'PN (subj.) . . . *ieuru* (verb 'dedicated'
vel sim.) (see Figure 6.1 (p. 200) for an example). Generally verbs are
relatively easy to identify, as are other elements such as subjects and
objects, even though overall understanding may not be clear. The problem arises with distinguishing sentences, since it is difficult to know
whether a verb is initial or final if we do not know where the sentence
begins or ends.

Some examples are presented in Table 9.1. Though broken, the first
example is illuminating; a verb *karnitou* can be identified and equated
with the *KARNITV* of the bilingual Todi inscription (see Figure 1.2
(p. 6) for text) where it corresponds to Lat *locavit et statuit* 'placed and
established'. The significance of this example is that, as is clear from
the photograph in Lejeune 1985: 199, the verb is the last word of the
inscription and the preceding word has a dative singular ending *-ouei*
/o:i/. The object of the verb may have been a word such as 'monument',
'stone', or simply 'this', or it may have been left unexpressed, as in
Table 9.1 (c). It is unclear, therefore, whether this inscription represents
an SOV order or simply SV. The example in Table 9.1 (b) contains the

TABLE 9.1   Examples of different word order in Gaulish

(a) Lejeune 1985: G-151
   . . . *oueimelikon . . ./. . . liouei*   *karnitou*
                      for X (dat. sg.) verb
   '. . . Y set (this) up for X . . .'
(b) Lejeune 1985: G-13 (see Lambert 1994: 89)
   Eskeggolati   aniateios   immi
   PN (gen. sg.) ?property I am
   'I am the ?property of E.'
(c) Dottin 1920: 162 (see Koch 1983: 183)
   Doiros   Segomari   ieuru Alisanu
   PN (nom. sg.) PN (gen. sg.) verb PN (dat. sg.)
   'D., son of S., dedicated (this) to A.'
(d) Marichal 1988: 14
   sioχti Albanos   panna extra tuθ CCC
   verb   PN (nom. sg.) obj.
   'A. supplied a lot of 300 vessels' (Koch 1985a: 3)

1st singular of the verb 'to be' *immi*, again in final position. In this case the genitive precedes the subject, perhaps as a fronted element (see below for fronting). We may compare the inscription recorded by Whatmough 1970: 496, *geneta imi daga uimpi* 'I am a good and pretty girl', where *daga* and *uimpi* seem to be adjectives agreeing with *geneta* 'girl' (cf. W *geneth*).[1] The graffito from Graufesenque in Table 9.1 (d), on the other hand, shows an initial verb *sioχti* in a sentence whose interpretation is uncertain but seems to display a VSO order.

When one turns to the longer inscriptions of Chamalières and Larzac for guidance about unmarked, standard word order, it is difficult to see what help they might offer (see 1.2.1; for details, see Chapter 1, n. 8). Generally verbs are identifiable but one needs to understand the context in order to establish their position in relation to the other constituents. For example, the first sentence of the Chamalières inscription begins *andedion* (adj. gen. pl.) *uediumi* (verb 1st sg.) *diiiuion* (noun gen. pl.) *ris* (prep.) [*s*]*unartiu* (noun dat. sg.) 'I pray to the good strength of the infernal gods' (for the reading, see Lambert 1987: 13). The verb is preceded by a fronted adjective agreeing with *diiiuion* 'gods' which may be dependent on *sunartiu* (see Koch 1985a: 22–4); the ordering would seem to imply that without fronting the verb would be in initial position. Similarly, in the second clause the verb(s) *lotites snieθθic*, whatever their interpretation (Lambert 1987: 15), again seem to be initial. The Larzac inscription (see Lejeune *et al.* 1985) presents some intriguing collocations. Lambert (in Lejeune *et al.* 1985: 162–3, 169) has wondered whether the forms *lunget-uton-id* and *biontutu*/*biietutu*, which are 3rd sg./pl. verbal forms followed by affixed pronouns, should be interpreted as being in initial position, and thus whether this point could be used as a starting point for interpretation (for arguments about enclitics and word order, see 9.2 below). There is an obvious danger of circularity here; rather than letting the context determine the sense, the difficulty of the context forces one to clutch at the straws of word order as a starting point.

Celtiberian word order, as illustrated by the Botorrita inscription (see 1.2.3), is clearly SOV (Eska 1989a: 176–7), e.g. *uTa ośCues* (subj.) *PouśTom-ue Coŕuinom-ue maCaśi*[*a*]*m-ue ailam-ue* (a list of objects) *amPiTiśeTi* (verb) 'and let him rebuild the cow stable . . ., etc.' (Eska 1989a: 21). However, to assume with Eichner 1989, that all verbs are final and to use this to divide the text into clauses again runs the risk of circularity. Similarly the inscription from Peñalba de Villastar (see Eska 1990a) seems to show a SOV order, provided the verbs *comeimv* and *sistat* have been correctly identified, and taking into account the complicated movement of indirect dative objects.

Inscriptions from Cisalpine Gaul (northern Italy) seem to display a range of different word orders. The bilingual inscription from Todi has a preposed dative and an order . . .VOS, i.e. *Ateknati Trutikni* (dat.)

TABLE 9.2   The Voltino inscription

TETVMVS | SEXTI | DVGIAVA |SAŚADIS |
tomedeclai Obalda natina
Koch 1985a: 24–5: 'I, the monument of Tetumus, son of Sextus, and of
   Dugiava, daughter of Saśadis, Obalda, (their) little daughter, had set me up'
Eska 1989c: 'T, son of S., and D, daughter of S., (are buried here). Obalda,
   (their) little daughter, set me (i.e. the monument) up'

UPPER CASE = 1st century BC Roman script,
lower case = local Lepontic script

karnitu (verb) *artuaš* (obj.) *Coisis Trutiknos* (subj.) 'C., son of Drutos
assembled (these) stones for A., son of D.' (see Figure 1.2 (p. 6) for
further details). It is difficult to come to any conclusions about
unmarked patterns since both initial and final position may be marked;
in other words, we cannot necessarily conclude with Koch 1985a: 19
that the underlying order is **Coisis Trutiknos karnitu artuaš Ategnati
Drutikni.*

As an illustration of the difficulties and potential circularities of
interpretation, the Cisalpine inscription from Voltino raises interesting
questions (see Table 9.2). Koch 1985a: 24–5 takes the inscription as
one sentence, disregarding the change in script. On such an interpretation, *TETVMVS*, etc. is not only fronted but also changes case from
genitive to nominative; the word order may well reflect an underlying
VS(O) but there are major difficulties. Eska's analysis is preferable in
that it pays due attention to the change in script; if it is accepted, it
provides clear evidence for VS(O) with the object pronoun infixed
between preverb and verb in *to-med-eclai* (cf. Old Irish infixed
pronouns, 2.2.6.2 above).

The evidence of Continental Celtic, then, presents a mixed picture,
ranging from SOV to SVO to VSO. As was noted above (9.0), inscriptional evidence of the type discussed here frequently puts a higher
premium on names than on actions; the activities are usually
predictable and formulaic, involving the setting up of tombs, giving
tithes, making dedications, etc. Koch 1985a has attempted to en-
capsulate this preoccupation with names by the application of the
theory of government and binding to these inscriptions. At some points,
this can be a fruitful exercise as it directs attention towards the process
of focus or topicalization of a particular element by bringing it to the
front of the sentence while leaving behind an empty slot. For example,
the Gaulish version of the Todi inscription is schematized by Koch as
in Figure 9.1. In Insular Celtic languages the fronted element might
well be picked up by a resumptive pronoun (see, for example, 3.5.4);
however, in Lepontic (Cisalpine Gaulish) the case endings seem to

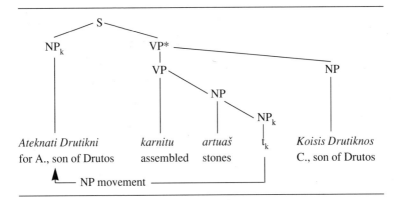

FIGURE 9.1   A schematization of the Todi inscription. See Koch 1985a: 18.

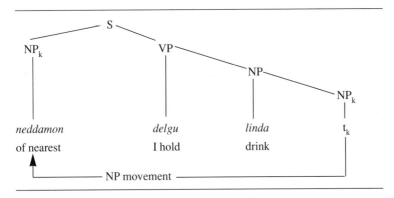

FIGURE 9.2: A schematization of the Banassac graffito. See Koch 1985a: 20.

perform that function (Koch 1985a: 18–19). Another brief example may be helpful. The brief graffito from Banassac reads *neddamon delgu linda* 'I hold the drink of the nearest ones' (see Figure 9.2 for a schematized analysis). Here the genitive plural *neddamon* (cf. W *nessaf* 'nearest') has been fronted; its unmarked position was probably after *linda* (cf. W *llyn* 'liquid'). Again in an Insular Celtic language the gap would be marked by a resumptive possessive pronoun, e.g. W *dyma'r rhai nessaf y daliaf eu diodydd* 'here are those nearest whose drink I hold' (lit. 'here are those nearest I hold their drinks'). The logical conclusion would seem to be that the unmarked version would have been **delgu linda neddamon*. However, Koch seems unwilling to take that step but rather claims that 'given the attested Gaulish preference for V-internal orders, it may be that **delgu linda neddamon* was a stylistically odd sentence' (Koch 1985a: 20). There is a danger here that the range of our evidence, all inscriptional and generally pre-occupied with personal names, could mislead us about what counts as stylistically acceptable or unacceptable, and whether within the language as a whole V-initial sentences were relatively common.

One aspect where Koch does encounter difficulty concerns his quest for cleft sentences in Gaulish. A cleft sentence is a more complicated process of fronting. Essentially it involves the fronting of an element which is marked by the verb 'to be' and the rest of the sentence is part of a relative clause; for example, in English a basic sentence 'the cat crossed the road' can be cleft as 'it was the cat which crossed the road' or as 'it was the road which the cat crossed'. Such patterns are widespread in Old Irish, particularly in the glosses, and common in early Welsh. As part of his attempt to link Continental Celtic patterns to early Brittonic (see 9.1 above), Koch identifies Gaulish *etic* with *eθθic* and derives them from **esti-kʷe* 'and it is'. The outcome is that the second part of the Alise-Sainte-Reine inscription *etic gobedbi* . . . 'and by the smiths . . .' becomes 'and it is by the smiths . . .' (Koch 1985a: 3–7; see Lejeune 1988: 147–55 (L-13), Meid 1992: 29–30). However, both *etic* and *eθθic* occur in the Chamalières inscription and Lambert 1987 has rightly objected to their equation:

> if the writer has written *eθθic* in the third line, and *etic* in the seventh, we are not allowed to suppose that he meant the same word in the two occurrences, unless we find other instances of this graphic variation in the same document. On the contrary, it would be sounder to suppose that he wrote the two words differently because they were different (Lambert 1987: 14).

Gaulish cleft sentences, therefore, remain uncertain and perhaps a figment. What is clear is that Continental Celtic, and particularly Gaulish and Lepontic, seemed to have a very flexible word order to the extent that it is difficult to establish the basic patterns. Koch would seem to prefer it to be, if anything, SV(O), but his own evidence also suggests that a case could be made for VS(O).

9.1.2   Insular Celtic

9.1.2.1 Goidelic

It is clear that the regular order in all the Goidelic languages is VSO and numerous examples have been quoted in Chapters 2 and 3 above. Even so, variation in word order is very common. The regular method of fronting an element is by clefting. We may use the artificial Old Irish example created by Greene 1977: 21 *sligid Níall slógu* 'N. slays hosts'; the range of possible cleft variants is presented in Table 9.3. When the subject or object is fronted as in (b) and (c), there is a special relative form of the verb. But with a fronted prepositional phrase or adverb the verb is non-relative, as in (d). Cleft sentences are very

TABLE 9.3   Cleft sentences in Old Irish

(a)	Basic	*sligid Níall slógu*
		'N. slays hosts'
(b)	Subject fronted	*is Níall sliges slógu*
		'It is N. who slays hosts'
(c)	Object fronted	*it slóig sliges Níall*
		'It is hosts which N. slays'
(d)	Other elements fronted	*is i cath sligid Níall slógu*
		'It is in battle that N. slays hosts'

common in the Old Irish glosses (see 2.1); indeed it is difficult, except in the longer comments, to find any sentences with an initial finite verb. In part, this has to do with the nature of the activity of glossing, which tends to focus on a particular word or phrase. Nevertheless, in some cases it is difficult to detect the precise force of the fronting and there is always a suspicion that it is as much a stylistic device as a marker of focus. Cleft sentences remain common in all stages of the languages as the usual method of topicalization, particularly in the spoken language. It is possible that their frequency in the Old Irish glosses may reflect a different register of language from that presented in literary texts.

Although the patterns from Old Irish onwards are fairly clear, Mac Cana 1973 has shown that at all periods, from the earliest evidence to the present day, other word order patterns, and particularly verb-final order, are permitted. Variant patterns are common in verse. A significant proportion of sentences in Early Modern Irish verse have a final verb which frequently alliterates with the preceding word; for one poem of 172 lines, Greene 1977: 21 has calculated that 10 per cent of the lines has a final verb.

In the earliest Old Irish texts there are similar types of variation which have been discussed at length.[2] Bergin 1934–8 offered one of the earliest discussions of a feature of Archaic Irish word order to which he was to give his name. 'Bergin's Law' is not a law in the usual linguistic sense in that it does not set out a clear linguistic environment in which a certain linguistic feature is predicted to occur; it simply provides a description of a particular pattern of word order which can occur in Archaic Irish but not in Classical Old Irish. Thurneysen 1946: 327 describes it as follows: 'simple and compound verbs may be placed at the end of their clause; the former then have conjunct flexion, the latter proto-tonic forms'. By contrast, the usual initial verb would have absolute flexion, if simplex, and deuterotonic, if compound (see 2.2.6.2 for the terminology). Carney 1977–9: 430–1, however, objected to this formulation on the basis that Bergin's own dictum referred simply to a

TABLE 9.4   Tmesis patterns in Archaic Irish

Tmesis I	(P . . . V (conjunct))
non-relative	* *to- boin -beir* 'he gives a cow'
	ad- cruth caín -cichither
	'fair form will be seen'
relative	* *in fer to- boin -beir*
	'the man who gives a cow'
	comarba liag imma- lann -lig
	'the heir of a gravestone which lies about lands'
Tmesis II	(Neg . . . PV (prototonic))
non-relative	* *ní tarb tabair* 'he does not give a bull'
	ní airged finn -foichmen
	'it cannot tarnish bright silver'
relative	* *in fer nad tarb tabair*
	'the man who does not give a bull'
	fíach na díre -dlig
	'a debt which does not give rise to *díre*'
Tmesis III	(Part (+ copula) . . . PV (prototonic))
	* *ceso tarb tabair* 'though he gives a bull'
	manip fri fasach fuirmider sceo fursantar fír Féne
	'unless the truth of Irish law be fixed and illuminated by
	precedent' (Greene 1977: 24)
Tmesis IV	(. . . (P)V (conjunct/prototonic))
	* *tarb tabair* 'he gives a bull'
(simplex verb)	*brechtaib ban mberar*
	'he is taken by the spells of women'
(compound verb)	*oenchairde fon Eilg n-áragar*
	'one peace treaty is established throughout Ireland'
	(Greene 1977: 24)

P = preverb, V = verb, Neg = negative, Part = particle.
Examples from C. Watkins 1963a: 32–4 unless otherwise indicated.

verb not standing at the head of its clause, and he has shown that there are numerous examples of SVO order in early Irish verse.

A related feature of Archaic Irish verse is the phenomenon known as 'tmesis', namely the separation of a compound verb into preverb and verb;[3] usually the preverb occurs at the beginning of the clause and the verb at the end where it follows the rules of Bergin's Law given above. An important aspect of both types, Bergin's Law and tmesis, is the regular alliteration between final verb and the preceding element. Greene 1977: 24–7 distinguished four types of tmesis formation and exemplified them with an artificial sentence corresponding to Classical Old Irish *do·beir boin/tarb* 'he gives a cow/bull' (the alternation of *boin/tarb* allows the required alliteration to be illustrated. The different types are set out in Table 9.4 and exemplified with variants of this sentence and other real language examples.

Only in Tmesis I is there genuine separation of preverb and verb, but Tmesis II involves a similar pattern, in that the negative and verb is the usual collocation at the beginning of the sentence; in Classical Old Irish we would expect to find *ní·tabair*. Tmesis III contains other types of particle, i.e. conjunctions, etc., but they are combined with the copula. It is important to understand the distinction between this type and the later cleft sentence which would contain a relative form of the verb; the formal correspondents to the examples in Table 9.4 would be in Classical Old Irish respectively *ceso tarb do·beir/do·mbeir* 'although it is a bull which he gives' and *manip fri fasach fo·ruimedar sceo for·osnadar fír Féine* 'unless it be by precedent that the truth of Irish law is fixed and illuminated' (Greene 1977: 24–5). The formal difference is in the form of the verbs, prototonic in a Tmesis III type but relative and deuterotonic in Classical Old Irish. There would, however, have been a difference in emphasis; the Classical Old Irish versions would have placed *tarb* and *fri fasach* in the topic position, while in the Tmesis III type no topicalization seems to be implied. On the other hand, the exact semantic equivalents of the Tmesis III type in Classical Old Irish would be *cía do·beir tarb* 'although he gives a bull' and *mani·fuirmider agus mani·fursantar fír Féine fri fasach* 'unless the truth of Irish law is fixed and illuminated by precedent'. F. Kelly 1986 has raised doubts about the distinction between types II and III, particularly on the grounds that Greene seems to exclude cases of negative and copula as a proper Archaic Irish construction, even though examples seem to be available.

Greene's Tmesis IV type is mis-named in that no tmesis occurs, although it is convenient to have them discussed under the same heading. Essentially, a simplex or compound verb can be found in final, or perhaps better non-initial, position in conjunct or prototonic form; these are the standard Bergin's Law forms. For simplex verbs, using Greene's artificial example from Table 9.3, they are the equivalent of *Níall slógu slig* 'N. slays hosts' with a final conjunct verb. However, the attested examples of simplex verbs in this position seem to show that the pattern is restricted to impersonal *r*-forms of the verb, e.g. *cóic conara fuigill fégaiter* 'five ways of judgement are surveyed', *molad coir canar* 'fitting praise is sung', etc. (Greene 1977: 27–8). Greene also draws attention to a difficulty with these *r*-forms, namely that the conjunct and relative forms in the 3rd person are identical; in theory, then, *cóic conara fuigill fégaiter* could be interpreted as '(there are) five ways of judgement which are surveyed' with the suppression of the copula. This interpretation only works where the preposed element is subject or object. The relative variant of *brechtaib ban mberar* (see Table 9.4), where the preposed element is prepositional, would be *brechtaib ban mberair* (Greene 1977: 28). However, Binchy 1979–80: 42 has argued that the restriction to *r*-forms may be illusory. He draws attention to at least one example of other forms of verbs in that position, such as *demin dom tríathaib tung* 'I swear firmly by my lords' (Binchy 1979–80: 44–5). Moreover, he also suggests that the rhyming patterns in Archaic Irish verse often required a final two or three syllable word. For simplex verbs the easiest way of providing the requisite number of syllables consistent with maintaining the sense of the line would have been to make it impersonal by using an *r*-form (see 2.2.6.3).

Binchy's observations touch upon important questions. As will be discussed and illustrated in 9.2, the verb-final patterns considered above have been thought to represent historically older word order patterns which have been preserved in the archaic poetical styles of language. The underlying assumption is that poetical language can preserve older features of the language than contemporaneous prose which is thought somehow to be a closer reflection of the contemporary spoken language. A number of difficulties arise if we are to take this as a blanket assumption.

First, there is a textual difficulty in that the manuscripts in which these apparently archaic patterns occur are often to be dated to as late as the 14th or 15th centuries. The possibility of scribal corruption must always, therefore, be taken into account. For example, the alternation between absolute *berair* and conjunct/relative *berar* is a tiny stroke beside the standard abbreviation for *ar*, which was *q* with a cross stroke on the descender, and could easily disappear. Moreover, archaic prototonic forms in sentence-final position could be a scribal modernization of a deuterotonic relative form; in 2.2.6.2 above it was shown that a widespread Middle Irish strategy for eliminating the absolute/conjunct distinction was to generalize a verbal stem based on the prototonic form of a compound verb. In some cases there would be potential for confusion (see, for example, Binchy 1979–80: 46, n. 1).

Secondly, as was noted briefly above in 9.0, in early Irish it is very difficult in some cases to distinguish verse from prose. There is material which is clearly verse, with a fixed number of syllables per line and a strict rhyming and alliterative pattern. There are also clear examples of prose. But there is an important grey area of alliterative, semi-metrical material which does not follow a strict metrical scheme but shows strong alliterative patterns, which is known as *rosc*. The verb-final word order patterns occur in verse and in this alliterative, semi-metrical prose but not in simpler prose registers. This intermediate style has generally been supposed to be old because it shows archaic patterns. However, Breatnach 1984 has demonstrated that some passages of *rosc* in the difficult *Bretha Nemed* collection of texts are based on excerpts from the Latin ecclesiastical text *Collectio Canonum Hibernensium*. The conclusion is that poets were capable of archaizing to a far greater extent than has previously been supposed, and that they were able to produce an archaic-looking version of material beside a Classical Old Irish version. This discovery has a number of ramifications; for example, the archaic verse sections of law tracts need not be supposed to contain the most legally archaic material. Similarly, an archaic-looking poem containing references to Christianity and Christian learning, such as the *Amra Choluim Chille* (Stokes 1899), should not necessarily be analysed as having an archaic core with later Christian accretions; the poem could be all of a piece, whether early or late.[4]

Thirdly, there is a danger that discussions which have focused on the origins of these verb-final patterns have tended to allow the conclusions to be driven in a certain direction. As will be seen in 9.2, views about the Indo-European background of these patterns have focused on the verb final examples and have rejected as artificial any formations which do not fit those views. A particular case in point is a group of verbal forms from the poem *Amra Choluim Chille*, which consist of a final absolute verb with a suffixed pronoun (see 2.2.6.2 above) which refers back to the stated nominal object, e.g. *libru Solman sexus* 'he followed the books of Solomon' (lit. 'the books of S., he followed them') (Stokes 1899: 254). It is generally interpreted as 'a blend of two constructions' (Thurneysen 1946: 327), the Bergin's Law final verb and the *nominativus pendens* (preposed nominative) construction (see 9.1.2.2 for a fuller discussion; see also Greene 1977: 29–30, Binchy 1979–80: 47). The point is that they are regarded as artificial because they do not fit the proposed scheme of things. They are not *per se* any more or less artificial than any other verb-final pattern considered here. Since it is clear that poets/scribes were capable of producing archaizing structures at any point in the Old Irish period, any verb-final pattern would have been an artificial construct. The question of which types reflect genuinely historical patterns is a separate question which should not influence our views of their position in the linguistic system of Archaic Irish.

The prevailing tenor of scholarship sees a link between these forms and patterns of SOV in other non-Celtic Indo-European languages. However, if one puts that view to one side for the present, it may be interesting briefly to explore other options. Wagner 1967 and 1977 was a major proponent of a sub-stratum theory which linked apparent non-Indo-European peculiarities in Celtic languages with Semitic languages, notably Berber, Egyptian and Arabic. Binchy 1979–80 has strongly rejected this approach in terms of its application to word order. Nevertheless, even if one rejects any form of substratum theory, it might be possible to argue that the use of verb-final patterns in Archaic Irish was maintained through the influence of Latin word order patterns. Recent views about the knowledge of Latin in early Ireland (see

6.3.2.5) suggest that there was a sophisticated degree of Latin literacy at a very early period. It might be argued, therefore, that an inherited pattern of verb final sentences was preserved by the influence of Latin. It is perhaps unlikely that the pattern was initiated from Latin but it could have helped continue a native pattern for a little longer. There are, however, substantial objections to this view, such as why the pattern should have died out except in obscure verse when the influence of Latin was, if anything, greater in the later Old Irish period than in the earlier. Even so, it is worth exploring possibilities which have generally been put to one side in the eagerness to demonstrate that the patterns are not only archaizing but genuinely archaic.

The bulk of this discussion of Goidelic has focused on the abnormalities of Archaic Irish word order. But it is important to recall that the overwhelmingly regular word order not only in Irish but also in Scottish Gaelic and Manx is VSO.

9.1.2.2   Brittonic

Word order in Modern Welsh has been discussed above (5.5.1) where it was shown that the predominant order is VSO, though elements can be fronted for topicalization in cleft sentences. Fife 1991 has shown that Classical Welsh, notionally Welsh from the 15th to the early 19th centuries (Fife 1991: 252), shows a similar predominance of verb initial clauses and, he claims, a move away from the predominant word order patterns of Middle Welsh. We encounter here one of the vexed problems of Welsh word order studies. As will emerge below, it seems that the predominant order in Old Welsh and Modern Welsh is VSO with appropriate variation for purposes of topicalization. However, Middle Welsh shows substantial differences with a significant preference for an unmarked order with an initial subject. If one opts to treat the development of Welsh word order in a linear fashion, it is necessary to account for the changes both from Old Welsh to Middle Welsh and from Middle Welsh to Modern Welsh, and in the latter case for changes which already seem to be in place by the 16th century. On the other hand, it may be possible to see the Middle Welsh patterns as a regional development, perhaps to be associated with similar patterns in Cornish and Breton (Mac Cana 1973). The following discussion will, therefore, consider Old Welsh first and then move on to Middle Welsh and comparison with the word order patterns of Cornish and Breton.

T. A. Watkins 1987 has examined the exiguous remains of continuous Old Welsh (for Old Welsh sources, see 4.1.1). It emerges very clearly from his discussion that VSO is the basic word order (see Table 9.5) but also that fronting of non-verbal constituents occurs fairly frequently. The basic order is found in verse as well as in prose. One standard variation is when the object is pronominal and is infixed before the verb (see Table 9.6 (b) for an example and also 5.3.5; cf.

TABLE 9.5   Examples of VSO in Old Welsh

Prose

VS	*agit eterin illud* 'that bird goes'
	retit loyr 'the moon runs'
V(S = pronoun)O	*diprotant gener tutri*
	'they dispossess T.'s son-in-law'
	tarnetor ir loc guac
	'the empty space is reckoned'
	(lit. 'there is a reckoning the space empty')
VSO	*imguodant i'r degion guragun tagc*
	'the nobles declared "let us make peace"'
	rodesit elcu . . . equs
	'Elgu gave . . . a horse'

Verse

V(S = pronoun)	*niguarcosam* 'I shall not boast'
	ceinmicun 'let us extol'
V(S = pronoun)O	*cet iben med* 'though we drink mead'
VSO	*nitarcup betid . . . tibertudou*
	'the world does not express . . . miracles'

For references to texts, see T. A. Watkins 1987: 53–4.

TABLE 9.6   Subject and object fronting in Old Welsh

(a) Relative (relative markers indicated in bold)
*is did ciman **ha** ci*
'it is a full day you will have'

*is aries is**id** in arcimeir*
'it is Aries that is opposite'

*[is] salt **emmi**-guollig hinnith*
'[it is] the Saltus which prevents that'

(b) Non-relative (resumptive pronoun indicated in bold)
*grefiat . . . **nis**-minn Tutbulc*
'a document of title . . . T. does not need [it]'

*ir pimphet eterin . . . hegit **hunnoid***
'the 5th bird . . . that one goes'

2.2.6.2 for the Old Irish situation). Examples of subject and object fronting are relatively rare but five examples are presented in Table 9.6. Two types are found; a relativized fronting where the fronted element is preceded by the copula and the verb is then marked as relative. The absence of the copula *is* before *salt* may be an error, or an early example of the deletion of the copula in relative order sentences (see T. A. Watkins 1987: 55, 59). The other type (Table 9.6 (b)) has neither copula nor relative verb but usually has a resumptive pronoun. The preposing of adverbial elements is relatively rare in Old Welsh but, when it occurs, the verb is not marked in any way, e.g. *ho diued diprotant* 'at last they deprive', *is cihun agit eterin illud* 'it is for the same amount that the bird goes'. In conclusion, the Old Welsh material shows a basic VSO but with fronting; however, elements can be fronted with or without relativization. The evidence is too exiguous to explore at length the question of stylistic choice between these variants, but T. A. Watkins 1987: 57–9 draws attention to factors such as sentence type and the stylistic category of the passage. For example, he notes that questions containing interrogative pronouns are always relative, as are answers to them, e.g. OW *pa sseren pigurth[r]et loyr? . . . ir seren hai bu in arcimeir o* 'which is the star to which the moon runs opposite? . . . the star which was facing *o*'. Moreover, the factual court record of the 'Surexit' Memorandum regularly tends to have verb-initial sentences, except for *grefiat . . . nis-minn Tutbulc* (see Table 9.6 (b)), where the object is topicalized as a new item in the discussion. On the other hand, the Computus fragment (a fragment of Old Welsh on the Latin computus) is didactic and therefore contains all kinds of contrastive devices and explanatory statements; not surprisingly it only contains three verb initial sentences and all are negative. Negation is an important factor in maintaining verb-initial patterns; it is striking that in Middle Welsh prose where verb-initial patterns are rare, the majority of cases are found in negative sentences (T. A. Watkins 1990).

Middle Welsh presents a very different picture. For the present we shall concentrate on prose; verse presents an even more complex picture which will be considered below. The most striking aspect of Middle Welsh word order is the relative rarity of verb initial patterns in declarative sentences.[5] There are two basic patterns found regularly in Middle Welsh prose, known traditionally but misleadingly as the 'abnormal' and 'mixed' order. Details of the two patterns are presented in Table 9.7. 'Abnormal' is a misnomer; it is by far the most common pattern in Middle Welsh (for examples, see T. A. Watkins 1988, Poppe 1989, etc.). It is, however, abnormal in relation to the usual patterns in Modern Welsh. Several aspects of these patterns are worthy of note. The 'abnormal' order in Middle Welsh does not convey any particular sense of emphasis, contrast or focus, while the 'mixed' type functions like any fronted clause in Old or Modern Welsh and marks the topic or focus of the sentence.

Formally, the two types are distinguished in three ways (see Table 9.7 (c)). First, the position of the negative is different; it is placed before the verb in the 'abnormal' order but initially before the preposed element in the 'mixed' type. Secondly, the early form of the 'mixed' order had a form of the copula before the preposed element, forming a standard cleft sentence with a following relative clause. Originally, the

TABLE 9.7   'Abnormal' and 'mixed' word order in Middle Welsh

(a) Abnormal (D. S. Evans 1964: 179–81)

Positive	subj./obj. + *a/ry/yr* + verb
	Gwydion y gerdwys yn y blaen
	'G. travelled in the fore-front'
	A'r gwyrda a doethant y gyt
	'and the nobles came together'
Negative	subj./obj. + neg. + verb
	y dyn ny doeth 'the man did not come'

(b) Mixed (D. S. Evans 1964: 140–1)

(i)	Positive	copula + noun + *a/y* + verb
		ys mi a'e heirch 'It is I who seek her'
		oed maelgwn a uelun in imuan
		'it was M. I could see fighting'
	Negative	neg. + copula + noun + *a/y* + verb
		Ny bu hir y buant yny doethant y Arberth
		'not long were they before they came to A.'
(ii)	Positive	noun + *a/y* + verb
		Mi a'e heirch '(it is) I who seek her'
		Kimri a oruit
		'(it shall be) the Welsh who shall conquer'
	Negative	neg. + copula + noun + *a/y* + verb
		Nyt tydi a gredaf 'it is not you I believe'

(c) Distinguishing features

	Abnormal	Mixed (i)	Mixed (ii)
Negative	before vb	initial	initial
Copula	–	+	–
Agreement of subject and verb	+	–	–

copula agreed with the relative clause verb in tense and mood but gradually the 3rd singular present *ys* was generalized irrespective of the tense of the other verb. The final stage was complete loss of the copula (see Table 9.7 (b) (ii)). At this point some 'mixed' order patterns, where the fronted element was singular, were indistinguishable from the 'abnormal' type. In other cases, they remained distinct by virtue of the third distinguishing feature, the difference in the rules of agreement. In 'abnormal' sentences there is agreement between the initial subject and the following verb, i.e. a plural subject requires a plural verb, etc. but in the 'mixed' order the verb is regularly the unmarked 3rd singular and does not agree in number or person.

In contrast, therefore, to Old Welsh and later Welsh, the unmarked word order in Middle Welsh prose declarative sentences was the so-called 'abnormal' sentence, while the 'mixed' type is used for the marked patterns of topicalization, focus, etc. Although the 'abnormal' pattern is generally thought to be unemphatic, Mac Cana 1973: 100–9 has drawn attention to a number of cases where fronted elements do convey some sort of emphasis, especially in responses, explanations and emotional expressions in prayers, blessings, etc. This aspect will be considered below. It is also worth reinforcing the point that in negative sentences the verb tends to revert to initial position following the negative particle (T. A. Watkins 1990).

Mac Cana 1973: 113–20 has argued that we need not attempt to build these patterns into a linear account of Welsh word order. He would prefer to see them as a literary pattern which has dialectal affiliations with south-east Wales (see also Mac Cana 1979–80, 1991); he notes the existence even in modern south-east dialects of forms such as *ni welsom* 'we saw', *nw ethon* 'they went', *ti golli* 'you lose', etc. where the order is [subject pronoun + verb] (C. H. Thomas 1973–4: 271–3). Strong support is adduced from the patterns of Cornish and Breton where SVO is regular with pronoun subjects. Koch 1991, however, suggests:

> it is possible that the abnormal order (with or without concord) was a pan-Brittonic innovation (slow to rise out of the spoken language to impress itself on the literary styles of Wales) which then collapsed in Early Modern W (but not in CB) in all dialects except for that of the far Southwest (where it survives with subject pronouns only) (Koch 1991: 20).

There is certainly a strong presumption that the pattern of [subject pronoun + verb] had a wider currency, e.g. *mi a welais* 'I saw', etc., since it lies behind the Modern Welsh usage of *mi* and *fe* as pre-sentential particles (see 5.5.2.3 above) but it does not necessarily mean that it was a pan-Welsh feature.

Recent work on Middle Welsh dialectology suggests that the range of features can expand and contract considerably between the Middle Welsh period and the present day. Moreover, to compare Middle Welsh literary texts with Modern Welsh colloquial usage is not necessarily very helpful. P. W. Thomas 1989: 295–9 has shown, for example, that the Middle Welsh 3rd singular preterite ending *-ws* /us/ was originally more widespread, though perhaps not common in the north, but its range has shrunk to the south-east dialects with the rise of the -/auð/, -/oð/ ending. On the other hand, he has shown that the presence or absence of /i̯/ in suffixes in Middle Welsh more or less corresponds to the modern dialectal distribution (P W Thomas 1989: 292–4, 1993: 26–8; see also Russell 1990: 39–60); here, however, the modern literary language tends to follow the northern pattern and use /i̯/. The lesson to be drawn from this for our present purposes is that features could have been more widespread or more narrowly confined at earlier stages of the language but that the evidence needs careful scrutiny to determine whether the precise distribution can be established.

One difficulty with Koch's view has to do with the supposed loss of SVO order in all dialects except the south-east. The work of Fife 1991 on Classical Welsh suggests that the SVO type must have disappeared remarkably rapidly so that by the 16th century the patterns were far more similar to Old and Modern Welsh. An important aspect of Fife's work is that he has narrowed down the time span of the *floruit* of Middle Welsh word order patterns. However, no one has yet come up with a satisfactory scheme of how the Middle Welsh patterns developed into the Classical Welsh patterns. The problem is resolved if we assume with Mac Cana that the basic VSO pattern co-existed in Middle Welsh with a south-east dialectal SVO pattern which, for whatever reasons, acquired literary status.

Questions concerning the origin of the pattern are examined below. But it may be appropriate at this point to consider word order patterns in Cornish and Breton. The geographical significance of the preservation of an SVO order in modern south-east Wales is that SVO seems to be the basic pattern in Cornish and Breton. George 1991 has shown that in the Middle Cornish play *Beunans Meriasek* (Stokes 1872) the commonest word order patterns are those presented in Table 9.8. There is an important distinction between positive and negative sentences. Only

TABLE 9.8   The commonest word order patterns in main clause statements in the Middle Cornish Beunans Meriasek

Object	Subject	
	Pronoun	Noun
(None)	*my a wel*	*an den a wel*
	'I see'	'the man sees'
	ny welav	*ny wel an den*
	'I do not see'	'the man does not see'
Pronoun	*my a's gwel*	*an den a's gwel*
	'I see it'	'the man sees it'
	ny's gwelav	*ny's gwel an den*
	'I do not see it'	'the man does not see it'
Noun	*my a wel an gath*	*an den a wel an gath*
	'I see the cat'	'the man sees the cat'
	ny welav an gath	*ny wel an den an gath*
	'I do not see the cat'	'the man does not see the cat'

After George 1991: 248.

TABLE 9.9   Word order patterns in Modern Breton

(a) *Tali 'zo traou hir*	'Tali are long things'
(b) *Ar re-se 'zo hir*	'Those are long'
(c) *Ar re-se 'zo ruz neuse*	'Those are red, then'
(d) *Bremañ e vezont sec' het*	'Now they are dried'

After Timm 1991: 285–6.

in the positive forms is the order SVO; the negative form reverts to
VSO.

While Old Cornish offers no evidence for word order, Old Breton
can provide examples of VSO, e.g. *es* (verb) *guel Argia hacet he guoer*
'A. is superior to her sister' and SVO, e.g. *ir doublidan a int* . . . 'the
two years are . . .' (Fleuriot 1964: 412–13). Timm 1989 and 1991 has
considered Modern Breton word order and concludes that statistically it
remains a VS(O) language despite the frequency of SV(O): 'about 1.8
times as many VS as SV clauses in main clauses, and about 2.5 times
as many VS as SV clauses in the count that included subordinate plus
main clauses' (Timm 1991: 280). She argues that the SV(O) pattern is
not unmarked but performs important pragmatic functions of marking
topic and focus. She includes a number of functions, such as responses
to questions which Mac Cana would acknowledge are emphatic, but
she also considers the use of fronted pronouns as topic continuers and
foci which 'are drawn on frequently to keep a topic going, and suggest
the continuing relevance of a given topic or theme in the speaker's
mind as the conversation unfolds' (Timm 1991: 285). She quotes the
conversation about seaweed collecting given in Table 9.9 as an
example of topic continuation. The pronominal phrase *ar re-se* 'those'
in sentences (b) and (c) is used without stress simply to keep the topic
going, while the new information *hir* and *ruz* is introduced in the
comment. In (d) the initial slot is filled by the adverb, while the topic is
only marked by the 3rd plural verb marker. A similar analysis by Poppe
1989 on a Middle Welsh tale has come to similar conclusions and it is
beginning to look as if the Middle Welsh patterns may not be as neutral
and unmarked as they first appear.

So far we have avoided two matters which some have argued are
inter-related, the word order patterns in Middle Welsh verse and the
question of the origin of the noun-initial pattern in Middle Welsh prose.
We may consider briefly the range of word order patterns attested in
early Welsh verse. H. Lewis 1942 was one of the first to draw attention
to a range of sentences with different orders in early Welsh verse (see
Table 9.10 for example). These sentences were used by Lewis, and subsequently by Koch 1988 and 1991, to argue that the SVO order in
Middle Welsh is a direct historical development from the SVO patterns

TABLE 9.10   Variant word order patterns in early Welsh verse

VOS

(a) *dygystud deurud dagreu*
      afflict   cheeks tears
      'tears afflict cheeks'

SV(O)

(b) *byssed brych   briwant barr*
      fingers speckled smash   head
      'the fingers of the speckled one smash heads'

(c) *Saeson   syrthyn*
      English fall
      'Englishmen fall'

(d) *Dewi differwys y   eglwysseu*
      PN   defended   his churches
      'Dewi defended his churches'

SOV

(e) *meiryon   eu   tretheu dychynnullyn*
      stewards their taxes   collect
      'stewards collect their taxes'

SO(pro)V

(f) *Duw am differo*
      God me deliver
      'May God deliver me'

See H. Lewis 1942: 22–4, T. A. Watkins 1987: 51.

attested in Gaulish, and indeed Koch would see the pattern as even more ancient (see 9.2). Koch 1991: 17–19 argues that the so-called 'abnormal' order acquired its Middle Welsh form by analogical remodelling from the relative clause pattern (the 'mixed' order). As they stand, the 'abnormal' sentences have a particle *a* in them. Koch argues that an example such as *Duw am difero* originally contained a syllabic form of the pronoun 'me', namely *am*, which was reanalysed as *a* + *m*, thus leading to the spread of *a* in the abnormal pattern. Substantial objections can be raised against this argument. At present we shall concentrate on those which concern Welsh. Mac Cana 1991: 49–51 (and elsewhere) has expressed considerable disquiet at the use of the evidence of verse for word order patterns. T. A. Watkins 1987: 52 makes the observation that the number of non-VSO sentences is insignificant in comparison with the number of VSO sentences in Middle Welsh. Moreover, such examples as *Duw am differo* (Table 9.10 (f)) are obviously relative, while in *Dewi differwys* . . . (Table 9.10

(d)) the relative marker may have been incorporated between the preverb and the verbal stem, as in OW *emmi-guollig* and regularly in Old Irish deuterotonic verbal forms.

As an alternative, Mac Cana 1973, 1990a, 1991 has argued that the SVO pattern may have arisen from an extension of the common *nominativus pendens* construction attested both in early Irish and in early Welsh, where the subject or object is fronted without any clear relative marker. Frequently, a resumptive pronoun refers back to the initial element. Mac Cana 1991: 62–72 argues that the 'abnormal' construction may have arisen from a combination of factor involving topicalization and focus together with cases where there was genuine contrast and emphasis. In contrast to Koch, who with Lewis claims it to be an archaism, Mac Cana sees it as a relatively recent development in southern Brittonic dialects which gained a particular literary significance in Middle Welsh by virtue of being the dialect of the composers of the earliest of the prose tales. In his view, therefore, the basic word order in Welsh remained at all periods VSO. Timm 1989 and 1991 similarly sees SVO order in Breton as secondary to a basic VSO.

There are important methodological considerations here. The matter of the uncertainties of word order in verse needs no reiteration. T. A. Watkins 1987 (and elsewhere) has emphasized the importance of considering all types of speech act before arriving at sweeping conclusions about word order. For example, though Middle Welsh positive sentences may be regularly SVO, negative sentences and subordinate clause patterns may ultimately be more revealing about the basic patterns.

9.2   The historical background

Until recently there was only one theory on offer which attempted to account for the development of word order in Celtic languages from the Indo-European situation, that of C. Watkins 1963a and 1964. However, in recent years Koch 1978, 1991 has offered us another approach. Any discussion of the origin of Celtic VSO patterns inevitably becomes tangled up with the question of absolute and conjunct verbal inflection in Old Irish (see 2.2.6.2 and 4.2.6). The aim here is to consider the matter from the point of view of word order leaving aside details specific to the absolute and conjunct question.

One difficulty about comparing the merits of these two theories is that they do not start from the same premisses. Both start from ideas about reconstructed word order patterns of Indo-European but the ideas are different. For Watkins, the basic word order of Indo-European was clearly SOV, to be reconstructed on the evidence of Latin, Hittite and Indo-Iranian (C. Watkins 1964). On the other hand, Koch 1987 takes the view that the word order and accentual patterns found in Vedic (the

TABLE 9.11   Patterns of verbal accent in Vedic

(a)	Unaccented main clause verb:
	agním īḷe puróhitam
	'I praise Agni, the domestic priest'
(b)	Accented main clause verb in initial position:
	hváyāmi *agním prathamám . . .*
	'I praise Agni first . . .'
(c)	Accented subordinate clause verb
	índraś ca **mṛḷáyāti** *no . . .*
	'if Indra be gracious to us . . .'
(d)	Unaccented main clause 'compound' verb
	pári spáśo ní **sedire**
	'the spies have sat down around . . .'
	úpa prá **yāhi**
	'come forth'
(e)	Accented subordinate clause 'compound' verb
	yád . . . **nisī́** *dathah*
	'when you two sit down'
	yó gā́ **udā́jad**
	'who drove the cows out . . .'

See Macdonell 1916: 466–8; verbs are indicated in bold.

oldest of the Indo-Iranian languages) reflects the Indo-European situation most accurately. In Vedic, a finite verb in a main clause is accented only if it stands at the head of the clause, but in subordinate clauses all verbs are accented (see Table 9.11 for examples). Where a preverb is present in a main clause it is accented and treated as a separate element from the verb even if it immediately precedes it (see Table 9.11 (d)). But in a subordinate clause the preverb and verb usually form a single unit in which the verb carries the accent. Tmesis, the separation and joining of preverbs and verbs, is common to a number of Indo-European languages; Archaic Irish examples are discussed above (9.1.2.1) but it also occurs in Greek and Archaic Latin as well as Vedic.

For Koch, the pattern of unaccented main verb is crucial for his view of Celtic developments. In his view an unaccented verb would follow the dictates of Wackernagel's Law (see 1.4.2.2 above) and go into second position in its clause. Removed to a Celtic context, he sees this pattern reflected in the dominant SVO pattern he would wish to reconstruct for Gaulish, early Welsh and early Irish (see above). He would, therefore, see the creation of initial patterns in Welsh and Irish as relatively late developments (see 2.2.6.2 above). We have seen that it is very doubtful whether an SVO pattern can be seen as basic for any stage of Celtic; in Gaulish SVO is only one of a number of attested patterns and Celtiberian shows a clear SOV pattern. In Welsh and Irish it is attested in early verse and considerable reservations have been expressed above about the relevance of word order patterns attested in verse for the reconstruction of basic types of word order.

Moreover, doubts may be raised about earlier stages of the argument. Koch's assumption is that the Vedic pattern of unaccented main clause verb beside an accented verb in subordinate clauses exactly continued the Indo-European pattern. A strong argument against an enclitic unaccented verb is precisely the appeal to Wackernagel's Law made by Koch for the verb in Celtic. For, if the verb was unaccented, we would expect to see it regularly occurring in second position in other Indo-European languages apart from Celtic, but, to judge from the evidence of Vedic, Hittite, Homeric Greek and Latin, the normal position for the verb was at the end of the clause with the option also of initial position as a marked alternative. Where a verb does appear in the middle of a sentence, it can generally be shown that the sentence is 'amplified', i.e. it is syntactically complete down to the verb and the remaining elements add further information such as prepositional phrases, indirect objects, adverbs, etc. (for the notion of 'amplification', see Gonda 1959, and also McCone 1979b). It would appear, then, that the Indo-European verb did not necessarily behave like an enclitic and therefore the loss of verbal accent in main clauses in Vedic is perhaps a later development. However, the unique accentual pattern of Greek verbs can also be explained as arising from an original unaccented verb. If this is not a common Indo-European inheritance it would suggest that at least the conditions under which both Greek and Vedic shifted the verbal accent onto a preverb must have already arisen at the stage of late Indo-European; the conditions are at the very least a tendency towards univerbation of preverb and verb into one unit (Kuryłowicz 1958: 93–5, 151–5). But the actual shift to unaccented verbs seems to have been an independent innovation in Greek and Vedic, that is, a similar but not identical response to similar conditions; the response is not identical because Greek does not show any variation between main and subordinate clauses.

The foundation, then, of Koch's arguments is less secure than might appear (see also Lindeman 1992). The evidence of other Indo-European languages strongly suggests that the basic order from which we may suppose the Celtic word order to have developed was SOV. C. Watkins 1963a, 1964 took this as a starting point and argued that it was possible in late Indo-European to find the sentence types set out in Table 9.12. Verb-final order was the unmarked order but initial verb could be used to mark focus or emphasis (as in Table 9.12 (a) and (b)). Compound verbs could be placed finally where verb and preverb(s) formed one accentual unit, as in (c). An alternative and perhaps older pattern would have been the tmesis type, as in (d); such a pattern might well have

TABLE 9.12   Sentence types in Proto-Celtic

(a)	#... 'V#
(b)	#'VE ... #
(c)	#... 'P(P$_2$)V#
(d)	#'PE ... '(P$_2$)V# (> #PE'(P$_2$)V ... #)
(e)	#'C(E) ... '(P)V# (> #'C(E)'(P)V ... #)

V = verb, E = enclitic, P = preverb, ' = stress, C = conjunction, () = optional element.

All five types are attested in early Old Irish; for examples, see 9.1.2.1.

occurred when the preverb was used to carry an unaccented enclitic particle, which was required by Wackernagel's Law to go in second position in the sentence. Type (e) in Table 9.12 is a variant of (c), where a conjunction (including negatives) rather than a preverb was used to carry the enclitic. The crucial shift was 'univerbation' of all the types where preverb and verb were separated. It is clear that univerbation was a gradual process which seems to have begun in late Indo-European but proceeded slowly and the final stages were not completed until after the separation of most of the language groups (Russell 1988e: 163–4). The univerbation of types (c) and (e) seem to have been completed at a relatively early stage. The final univerbation of the tmesis types probably occurred within Celtic itself and possibly within Italic; for in both language groups there are surviving examples of tmesis patterns in archaic material (for Irish, see 9.1.2.1 above). In Italic, or at least in Latin, the second univerbation brought the tmesis type into line with the pre-existing compound verbs. Uniquely in Celtic, however, univerbation brought the verb to the front of the sentence to join with the preverb. The direction of univerbation seems to have been determined by the particular refinement of Wackernagel's Law, known as Vendryes' Restriction (see 1.4.2.2), which operated in Celtic, whereby enclitics should remain in second position but be embedded in verbs or attached to simplex verbs. Types (d) and (e) in Table 9.12 were 'univerbated' forwards to the front of the sentence, conforming to the pre-existing marked type (b). At this point, the markedness of initial verbs would probably have become lost, since the motivation for fronting was no longer only for marking. At a later stage still, types (a) and (c) would have conformed to the widespread pattern. McCone 1979a has claimed that the univerbation of type (d) produced a different accentual pattern, namely the PE'V pattern in contrast to the 'PV type, and that this with refinements was the origin of the deutero-tonic and prototonic distinction in Old Irish verbs (see 2.2.6.2).

This pattern of development gains support from another aspect of compound verb morphology. Russell 1988c, 1988e has shown that a curious distribution of preverbs with and without -*s* in Old Irish, and probably in Brittonic, can be accounted for within the pattern of word order changes discussed above. For example, Old Irish shows an alternation in the form of the preverb between deuterotonic *fris·gair* 'he answers' (< *u̯rits-gar-*) and prototonic *·frecair* (< *u̯rit-gar-*) (Russell 1988e: 160). The -*s* can be compared with various *s*-markers in other Indo-European languages which mark adverbs, prepositions and preverbs. It seems that particularly in western Indo-European languages, preverbs or adverbs which remained independent of the verb, possibly because they were in initial position, as in type (d) in Table 9.12, were marked with -*s*, while those which were amalgamated with verbs in late Indo-European were not so marked. According to the scheme outlined above by Watkins and McCone, the *s*-marked preverbs were subsequently 'univerbated' to produce Old Irish deuterotonic forms, while prototonic forms represented the outcome of earlier univerbation, thus neatly accounting for the observable distribution of preverbs with and without -*s* (Russell 1988e: 163–4). Similar arguments can be used to explain the preverbs marked with -*s* in Latin.

The theory of C. Watkins 1963a, 1964 does have considerable explanatory power and does start from a more coherent view of the Indo-European background. Nevertheless, it does in part depend on taking the Archaic Irish tmesis forms as representatives of an archaic pattern, even if the attested example are part of an archaizing tradition (see 9.1.2.1). However, in defence of the tmesis pattern, it has to be said that they do not stand on a par with other aberrant word order patterns, such as SVO, VOS or SOV, which can be justified on the basis of rhyme or emphasis, or the like. If the tmesis pattern is not archaic, it is difficult to see how it could have arisen independently in Irish. The possibility of Latin influence as tentatively canvassed above (9.1.2.1) as an alternative source of influence for verb-final patterns. But, even though a few cases of tmesis are attested in Archaic Latin, they would not have occurred in any of the Latin with which the Irish came into contact. There seems to be little option, therefore, but to regard them as archaisms.

Notes

1. Koch 1985a 14–15 suggests that *geneta* has been fronted from its 'underlying' position 'in the post-verbal predicate'; it is not clear how he can be sure that this is its underlying position.
2. For the earliest statement on the word order patterns in Archaic Irish, see Bergin 1934–8; the question has been taken further by C. Watkins 1963a, Greene 1977, Binchy 1979–80, F. Kelly 1986. For a more critical approach, see Wagner 1967, 1977. See also Carney 1977–9, 1989.

3. 'Tmesis' (lit. 'cutting') is not a very helpful term as it implies the pre-existence of a compound verb which undergoes splitting or 'cutting'. However, as will emerge, it is not clear that in historical terms we should think of the process as one of splitting but rather as one of joining separate elements.

4. There has been considerable discussion on the possibility of distinguishing in Ireland a pre-Christian and pagan society from the later Christian society; for a strong anti-nativist view, see McCone 1990.

5. The literature on Middle Welsh word order is extensive. For general discussions, see H. Lewis 1942, Mac Cana 1973, 1979–80, 1990a, 1991, T. A. Watkins 1977–8b, Poppe 1991a, Fife 1988, Fife and King 1991. Several studies focus on particular texts; see T. A. Watkins 1983–4 (*Branwen*), 1988 and 1990 (*Kulhwch ac Olwen*), Poppe 1989 (*Breudwyt Macsen*), 1990 (*Breudwyt Ronabwy*), 1991b (*Cyfranc Lludd a Llefelys*), 1993 (*Kedymdeithas Amlyn ac Amic*). For early verse, see Koch 1988 and 1991.

References

Abbreviations of periodical titles used below:

BBCS	Bulletin of the Board of Celtic Studies
CMCS	Cambridge Medieval Celtic Studies (vols. 1–25), Cambrian Medieval Celtic Studies (vols. 26–)
EC	Etudes celtiques
JCeltL	Journal of Celtic Linguistics
NLWJ	National Library of Wales Journal
NTS	Norsk Tidsskrift for Sprogvidenskap
PBA	Proceedings of the British Academy
PHCC	Proceedings of the Harvard Celtic Colloquium
PRIA	Proceedings of the Royal Irish Academy (Section C)
SC	Studia Celtica
SGS	Scottish Gaelic Studies
TPhS	Transactions of the Philological Society
RC	Revue celtique
ZCP	Zeitschrift für celtische Philologie

AITCHISON, J., CARTER, H. (1994) *A Geography of the Welsh Language.* University of Wales Press

ALLEN, W. S. (1974) *Vox Graeca. The Pronunciation of Classical Greek* 2nd edn. Cambridge University Press

ALLEN, W. S. (1978) *Vox Latina. The Pronunciation of Classical Latin* 2nd edn. Cambridge University Press

ANDERSEN, H. (ed) (1986) *Sandhi Phenomena in the Languages of Europe.* Mouton de Gruyter, Berlin (Trends in Linguistics, Studies and Monographs, 33)

ANDERSON, A. O., ANDERSON, M. O. (eds) (1991) *Adomnán's Life of Columba* revised edn. Oxford University Press (Oxford Medieval Texts)

ANDERSON, S. R. (1981) Topicalization in Breton. *Proceedings of the Berkeley Linguistics Society* **7**: 27–39

ANDREWS, R. M. (1994) Review of King 1993. *JCeltL* **3**: 165–9

ARMSTRONG, J. (1987–8) On some Middle Welsh relative constructions. *SC* **22-23**: 10–28

AWBERY, G. M. (1976) *The Syntax of Welsh. A Transformational Study of the Passive*. Cambridge University Press

AWBERY, G. M. (1984) Phonotactic Constraints in Welsh. In Ball and Jones 1984: 65–104

AWBERY, G. M. (1986a) *Pembrokeshire Welsh. A Phonological Study*. Welsh Folk Museum

AWBERY, G. M. (1986b) Moves Towards a Simpler, Binary Mutation System in Welsh. In Andersen 1986: 161–6

AWBERY, G. M. (1986c) Survey of Sandhi Types in Welsh. In Andersen 1986: 415–34

AWBERY, G. M. (1988) Pembrokeshire Negatives. *BBCS* **35**: 37–49

AWBERY, G. M. (1990) Dialect Syntax: A Neglected Resource for Welsh. In Hendrick 1990a: 1–25

BALL, M. J. (1984) Phonetics for Phonology. In Ball and Jones 1984: 5–39.

BALL, M. J. (1987) Analogic Levelling in Welsh Prepositions. *ZCP* **42**: 362–5

BALL, M. J. (ed) (1988a) *The Uses of Welsh. A Contribution to Sociolinguistics*. Multilingual Matters, Philadelphia

BALL, M. J. (1988b) Accounting for Linguistic Variation: Dialectology. In Ball 1988a: 7–23

BALL, M. J. (1990) The Lateral Fricative: Lateral or Fricative? In Ball, Fife *et al.* 1990: 109–25

BALL, M. J., FIFE, J. (eds) (1993) *The Celtic Languages*. Routledge (Routledge Language Family Descriptions)

BALL, M. J., FIFE, J., POPPE, E., ROWLAND, J. (eds) (1990) *Celtic Linguistics. Ieithyddiaeth Geltaidd. Readings in the Brythonic Languages. Festschrift for T. Arwyn Watkins*. Benjamins, Amsterdam

BALL, M. J., GRIFFITHS, T., JONES, G. E. (1988) Broadcast Welsh. In Ball 1988a: 182–99

BALL, M. J., JONES, G. E. (eds) (1984) *Welsh Phonology. Selected Readings*. University of Wales Press

BALL, M. J., MÜLLER, N. (1992) *Mutation in Welsh*. Routledge

BAMMESBERGER, A. (1982) *A Handbook of Irish: 1. Essentials of Modern Irish*. Winter, Heidelberg

BAMMESBERGER, A. (1983) *A Handbook of Irish: 2. An Outline of Modern Irish Grammar*. Winter, Heidelberg

BAMMESBERGER, A. WOLLMANN, A. (eds) (1990) *Britain 400–600: Language and History*. Winter, Heidelberg (Anglistische Forschungen)

BAUDIŠ, J. (1924) *Grammar of Early Welsh*. Oxford University Press (Philological Society, Philologica, vol. II)

BAUMGARTEN, R. (1986) *Bibliography of Irish Linguistics and Literature 1942–71*. Dublin Institute for Advanced Studies

BEDNARCZUK, L. (1988) The Italo-Celtic Hypothesis. In Maclennan 1988: 175–89

BEELER, M. S. (1966) The Inter-Relationships within Italic. In Birnbaum H, Puhvel J (eds) *Ancient Indo-European Dialects*. University of California Press, Berkeley, pp. 51–8

BELTRÁN, A., TOVAR A. (eds) (1982) *Contrebia Belaisca I. El Bronze con Alfabeto 'ibérico' de Botorrita*. Universidad de Zaragoza

BERGIN, O. J. (1902) The Future Tense in Modern Irish. *Ériu* **2**: 36–48
BERGIN, O. J. (1934–8) On the Syntax of the Verb in Old Irish. *Ériu* **12**: 197–214
BERGIN, O. J. (ed) (1970) *Irish Bardic Poetry*. Dublin Institute for Advanced Studies
BEST, R. I. (1913) *Bibliography of Irish Philology and of Printed Irish Literature*. National Library of Ireland, Dublin
BEST, R. I. (1942) *Bibliography of Irish Philology and Manuscript Literature. Publications 1913–1941*. Dublin Institute for Advanced Studies
BEST, R. I., BERGIN O. J. (eds) (1929) *Lebor na h-Uidre*. Royal Irish Academy, Dublin
BEST, R. I., O'BRIEN, M. A., O'SULLIVAN, A. (eds) (1954–83) *The Book of Leinster* 6 vols. Dublin Institute for Advanced Studies
BIELER, L. (ed) (1979) *The Patrician Texts in the Book of Armagh*. Dublin Institute for Advanced Studies (Scriptores Latini Hibernici, vol. X)
BILLY, P-H. (1993) *Thesaurus Linguae Gallicae*. Olms-Weidmann, Hildesheim
BINCHY, D. A. (1960) IE *q^ue in Irish. *Celtica* **5**: 77–94
BINCHY, D. A. (1978) *Corpus Iuris Hibernici*. 6 vols. Dublin Institute for Advanced Studies
BINCHY, D. A. (1979–80) Bergin's Law. *SC* **14-15**: 36–53
BIRLEY, A. (1979) *The People of Roman Britain*. Batsford
BISCHOFF, B. (1990) *Latin Palaeography*. Cambridge University Press
BOLING, B. D. (1972) Some Problems of the Phonology and Morphology of the Old Irish Verb. *Ériu* **23**: 73–101
BOLINGER, D. (1952) Linear Modification. *Proceedings of the Modern Languages Association of America* **67**: 1117–44
BONFANTE, G. (1956) A Contribution to the History of Celtology. *Celtica* **3**: 17–34
BORGSTRØM, C. HJ. (1937) The Dialect of Barra in the Outer Hebrides. *Norsk Tidsskrift for Sprogvidenskap* **8**: 71–242
BORGSTRØM, C. HJ. (1940) *The Dialects of the Outer Hebrides*. Norwegian Universities Press (A Linguistic Survey of the Scottish Gaelic Dialects, vol. I)
BORGSTRØM, C. HJ. (1941) *The Dialects of Skye and Ross-shire*. Norwegian Universities Press (A Linguistic Survey of the Scottish Gaelic Dialects, vol. II)
BORSLEY, R. D. (1983) A Welsh Agreement Process and the Status of VP and S. In Gazdar, Klein *et al.* 1983: 57–74
BORSLEY, R. D. (1984) VP complements: evidence from Welsh. *Journal of Linguistics* **20**: 277–302
BORSLEY, R. D. (1987) A Note on 'Traditional Treatments' of Welsh. *Journal of Linguistics* **23**: 185–90
BORSLEY, R. D. (1990a) Welsh Passives. In Ball, Fife, *et al.* 1990: 89–107
BORSLEY, R. D. (1990b) A GPSG Approach to Breton Word Order. In Hendrick 1990a: 81–95
BORSLEY, R. D. (1993) On So-called 'Verb-Nouns' in Welsh. *JCeltL* **3**: 35–64
BOSCH, A. (1990) A Brief Historiography of Scottish Gaelic Dialects. In Matonis and Melia 1990: 199–206
BREATNACH, L. (1977) The Suffixed Pronouns in Early Irish. *Celtica* **12**: 75–107
BREATNACH, L. (1980) Some Remarks on the Relative in Old Irish. *Ériu* **31** : 1–9

BREATNACH, L. (1984) Canon Law and Secular Law in Early Ireland: The Significance of *Bretha Nemed*. *Peritia* **3**: 439–59

BRODERICK, G. (1981) Manx Stories and Reminiscences of Ned Beg Hom Ruy. *ZCP* **38**: 113–78

BRODERICK, G. (1982) Manx Stories and Reminiscences of Ned Beg Hom Ruy. *ZCP* **39**: 117–94

BRODERICK, G. (1984–6) *A Handbook of Late Spoken Manx.* 3 vols. Niemeyer, Tübingen (Buchreihe der *ZCP*, Bd 3–5)

BRODERICK, G. (1993) Manx. In Ball and Fife 1993: 228–85

BROMWICH, R. (ed) (1972) *The Beginnings of Welsh Poetry. Studies by Sir Ifor Williams D Litt, LlD, FBA.* University of Wales Press

BROMWICH, R. (1974) *Medieval Celtic Literature. A Select Bibliography.* University of Toronto Press

BROWN, W. (1984) *A Grammar of Modern Cornish.* Cornish Language Board, Saltash

BYNON, T. (1977) *Historical Linguistics.* Cambridge University Press

CAESAR (see du Pontet 1900)

CALDER, G. (1923) *A Gaelic Grammar.* Maclaren, Glasgow (repr. 1972, Gairm, Glasgow)

CAMPANILE, E. (ed) (1961) Vocabularium Cornicum. *Annali della Scuola Normale Superiore di Pisa (serie II)* **30**: 299–325

CAMPANILE, E. (1974) *Profilo etimologico de Cornico antiquo.* Pacini, Pisa (Biblioteca dell'Italia Dialettale e di Studi e Saggi Linguistici, 7)

CAMPANILE, E. (ed) (1981) *I Celti d'Italia.* Giardini, Pisa

CAMPBELL, A. (1957) *Old English Grammar.* Oxford University Press

CARNEY, J. P. (1977–9) Aspects of Archaic Irish. *Eigse* **17**: 417–35

CARNEY, J. P. (1989) The Dating of Archaic Irish Verse. In Tranter S, Tristram H (eds) *Early Irish Literature – Media and Communication.* Gunter Narr, Tübingen, pp. 39–55

CHADWICK, N. K. (1965) The Colonization of Brittany from Celtic Britain. *PBA* **51**: 235–99

CHADWICK, N. K. (1969) *Early Brittany.* University of Wales Press

CHARLES, B. G. (1993) *The Place-Names of Pembrokeshire.* National Library of Wales, Aberystwyth

CHARLES-EDWARDS, T. M. (1971) Varia IV: Wb. 28c14 and the 'exclusive' use of the equative in Old Irish. *Ériu* **22**: 188–9

CHARLES-EDWARDS, T. M. (1992) Review of Bammesberger and Wollmann 1990. *JCeltL* **1**: 145–55

CHARLES-EDWARDS, T. M. (1993) The new edition of Adomnán's *Life of Columba. CMCS* **26**: 65–73

CHARLES-EDWARDS, T. M., RUSSELL, P. (1993–4) The Hendregadredd Manuscript and the Orthography and Phonology of Welsh in the Early Fourteenth Century. *NLWJ* **28**: 349–92

CLANCY, J. P. (1965) *Medieval Welsh Lyrics.* Macmillan

CLANCY, J. P. (1970) *The Earliest Welsh Poetry.* Macmillan

COLLINGE, N. E. (1985) *The Laws of Indo-European.* Benjamins, Amsterdam (Current Issues in Linguistic Theory)

COLLINGWOOD, R. G., WRIGHT, R. P. (eds) (1965) *The Roman Inscriptions of Britain I: Inscriptions on Stone.* Oxford University Press

COMRIE, B. (1976) *Aspect*. Cambridge University Press

CONRAN, T. (1986) *Welsh Verse*. Poetry Wales Press, Bridgend

CONWAY, R. S., JOHNSON, S. E., WHATMOUGH, J. 1933 *The Prae-Italic Dialects of Italy* 3 vols. Harvard University Press (repr. 1968, Olms, Hildesheim)

COWGILL, W. (1970) Italic and Celtic Superlatives and the Dialects of Indo-European. In Cardona G, Hoenigswald H M, Senn A (eds) *Indo-European and the Indo-Europeans*. University of Pennsylvania Press, Philadelphia

COWGILL, W. (1975a) The Origins of the Insular Celtic Conjunct and Absolute Verbal Endings. In Rix H (ed) *Flexion und Wortbildung (Akten der V. Fachtagung der Indogermanischen Gesellschaft, Regensburg)*. Reichert, Wiesbaden, pp. 40–70

COWGILL, W. (1975b) Two Further Notes on the Origin of the Insular Celtic Absolute and Conjunct Verb Endings. *Ériu* **26**: 27–32

COWGILL, W. (1980) The Etymology of Irish *guidid* and the Outcome of *$g^w h$* in Celtic. In Mayrhofer M, Peters M, Pfeiffer O E (eds) *Lautgeschichte und Etymologie. Akten der Vi. Fachtagung der Indogermanischen Gesellschaft, Wien*. Reichert, Wiesbaden, pp. 49–78

COWGILL, W. (1983) On the Prehistory of the Celtic Passive and Deponent Inflection. *Eriu* **34**: 73–111

CUNLIFFE, B. (1988) *Greeks, Romans and Barbarians*. Batsford

CYMRAEG BYW, *Rhifyn 1* (1964). Llyfrau'r Dryw (for the Education Faculty of University College Swansea)

CYMRAEG BYW, *Rhifyn 2* (1967). Welsh Joint Education Committee

CYMRAEG BYW, *Rhifyn 3* (1970). Welsh Joint Education Committee

DAVIES, C. (1988) Cymraeg Byw. In Ball 1988a: 200–10

DAVIES, E. (ed) (1967) *Rhestr o Enwau Lleoedd / A Gazetteer of Welsh Place-names* 3rd edn. University of Wales Press

DAVIES, J. (1621) *Antiquae Linguae Britannicae Rudimenta*. London (repr. 1968, Scolar Press, Menston, English Linguistics 1500–1800: a Collection of Facsimile Reprints, 7)

DAVIES, J. (1993) *The Welsh Language*. University of Wales Press

DAVIES, W. (1979) *The Llandaff Charters*. National Library of Wales, Aberystwyth

DAVIES, W. (1982) *Wales in the Early Middle Ages*. Leicester University Press (Studies in the Early History of Britain)

DAVIES, W. (1988) *Small Worlds. The Village Community in Early Medieval Brittany*. Duckworth

DE BERNARDO STEMPEL, P. (1987) *Die Vertretung der indogermanischen liquiden und nasalen Sonanten im keltischen*. Institut für Sprachwissenchaft der Universität Innsbruck, Innsbruck (Innsbrucker Beiträge zur Sprachwissenschaft, Bd 54)

DE BHALDRAITHE, T. (1945) *The Irish of Cois Fhairrge, County Galway*. Dublin Institute for Advanced Studies

DE BHALDRAITHE, T. (1953) *Gaeilge Chois Fhairrge: an Deilbhíocht*. Dublin Institute for Advanced Studies

DE BHALDRAITHE, T. (1981) *Innéacs Nua-Ghaeilge don Dictionary of the Irish Language*. Royal Irish Academy, Dublin (Deascán Foclóireachta, 1)

DE BHALDRAITHE, T. (1985) *Foirisiún Focal as Gaillimh*. Royal Irish Academy, Dublin

DE BHALDRAITHE, T. (1990) Notes on the Diminutive Suffix -ín in Modern Irish. In Matonis and Melia 1990: 85–95

DE BÚRCA, S. (1958) *The Irish of Tourmakeady, Co. Mayo*. Dublin Institute for Advanced Studies

DE COENE, A. (1972–4) Some notes on 'Italo-Celtic'. *BBCS* **25**: 359– 69

DE COENE, A. (1976–8) Italo-Celtic after W. Cowgill: some remarks. *BBCS* **27**: 406–12

DE COURSON, A. (1863) *Cartulaire de l'Abbaye de Redon*. Imprimerie impériale, Paris (Collection des Documents Inédits sur l'Histoire de la France)

DE HOZ, J. (1983) Origine ed evoluzione delle scritture ispaniche. *Annali (sez. ling.) dell' Istituto Orientale di Napoli* **5**: 27–61

DE HOZ, J. (1985) El nuevo plomo inscrito de Castell y el problema de las oposiciones de sonoridad en Ibérico. In Melena J L (ed) *Symbolae Ludovico Mitxelena septuagenario oblatae* 2 vols. Instituto de Ciencias de la Antiguedad, Universidad del Pais Vasco, Vitoria, pp. 443–53

DE HOZ, J., MICHELENA, L. (1974) *La inscripción celtiberica de Botorrita*. Universidad de Salamanca

DELAPORTE, R. (1979) *Elementary Breton–English Dictionary. Geriadurig Brezhoneg–Saozneg*. Cork University Press

DEPREZ, V., HALE, K. (1985) Resumptive Pronouns in Irish. *PHCC* **5**: 38–47

DILLON, M. (1943) On the Structure of the Celtic Verb. *Language* **19**: 252–5

DINNEEN, P. S. (1934) *Foclóir Gaedhilge agus Béarla. An Irish–English Dictionary*. Educational Co. of Ireland, Dublin (Irish Texts Society)

DIRINGER, D. (1968) *The Alphabet: A Key to the History of Mankind*. 3rd edn. Hutchinson

DISTERHEFT, D. (1980) *The Syntactic Development of the Infinitive in Indo-European*. Slavica, Columbus, Oh

DORIAN, N. C. (1977) A Hierarchy of Morphophonemic Decay in Scottish Gaelic Language Death. *Word* **28**: 96–109

DORIAN, N. C. (1978) *East Sutherland Gaelic*. Dublin Institute for Advanced Studies

DORIAN, N. C. (1981) *Language Death: The Life Cycle of a Scottish Gaelic Dialect*. University of Pennsylvania Press, Philadelphia

DORIAN, N. C. (1991) Review of Hindley 1990. *Language* **67**: 823–8

DOTTIN, G. (1913) *Manuel d'irlandais moyen*. 2 vols. Honoré Champion, Paris

DOTTIN, G. (1920) *La langue gauloise*. Klincksieck, Paris (repr. 1980, Slatkine, Geneva; Collections pour l'étude des antiquités nationales)

DOWNING, P. (1978) Some Universals of Relative Clause Structure. In Greenberg J (ed) 1978 *Universals of Human Language, vol. 4 Syntax*. Stanford University Press, Palo Alto, pp. 376–418

DOYLE, A. (1992) *Noun derivation in Modern Irish. Selected Categories, Rules and Suffixes*. Redakja Wydawnictw Katolickiego Uniwersytetu Lubelskiego, Lublin

DRESSLER, W. (1972) On the Phonology of Language Death. In Peranteau P M, Levi J N, Phares G C (eds) *Papers from the 8th Regional Meeting, Chicago Linguistic Society*. Chicago University Press, pp. 448–57

DRESSLER, W. (1981) Language Shift and Language Death: A Protean Challenge for the Linguist. *Folia Linguistica* **15**: 5–28

DUMVILLE, D. N. (ed) (1993) *Saint Patrick, AD. 493–1993*. Boydell

DU PONTET, E. (1900) *C. Iuli Caesaris Commentariorum pars prior qua continentur libri vii de Bello Gallico cum A. Hirti supplemento.* Oxford University Press (Oxford Classical Texts)

DUVAL, P-M., PINAULT, G. (eds) (1986) *Recueil des inscriptions gauloises. Vol. III Les calendriers.* CNRS, Paris (xlve supplément à *Gallia*)

EICHNER, H. (1989) Damals und heute: Probleme der Erschliessung des Altkeltischen zu Zeussens Zeit und in der Gegenwart. In Forssman B (ed) *Erlanger Gedenkfeier für Johann Kaspar Zeuss.* Universitätsbund Erlangen-Nürnberg, Erlangen (Erlanger Forschungen Reihe A – Geisteswissenschaften, Bd 49), pp. 9–56

ELLIS, T. (1972) Yr Ymadrodd Berfol. *BBCS* **24**: 465–77

ERNAULT, E. (1895–6) *Glossaire moyen-breton.* Bouillon, Paris (repr. 1976, Lafitte, Marseilles)

ESKA, J. F. (1989a) *Towards an Interpretation of the Hispano-Celtic Inscription of Botorrita.* Institut für Sprachwissenchaft der Universität Innsbruck, Innsbruck (Innsbrucker Beiträge zur Sprachwissenschaft, Bd 59)

ESKA, J. F. (1989b) The Verbal Desinence -*Tus* in the Hispano-Celtic Inscription of Botorrita. *ZCP* **43**: 214–22

ESKA, J. F. (1989c) Interpreting the Gaulish Inscription of Voltino. *BBCS* **36**: 106–7

ESKA, J. F. (1990a) Syntactic Notes on the Great Inscription of Peñalba de Villastar. *BBCS* **37**: 104–7

ESKA, J. F. (1990b) The So-called Weak Dental Preterite in Continental Celtic, Watkins' law, and Related Matters. *Historische Sprachforschung* **103**: 81–91

ESKA, J. F., EVANS. D. E. (1993) Continental Celtic. In Ball and Fife 1993: 26–63

EVANS, C., FLEURIOT, L. (1985) *A Dictionary of Old Breton. Dictionnaire du vieux breton.* 2 vols. University of Toronto Press

EVANS, D. E. (1967) *Gaulish Personal Names.* Oxford University Press

EVANS, D. E. (1970–2) A Comparison of the Formation of Some Continental and Early Insular Celtic Personal Names. *BBCS* **24**: 415–34

EVANS, D. E. (1979) The Labyrinth of Continental Celtic. *PBA* **65**: 497–538

EVANS, D. E. (1980–2) Celts and Germans. *BBCS* **29**: 230–55

EVANS, D. E. (1983) Language Contact in Pre-Roman and Roman Britain. In Temporini H, Haase W (eds) *Aufstieg und Niedergang der römischen Welt, Vol. II Principät* Band 29.2. De Gruyter, Berlin, pp. 949–87

EVANS, D. E. (1988) Celtic Origins. In Maclennan 1988: 209–22

EVANS, D. E. (1990) Insular Celtic and the Emergence of the Welsh Language. In Bammesberger and Wollmann 1990: 149–77

EVANS, D. S. (1964) *A Grammar of Middle Welsh.* Dublin Institute for Advanced Studies

EVANS, D. S. (1988) Dylanwad y Beibl ar yr Iaith Gymraeg. In Gruffydd 1988: 67–86

EVANS, E. 1987 *Termau Ieithyddiaeth.* University College, Aberystwyth

EVANS, J. G., RHŶS, J. (eds) (1893) *The Text of the Book of Llan Dâv.* Clarendon Press

EVANS, H. H., THOMAS, W. O. (eds) (1968) *Y Geiriadur Mawr* 2nd edn. Gwasg Gomer, Llandysul

EWERT, A. (1961) *The French Language* 2nd edn. Faber

FALC'HUN, F. (1951) *Le système consonantique du breton.* Plihon, Rennes

FALC'HUN, F. (1963) *L'histoire de la langue bretonne d'après la géographie linguistique*. 2nd edn. Presses universitaires de la France, Paris

FIFE, J. (1986a) The Semantics of *gwneud*-Inversions. *BBCS* **33**: 133–44

FIFE, J. (1986b) Additional Facts about Welsh VPs. *Journal of Linguistics* **22**: 179–86

FIFE, J. (1987) Review of Ball and Thomas 1984. *ZCP* **42**: 374–84

FIFE, J. (1988) *Functional Syntax: A Case Study in Middle Welsh*. Redakja Wydawnictw Katolickiego Uniwersytetu Lubelskiego, Lublin

FIFE, J. (1990) *The Semantics of the Welsh Verb*. University of Wales Press

FIFE, J. (1991) Some Constituent-order Frequencies in Classical Welsh Prose. In Fife and Poppe 1991: 251–74

FIFE, J. (1993) Introduction. In Ball and Fife 1993: 3–25

FIFE, J., KING, G. (1991) Focus and the Welsh 'Abnormal Sentence': A Cross-linguistic Perspective. In Fife and Poppe 1991: 81–153

FIFE, J., POPPE, E. (eds) (1991) *Studies in Brythonic Word Order*. Benjamins, Amsterdam (Current Issues in Linguistic Theory, 83)

FLEURIOT, L. (1964) *Le vieux breton: éléments d'une grammaire*. Klincksieck, Paris

FLEURIOT, L. (1967) L'importance du dialecte de Vannes pour l'étude diachronique et comparative du breton armoricain. In Meid 1967b: 159–70

FLEURIOT, L. (1975) La grande inscription celtibère de Botorrita. *EC* **14**: 51–62

FLEURIOT, L. (1976–7) Le vocabulaire de l'inscription gauloise de Chamalières. *EC* **15**: 173–90

FLEURIOT, L. (1978) Brittonique et gaulois durant les premiers siècles de notre ère. In *Etrennes de septentaine. Travaux de linguistique et de grammaire comparée offerts à Michel Lejeune par un groupe de ses élèves*. Klincksieck, Paris, pp. 75–83

FLEURIOT, L. (1979) L'inscription gauloise de Thiaucourt et le problème des désinences verbales en *-seti* et en *-setu* du celtique antique. *EC* **16**: 123–39

FLEURIOT, L. (1980) *Les origines de la Bretagne*. Payot, Paris

FLEURIOT, L. (1988) New Documents on Ancient Celtic and the Relationship between Brittonic and Continental Celtic. In Maclennan 1988: 223–30

FORD, P. K., HAMP, E. P. (1974–6) Welsh *asswynaw* and Celtic Legal Idiom. *BBCS* **26**: 147–60

FÖRSTER, M. (1930) Die Freilassungsurkunden des Bodmin Evangeliars. In Bøgholm N, Brusendorff A, Bodelsen C A (eds) *A Grammatical Miscellany Offered to Otto Jespersen on his Seventieth Birthday*. Levin and Munksgaard, Copenhagen, pp. 77–99

FÖRSTER, M. (1942) *Der Flussname Themse und seine Sippe, Studien zur Anglisierung keltischer Eigennamen und zur Lautchronologie des Altbritischen*. Sitzungberichte der Bayerischen Akademie der Wissenschaften, philosophisch-historischen Abteilung, Jahrgang 1941, Munich

FOWKES, R. A. (1991) Verbal Noun as 'equivalent' of Finite Verb in Welsh. *Word* **42**: 19–29

FRERE, S. S., ROXAN, M., TOMLIN, R. S. O. (eds) (1990) *The Roman Inscriptions of Britain II.1: instrumentum domesticum*. Alan Sutton

FRERE, S. S., TOMLIN, R. S. O. (eds) (1991a) *The Roman Inscriptions of Britain II.2: instrumentum domesticum*. Alan Sutton

FRERE, S. S., TOMLIN, R. S. O. (eds) (1991b) *The Roman Inscriptions of Britain II.3: instrumentum domesticum*. Alan Sutton

FRERE, S. S., TOMLIN, R. S. O. (eds) (1992) *The Roman Inscriptions of Britain II.4: instrumentum domesticum.* Alan Sutton

FRERE, S. S., TOMLIN, R. S. O. (eds) (1993) *The Roman Inscriptions of Britain II.5: instrumentum domesticum.* Alan Sutton

FRERE, S. S., TOMLIN, R. S. O. (eds) (1994) *The Roman Inscriptions of Britain II.6: instrumentum domesticum.* Alan Sutton

FURNEAUX, H., ANDERSON, J. G. C. (eds) (1939) *Cornelii Taciti Opera Minora.* Oxford University Press (Oxford Classical Texts)

FYNES-CLINTON, O. H. (1913) *The Welsh Vocabulary of the Bangor District.* Oxford University Press

GAGNEPAIN, J. (1963) *La syntaxe du nom verbal dans les langues celtiques, I. Irlandais.* Klincksieck, Paris (Collection linguistique, LXI)

GAMBARI, F. M., COLONNA, G. (1988) Il bicchiere con iscrizione arcaica de Castelletto Ticino e l'adozione della scrittura nell'Italia nord-occidentale. *Studi Etruschi* **54**: 119–64

GAZDAR, J., KLEIN, E., PULLUM, G. K. (eds) (1983) *Order, Concord and Constituency.* Foris, Dordrecht

GELB, I. J. (1963) *A Study of Writing.* Chicago University Press

GENEE, I. (1994) Pragmatic Aspects of Verbal Noun Complements in Early Irish: *do* + verbal noun in the Würzburg Glosses. *JCeltL* **3**: 41–73.

GEORGE, K. J. (1985) A Phonological History of Cornish. PhD dissertation, Brest

GEORGE, K. J. (1991) Notes on Word-Order in *Beunans Meriasek.* In Fife and Poppe 1991: 205–50

GEORGE, K. J. (1993a) Cornish. In Ball and Fife 1993: 410–68

GEORGE, K. J. (1993b) *Gerlyvyr Kernewek Kemmyn.* Kesva an Taves Kernewek / The Cornish Language Board, Callington

GEORGE, K. J., BRODERICK, G. (1993) The Revived Languages: Modern Cornish and Modern Manx. In Ball and Fife 1993: 644–63

GILLIES, W. (1993) Scottish Gaelic. In Ball and Fife 1993: 145–227

GLEASURE, J. W. (1968) Consonant Quality in Irish and a Problem of Segmentation. *SC* **3**: 79–87

GLEASURE, J. W. (1990) The Evolution of the Present/Future Tense in Scottish Gaelic. *SGS* **16**: 181–90

GÓMEZ-MORENO, M. (1922) De epigrafía ibérica: el plomo del Alcoy. *Revista de Filología Española* **9**: 341–66

GONDA, J. (1959) On Amplified Sentences and Similar Structures in the Veda. In Gonda J *Four Studies in the Language of the Veda.* Mouton, 'S-Gravenhage, pp. 7–70

GOODBURN, R., WAUGH, H. (1983) *The Roman Inscriptions of Britain, I: Epigraphic Indexes.* Alan Sutton

GRATWICK, A. S. (1982) *Latinitas Britannica.* Was British Latin Archaic? In Brookes N (ed) *Latin and the Vernacular Languages in Early Medieval Britain.* Leicester University Press (Studies in the Early History of Britain)

GRAVES, C. (1876) The Ogham Alphabet. *Hermathena* **2**: 443–72

GRAVES, E. VAN T. (1962) *The Old Cornish Vocabulary.* Ann Arbor, Michigan

GRAY, L. H. (1944) Mutation in Gaulish. *Language* **20**: 223–30

GREENBERG, J. (1966) Some Universals of Grammar with Particular Reference to the Order of Meaningful Elements. In Greenberg J (ed) *Universals of Human Language.* MIT, Cambridge, Ma, pp. 73–113

GREENE, D. (1952–4) Miscellanea. *Celtica* **2**: 334–40

GREENE, D. (1956) Gemination. *Celtica* **3**: 284–9

GREENE, D. (1962) The Colouring of Consonants in Old Irish. Sovijärvi A, Aalto P (eds) *Proceedings of the IVth International Congress of Phonetic Sciences*, Mouton, The Hague, pp. 622–4

GREENE, D. (1966) The Spirant Mutation in Brythonic. *Celtica* **7**: 116–19

GREENE, D. (1971) Linguistic Considerations in the Dating of Early Welsh Verse. *SC* **6**: 1–11

GREENE, D. (1973) The Growth of Palatalization in Irish. *TPhS* **72**: 127–36

GREENE, D. (1974) Distinctive Plural Forms in Old and Middle Irish. *Ériu* **25**: 190–99

GREENE, D. (1976) The Diphthongs of Old Irish. *Ériu* **27**: 26–45

GREENE, D. (1977) Archaic Irish. In Schmidt 1977b: 11–33

GREENE, D. (1992) Celtic. In Gvozdanovič J (ed) *Indo-European Numerals*. De Gruyter, Berlin / New York (*Trends in Linguistics*, Studies and Monographs 57), pp. 497–554

GREGOR, D. B. (1980) *Celtic. A Comparative Study*. Oleander Press

GRIFFEN, T. D. (1975) Lenis Initials in Welsh Borrowing. *Language Sciences* **36**: 6–12

GRIFFEN, T. D. (1984) Early Welsh Eclipsis: A Dynamic Analysis. *BBCS* **31**: 48–59

GRIFFEN, T. D. (1985) Early Welsh Aspiration: A Dynamic Perspective. *Word* **36**: 211–35

GRIFFEN, T. D. (1990) Old Welsh *ll* and *rh*. *BBCS* **37**: 89–103

GRUFFYDD, R. G. (ed) (1988) *Y Gair ar Waith. Ysgrifau ar Etifeddiaeth Feiblaidd yng Nghymru*. University of Wales Press

GRUFFYDD, R. G. (1990) The Renaissance and Welsh Literature. In Williams G and Jones R O (eds) *The Celts and the Renaissance: Tradition and Innovation. Proceedings of the Eighth International Congress of Celtic Studies 1987*. University of Wales Press, pp. 17–39

GUILLEVIC, A., LE GOFF, P. (1902) *Grammaire bretonne du dialecte de Vannes*. Lafolye, Vannes

GUYONVARC'H, C-J. (ed) (1975) *The Catholicon de Jehan Lagadeuc*. Ogam, Rennes (Celticum 22)

HAARMANN, H. (1970) *Der lateinische Lehnwortschatz im Kymrischen*. Romanisches Seminar der Universität Bonn (Romanistische Versuche und Vorarbeiten)

HAARMANN, H. (1973) *Der lateinische Lehnwortschatz im Bretonischen*. Buske, Hamburg (Hamburger philologische Studien)

HAMILTON, J. N. (1974) *The Irish of Tory Island*. Institute of Irish Studies, Queen's University, Belfast

HAMP, E. P. (1951) Morphophonemes of the Keltic Mutations. *Language* **27**: 230–47

HAMP, E. P. (1954) Old Irish *gaib-*, Welsh *gafael, caffael, cael, cahel*. *ZCP* **24**: 229–33

HAMP, E. P. (1958) Consonant Allophones in Proto-Keltic. *Lochlann* **1**: 209–17

HAMP, E. P. (1965) Evidence in Keltic. In Winter W (ed) *Evidence for Laryngeals*. Mouton, The Hague

HAMP, E. P. (1974) The MacNeill-O'Brien Law. *Eriu* **25**: 172–80

HAMP, E. P. (1975a) Social Gradience in British Latin. *Britannia* **6**: 150–61

HAMP, E. P. (1975b) **DIEU*- 'day' in Celtic. *EC* **14**: 472–7

HAMP, E. P. (1975c) Varia II. *Eriu* **26**: 168–74

HAMP, E. P. (1975–6) Miscellanea Celtica. *SC* **10-11**: 54–73

HAMP, E. P. (1976) On some Gaulish Names in -*ant*- and the Celtic Verbal Nouns. *Ériu* **27**: 1–20

HAMP, E. P. (1977–8) Intensives in British Celtic and Gaulish. *SC* **12-13**: 1–13

HAMP, E. P. (1991a) Varia. *Celtica* **22**: 33–47

HAMP, E. P. (1991b) A Simplicity Metric: Welsh Prepositions. *ZCP* **44**: 236–8

HANDFORD, S. A. (1951) *Caesar: the Conquest of Gaul*. Penguin

HARLOW, S. (1981) Government and Realization in Celtic. In Heny F (ed) *Binding and Filtering*. Croom Helm, pp. 213–54

HARVEY, A. (1984) Aspects of Lenition and Spirantization. *CMCS* **8**: 87–100

HARVEY, A. (1985) The Significance of *Cothraige*. *Ériu* **36**: 1–9

HARVEY, A. (1987a) The Ogam Inscriptions and their Geminate Consonants. *Ériu* **38**: 45–71

HARVEY, A. (1987b) Early Literacy in Ireland: the Evidence from Ogam. *CMCS* **14**: 1–15

HARVEY, A. (1989) Some Significant Points of Early Insular Celtic Orthography. In Ó Corráin D, Breatnach L, McCone K R (eds) *Sages, Saints and Storytellers. Celtic Studies in Honour of Profesor James Carney*. An Sagart, Maynooth, pp. 56–66

HARVEY, A. (1992) Review of Bammesberger and Wollmann 1990. *CMCS* **24**: 102–4

HAYWOOD, N. R. (1982) Studies in the Historical Grammar of Cornish. MPhil dissertation, Oxford

HEMON, R. (1941) *Grammaire breton*. Gwalarn, Brest

HEMON, R. (1947) *La langue bretonne et ses combats*. Editions de Bretagne, La Baule

HEMON, R. (1954) The Breton Personal Pronoun as Direct Object of the Verb. *Celtica* **2**: 229–44

HEMON, R. (ed) (1956) *Christmas Hymns in the Vannes Dialect of Breton*. Dublin Institute for Advanced Studies

HEMON, R. (ed) (1962) *Trois poèmes en moyen-breton*. Dublin Institute for Advanced Studies (Modern and Medieval Breton Series, vol. I)

HEMON, R. (1975) *A Historical Morphology and Syntax of Breton*. Dublin Institute for Advanced Studies

HEMON, R. (ed) (1976–) *Geriadur istorel ar brezhoneg. Dictionnaire historique du breton*. Preder, Quimper

HEMON, R. (ed) (1977) *Doctrin an Christienen*. Dublin Institute for Advanced Studies (Modern and Medieval Breton Series, vol. IV)

HEMON, R. (ed) (1978) *Nouveau dictionnaire breton–français* 6th edn. Al Liamm, Brest

HEMON, R., LE MENN, G. (eds) (1969) *Les fragments de la destruction de Jérusalem et des Amours du Vieillard*. Dublin Institute for Advanced Studies (Modern and Medieval Breton Series, vol. II)

HENDRICK, R. (1988) *Anaphora in Celtic and Universal Grammar*. Kluwer, Dordrecht (Studies in Natural Language and Linguistic Theory)

HENDRICK, R. (ed) (1990a) *The Syntax of the Modern Celtic Languages*. Academic Press, San Diego (Syntax and Semantics, vol. 23)

HENDRICK, R. (1990b) Breton Pronominals, Binding and Barriers. In Hendrick 1990a: 121–65

HENNESSEY, J. S. (1990) Spirantization to Lenition in Breton: Interpretation of Morphophonological Variability. In Ball, Fife *et al.* 1990: 209–24

HEWITT, S. (1990) The Progressive in Breton in the Light of the English Progressive. In Ball, Fife *et al.* 1990: 167–88

HICKEY, R. (1985) Reduction of Allomorphy and the Plural in Irish. *Ériu* **36**: 143–62

HINDLEY, R. (1990) *The Death of the Irish Language.* Routledge

HOCK, H. H. (1986) *Principles of Historical Linguistics.* Mouton de Gruyter, Berlin

HOENIGSWALD, H. M. (1973) Indo-European **p* in Celtic and the Claim for Relative Chronologies. *Journal of Indo-European Studies* **1**: 324–9

HOLDER, A. (ed) (1891–1913) *Alt-celtischer Sprachschatz.* 3 vols. Teubner, Leipzig

HOLMER, N. M. (1957) *The Gaelic of Arran.* Dublin Institute for Advanced Studies

HOLMER, N. M. (1962) *The Gaelic of Kintyre.* Dublin Institute for Advanced Studies

HOLMER, N. M. (1962–5) *The Dialects of Co. Clare.* 2 vols. Royal Irish Academy, Dublin

HOOKER, J. T. (ed) (1990) *Reading the Past.* British Museum Publications

HOWELLS, D. (1971) Miscellanea II. The Nom. Pl. of the Noun in the Gaelic of the Isle of Lewis. *SC* **6**: 90–7

HUGHES, A. J. (1992) Review of Ó Siadhail 1989. *JCeltL* **1**: 162–9

HUGHES, R. E. (ed) (1990) *Nid am Un Harddwch Iaith. Rhyddiaith Gwyddoniaeth y Bedwaredd Ganrif ar Bymtheg.* University of Wales Press

HUMPHREYS, H. LL. (1992) The Breton Language. In Price 1992a: 245– 75

HUMPHREYS, H. LL. (1993) The Breton Language: its Present Position and Historical Background. In Ball and Fife 1993: 606–43

IFANS, D., THOMSON, R. L. (1979–80) Edward Lhuyd's *Geirieu Manaweg. SC* **14-15**: 129–67

ISAAC, G. R. (1991) Non-lenition in the Neo-Celtic Verbal Complex. *BBCS* **38**: 93–7

ISAAC, G. R. (1993) Issues in the Reconstruction and Analysis of Insular Celtic Syntax and Phonology. *Ériu* **44**: 1–32

JACKSON, K. H. (1951) Common Gaelic. *PBA* **37**: 71–97

JACKSON, K. H. (1953) *Language and History in Early Britain.* Edinburgh University Press

JACKSON, K. H. (1960) Gemination and the Spirant Mutation. *Celtica* **5**: 127–34

JACKSON, K. H. (1960–1) The Phonology of the Breton Dialect of Plougrescant. *EC* **9**: 327–404

JACKSON, K. H. (1963) Angles and Britons in Northumbria and Cumbria. In *Angles and Britons.* University of Wales Press, pp. 60–84

JACKSON, K. H. (1967a) *A Historical Phonology of Breton.* Dublin Institute for Advanced Studies

JACKSON, K. H. (1967b) Palatalization of Labials in the Gaelic Languages. In Meid 1967b: 179–92

JACKSON, K. H. (1968) The Breaking of Long *ē* in Scottish Gaelic. In Carney J, Greene D (eds) *Celtic Studies. Essays in Memory of Angus Matheson 1912–1962*. Routledge, Kegan, Paul, pp. 65–71

JACKSON, K. H. (1969) *The Gododdin. The Oldest Scottish Poem.* Edinburgh University Press

JACKSON, K. H. (1972) *The Gaelic Notes in the Book of Deer.* Cambridge University Press

JACKSON, K. H. (1973–4) Some Questions in Dispute about Early Welsh Literature and Language. *SC* **8-9**: 1–32

JACKSON, K. H. (1975–6) The Date of the Old Welsh Accent Shift. *SC* **10-11**: 40–53

JACKSON, K. H. (1980) The Pictish Language. In Wainwright 1980: 129–66

JACKSON, K. H. (ed) (1990) *Aislinge Meic Con Glinne.* Dublin Institute for Advanced Studies

JARMAN, A. O. H. (ed) (1988) *Aneirin: Y Gododdin.* Gwasg Gomer, Llandysul

JARMAN, A. O. H., HUGHES, G. R. (eds) (1976) *A Guide to Welsh Literature* Vol 1. Christopher Davies, Swansea

JARMAN, A. O. H., HUGHES, G. R. (eds) (1979) *A Guide to Welsh Literature* Vol 2. Christopher Davies, Swansea

JEFFERS, R. J. (1973) Problems in the Reconstruction of Proto-Italic. *Journal of Indo-European Studies* **1**: 330–44

JEFFERS, R. J. (1975) Remarks on Indo-European Infinitives. *Language* **51**: 133–48

JEFFERS, R. J. (1978) Old Irish Verbal Nouns. *Eriu* **29**: 1–12

JENKINS, D., OWEN, M. E. (1983) The Welsh Marginalia in the Lichfield Gospels. Part I. *CMCS* **5**: 37–66

JENKINS, D., OWEN, M. E. (1984) The Welsh Marginalia in the Lichfield Gospels. Part II: the 'Surrexit' Memorandum. *CMCS* **7**: 91–120

JENNER, H. (1904) *A Handbook of the Cornish Language.* David Nutt

JOHNSTON, D. R. (1992) Welsh Literature. In Price 1992a: 216–44

JONES, B. P. (1988) Official Welsh. In Ball 1988a: 172–81

JONES, D. G. (1988) Literary Welsh. In Ball 1988a: 125–71

JONES, G. E. (1982) Central Rounded and Unrounded Vowels in Sixteenth Century Welsh. *Cardiff Working Papers in Welsh Linguistics* **2**: 43–52

JONES, G. E. (1984) The Distinctive Vowels and Consonants of Welsh. In Ball and Jones 1984: 40–64

JONES, G. E. (1988) Some Features of the Welsh of Breconshire. In Ball 1988a: 97–103

JONES, G. E. (1989–90) Ffin y Llafariad Ganol yng Nganolbarth Cymru: Tystiolaeth Brycheiniog. *SC* **24-25**: 108–16

JONES, G. R. J. (1972) Post-Roman Wales. In Finberg H P R (ed) *The Agrarian History of England and Wales. Vol. I.ii (AD 43 – 1042).* Cambridge University Press, pp. 279–382

JONES, M., THOMAS, A. R. (1977) *The Welsh Language. Studies in its Syntax and Semantics.* University of Wales Press

JONES, R. M. (1965) *Cymraeg i'r Oedolion.* University of Wales Press

JONES, R. O. (1986) Datblygiad Gwyddor Tafodieitheg yng Nghymru. *BBCS* **33**: 18–40

JONES, R. O. (1993) The Sociolinguistics of Welsh. In Ball and Fife 1993: 536–605

JOSEPH, L. (1987) The Origin of the Celtic Denominatives in *sag-. In Watkins C (ed) *Studies in Memory of Warren Cowgill (1929–1985)*. *Papers from the East Coast Indo-European Conference*, Cornell University, June 6–9, 1985. De Gruyter, Berlin/New York, pp. 113–59

JUSTESON, J. S., STEPHENS, L. D. (1991–3) The Evolution of Syllabaries from Alphabets: Transmission, Language Contrast, and Script Typology. *Die Sprache* 35: 2–46

KELLY, F. (1986) Two Notes on Final-Verb Constructions. *Celtica* 18: 1–12

KELLY, F. (1988) *A Guide to Early Irish Law*. Dublin Institute for Advanced Studies (Early Irish Law Series, vol. III)

KELLY, J. (1804) *A Practical Grammar of the Ancient Gaelic or Language of the Isle of Man usually called Manks*. The Manx Society, Douglas

KERVELLA, F. (1947) *Yezhadhur bras ar Brezhoneg*. Skridou Breizh, La Baule

KING, G. (1993) *Modern Welsh. A Comprehensive Grammar*. Routledge (Routledge Grammars)

KNOTT, E. (ed) (1962) *Irish Syllabic Poetry 1200–1600* 2nd edn. Dublin Institute for Advanced Studies

KOCH, J. T. (1982–3) The Loss of Final Syllables and Loss of Declension in Brittonic. *BBCS* 30: 201–33

KOCH, J. T. (1983) The Sentence in Gaulish. *PHCC* 3: 169–215

KOCH, J. T. (1985a) Movement and Emphasis in the Gaulish Sentence. *BBCS* 32: 1–37

KOCH, J. T. (1985b) Linguistic Preliminaries to the Dating and Analysis of Archaic Welsh Verse. PhD dissertation, Harvard

KOCH, J. T. (1985–6) When was Welsh Literature First Written Down? *SC* 20-21: 43–66

KOCH, J. T. (1987) Prosody and the Old Celtic Verbal Complex. *Ériu* 38: 143–76

KOCH, J. T. (1988) The Cynfeirdd Poetry and the Language of the Sixth Century. In Roberts 1988: 17–41

KOCH, J. T. (1990) *Cothairche, Esposito's Theory, and neo-Celtic Lenition. In Bammesberger and Wollmann 1990: 179–202

KOCH, J. T. (1991) On the Prehistory of Brittonic Syntax. In Fife and Poppe 1991: 1–43

KOCH, J. T. (1992) Gallo-Brittonic *Tasc(i)ouanos* 'Badger-slayer' and the Relex of Indo-European $g^w h$. *JCeltL* 1: 101–18

KORTLANDT, F. (1979) The Old Irish Absolute and Conjunct Endings and Questions of Relative Chronology. *Ériu* 30: 35–53

KORTLANDT, F. (1981) More Evidence for Italo-Celtic. *Ériu* 32: 1–22

KURYŁOWICZ, J. (1958) *L'accentuation des langues indo-européennes* 2nd edn. Polska Akademia Nauk, Wrocław

KURYŁOWICZ, J. (1971) Morphophonological Palatalization in Old Irish. *Travaux linguistiques de Prague* 4: 67–73 (= Kuryłowicz J (ed) 1973–5 *Esquisses linguistiques* 2 vols. Wilhelm Fink, Munich, pp. 323–9)

LAMBERT, P-Y. (1978) Restes de la flexion hétéroclitique en celtique. In *Etrennes de septentaine. Travaux de linguistique et de grammaire comparée offerts à Michel Lejeune par un groupe de ses élèves*. Klincksieck, Paris, pp. 115–22

LAMBERT, P-Y. (1979a) La tablette gauloise de Chamlières. *EC* 16: 141–69

LAMBERT, P-Y. (1979b) Gaulois *IEVRV*: irlandais *(ro)·ír* 'dicavit'. *ZCP* **37**: 207–13

LAMBERT, P-Y. (1986) The New Dictionary of Old Breton. *CMCS* **12**: 99–113

LAMBERT, P-Y. (1987) A Restatement on the Gaulish Tablet of Chamalières. *BBCS* **34**: 10–17

LAMBERT, P-Y. (1990) Welsh *Caswallawn*: The Fate of British **au*. In Bammesberger and Wollmann 1990: 203–15

LAMBERT, P-Y. (1994) *La langue gauloise*. Editions Errance, Paris

LAPIDGE, M., SHARPE, R. (1985) *A Bibliography of Celtic-Latin Literature 400–1200*. Royal Irish Academy, Dublin (Royal Irish Academy Dictionary of Medieval Latin from Celtic Sources. Ancillary Publications 1)

LE BIHAN, A. (1957) *Brud ar Brezhoneg. Monuments de la langue bretonne*. Emgleo Breiz, Brest

LE CLERC, L. (1911) *Grammaire breton du dialecte de Tréguier*. 2nd edn. René Prud'homme, Saint Brieuc

LE DÛ, J. (1986) A Sandhi Survey of the Breton Language. In Andersen 1986: 435–50

LE GONIDEC, J. F. M. M. A. (1807) *Grammaire Celto-Bretonne contenant les principes de l'orthographe, de la prononciation, de la construction des mots et des phrases, selon la génie de la language celto-bretonne*. Rougeron, Paris

LE GONIDEC, J. F. M. M. A. (1821) *Dictionnaire celto-breton ou breton- français*. Trémeau, Angoulême

LEJEUNE, M. (1955) *Celtiberica*. Universidad de Salamanca (Acta Salmanticensia, Filosofía y Letras, vol. VII, no. 4)

LEJEUNE, M. (1971) Documents gaulois et paragaulois de Cisalpine. *EC* **12**: 337–500 (reprinted as *Lepontica*. Société d'édition 'Les Belles Lettres' Paris)

LEJEUNE, M. (1972) Un problème de nomenclature: Lépontiens et Lepontique. *Studi Etruschi* **40**: 259–70

LEJEUNE, M. (1973) La grande inscription celtibère de Botorrita (Saragosse). *Comptes-rendus de l'Académie des Inscriptions et Belles-Lettres*: 622–47

LEJEUNE, M. (1985) *Recueil des inscriptions gauloises: I. Textes gallo-grecs*. CNRS, Paris (xlveᵉ supplément à *Gallia*)

LEJEUNE, M. (1988) *Recueil des inscriptions gauloises: II.1 Textes gallo-étrusques. Textes gallo-latins sur pierre*. CNRS, Paris (xlveᵉ supplément à *Gallia*)

LEJEUNE, M. (1993) D'Alcoy à Espanca: réflexions sur les écritures paléo-hispaniques. In Duhoux Y, Swiggers P (eds) *Michel Lejeune. Notice biographique et bibliographique*. Centre internationale de dialectologie générale, Leuven (Biobibliographies et exposés N.S. 3), pp. 53–86

LEJEUNE, M., FLEURIOT, L., LAMBERT, P-Y., MARICHAL, R., VERNHET, A. (1985) Textes gaulois et gallo-romains en cursive latine, 3. le plomb de Larzac. *EC* **22**: 95–177

LEJEUNE, M., MARICHAL, R. (1976–7) Textes gaulois et gallo-romains en cursive latine, 2. Chamalières. *EC* **15**: 151–68

LE ROUX, P. (1924–63) *Atlas linguistique de la Basse-Bretagne*. 6 vols. Plihon, Rennes/Champion, Paris

LEUMANN, M. (1977) *Lateinische Laut- und Formenlehre*. Oscar Beck, Munich

LEWIS, C. W. (1976) The Historical Background of Early Welsh Verse. In Jarman and Hughes 1976: 11–50

LEWIS, H. (1942) The Sentence in Welsh. *PBA* **28**: 259–80

LEWIS, H. (1943) *Yr Elfen Ladin yn yr Iaith Gymraeg*. University of Wales Press

LEWIS, H. (1946) *Llawlyfr Cernyweg Canol*. 2nd edn. University of Wales Press (transl. Zimmer 1990a)

LEWIS, H. (1967) Welsh *oes* 'is'. In Meid 1967b: 215–16

LEWIS, H., PEDERSEN, H. (1961) *A Concise Comparative Celtic Grammar*. 2nd edn. Vandenhoeck and Ruprecht, Göttingen

LEWIS, H., PIETTE, J. R. F. (1966) *Llawlyfr Llydaweg Canol*. 3rd edn. University of Wales Press (transl. Meid 1990)

LEWIS, M. (1961) Disgrifiad o Orgraff Hen Gymraeg gan ei Chymharu ag Orgraff Hen Wyddeleg. MA dissertation, University of Wales, Aberystwyth

LEWIS, S. (1968) Rhagair. In *Problemau Prifysgol*. Llyfrau'r Dryw, Llandybie

LHUYD, E. (1707) *Archaeologia Britannica*. Clarendon Press, Oxford (repr. 1971, Irish University Press, Dublin)

LI, C. (ed) (1976) *Subject and Topic*. Academic Press, New York

LI, C., THOMPSON, S. (1976) Subject and Topic: A New Typology of Language. In Li 1976: 459–89

LINDEMAN, F. O. (1987) *Introduction to the 'Laryngeal Theory'*. Norwegian University Press, Oslo (The Institute for Comparative Research in Human Culture, Series B, LXXIV)

LINDEMAN, F. O. (1992) L'accent indo-européen et le verbe celtique. *EC* **29**: 43–9

LLOYD-JONES, J. (1928) *Enwau Lleoedd Sir Gaernarfon*. University of Wales Press

LOCKWOOD, W. B. (1969) *Indo-European Philology*. Hutchinson

LOCKWOOD, W. B. (1972) *A Panorama of Indo-European Languages*. Hutchinson

LOOMIS, R., JOHNSTON, D. R. (1992) *Medieval Welsh Poems. An Anthology*. Pegasus, Binghampton, NY (Medieval and Renaissance Texts and Studies)

LOTH, J. (1884) *Vocabulaire vieux-breton*. Champion, Paris (repr. 1982 Slatkine, Geneva)

LOTH, J. (1890) *Chrestomathie bretonne*. Bouillon, Paris

LOTH, J. (1892) *Les mots latins dans les langues brittoniques (gallois, armoricain, cornique), phonétique et commentaire*. Bouillon, Paris

LOTH, J. (1905) Etudes corniques. *RC* **26**: 218–67

LOTH, J. (1930) Persistance des institutions et de la langue des Brittons du nord (ancien royaume de Statclut) au XII\u1d49 siècle. *RC* **47**: 383–400

LUCAS, L. W. (1979) *Grammar of Ros Goill Irish, Co. Donegal*. Institute of Irish Studies, Queen's University, Belfast (Studies in Irish Language and Literature)

LUCAS, L. W. (1986) *Cnuasach Focal as Ros Goill*. Royal Irish Academy, Dublin (Deascán Foclóireachta 5)

MACALISTER, R. A. S. (1945–9) *Corpus Inscriptionum Insularum Celticarum*. 2 vols. Stationery Office, Dublin

MHAC AN FHAILLIGH, E. (1968) *The Irish of Erris, Co. Mayo*. Dublin Institute for Advanced Studies

MACAULAY, D. (1966) Palatalization of Labials in Scottish Gaelic and some Related Problems in Phonology. *SGS* **11**: 72–84

MACAULAY, D. (1992a) *The Celtic Languages*. Cambridge University Press
MACAULAY, D. (1992b) The Scottish Gaelic Language. In MacAulay 1992a: 137–248
MCBREARTY, J. R. (1976) Initial Mutations in a Generative Phonology of Modern Irish. In D P Ó Baoill 1976: 39–53
MAC CANA, P. (1973) On Celtic Word-order and the Welsh 'Abnormal' Sentence. *Ériu* **24**: 90–120
MAC CANA, P. (1975–6) Notes on the Affixed Pronouns in Welsh. *SC* **10-11**: 318–25
MAC CANA, P. (1976) Latin Influence on British: the Pluperfect. In O'Meara J J, Naumann B (eds) *Latin Script and Letters AD 400–900: Festschrift Presented to Ludwig Bieler on the Occasion of his 70th Birthday*. Brill, Leiden, pp. 194–206
MAC CANA, P. (1979–80) Notes on the 'Abnormal' Sentence. *SC* **14-15**: 174–87
MAC CANA, P. (1990a) Word-order in Old Irish and Middle Welsh: an Analogy. In Matonis and Melia 1990: 253–60
MAC CANA, P. (1990b) On the Uses of the Conjunctive Pronouns in Middle Welsh. In Ball, Fife *et al.* 1990: 411–33
MAC CANA, P. (1991) Further Notes on Constituent Order in Welsh. In Fife and Poppe 1991: 45–80
MCCLOSKEY, J. (1977) An Acceptable Ambiguity in Modern Irish? *Linguistic Inquiry* **8**: 604–9
MCCLOSKEY, J. (1979) *Transformational Syntax and Model Theoretic Semantics: A Case Study in Modern Irish*. Reidel, Dordrecht
MCCLOSKEY, J. (1980) Modern Irish Nouns and the VP-Complement Analysis. *Linguistic Inquiry* **6**: 345–57
MCCLOSKEY, J. (1983) A VP in a VSO Language? In Gazdar Klein *et al.* 1983: 9–55
MCCLOSKEY, J. (1985) The Modern Irish Double Relative and Syntactic Binding. *Ériu* **36**: 45–84
MCCLOSKEY, J. (1990) Resumptive pronouns, Ā-Binding, and Levels of Representation in Irish. In Hendrick 1990a: 199–248
MCCONE, K. R. (1978) The Dative Singular of Old Irish Consonant Stems. *Ériu* **29**: 26–38
MCCONE, K. R. (1979a) Pretonic Preverbs and the Absolute Verbal Endings in Old Irish. *Ériu* **30**: 1–34
MCCONE, K. R. (1979b) The Diachronic Possibilities of the IE 'Amplified' Sentence: a Case History from Anatolian. In Broganyi B *Festschrift for Oswald Szemerényi on the Occasion of his 65th Birthday*. Benjamins, Amsterdam, pp. 467–87
MCCONE, K. R. (1980) The Nasalizing Relative Clause with Object Antecedent in the Glosses. *Ériu* **31**: 10–27
MCCONE, K. R. (1981) Final /t/ to /d/ after Unstressed Vowels, and an Old Irish Sound Law. *Ériu* **32**: 29–44
MCCONE, K. R. (1982) Further to Absolute and Conjunct. *Ériu* **33**: 1–29
MCCONE, K. R. (1984) Review of Disterheft 1980. *Celtica* **16**: 179–82
MCCONE, K. R. (1985) The Würzburg and Milan Glosses: Our Earliest Source of 'Middle Irish'. *Ériu* **36**: 85–106
MCCONE, K. R. (1986) From Indo-European to Old Irish: Conservation and Innovation in the Verbal System. In Evans D E, Griffith J G, Jope E M (eds)

Proceedings of the Seventh International Congress of Celtic Studies. Oxbow, pp. 222–66.

MCCONE, K. R. (1987) *The Early Irish Verb.* An Sagart, Maynooth (Maynooth Monographs)

MCCONE, K. R. (1990) *Pagan Past and Christian Present.* An Sagart, Maynooth (Maynooth Monographs)

MCCONE, K. R. (1991a) *The Indo-European Origins of the Old Irish Nasal Presents, Subjunctives and Futures.* Institut für Sprachwissenchaft der Universität Innsbruck, Innsbruck (Innsbrucker Beiträge zur Sprachwissenchaft, Bd 66)

MCCONE, K. R. (1991b) The PIE Stops and Syllabic Nasals in Celtic. *Studia Celtic Japonica* 4: 37–69

MCCONE, K. R. (1992) Relative Chronologie: Keltisch. In Beekes R, Lubotsky A, Weitenberg J (eds) *Rekonstruktion und relative Chronologie. Akten der VIII. Fachtagung der indogermanischen Gesellschaft, Leiden.* Institut für Sprachwissenchaft der Universität Innsbruck, Innsbruck (Innsbrucker Beiträge zur Sprachwissenchaft, Band 65), pp. 11–39

MCCONE, K. R. (1993a) Old Irish 'three' and 'four': A Question of Gender. *Ériu* 44: 53–74

MCCONE, K. R. (1993b) Old Irish *co, cucci* 'as far as (him, it)' and Latin *usque* 'as far as'. *Ériu* 44: 171–6

MCCONE, K. R., MCMANUS, D., Ó HÁINLE, C., WILLIAMS, N., BREATNACH, L. (1994) *Stair na Gaeilge in ómós do Pádraig Ó Fiannachta.* Roinn na Sean-Ghaeilge, Coláiste Phádraig, Maigh Nuad

MACDONELL, A. A. (1916) *A Vedic Grammar for Students.* Oxford University Press

MAC EOIN, G. (1993) Irish. In Ball and Fife 1993: 101–44

MAC GILL-FHINNAIN, G. (1966) *Gaidhlig Uidhist a Deas.* Dublin Institute for Advanced Studies

MACINNES, J. (1992) The Scottish Gaelic Language. In Price 1992a: 101–30

MCKENNA, C. A. (ed) (1991) *The Medieval Welsh Religious Lyric. Poems of the Gogynfeirdd, 1137–1282.* Ford and Bailie, Belmont, MA

MCKENNA, M. (1988) *A Handbook of Modern Spoken Breton.* Niemeyer, Tübingen (Buchreihe der *ZCP*, Bd 6)

MCKENNA, M. (1992) Conjugation of the Verb in Areas of East Ulster Irish: Now You See It, Now You Don't. *JCeltL* 1: 23–60

MACKINNON, K. (1993) Scottish Gaelic Today: Social History and Contemporary Status. In Ball and Fife 1993: 491–535

MACLENNAN, G. W. (ed) (1988) *Proceedings of the First North American Congress of Celtic Studies, Ottawa 1986.* Chair of Celtic Studies, Ottawa

MCMANUS, D. (1983) A Chronology of the Latin Loan-words in Early Irish. *Ériu* 34: 21–72

MCMANUS, D. (1984) On Final Syllables in the Latin Loan-words in Early Irish. *Ériu* 35: 137–62

MCMANUS, D. (1986) Ogam; Archaizing Orthography and the Authenticity of the Manuscript Key to the Alphabet. *Ériu* 37: 1–32

MCMANUS, D. (1991) *A Guide to Ogam.* An Sagart, Maynooth (Maynooth Monographs)

MAC MATHÚNA, L. (1990) Thirty Years a-floundering? Official Policy and Community Use of Irish in the Republic of Ireland. In Bramsbäck B (ed)

Homage to Ireland. Aspects of Culture, Literature and Language. Acta Universitatis Upsaliensis, Uppsala (Studia Anglistica Upsaliensia), pp. 65–80

MAC MATHÚNA, S. (1992) Post-Norman Irish Literature. In Price 1992a: 81–100

MAC NEILL, J. (1909) Notes on the Distribution, History, Grammar, and Import of the Irish Ogham Inscriptions. *PRIA* **27**: 329–70

MANN, J. C. (1971) Spoken Latin in Britain as Evidenced in the Inscriptions. *Britannia* **2**: 218–24

MARICHAL, R. (ed) (1988) *Les graffites de la Graufesenque.* CNRS, Paris (xlviiᵉ supplément à *Gallia*)

MARTINET, A. (1952) Celtic Lenition and Western Romance Consonants. *Language* **28**: 192–217 (translated and revised in Martinet 1955)

MARTINET, A. (1955) La lénition en celtique et les consonnes du roman occidental. In Martinet A *Economie des changements phonétiques.* Francke, Berne, pp. 257–96

MATONIS, A. T. E. (ed) (1987) *A Celtic Studies Bibliography for 1983–1985.* Celtic Studies Association of North America, Philadelphia

MATONIS, A. T. E., MELIA, D. F. (eds) (1990) *Celtic Language. Celtic Culture. A festschrift for Eric P. Hamp.* Ford and Bailie, Van Nuys

MATTINGLY, H., HANDFORD, S. A. (1970) *Tacitus: The Agricola and the Germania.* Penguin

MEID, W. (1963) *Die indogermanischen Grundlagen der altirischen absoluten und konjunkten Verbalflexion.* Harassowitz, Wiesbaden

MEID, W. (1967a) Zum Aequativ der keltischen Sprachen, besonders des Irischen. In Meid 1967b: 223–42

MEID, W. (ed) (1967b) *Beiträge zur Indogermanistik und Keltologie. Julius Pokorny zum 80. Geburtstag gewidmet.* Institut für Sprachwissenchaft der Universität Innsbruck, Innsbruck (Innsbrucker Beiträge zur Kulturwissenschaft, Bd 13)

MEID, W. (1990) *Handbuch des Mittelkornischen.* Institut für Sprachwissenchaft der Universität Innsbruck, Innsbruck (Innsbrucker Beiträge zur Sprachwissenschaft, Bd 62) (translation of H. Lewis and Piette 1966)

MEID, W. (1992) *Gaulish Inscriptions.* Archaeolingua, Budapest

MEILLET, A. (1933) *Esquisse d'une histoire de la langue latine.* 3rd edn. Hachette, Paris

MEILLET, A. (1937) *Introduction à l'étude comparative des langues indo-européenes.* 8th edn. Klincksieck, Paris

MEILLET, A. (1967) *The Indo-European Dialects.* University of Alabama Press (Alabama Linguistic and Philological Society)

MITCHELL, S. (1993) *Anatolia. Land, Man and Gods in Asia Minor. Vol. I The Celts and the Impact of Roman Rule.* Oxford University Press

MOORE, A. W., RHŶS, J. (eds) (1893–4) *The Book of Common Prayer in Manx Gaelic being translations made by Bishop Phillips in 1610 and by the Manx Clergy in 1765.* Manx Society, Douglas

MORGAN, D. LL. (1988) Y Beibl a Llenyddiaeth Gymraeg. In Gruffydd 1988: 87–112

MORGAN, T. J. (1952) *Y Treigladau a'u Cystrawen.* University of Wales Press

MORGAN, T. J. (1987) Simo i'n gwbod. Sana i'n gwbod. *BBCS* **34**: 88–93

MORRIS-JONES, J. (1913) *A Welsh Grammar.* Oxford University Press

MÜLLER, N. (1990) *Zur altirische Präposition* la. In Tristram H L C (ed) *Deutsche, Kelten und Iren. 150 Jahre deutsche Keltologie. Gearóid Mac Eoin zum 60. Geburtstag gewidmet.* Buske, Hamburg, pp. 115–23

MÜLLER, N. (1994) Review of MacAulay 1992, Price 1992, Ball and Fife 1993. *JCeltL* **3**: 171–4

NANCE, R. M. (ed) (1978) *An English–Cornish and Cornish–English Dictionary.* Cornish Language Board, Marazion

NASH-WILLIAMS, V. E. (1950) *The Early Christian Monuments of Wales.* University of Wales Press

NATIONAL LIBRARY OF WALES (1909–84) *Bibliotheca Celtica.* National Library of Wales, Aberystwyth

NIC PHÁIDÍN, C. (1987) *Cnuasach Focal ó Uibh Ráthach.* Royal Irish Academy, Dublin (Deascán Foclóireachta 6)

NORRIS, E. (1859) *The Ancient Cornish Drama.* Oxford University Press

Ó BAÓILL, C. (1978) *Contributions to a Comparative Study of Ulster Irish and Scottish Gaelic.* Institute of Irish Studies, The Queen's University, Belfast

Ó BAOILL, D. P. (1979) *Papers in Celtic Phonology.* New University of Ulster (Occasional Papers in Linguistics and Language Learning, 6)

O'BRIEN, M. A. (1956) Etymologies and Notes. *Celtica* **3**: 168–84

O'BRIEN, M. A. (1962) *Corpus Genealogiarum Hiberniae.* vol. 1. Dublin Institute for Advanced Studies

Ó BUACHALLA, B. (1977) *Ní* and *cha* in Ulster Irish. *Ériu* **28**: 92–141

Ó BUACHALLA, B. (1985) The *f*-future in Modern Irish: A Re-assessment. *PRIA* **85**: 1–36

Ó CORRÁIN, A. (1992) On Certain Modal and Aspectual Values of the Future Category in Irish. *JCeltL* **1**: 1–21

Ó CUÍV, B. (1944) *The Irish of West Muskerry.* Dublin Institute for Advanced Studies

Ó CUÍV, B. (1951) *Irish Dialects and Irish-speaking Districts.* Dublin Institute for Advanced Studies

Ó CUÍV, B. (1980) The Verbal Noun Ending *-áil* and Related Forms. *Celtica* **13**: 125–45

Ó CUÍV, B. (1986) Sandhi Phenomena in Irish. In Andersen 1986: 396–414

Ó CUÍV, B. (1990) Vowel Hiatus in Early Modern Irish. In Matonis and Melia 1990: 96–107

Ó DOCHARTAIGH, C. (1976) Aspects of Cluster Modification in Irish. In D. P. Ó Baoill 1976: 124–33

Ó DOCHARTAIGH, C. (1987) *Dialects of Ulster Irish.* Institute of Irish Studies, Queen's University, Belfast

Ó DOCHARTAIGH, C. (1992) The Irish Language. In MacAulay 1992a: 11–99

Ó DÓNAILL, N. (ed) (1977) *Foclóir Gaeilge : Béarla.* Oifig an tSoláthair, Dublin

OFTEDAL, M. (1956) *The Gaelic of Leurbost, Isle of Lewis.* Norwegian University Press, Oslo (*NTS* Supplement, Bd iv)

OFTEDAL, M. (1962) A Morphemic Evaluation of the Celtic Initial Mutations. *Lochlann* **2**: 93–102

OFTEDAL, M. (1963) On 'Palatalised' Labials in Scottish Gaelic. *SGS* **10**: 71–81

Ó hAIRT, D. (1988) *Díolaim Dhéiseach.* Royal Irish Academy, Dublin (Deascán Focloireachta 7)

Ó hÓGÁIN, D. (1984) *Díolaim Focal (A) ó Chorca Dhuibhne.* Royal Irish Academy, Dublin (Deascán Foclóireachta 3)

OKASHA, E. (1993) *Corpus of Early Christian Inscribed Stones of South-west Britain*. Leicester University Press (Studies in the Early History of Britain)

OLSEN, B. L., PADEL, O. J. (1986) A Tenth-century List of Cornish Parochial Saints. *CMCS* **12**: 33–71

Ó MÁILLE, T. (1911) Contributions to the History of the Verbs of Existence in Irish. *Ériu* **6**: 1–102

Ó MÁILLE, T. S. (1974) *Liosta Focal as Ros Muc*. Irish University Press

Ó MUIRI, D. (1982) *Comhréir Ghaeilge Ghaoth Dobhair*. Coiscéim, Dublin

Ó MURCHÚ, M. (1985) *The Irish Language*. Government of Ireland, Dublin (Aspects of Ireland, 10)

Ó MURCHÚ, M. (1989) *East Perthshire Gaelic*. Dublin Institute for Advanced Studies

Ó MURCHÚ, M. (1992) The Irish Language. In Price 1992a: 30–64

Ó MURCHÚ, M. (1993) Aspects of the Societal Status of Modern Irish. In Ball and Fife 1993: 471–90

O'NEILL, T. (1984) *The Irish Hand*. Dolmen, Portlaoise

O'RAHILLY, C. (1976) *Táin Bó Cúailnge, Recension I*. Dublin Institute for Advanced Studies

O'RAHILLY, T. F. (1932) *Irish Dialects Past and Present*. Browne and Nolan, Dublin (repr. 1972, 1976, Dublin Institute for Advanced Studies)

O'RAHILLY, T. F. (1946) *Early Irish History and Mythology*. Dublin Institute for Advanced Studies

O'RAHILLY, T. F. (1946–50) *Do-ním, déanim* 'I proceed, go'. *Celtica* **1**: 318–21

Ó RIAGÁIN, P. (1992) *Language Maintenance and Language Shift as Strategies of Social Reproduction. Irish in the Corca Dhuibhne Gaeltacht 1926–86*. Institúid Teangeolaíochta Eireann, Dublin

Ó RIAIN, P. (1992) Early Irish Literature. In Price 1992a: 65– 80

Ó SIADHAIL, M. (1973) Abairtí freagartha agus míreanna freagartha sa Nua-Ghaeilge. *Ériu* **24**: 134–59

Ó SIADHAIL, M. (1982) Cardinal Numbers in Modern Irish. *Ériu* **23**: 101–7

Ó SIADHAIL, M. (1983) The Erosion of the Copula in Modern Irish Dialects. *Celtica* **15**: 117–27

Ó SIADHAIL, M. (1989) *Modern Irish: Grammatical Structure and Dialectal Variation*. Cambridge University Press

Ó SIADHAIL M., WIGGER, A. (1975) *Coras na Fuaimeanna Gaeilge*. Dublin Institute for Advanced Studies

PADEL, O. J. (1985) *Cornish Place-name Elements*. Nottingham (English Place Name Society)

PADEL, O. J. (1988) *A Popular Dictionary of Cornish Place-names*. Alison Hodge, Penzance

PALMER, L. R. (1954) *The Latin Language*. Faber and Faber

PANDOLFINI M., PROSDOCIMI, A. L. (1990) *Alfabetari e insegnamento della scritture in Etruria e nell'Italia antica*. Florence

PARRY, T. (1962) *A History of Welsh Literature*. Oxford University Press

PARRY-WILLIAMS, T. H. (1923) *The English Element in Welsh*. Honourable Society of Cymmrodorion, London

PEDERSEN, H. (1909–13) *Vergleichende Grammatik der keltischen Sprachen*. 2 vols. Vandenhoek and Ruprecht, Göttingen

PIERCE, G. O. (1968) *The Place-names of Dinas Powys Hundred*. University of Wales Press

PILCH, H. (1986) Typology of Celtic Mutations. In Andersen 1986: 105–13

POKORNY, J. (1969) *Altirische Grammatik*. 2nd edn. De Gruyter, Berlin

POPE, M. K. (1934) *From Latin to Modern French with Especial Consideration of Anglo-Norman*. Manchester University Press

POPPE, E. (1989) Constituent Ordering in *Breudwyt Macsen Wledig*. BBCS **37**: 46–63

POPPE, E. (1990) Word Order Patterns in *Breudwyt Ronabwy*. In Ball and Fife *et al.* 1990: 445–60

POPPE, E. (1991a) *Untersuchungen zur Wortstellung im Mittelkymrischen*. Helmut Buske, Hamburg

POPPE, E. (1991b) Word Order in *Cyfranc Lludd a Llefelys*: Notes on the Pragmatics of Constituent Ordering in Middle Welsh Narrative Prose. In Fife and Poppe 1991: 157–204

POPPE, E. (1993) Word Order in Middle Welsh: the case of *Kedymdeithas Amlyn ac Amic*. BBCS 40: 95–117

PRESS, I. (1986) *A Grammar of Modern Breton*. Mouton de Gruyter, Berlin (Mouton Grammar Library 2)

PRICE, G. (1984) *The Languages of Britain*. Edward Arnold

PRICE, G. (ed) (1992a) *The Celtic Connection*. Colin Smythe (Princess Grace Irish Library, 6)

PRICE, G. (1992b) The Celtic Languages. In Price 1992a: 1–9

PRICE, G. (1992c) The Welsh Language Today. In Price 1992a: 206–15

PRICE, G. (1992d) Cornish Language and Literature. In Price 1992a: 302–14

QUIGGIN, E. C. (1906) *A Dialect of Donegal*. Cambridge University Press

QUIGGIN, E. C. (1937) *Poems from the Book of the Dean of Lismore*. Cambridge University Press

QUIN, E. G. (1969) On the Modern Irish *f*-future. *Ériu* **21**: 32–41

QUIN, E. G. (1978) The Origin of the *f*-future: an Alternative Explanation. *Ériu* **29**: 13–25

QUIN, E. G. *et al.* (1913–76) (*Contributions to a*) *Dictionary of the Irish Language based mainly on Old and Middle Irish Materials*. Royal Irish Academy, Dublin

RANKIN, H. D. (1987) *Celts and the Classical World*. Croom Helm

RHŶS, J. (1906) The Celtic Inscriptions of France and Italy. *PBA* **2**: 273–373

RICHARDS, M. (1935) *Llawlyfr Hen Wyddeleg*. University of Wales Press

RICHARDS, M. (1969) *Welsh Administrative and Territorial Units*. University of Wales Press

RIVET, A. L. F. (1988) *Gallia Narbonensis*. Batsford

RIVET, A. L. F., SMITH, C. (1979) *The Place-names of Roman Britain*. Batsford

ROBERTS, B. F. (ed) (1988) *Early Welsh Poetry: Studies in the Book of Aneirin*. National Library of Wales, Aberystwyth

ROBERTS, M. E., JONES, R. M. (1974) Iaith Lafar. In *Cyfeiriadur i'r Athro Iaith, Rhan II, D-N*. University of Wales Press

ROBINS, R. H. (1987) The Life and Work of Sir William Jones. *TPhS*: 1–23

ROGERS, H. (1992) The Initial Mutations in Modern Scottish Gaelic. *Celtica* **7**: 63–85

ROSÉN, H. (1981) *Studies in the Syntax of the Verbal Noun in Early Latin*. Fink, Munich

ROUVERET, A. (1990) X-Bar Theory, Minimality and Barrierhood in Welsh. In Hendrick 1990a: 27–79

RUSSELL, P. (1982) The Origin of the Welsh Conjunctive Pronouns. *BBCS* **30**: 30–8

RUSSELL, P. (1984) Welsh *anadl/anaddl, gwadn/gwaddn*. *BBCS* **31**: 104–12

RUSSELL, P. (1985a) A Footnote to Spirantization. *CMCS* **10**: 53–6

RUSSELL, P. (1985b) Middle Welsh *brodorion*. *BBCS* **32**: 168–71

RUSSELL, P. (1985c) Recent Work in British Latin. *CMCS* **9**: 19–29

RUSSELL, P. (1988a) The Suffix *-āko-* in Continental Celtic. *EC* **25**: 131–73

RUSSELL, P. (1988b) The Sounds of a Silence: The Growth of Cormac's Glossary. *CMCS* **15**: 1–30

RUSSELL, P. (1988c) The Celtic Preverb **uss* and Related Matters. *Ériu* **39**: 95–126

RUSSELL, P. (1988d) Review of Zimmer 1987. *CMCS* **15**: 108–9

RUSSELL, P. (1988e) Preverbs, Prepositions and Adverbs: Sigmatic and Asigmatic. *TPhS* **86**: 144–72

RUSSELL, P. (1989) Agent Suffixes in Welsh: Native and Non-native. *BBCS* **36**: 30–42

RUSSELL, P. (1990) *Celtic Word Formation: the Velar Suffixes*. Dublin Institute for Advanced Studies

RUSSELL, P. (1991–2) Review of Bammesberger and Wollmann 1990. *SC* **26-27**: 265–70

RUSSELL, P. (1992a) Some Neglected Sources for Middle Welsh Phonology. *EC* **29**: 383–90

RUSSELL, P. (1992b) Review of Eska 1989a. *JCeltL* **1**: 175–7

RUSSELL, P. (1993a) Review of McCone 1991a. *JCeltL* **2**: 157–68

RUSSELL, P. (1993b) Orthography as a Key to Codicology: Innovation in the Work of a Thirteenth Century Welsh Scribe. *CMCS* **25**: 77–85.

RUSSELL, P. (1993c) Modern Welsh *-og* and Productivity in Derivational Patterns. *JCeltL* **2**: 151–6

RUSSELL, P. (1994) Review of Salmons 1992. *JCeltL* **3**: 177–9

RUSSELL, P. (forthcoming) Scribal (In)competence in 13th Century North Wales: The Orthography of the Black Book of Chirk (Peniarth MS 29). *NLWJ*

SADLER, L. (1988) *Welsh Syntax. A Government-binding Approach*. Croom Helm (Croom Helm Linguistics Series)

SALMONS, J. (1992) *Accentual Change and Language Contact*. Routledge

SCHMIDT, K. H. (1957) Die Komposition in gallischen Personennamen. *ZCP* **26**: 33–301

SCHMIDT, K. H. (1958) Gallisch *nemeton* und Verwandtes. *Münchener Studien zur Sprachwissenchaft* **12**: 49–51

SCHMIDT, K. H. (1971) Partizip und passives Präteritum im Keltischen. In Schmidt-Brandt R (ed) *Donum Indogermanicum. Festgabe für Anton Scherer zum 70. Geburtstag*. Winter, Heidelberg

SCHMIDT, K. H. (1976a) Zur keltiberischen Inschrift von Botorrita. *BBCS* **26**: 375–94

SCHMIDT, K. H. (1976b) Historische-vergleichende Analyse des keltiberischen Inschrift von Botorrita zu Grunde liegenden Morpheminventars. In Davies A M, Meid W (eds) *Studies in Greek, Italic and Indo-European Linguistics Offered to Leonard R. Palmer*. Institut für Sprachwissenchaft der Universität Innsbruck, Innsbruck, pp. 359–71 (Innsbrucker Beiträge zur Sprachwissenchaft, Bd 16)

SCHMIDT, K. H. (1977a) *Die festlandkeltischen Sprachen*. Institut für Sprachwissenchaft der Universität Innsbruck, Innsbruck (Innsbrucker Beiträge zur Sprachwissenschaft, Vorträge und kleinere Schriften 18)

SCHMIDT, K. H. (ed) (1977b) *Indogermanisch und Keltisch*. Reichart, Wiesbaden

SCHMIDT, K. H. (1978–80) On the Celtic Languages of Continental Europe. *BBCS* **28**: 189–205 (English version of Schmidt 1977a)

SCHMIDT, K. H. (1980–2) The Gaulish Inscription of Chamalières. *BBCS* **29**: 256–68

SCHMIDT, K. H. (1988) On the Reconstruction of Proto-Celtic. In Maclennan 1988: 231–48

SCHMIDT, K. H. (1990) Zum plomb du Larzac. In Matonis and Melia 1990: 16–25

SCHMIDT, K. H. (1991) Latin and Celtic: Genetic Relationship and Areal Contacts. *BBCS* **38**: 1–19

SCHMIDT, K. H. (1993) Insular Celtic: P and Q Celtic. In Ball and Fife 1993: 64–98

SHARPE, R. (1991) *Medieval Irish Saints' Lives. An Introduction to Vitae Sanctorum Hiberniae*. Oxford University Press

SHUKEN, C. (1976) Some Physiological and Acoustic Characteristics of Scottish Gaelic Stop Consonants. In D P Ó Baoill 1976: 134–52

SIMS-WILLIAMS, P. (1982) The Development of the Indo-European Voiced Labio-velars in Celtic. *BBCS* **29**: 201–29

SIMS-WILLIAMS, P. (1984) The Double System of Verbal Inflexion in Old Irish. *TPhS*: 138–201

SIMS-WILLIAMS, P. (1990) Dating the Transition to Neo-Brittonic: Phonology and History, 400–600. In Bammesberger and Wollmann 1990: 217–61

SIMS-WILLIAMS, P. (1991) The Emergence of Old Welsh, Cornish and Breton Orthography, 600–800: The Evidence of Archaic Old Welsh. *BBCS* **38**: 20–86

SIMS-WILLIAMS, P. (1992) The Additional Letters of the Ogam Alphabet. *CMCS* **23**: 29–75

SIMS-WILLIAMS, P. (1993) Some Problems in Deciphering the Early Irish Ogam Alphabet. *TPhS* **91**: 133–80

SJOESTADT, M. L. (1931) *Phonétique d'un parler irlandais de Kerry*. Ernest Leroux, Paris

SJOESTADT-JONVAL, M. L. (1938) *Description d'un parler irlandais de Kerry*. Champion, Paris

SOMMERFELT, A. (1922) *The Dialect of Torr, Co. Donegal*. Dybwald, Oslo

SOMMERFELT, A. (1925a) *Studies in Cyfeiliog Welsh. A Contribution to Welsh Dialectology*. Dybwald, Oslo (Det Norske Videnskap-Akademi, Hist.-Filos. Klasse, No. 3)

SOMMERFELT, A. (1925b) Sur le système consonantique du celtique. In *Mélanges linguistiques offerts à M. J. Vendryes par ses amis et ses élèves*. Champion, Paris, pp. 341–6 (Collection linguistique publiée par la Société de Linguistique de Paris) (= Sommerfelt 1962: 325–8)

SOMMERFELT, A. (1954) Consonant Quality in Celtic. *NTS* **17**: 102–18 (= Sommerfelt 1962: 349–59)

SOMMERFELT, A. (1957) Some Notes on the Influence of Latin on the Insular Celtic Languages. In *Acta Congressus Madvigiani. Proceedings of the*

Second International Congress of Classical Studies, vol. V, pp. 157–62 (= Sommerfelt 1962: 360–4)

SOMMERFELT, A. (1962) *Diachronic and Synchronic Aspects of Language.* Mouton, The Hague (Ianua Linguarum, series major VII)

SOMMERFELT, A. (1978) *Le breton parlé de Saint-Pol-de-Léon.* new edn by Falc'hun F, Oftedal M. Universitetsforlaget, Oslo

SPROAT, R. (1985) Welsh Syntax and VSO Structure. *Natural Language and Linguistic Theory* **3**: 173–216

STENSON, N. (1981) *Studies in Irish Syntax.* Gunter Narr, Tübingen (Ars Linguistica 8, commentationes analyticae et criticae)

STENSON, N. (1991) Review of Ó Siadhail 1989. *Journal of Linguistics* **27**: 274–7

STEPHENS, J. (1993) Breton. In Ball and Fife 1993: 349–409

STEPHENS, M. (ed) (1986) *The Oxford Companion to the Literature of Wales.* Oxford University Press

STEPHENS, R. (1978) *Yr Odliadur.* Gwasg Gomer

STEPHENS, R. (1989–90) Review of Zimmer 1987. *SC* **24-25**: 236–7

STEVENSON, J. (1989) The Beginnings of Literacy in Ireland. *PRIA* **89**: 127–65

STOCKMAN, G. (1974) *The Irish of Aichill, Co. Mayo.* Institute of Irish Studies, Queen's University, Belfast

STOKES, W. (ed) (1860–1) The Passion: A Middle Cornish Poem. *TPhS* (appendix): 1–100

STOKES, W. (ed) (1864) *Gwreans an Bys: The Creation of the World.* Williams and Norgate.

STOKES, W. (ed) (1872) *The Life of Saint Meriasek, Bishop and Confessor: A Cornish Drama.* Trübner

STOKES, W. (ed) (1883) *Saltair na Rann.* Clarendon Press (Anecdota Oxoniensia, Medieval and Modern series, vol. 1, part iii)

STOKES, W. (1899) The Bodleian *Amra Choluimb Cille. RC* **20**: 30–55, 132–83, 248–87, 400–37

STOKES, W. (1900) A Collation of Norris' *Ancient Cornish Drama. Archiv für celtische Lexicographie* **1**: 161–74 (see Norris 1859)

STOKES, W. (1902) On the Death of Some Irish Heroes. *RC* **23**: 303–48

STOKES, W., STRACHAN, J. (1901–3) *Thesaurus Palaeohibernicus. A Collection of Old-Irish Glosses, Scholia, Prose and Verse.* 2 vols. Cambridge University Press

STRACHAN, J. (1903–6) Contributions to the History of the Middle Irish Declension. *TPhS*: 202–46

STRACHAN, J. (1908) *An Introduction to Early Welsh.* Manchester University Press

STRACHAN, J., BERGIN, O. J. (1949) *Old-Irish Paradigms and Selections from the Old-Irish Glosses.* 4th edn. Royal Irish Academy, Dublin

STUMP, G. T. (1990) Breton Inflection and the Split Morphology Hypothesis. In Hendrick 1990a: 97–119

SWEET, H. (1882–4) Spoken North Welsh. *TPhS* **19**: 409–84

SZEMERÉNYI, O. (1974) A Gaulish Dedicatory Formula. *Kuhns Zeitschrift für vergleichende Sprachforschung* **88**: 246–86

SZEMERÉNYI, O. (1978) Review of Schmidt 1977a. *ZCP* **36**: 293–7

SZEMERÉNYI, O. (1990) *Einführung in die vergleichende Sprachwissenschaft.*

4th edn. Wissenschaftliche Buchgesellschaft, Darmstadt

SZEMERÉNYI, O. (1991) Review of de Bernardo Stempel 1987. *ZCP* **44**: 299–312

TERNES, E. (1970) *Grammaire structurale du breton parlé de l'Ile de Groix.* Winter, Heidelberg

TERNES, E. (1992) The Breton Language. In MacAulay 1992a: 371–452

THOMAS, A. R. (1966) Systems in Welsh Phonology. *SC* **1**: 93–127

THOMAS, A. R. (1973) *The Linguistic Geography of Wales.* University of Wales Press

THOMAS, A. R. (1977) Derivational Complexity in Varieties of Contemporary Spoken Welsh. *Word* **28**: 166–86

THOMAS, A. R. (1984) A Lowering Rule for Vowels and its Ramifications in a Dialect of North Welsh. In Ball and Jones 1984: 105–24

THOMAS, A. R. (1992a) The Welsh Language. In MacAulay 1992: 251– 345

THOMAS, A. R. (1992b) The Cornish Language. In MacAulay 1992: 346– 70

THOMAS, B. (1984) Linguistic and Non-linguistic Boundaries in North-east Wales. In Ball and Jones 1984: 189–207

THOMAS, B., THOMAS, P. W. (1989) *Cymraeg, Cymrâg, Cymrêg . . . Cyflwyno'r Tafodieithoedd.* Gwasg Taf

THOMAS, C. (1994) *And Shall These Mute Stones Speak? Post-Roman Inscriptions in Western Britain.* University of Wales Press

THOMAS, C. H. (1966) Review of Joncs R M 1965. *Y Traethodydd* **121** (3rd series **34**): 174–80

THOMAS, C. H. (1967) Review of *Cymraeg Byw Rhifyn 2. Llên Cymru* **9**: 242–9

THOMAS, C. H. (1973–4) The Verbal System and the Responsive in a Welsh Dialect of South-east Glamorgan. *SC* **8-9**: 271–86

THOMAS, C. H. (1975–6) Some Phonological Features of Dialects in South-east Wales. *SC* **10-11**: 345–66

THOMAS, C. H. (1979) Y Tafodieithegydd a 'Cymraeg Cyfoes'. *Llên Cymru* **13**: 113–59

THOMAS, C. H. (1993) *Tafodiaith Nantgarw. Astudiaeth Gymraeg Llafar Nantgarw yng Nghwm Taf, Morgannwg* 2 vols. University of Wales Press

THOMAS, G. C. G. (ed) (1988) *A Welsh Bestiary of Love.* Dublin Institute for Advanced Studies

THOMAS, P. W. (1984) Variation in South Glamorgan Consonant Mutation. In Ball and Jones 1984: 208–36

THOMAS, P. W. (1989) In Search of Middle Welsh Dialects. In Byrne C J, Henry M, Ó Siadhail P (eds) *Celtic Languages and Celtic Peoples. Proceedings of the Second North American Congress of Celtic Studies.* St Mary's University, Halifax, pp. 287–303

THOMAS, P. W. (1990) The Brythonic Consonant Shift and the Development of Consonant Mutation. *BBCS* **37**: 1–42

THOMAS, P. W. (1993) Middle Welsh Dialects: Problems and Perspectives, *BBCS* **40**: 17–50

THOMAS, R. J. *et al.* (eds) (1950–) *Geiriadur Prifysgol Cymru. A Dictionary of the Welsh Language.* University of Wales Press

THOMAS, S. E. (1988) A Study of *Calediad* in the Upper Swansea Valley. In Ball 1988a: 85–96

THOMSON, D. S. (1989) *An Introduction to Gaelic Poetry.* 2nd edn. Edinburgh University Press

THOMSON, D. S. (1992 Scottish Gaelic Literature. In Price 1992a: 131–53

THOMSON, R. L. (ed) (1961) The Manx *Traditionary Ballad*. *EC* **9**: 521–48, **10**: 60–87

THOMSON, R. L. (1969) The Study of Manx Gaelic. *PBA* **55**: 177–210

THOMSON, R. L. (1992a) The Manx Language. In MacAulay 1992a: 100–36

THOMSON, R. L. (1992b) Manx Language and Literature. In Price 1992a: 154–70

THORNE, D. A. (1985) *Cyflwyniad i Astudio'r Iaith Gymraeg*. University of Wales Press

THORNE, D. A. (1992) The Welsh Language, its History and Structure. In Price 1992a: 171–205

THORNE, D. A. (1993) *A Comprehensive Welsh Grammar*. Blackwell (Reference Grammars)

THURNEYSEN, R. (1907) On Certain Initial Changes in the Irish Verb after Preverbal Particles. *Ériu* **3**: 18–19

THURNEYSEN, R. (1909) *Handbuch des Altirischen*. vol. I. Winter, Heidelberg

THURNEYSEN, R. (1946) *A Grammar of Old Irish*. 2nd edn revised and translated by Binchy D A and Bergin O J. Dublin Institute for Advanced Studies

TIBILETTI BRUNO, M. G. (1978) Ligure, Leponzio e Gallico. In Prosdocimi A. L., (ed) *Popoli e Civilta dell'Italia Antica, vol. 6 Lingue e Dialetti*. Biblioteca di Storia Patria, Rome

TIERNEY , J. J. (1960) The Celtic Ethnography of Posidonius. *PRIA* **60**: 189–275

TIMM, L. A. (1985) Breton Mutations: Literary vs Vernacular Usages. *Word* **35**: 95–107

TIMM, L. A. (1989) Word Order in Twentieth Century Breton. *Natural Language and Linguistic Theory* **7**: 361–78

TIMM, L. A. (1990) Some Observations on the Syntax of the Breton Verbal Noun. In Ball, Fife *et al.* 1990: 189–208

TIMM, L. A. (1991) The Discourse Pragmatics of NP-initial Sentences in Breton. In Fife and Poppe 1991: 274–310

TOMLIN, R. S. O. (1987) Was Ancient British Celtic ever a Written Language? Two texts from Roman Bath. *BBCS* **34**: 18–25

TOMLIN, R. S. O. (1988) Tabellae Sulis. Roman Inscribed Tablets on Tin and Lead from the Sacred Spring at Bath. In Cunliffe B (ed) *The Temple of Sulis Minerva at Bath* vol. II. Oxford University Committee for Archaeology

TOORIANS, L. (1991) *The Middle Cornish Charter Endorsement. The Making of a Marriage in Medieval Cornwall*. Institut für Sprachwissenschaft der Universität Innsbruck, Innsbruck (Innsbrucker Beiträge zur Sprachwissenschaft, Bd 67)

TOVAR, A. (1949) *Estudios sobre las primitivas lenguas hispánicas*. Ministerio de Educación, Buenos Aires

TOVAR, A. (1951) La sonorisation et la chute des intervocaliques: phénomène latin occidental. *Revue des Etudes Latines* **29**: 102–20

TOVAR, A. (1972–3) Kollektiva auf *r* im Keltischen. *EC* **13**: 411–27

TRÉPOS, P. (1957) *Le pluriel breton*. Emgleo Breiz, Brest

TRISTRAM, H. L. C. (1983) *Tense and Time in Early Irish Narrative*. Institut für Sprachwissenchaft der Universität Innsbruck, Innsbruck (Innsbrucker Beiträge zur Sprachwissenchaft, Vorträge und kleinere Schriften 32)

UHLICH, J. (1989) *DOV(A)* and lenited *-B-* in Ogam. *Ériu* **40**: 129–34

UÍ BHEIRN Ú. M. (1989) *Cnuasach Focal as Teileann*. Royal Irish Academy, Dublin (Deascán Foclóireachta 8)

UNIVERSITY OF WALES PRESS, (1928) *Orgraff yr Iaith Gymraeg*. Cardiff

UNTERMANN J. (1980) *Monumenta Linguarum Hispanicarum, band II, Die Inschriften in iberischer Schrift aus Südfrankreich.* Reichert, Wiesbaden

UNTERMANN, J. (1990) *Monumenta Linguarum Hispanicarum, Band III, Die iberischen Inschriften aus Spanien* (2 vols). Reichert, Wiesbaden

VÄÄNÄNEN, V. (1981) *Introduction au latin vulgaire* 3rd edn. Klincksieck, Paris

VENDRYES, J. (1908) *Grammaire du vieil irlandais.* Guilmoto, Paris

VENDRYES, J. (1951) Sur le traitment brittonique de *i* en hiatus. *Bulletin de la Société de Linguistique de Paris* **47**: 1–10

VENDRYES, J., BACHELLERY, E., LAMBERT, P-Y. (eds) (1959–) *Lexique étymologique de l'irlandais ancien* vols *A-C, M-U.* Dublin Institute for Advanced Studies/CNRS, Paris

WAGNER, H. (1958–69) *Linguistic Atlas and Survey of Irish Dialects.* 4 vols. Dublin Institute for Advanced Studies

WAGNER, H. (1959) *Gaeilge Theilinn.* Dublin Institute for Advanced Studies

WAGNER, H. (1967) Zur unregelmässigen Wordstellung in der altirischen Alliterationsdichtung. In Meid 1967b: 289–314

WAGNER, H. (1977) Wortstellung im Keltischen und Indogermanischen. In Schmidt 1977: 204–35

WAINWRIGHT, F. T. (ed) (1980) *The Problem of the Picts.* 2nd edn. Nelson

WALDE, A. (1917) *Über älteste sprachliche Beziehungen zwischen Kelten und Italikern.* Kiesel, Innsbruck

WAKELIN, M. F. (1975) *Language and History in Cornwall.* Leicester University Press

WATKINS, C. (1955) The Phonemics of Gaulish: the Dialect of Narbonensis. *Language* **31**: 9–19

WATKINS, C. (1962) *The Indo-European Origins of the Celtic Verb: I the Sigmatic Aorist.* Dublin Institute for Advanced Studies

WATKINS, C. (1963a) Preliminaries to the Historical and Comparative Analysis of the Syntax of the Old Irish Verb. *Celtica* **6**: 11–49

WATKINS, C. (1963b) Indo-European Metrics and Archaic Irish Verse. *Celtica* **6**: 194–249

WATKINS, C. (1964) Preliminaries to the Reconstruction of the Indo-European Sentence Structure. In Lunt H G (ed) *Proceedings of the Ninth International Congress of Linguistics.* Mouton, The Hague, pp. 1035–42

WATKINS, C. (1966a) Italo-Celtic Revisited. In Birnbaum H, Puhvel J (eds) *Ancient Indo-European Dialects.* University of California Press, Berkeley/ Los Angeles, pp. 29–50

WATKINS, C. (1966b) The Origin of the *f*-future. *Ériu* **20**: 67–81

WATKINS, C. (1966c) The Indo-European Word for 'day' in Celtic and Related Topics. *Trivium* **1**: 102–20

WATKINS, C. (1976) The Etymology of Irish *dúan. Celtica* **11**: 270–9

WATKINS, T. A. (1961) *Ieithyddiaeth. Agweddau ar Astudio Iaith.* University of Wales Press

WATKINS, T. A. (1967) Some Phonological Features of the Welsh Dialect of Llansamlet. In Meid 1967b: 315–22

WATKINS, T. A. (1972) The Accent in Old Welsh – its Quality and its Development. *BBCS* **25**: 1–11

WATKINS, T. A. (1977) The Welsh Personal Pronouns. *Word* **28**: 146–65

WATKINS, T. A. (1977–8a) Y Rhagenw Ategol. *SC* **12-13**: 349–66

WATKINS, T. A. (1977–8b) Trefn yn y Frawddeg Gymraeg. *SC* **12-13**: 367–95

WATKINS, T. A. (1983–4) Trefn y Constitwentau Brawddegol yn *Branwen*. *SC* **18-19**: 147–57

WATKINS, T. A. (1987) Constituent Order in the Old Welsh Verbal Sentence. *BBCS* **34**: 51–60

WATKINS, T. A. (1988) *Constituent Order in the Positive Declarative Sentence in the Medieval Welsh Tale 'Kulhwch ac Olwen'*. Institut für Sprachwissenchaft der Universität Innsbruck, Innsbruck (Innsbrucker Beiträge zur Sprachwissenschaft, Vorträge und kleinere Schriften 41)

WATKINS, T. A. (1990) Constituent Order in the Negative Declarative Sentence in the White Book Version of *Kulhwch ag Olwen*. In Matonis and Melia 1990: 247–52

WATKINS, T. A. (1991) The Functions of Cleft and Non-cleft Constituent Orders in Modern Welsh. In Fife and Poppe 1991: 329–51

WATKINS, T. A. (1993) Welsh. In Ball and Fife 1993: 289–348

WELLS, J. C. (1979a) Final Voicing and Vowel Length in Welsh. *Phonetica* **36**: 344–60

WHATMOUGH, J. (1963) Continental Celtic. In *Proceedings of the International Congress of Celtic Studies 1963*. University of Wales Press, pp. 101–20

WHATMOUGH, J. (1970) *The Dialects of Ancient Gaul*. Harvard University Press, Cambridge, Mass.

WIGGER, A. (1972) Preliminaries to a Generative Morphology of the Modern Irish Verb. *Ériu* **23**: 162–213

WIGGER, A. (1976) Irish Dialect Phonology and Problems of Irish Orthography. In D P Ó Baoill 1976: 173–99

WILLIAMS, B. (1982–3) An Approach to the Welsh Vowel System. *BBCS* **30**: 239–52

WILLIAMS, G. J., JONES, E. J. (eds) (1934) *Gramadegau Pennceirddiaid*. University of Wales Press

WILLIAMS, I. (ed) (1926–7) The Computus Fragment. *BBCS* **3**: 245–72

WILLIAMS, I. (ed) (1930) *Pedeir Keinc y Mabinogi*. University of Wales Press

WILLIAMS, I. (ed) (1938) *Canu Aneirin*. University of Wales Press

WILLIAMS, I. (ed) (1941) An Old Welsh Verse. *NLWJ* **2**: 69–75 (reprinted in Bromwich 1972: 181–9)

WILLIAMS, I. (1945) *Enwau Lleoedd*. Gwasg y Brython, Liverpool

WILLIAMS, I. (ed) (1968) *The Poems of Taliesin* translated and annotated by Williams J E C. Dublin Institute for Advanced Studies

WILLIAMS, J. E. C., FORD, P. K. (1992) *The Irish Literary Tradition*. University of Wales Press

WILLIAMS, J. E. C., HUGHES, M. B. (eds) 1988 *Llyfryddiaeth yr Iaith Gymraeg*. University of Wales Press

WILLIAMS, R. (1992) Breton Literature. In Price 1992a: 276–300

WILLIAMS, S. J. (1980) *A Welsh Grammar*. University of Wales Press

WILLIS, P. (1986) *The Initial Consonant Mutations in Welsh and Breton*. Indiana University Linguistics Club, Bloomington

WILLIS, P. (1987) A Reply to T D Griffen, 'Early Welsh Aspiration ...'. *Word* **38**: 47–55

WILLIS, P. (1988) Is the Welsh Verbal Noun a Verb or a Noun? *Word* **39**: 201–24

ZIEGLER, S. (1994) *Die Sprache der altirischen Ogam-Inschriften*. Vandenhoeck und Ruprecht, Göttingen (*Historische Sprachforschung*, Ergänzungsheft 36)

ZIMMER, S. (1987) *Geiriadur Gwrthdroadol Cymraeg Diweddar. A Reverse Dictionary of Modern Welsh*. Buske, Hamburg

ZIMMER, S. (1990a) *Handbuch des Mittelkornischen*. Institut für Sprachwissenchaft der Universität Innsbruck, Innsbruck (Innsbrucker Beiträge zur Sprachwissenschaft; translation of Lewis 1946)

ZIMMER, S. (1990b) Dating the Loanwords: the Latin Suffixes in Welsh. In Bammesberger and Wollmann 1990: 263–82

ZIMMER, S. (1992) On the Productivity of the Welsh Suffix *-og*. *JCeltL* **1**: 139–44

ZIMMER, S. (1994) Zum britischen *s-*. *JCeltL* **3**: 149–64

Index

Page references in italics refer to tables, figures or maps.

abnormal order, 294–6
  see also word order, Middle Welsh
absolute verbal conjugation, 49–55,
  60, 65, 263
  Brittonic, 126, 127
  see also conjunct verbal conjugation, deuterotonic, prototonic
accent, 15
  Brittonic, 119–21
  Goidelic, 29–31
  Modern Irish, 72–3, 77–8
active and passive, in verbal nouns,
  268–9
adjective
  degrees of comparison
    Irish, 87
    Welsh, 164–6
  modifying verbal noun, 263
  possessive
    Irish, 86–7
    Welsh, 161
  Welsh, 164–6
  see also comparative, equative,
  superlative
adverb, with verbal noun, 269
agreement
  of adjective and noun
    Irish, 87
    Welsh, 164
  of subject and verb, 131
Alise-Sainte-Reine, 286
amplification, 302
Amra Choluim Chille, 291
analytic verbal formation
  Irish, 71–2, 92–4
  Welsh, 130–1, 170–1, 174–6

Aneirin, 9
apocope
  Brittonic, 122–5
  Goidelic, 38–42
Arabic, 291
archaizing, Old Irish, 26
Argyll, 9
Asia Minor, 3
aspect
  Welsh, 174–7
  in verbal nouns, 269–70
athematic conjugation, in Indo-
  European, 52
Athenaeus, 21 n6
auxiliary verbs, see verbal system
Avestan, 2

Ballymacoda, 70, 73
Banassac, 285
Bath, curse tablets, 212
Berber, 291
Berehaven, 70, 73
Bergin's Law, 287–92
Beunans Meriasek, 14
bibliography, general, 21 n3
binding, Modern Irish relatives,
  106–9
Black Book of Chirk, 217–18
Blasket Island, 70, 73
Book of the Dean of Lismore, 28, 63,
  227–8
Book of Llandaf, 112, 213
Botorrita, 6–7, 202–3, 279, 283
breaking of vowels
  Old Irish, 33
  Scottish Gaelic, 63

Breconshire, 139, 141
Breint Teilo, *215*–16
Bretha Nemed, 290
Breton, 1, 7, 9, *16*, *128*, *134*
  dialects, 115, 121, 126
  orthography, 220–1
  Vannetais, 121, 126, 128
  infixed pronouns, 126
  mutations, 231–6
  possessive adjectives, 252
  spirant mutation, 255–6
  orthography, 219–22
  sources, 114–15
Britain, 7–9
British, 8
  orthography, 211–13
Brittonic, 6–9, *16*–*17*, Ch. 4
  111–36
  accent, 15
  distinctive features, 14–15
  inter-relationship of languages,
    127–34
  morphology, 122–7, 130–2
  apocope, 122–5
  cases, 122–5
  distinctive developments,
    130–2
  verbal system, 125–7
  infixed pronouns, 126
  P and Q, 14–15
  phonology
    accent, 119–21
    Old Welsh accent shift,
      119–21
    apocope, 122–5
    diphthongs, 116–18
    distinctive sound changes,
      129–30
    long vowels, 116–18
    quantity system, 121–2
    vowel affection, 118
  sources, 111–15
Burgos, 6
Bute, 9

Caighdeán na Gaeilge, 227
Cardiganshire, 151–2
Carna, *70*, *72*
Cartulary of Redon, 114

cases, 2
case forms
  Irish, 82–4
  mutations, 234
Celtiberian, 6–7, *16*–*17*
  orthography, 202–4
Celto-Ligurian, 22 n11
central vowels
  Welsh, 141–3, 151–3
  orthography, 214
Chamalières, 4, 206, 279, 283
chronology of sound changes
  early Irish, *43*
Cisalpine Gaul, 5
Clear Island, *70*, *73*
cleft sentences, 286–7
Co. Clare, 69
Cognitive Grammar, 194–5
Cois Fhairrge, *70*, *72*
Collection Canonum Hibernensium,
  290
comment, 279
comparative adjective
  Irish, 87
  Welsh, 164–6
compound preposition, *see*
  preposition
Computus fragment, 294
conjunct verbal conjugation, 49–55,
  60, 65, 263
  Brittonic, 126, 127
  see also absolute verbal
    conjugation, deuterotonic,
    prototonic
conjunctive pronoun, *see* pronoun
Connacht, 69–73
consonant clusters
  Irish, 79
  Welsh, 154–6
Continental Celtic, 2–7, 14
  orthography, 198–207
  Greek, 198–202
  Iberian, 202–4
  Lugano, 204–6
  Latin, 206–7
  word order, 278–9, 281, 282–6,
    301–2
copula
  Irish, 58–9, 96–8

Cornish, 7, 8, 9, *16*, *128*, *134*
  mutations, 231–6
  orthography, 222–3
  sources, 113–14
Cumbric, 8–9, *16*, *128*, *134*
curse tablets
  Bath, 8, 212
  Gaul, 4
Cymraeg Byw, 145
Cyrillic, 197

Dál Riada, 9
declaratives
  Irish, 104
  Welsh, 186
definite article
  Irish, 85
  with verbal noun, 263
  Welsh, 160
definiteness
  Irish, 85–7
  Welsh, 160–3
defixiones, 4
  see also curse tablets
demonstratives
  Irish, 85–6
  Welsh, 160–1
denominative verbs, 60, 262–3
deontas, 74
deponent verbs
  Old Irish, 46, 55–6
determination
  Irish, 85–7
  Welsh, 160–3
deuterotonic, 50–5, 288–9
  see also conjunct verbal
    conjugation, deuterotonic,
    prototonic
devoicing
  Scottish Gaelic, 62, 63
  see also provection
dialects
  Breton, 115
  Irish, 69–73
  Scottish Gaelic, 61–2
  Welsh, 139–45
Diodorus Siculus, 21 n6
diphthongs
  Brittonic, 116–18

Goidelic, 33
  Proto-Celtic, 10–11
  Welsh, *147*, 151
    notation, 196 n5
direct object mutation
  Welsh, 251
Donegal, 69–73
drag-chain, 247
druids, 198
Dunquin, *70*, *73*
Dutch, 270
Dyfi, 139

East Carbery, *70*, *73*
Egyptian, 291
emphasizing particles, Irish, 89
English, 9
  in Radnorshire, 141
  loanwords in Irish, 78
epenthesis
  Irish, 79
  Welsh, 154–6
equative,
  Old Irish, 87
  Welsh, 164–6
Erris, *70*, 72
Etruscan, 22 n11
  script, 197
  north Etruscan script, 205

Faliscan, 18
feminine nouns, mutation, 232–4
final syllables, *see* apocope
focus, 280
French, 270
  influence on Breton orthography,
    220–2
  model for Breton perfect and
    pluperfect, 131
fronting, 293
  Welsh, 179–81
future tense
  Modern Irish, 93–5

Gaeltacht, 74
Galatia, 2
Gallic, 22 n11
Gallo-Romance, 128
Gaul, 3–5, 7

Gaulish, 3–5, *17*
  in Italy, 5–6
  orthography, 198–202, 204–7
  substratum in France, 20
gender
  Irish, 81–2
  verbal noun, 266–7
  Welsh, 158–9
'genitival' construction
  Welsh, 161
genitive case
  with verbal nouns, 263–5
Georgian, 270
Glagolithic, 197
Glamorgan, 141
Glencolumbkille, *70, 72*
Glenfin, *70, 72*
glosses
  Old Breton, 114
  Old Irish, 26
  orthography of Würzburg
    glosses, 224
  Old Welsh, 112
Gododdin, 8
Goidelic, 7, 9–10, *16–17*, Ch. 2
  25–68
  distinctive features, 14–15
  general features, 28–60
  Manx developments, 61–5
  morphology,
    nominal declension, 38–42
    verbal system, 45–60
      absolute and conjunct
        conjugation, 49–55
      copula, 58–9
      deponents and passives, 55–6
      Middle Irish developments,
        59–60
      relative forms, 56–8
      substantive verb, 58–9
      tenses and moods, 45–9
      verbs 'to be' 58–9
  phonology,
    accent, 15, 29–31
    apocope, 38–42
    chronology of sound changes,
      42–5
    diphthongs, 33
    Latin loanwords in Irish, 42–5

lenition, 28–9
long vowels, 33
Mac Neill's law, 38
mutations, 28–9, 231–6
P and Q Celtic, 14–15
palatalization, 35–8
resonants, 38
vowel affection, 34–5
Scottish Gaelic developments,
  61–5
sources, 35–8
word order, 286–92
Greek, 2, 39
  Hellenistic, 201
  script for Continental Celtic,
    198–202
Gweedore, *70, 72*
Gwent, 141
Gwreans an Bys, 114

Helvetii, 198
hiatus, 62, 227
Hittite, 300, 302

Iberian peninsula, 6–7
Iberian scripts, 197, 203–4
impersonal
  early Irish, 55–6
  Modern Irish, 101–2
  r-forms, 289–90
Indo-European, 2, 47–9, 50, 55,
  275–6, 300–4
Indo-Iranian, 2, 300
infinitives, 258–60, 275–6
infixed pronouns, *see* pronouns
Inishmaan, *70, 72*
Inisheer, *70, 72*
Inishmore, *70, 72*
inscriptions
  Alise-Sainte-Reine, 286
  Banassac, *285*
  Botorrita, 6–7, 202–*3*, 279, 283
  Chamalières, 4, 206, 279, 283
  Gallo-Greek, 3–4
  Larzac, 4, 206, 279, 283
  Luzaga, 6, 202
  Peñalba de Villastar, 6, 202
  post-Roman Britain, 135 n1
  Roman Britain, 22 n15

in Roman cursive, 4–5
South-west Britain, 135 n1
Todi, 5–6, 282, 283, *285*,
Voltino, *284*
Insular Celtic, 7–10
orthography, 207–29
inter-relationship
of Brittonic languages, 127–34
of Celtic and Italic, 18–20, 47
of Celtic languages, 15–18
of Goidelic languages, 27, 61–5
interrogatives
Irish, 103–4
Welsh, 184–5
intransitive verbs, 55–6
Irish, 1, 7, 9, *16*, Ch. 3 69–110
dialects, 27, 61–2, 69, 73
morphology, 81–102
adjectives, 87
case system, 82–4
definite article, 85
demonstratives, 85–6
gender, 81
mutations, 231–6
nominal system, 81–6
number, 84–5
numerals, 90–2
plural formation, 84–5
possessive adjectives, 86–7
pronouns, 88–90
verbal system, 92–102
aspect, 98–101
auxiliaries, 98–101
forms, 92–6
impersonals, 101–2
passives, 101–2
tenses, 98–101
'to be', 96–8
orthography, 223–7
accents on long vowels, 224–5
glide vowels, 226
origin of *h*, 224
palatalization, 211, 225–6
prima manus of the Würzburg
glosses, 223–4
phonology, 74–81
accent, 77–8
consonants, 76–7
clusters, 79

diphthongs, 75–6
epenthesis, 79
framework, 74–7
lowering, 79–80
palatalization, 80–1
raising, 79–80
stress, 77–8
vowels, 75–6
sources, 25–7
survival, 73–4
syntax,
declaratives, 104
interrogatives, 103–4
negatives, 102–3
subordination, 104–6
relative clauses, 105–9
reported speech, 104–5
word order, 102
'islands',
Modern Irish relative clauses,
106–9
Isle of man, 9
Italo-Celtic hypothesis, 18–20, 47
Iveragh, *70*, *73*

Julius Caesar, 7, 198
Juvencus poems, 112

Kernewek Kemmyn, 223

labialization of /g^w/, 12
labiovelars, 12, 14
laryngeals, 48, 67 n16
Larzac, 4, 206, 279, 283
Latin, 2, 9, 18, 22 n11, 39
gerunds, 258, 277 n8
influence on Irish word order,
291–2
influence on word order patterns,
304
loanwords in Irish, 42–5
model for Welsh pluperfect, 131
script, 206–7, 211–29
Lebor na h-Uidre, 26
Leenane, *70*, *72*
Leges inter Brittos et Scottos, 8–9
lenition, Ch. 7 231–57
British, 212
Brittonic, 115–16

lenition *cont.*
    functional load, 252–6
    in Gaulish, 206–7, 246–7
    Goidelic, 28–9
    grammatical function of initial
        mutations, 232–6
    grammaticalization, 249–51
    modern mutations, 252–6
    mutations in the consonant system,
        236–8
    in Ogam, 211
    phonological data, 231–2
    theories, 238–49
        Greene, 239–42
        Harvey, 242
        Jackson, 239–42
        Koch, 246–9
        Martinet, 246–9
        Sims-Williams, 242–5
        P W Thomas, 242–5
Lepontic, 5, *17*, 22 n11, 204–5
Lettermore, *70*, *72*
Ligurian, 22 n11
long vowels
    Brittonic, 116–18
    Goidelic, 33
    Proto-Celtic, 10–11
loss of final syllables, *see* apocope
loss of /p/, 10, 11–12, 19–20
lowering, 66 n12
    in Modern Irish, 79–80
Luganian, 22 n11
Luzaga, 6, 202

Mandarin Chinese, 270
Manx, 1, 7, 9–10, *16*
    mutations, 231–2
    orthography, 228–9
    phonology, 64
    sources, 28
    word order, 292
Massalia, 3, 199
Meenawania, *70*, *72*
Middle Irish, *16*
    adjective derivation, 42
    plural formation, 42
    sources, 27
    verb formation, 59–60
    see also Irish

Middle Welsh,
    word order, 292, 294–6,
        298–300
    mixed order, 294–6
Modern Irish
    dialects, 27, 61–2, 69, 73
    morphology, 81–102
        adjectives, 87
        case system, 82–4
        definite article, 85
        demonstratives, 85–6
        gender, 81
        mutations, 231–6
        nominal system, 81–6
        number, 84–5
        numerals, 90–2
        plural formation, 84–5
        possessive adjectives, 86–7
        pronouns, 88–90
        verbal system, 92–102
            aspect, 98–101
            auxiliaries, 98–101
            forms, 92–6
            impersonals, 101–2
            passives, 101–2
            tenses, 98–101
            'to be', 96–8
    phonology, 74–81
        accent, 77–8
        consonants, 76–7
        clusters, 79
        diphthongs, 75–6
        epenthesis, 79
        framework, 74–7
        lowering, 79–80
        palatalization, 80–1
        raising, 79–80
        stress, 77–8
        vowels, 75–6
modern literary Welsh, 138–9
Modern Welsh
    word order, 292
mood,
    early Irish, 45–9
morphology
    Brittonic, 130–2
    Common Gaelic features, 12–14
        nominal inflection, 13
        verbal system, 13

Irish, 81–102
    adjectives, 87
    case system, 82–4
    definite article, 85
    demonstratives, 85–6
    gender, 81
    mutations, 231–6
    nominal system, 81–6
    number, 84–5
    numerals, 90–2
    plural formation, 84–5
    possessive adjectives, 86–7
    pronouns, 87–90
    verbal system, 92–102
        aspect, 98–101
        auxiliaries, 98–101
        forms, 92–6
        impersonals, 101–2
        passives, 101–2
        tenses, 98–101
        'to be', 96–8
    possession, 13–14
Welsh
    determination, 160–3
        definite article, 160
        demonstratives, 160–1
        'genitive' construction, 161
    gender, 158–9
    nominal system, 158–69
    number 159–60
    numerals, 169–70
    plural formation, 159–60
    possessive adjectives, 161–3
    pronouns
        affixed, 162
        personal, 166–9
        reflexive, 162–3
    verbal system, 169–79
        aspect, 174–7
        auxiliaries, 174–7
        forms, 170–5
        passives, 177–9
        tenses, 174–7
        'to be', 173–4
mutations, Ch. 7 231–57
    direct object mutation, 251
    functional load, 252–6
    grammaticalization, 249–51
    of initial vowels, 236

nasal mutation, 250
spirant mutation, 250
verb mutation in Middle Irish,
    251
see also lenition

nasal mutation, 250
negatives
    Irish, 65, 102–3
    mutations, 235
    Scottish Gaelic, 61
    Welsh, 181–4
        Pembrokeshire, 182–4
Nervii, 199
nominal declension, see nominal
    inflection
nominal inflection
    Brittonic, 122–5
    Common Celtic, 13
    Goidelic, 38–42
    Modern Irish, 82–4
nominal system
    verbal nouns, Ch. 8 258–77
        nominal features, 259, 263–9
    Welsh, 158–69
nominativus pendens, 291
Northern Italy, 5–6
North Welsh, 134
number
    Irish, 84–5
    Welsh, 159–60
numerals
    Irish, 90–2
        cardinals, 90–1
        ordinals, 91
        'personal' numbers, 91–2
    mutations, 234
    Welsh, 169–70
        cardinals, 169
        ordinals, 169

Ogam, 9, 14, 25
    orthography, 208–11
Old Irish, 16
    sources, 26–7
        Glosses, 26
        law texts, 26–7
    word order, 286–92
Old Welsh, 112–13

accent shift, 119–21
word order, 292–4
Ordinalia, 114
orthographie universitaire, 221
orthography, Ch. 6 197–230
  Continental Celtic, 198–202
    Celtiberian, 202–4
    Greek, 198–202
    Latin, 206–7
    Lugano script, 204–6
    Gallo-Greek, 3–4
    Iberian, 6
  Insular Celtic, 207–9
    Latin, 211–29
    Breton, 219–22
    British, 211–13
    Cornish, 222–3
    Irish, 223–7
    Manx, 228–9
    Scottish Gaelic, 227–8
    Welsh, 213–19
    Ogam, 208–11
  and phonology, 197–8
  reforms
    Breton, 220–2
    Irish, 226–7
    Welsh, 219
  Roman cursive, 4–5
Oscan, 18

P and Q Celtic, 14–15
palatalization
  Goidelic, 35–8
  'first' palatalization, *36*
  Modern Irish, 80–1
paradigmatic variation, 79–80
participles, 258
  past, 46, 258–9
  present, 276 n1
Pascon agan Arluth, 114
passive
  early Irish, 55–6
  Modern Irish, 101–2
  past participle, 46
  Welsh, 177–9
  theoretical treatments, 189–95
Pembrokeshire, 151–2, 182–4
  central vowel, 151–2
  negatives, 182–4
Peñalba de Villastar, 6, 202

periphrasis
  Modern Irish, 96, 98–101
  with verbal nouns, 269–70
  Welsh, 130–2
Persian, 2
Phoenician, 204
  script, 197
phonology
  Brittonic
    accent, 119–21
    apocope, 122–5
    distinctive features, 129–30
    diphthongs, 116–18
    long vowels, 116–18
    quantity system, 121–2
    stress, 119–21
    vowel affection, 118
  Celtic
    diphthongs, 10–11
    distinctive features, 10–12
    labialization of /g^w/, 12
    long vowels, 10–11
    loss of /p/, 10, 11–12
    vocalic liquids, 12
  Goidelic, 28–45
    accent, 29–32
    apocope, 38–42
    lenition, 42–5
    long vowels, 33
    palatalization, 35–8
    stress, 29–32
    syncope, 30–1
    vowel affection, 34–5
  lenition, 231–57
  lowering, 66 n12
  Modern Irish, 74–81
    accent, 77–8
    consonants, 76–7
    clusters, 79
    diphthongs, 75–6
    epenthesis, 79
    framework, 74–7
    lowering, 79–80
    palatalization, 80–1
    raising, 79–80
    stress, 77–8
    vowels, 75–6
  raising, 66 n12
  spirantization, 231–57

Welsh, 146–58
  central vowels, 151–3
  consonantal clusters, 154–6
  framework, 146–51
  grammatical alternations, 156–7
    theoretical treatments, 157–8
  vowels, 146–51
Phrase Structure Grammar, 194
place names
  Cornish, 114
  Welsh, 13, 136 n7
plural formation
  Breton, 132–3
  Modern Irish, 72, 84–5
  Welsh, 159–60
polite requests, 177
Portuguese, 270
possession
  Brittonic, 14
  Celtic, 13–14
  Irish, 86–7
possessive adjectives, mutations, 235
prepositions
  compound, 20
  Brittonic, 127
  conjugated
    Irish, 86–7, 88, 90
    Welsh, 168–9
  with verbal nouns, 266, 280–1
pre-sentential particles
  Irish
    declaratives, 104
    interrogatives, 103
    negatives, 102–4
  Welsh
    declaratives, 186
    interrogatives, 184–5
    negatives, 181–4
preverbs, 49–54, 302–4
Pritenic, see Cumbric
pronouns
  affixed
    Welsh, 162, 166–8
  in conjugated prepositions
    Irish, 88, 90
    Welsh, 168–9
  conjunctive
    Welsh, 166–7

    Irish, 87–90
  infixed
    Brittonic, 126
    Old Irish, 50–1, 53–4
  independent
    Irish, 88
    Welsh, 166–7
  interrogative
    Irish, 103
    Welsh, 184
  possessive
    Irish, 87
    Welsh, 161–2
  reduplicated
    Welsh, 166–7
  reflexive
    Irish, 89–90
    Welsh, 162–3
  resumptive
    Irish, 106, 108–9
    Welsh, 188–9
  suffixed
    Old Irish, 50–1
  with verbal nouns, 263–4
Proto-Celtic, 10–14, 16–17
Proto-Ligurian, 22 n11
prototonic, 50–5
  see also absolute, conjunct, deuterotonic
provection, 144, 235–6
  see also devoicing
Ptolemy, 9
Punic script, 197
pull-chain, 247
push-chain, 247

quantity system
  Brittonic, 121–2

Radnorshire, 141
raising, 66 n12
  Irish, 79–80
Rannafast, 70, 72
Red Book of Hergest, 217
reduction of vowels
  Goidelic, 29–30
  Scottish Gaelic, 62–3
reduplicated futures, 2
  early Irish, 49

reduplicated preterite, 2
  Brittonic, 126
  early Irish, 48–9
reduplicated pronouns, *see* pronouns
reflexive pronouns, *see* pronouns
relative clauses
  Irish, 56–8, 105–9
  Welsh, 188–9
reported speech
  Irish, 104–5
  Welsh, 186–8
responsives
  Irish, 93–4, 100, 103–4
  Welsh, 185
Rheged, 8
rheme, 179
Ring, *70, 73*
Romance languages, 2
Rosguill, *70, 72*
Rosmuck, *70, 72*

Sanskrit, 2, 39
s-aorist, 47
Scottish Gaelic, 1, 7, 9–10, *16*
  dialects, 28, 61–2
  morphology, 65
  mutations, 321–6
    in East Sutherland, 254–5
  orthography, 227–8
    hiatus, 227
  phonology, 62–4
  sources, 27–8
  word order, 292
Semitic languages, 291
sociolinguistics, 21 n1
South Welsh, *134*
Spain, *see* Iberian peninsula
Spanish, 270
spelling
  reforms
    Breton, 220–2
    Irish, 226–7
    Welsh, 219
  see also orthography
spirantization
  Brittonic, 116
  first, *243*
  second, *243*
  theories, 238–49

'voiced', *243*
voiceless, *243*
standard spoken Welsh, 145
Strabo, 21 n6
Strathclyde, 8
stress, *see* accent
subordination
  Irish, 104–6
  verbal nouns, 270–1
  Welsh, 186–9
substantive verb, 58–9
  Modern Irish, 96–8
suffixation, 296–7
  verbal nouns, 260–1
superlatives
  Celtic, 20
  Irish, 87
  Welsh, 164–6
'Surexit' memorandum, 112, 294
syllabary, 203
syncope, Goidelic, 30–1, 36–7
syntax
  Common Celtic features, 12–14
  Irish, 102–9
    declaratives, 104
    interrogatives, 103–4
    negatives, 102–3
    subordination, 104–6
      relative clauses, 56–8, 105–9
      reported speech, 104–5
    theoretical treatments, 106–9
    word order, 102
  Welsh, 179–95
    declaratives, 186
    interrogatives, 184–5
    negatives, 181–4
    subordination, 186–9
      relative clauses, 188–9
      reported speech, 186–8
    theoretical treatments, 189–95
    word order, 179–81
  word order, Ch. 9 278–305
synthetic
  Irish, 71–2, 92–4
  Welsh, 170–1, 174–6

Tacitus, 7–8
tag questions
  Irish, 103
  Welsh, 184–5

Táin Bó Cúailnge, 208
Taliesin, 9
tau Gallicum, 202, 207
Teelin, *70, 72*
tense
  Irish, 45–9
    past, 93–4
  Welsh, 174–7
thematic conjugation
  in Indo-European, 52
theme, 279
theoretical treatments
  Irish syntax, 106–9
  Welsh phonology, 157–8
  Welsh syntax, 189–95
tmesis, 288–9, 301
Todi, 5–6, 282, 283, *285*
topic, 279–80
topicalization, 287, 289
Tourmakeady, *70, 72*
typology, 280–1

Umbrian, 18
univerbation, 53–4, 302, 303

Vannetais, 121, 126
Vedic, 300–*1*, 302
Vendryes' Restriction, 50, 303
  see also word order
Venetic, 22 n11
verb, *see* verbal system
verbal noun, Ch. 8 258–77
  formal characteristics, 260–3
  historical background, 275–6
  Irish, 46, 60
  nominal features, *259*, 263–9
    gender and declension, 266–7
    modified by
      article and genitive, 263
      noun and pronoun, 263–5
      preposition, 266
    neutral to active/passive distinc-
    tions, 268–9
    as subject/object of verb, 267–8
  and verbal adjectives, 258–60
  verbal features, *259*, 269–74
    modified by adverb, 269
    periphrastic use, 269–70
    replacing finite verbs, 271
    in subordinate clauses, 270–1

verbs or nouns, 271–4
Welsh
  reported speech, 186–8
verbal of necessity, 258–9
verbal system, 2
  absolute and conjunct, 49–55, 60, 65, 263
  auxiliary verbs
    Irish, 98–102
    with verbal nouns, 269–70
    Welsh, 174–7, 178
  Brittonic, 125–7
  Common Celtic, 13
  conjunct (and absolute), 49–55, 60, 65, 263
  denominative verbs, 262–3
  endings
    primary, 52–3
    secondary, 52–3
  Irish, 92–102
    analytic, 71–2
    aspect, 98–101
    auxiliaries, 98–101
    forms, 92–6
    impersonals, 101–2
    passives, 101–2
    synthetic, 71–2
    tenses, 98–101
    'to be', 58–9, 96–8
  Old Irish, 45–60
    absolute and conjunct, 49–55, 60, 65, 263
    deponents, 55–6
    impersonals, 55–6
    moods, 45–9
    passives, 55–6
    tenses, 45–9
  Scottish Gaelic, 65
  verbal nouns, Ch. 8 258–77
  'to be'
    Irish, 58–9, 96–8
    Welsh, 173–4
  Welsh, 169–79
    aspect, 174–7
    auxiliaries, 174–7
    forms, 170–5
    passives, 177–9
    tenses, 174–7
    'to be', 173–4

vigesimal counting system
  Irish, 90
  Welsh, 169–70
Vikings, 9
Vocabularium Cornicum, 114, 222
vocalic liquids, 12
Voltino, *284*
vowel affection
  Brittonic, 118
  Goidelic, 34–5
Vulgar latin, 20

Wackernagel's Law, 50, 302, 303
  see also word order
Waterville, *70, 73*
Welsh, 1, 7, 8, *16, 128*, Ch. 5 137–96
  Cymraeg Byw, 145
  dialects, 139–45
  modern literary Welsh, 138–9
  morphology, 158–79
    determination, 160–3
      definite article, 160
      demonstratives, 160–1
      'genitive' construction, 161
    gender, 158–9
    nominal system, 158–69
    number 159–60
    numerals, 169–70
    plural formation, 159–60
    possessive adjectives, 161–3
    pronouns
      affixed, 162
      personal, 166–9
      reflexive, 162–3
    verbal system, 169–79
      aspect, 174–7
      auxiliaries, 174–7
      forms, 170–5
      passives, 177–9
      tenses, 174–7
      'to be', 173–4
  mutations, 231–6
  orthography, 213–19
    Middle Welsh, 217–19
    Old Welsh, 213–17
  phonology, 146–58
    central vowels, 151–3

consonantal clusters, 154–6
framework, 146–51
grammatical alternations, 156–7
  theoretical treatments, 157–8
vowels, 146–51
syntax, 179–95
  declaratives, 186
  interrogatives, 184–5
  negatives, 181–4
  subordination, 186–9
    relative clauses, 188–9
    reported speech, 186–8
  theoretical treatments, 189–95
  word order, 179–81
word order, Ch. 9 278–305
  types of, 137–45
  sources, 111–13
West Carbery, *70, 73*
West Muskerry, *70, 73*
word order, Ch. 9 278–305
  Brittonic, 292–300
    Breton, 298
    Classical Welsh, 297
    Cornish, 297–8
    Middle Welsh, 292, 294–7
      verse, 208–300
    Old Welsh, 292–4
    Welsh, 179–81
  Continental Celtic, 278–9, 281, 282–6
  the evidence, 281–300
  Goidelic, 286–92
    Manx, 292
    Modern Irish, 102
    Old Irish, 286–92
    Scottish Gaelic, 292
  historical background, 300–4
  varieties, 278–9
  Vendryes' Restriction, 50, 303
  in verse, 278–9, 298–300
  Wackernagel's Law, 50, 302, 303

Yoruba, 270
Ystwyth, 139

Zaragoza, 6
zedachek, 221